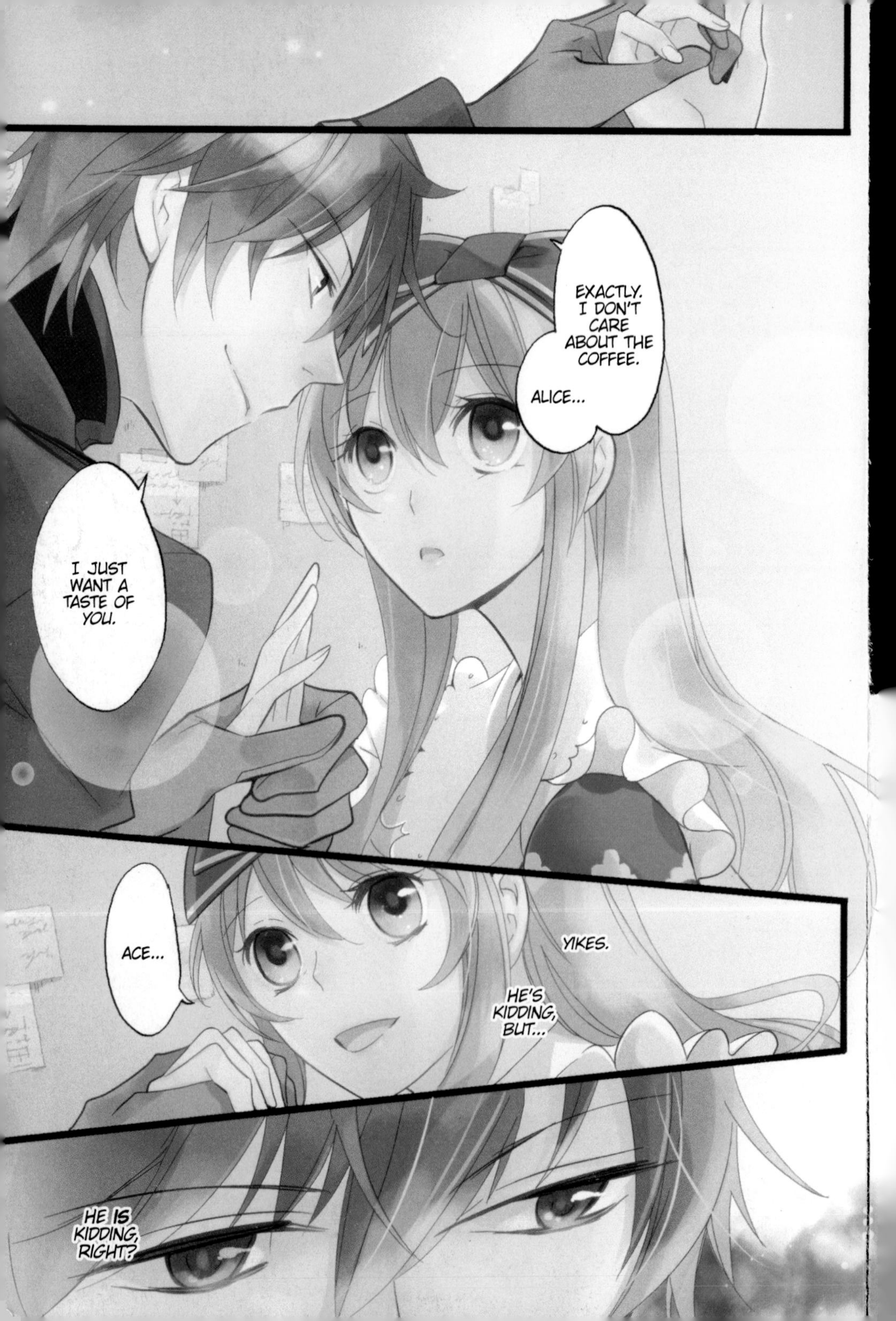
EXACTLY. I DON'T CARE ABOUT THE COFFEE.
ALICE...
I JUST WANT A TASTE OF YOU.
YIKES.
HE'S KIDDING, BUT...
ACE...
HE IS KIDDING, RIGHT?

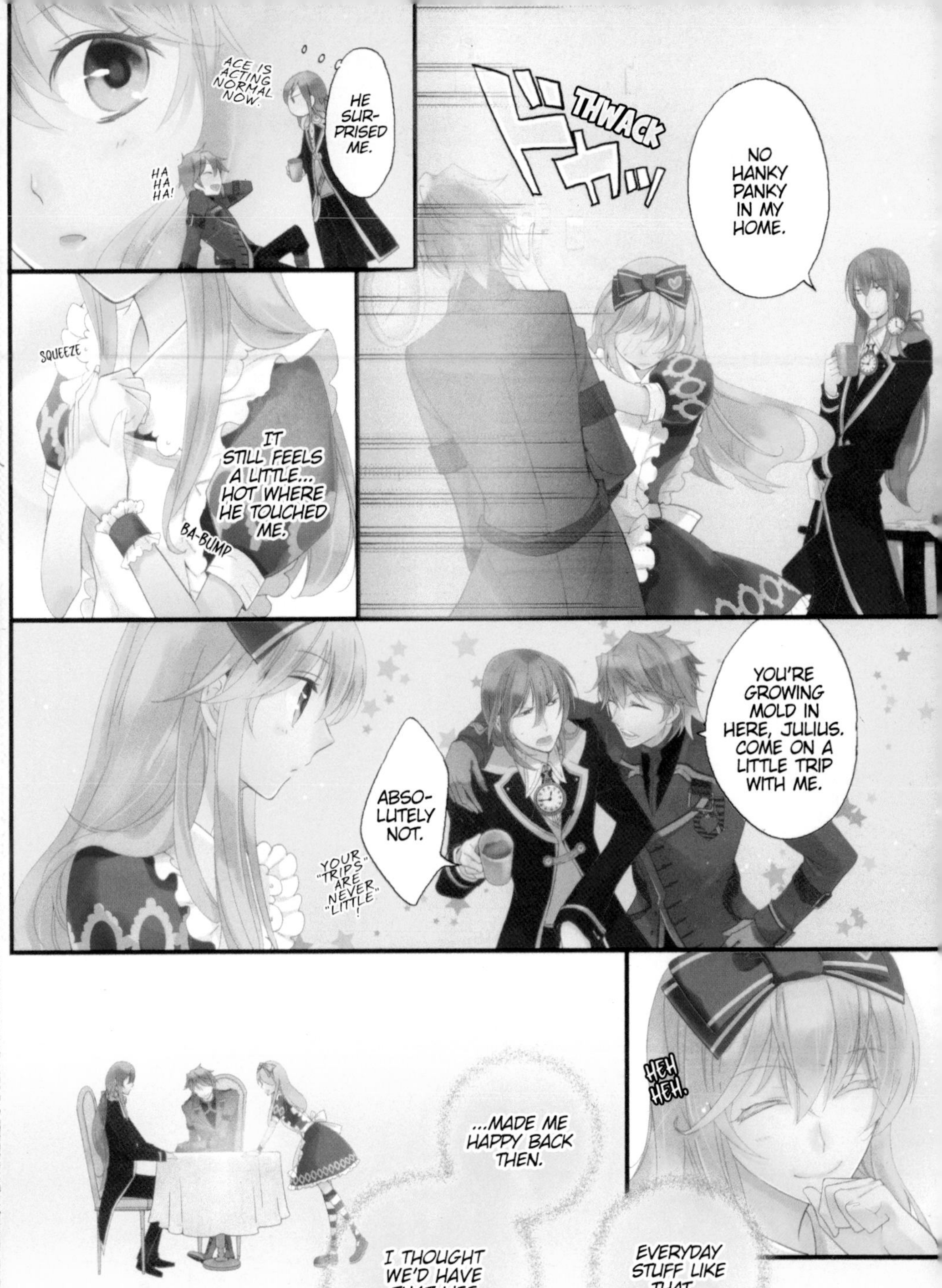
THWACK
NO HANKY PANKY IN MY HOME.
HE SUR-PRISED ME.
ACE IS ACTING NORMAL NOW.
HA HA HA!
SQUEEZE
IT STILL FEELS A LITTLE... HOT WHERE HE TOUCHED ME.
BA-BUMP
YOU'RE GROWING MOLD IN HERE, JULIUS. COME ON A LITTLE TRIP WITH ME.
ABSO-LUTELY NOT.
YOUR "TRIPS" ARE NEVER "LITTLE"!
HEH HEH.
EVERYDAY STUFF LIKE THAT...
...MADE ME HAPPY BACK THEN.
I THOUGHT WE'D HAVE THAT LIFE FOREVER.

ALICE IN THE COUNTRY OF CLOVER
~Knight's Knowledge~

1

SAI ASAI

浅井 西

SEVEN SEAS ENTERTAINMENT PRESENTS

Alice IN THE COUNTRY OF Clover
KNIGHT'S KNOWLEDGE VOL. 1

art by SAI ASAI / story by QUINROSE

TRANSLATION
Angela Liu

ADAPTATION
Lianne Sentar

LETTERING AND LAYOUT
Laura Scoville

LOGO DESIGN
Courtney Williams

COVER DESIGN
Nicky Lim

PROOFREADER
Rebecca Scoble
Conner Crooks

MANAGING EDITOR
Adam Arnold

PUBLISHER
Jason DeAngelis

ALICE IN THE COUNTRY OF CLOVER: KNIGHT'S KNOWLEDGE VOL. 1
Copyright © Sai Asai / QuinRose UnderGarden 2012
First published in Japan in 2012 by ICHIJINSHA Inc., Tokyo.
English translation rights arranged with ICHIJINSHA Inc., Tokyo, Japan.

No portion of this book may be reproduced or transmitted in any form without
written permission from the copyright holders. This is a work of fiction. Names,
characters, places, and incidents are the products of the author's imagination
or are used fictitiously. Any resemblance to actual events, locals, or persons,
living or dead, is entirely coincidental.

Seven Seas books may be purchased in bulk for educational, business, or
promotional use. For information on bulk purchases, please contact Macmillan
Corporate & Premium Sales Department at 1-800-221-7945 (ext 5442)
or write specialmarkets@macmillan.com.

Seven Seas and the Seven Seas logo are trademarks of
Seven Seas Entertainment, LLC. All rights reserved.

ISBN: 978-1-626920-57-6

Printed in Canada

First Printing: July 2014

10 9 8 7 6 5 4 3 2 1

FOLLOW US ONLINE: www.gomanga.com

READING DIRECTIONS

This book reads from *right to left*, Japanese style. If
this is your first time reading manga, you start
reading from the top right panel on each page and
take it from there. If you get lost, just follow the
numbered diagram here. It may seem backwards at
first, but you□ll get the hang of it! Have fun!!

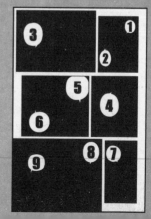

Alice in the Country of Clover
クローバーの国の
アリス
~Wonderful Wonder World~

- STORY -

In *Alice in the Country of Clover,* the game starts with Alice having not fallen in love,
but still deciding to stay in Wonderland.

She's acquainted with all the characters from the previous game, *Alice in the Country of Hearts.*

Since love would now start from a place of friendship rather than passion with a new stranger, she can experi-
ence a different type of romance from that in the previous game. Her dynamic with the characters is different
because of this friendship—characters can't always be forceful with her, and in many ways it's more comfort-
able to grow intimate. The relationships *between* the Ones With Duties have also become more of a factor.

In this game, the story focuses on Heart Castle. Alice attends the suited meetings (forcefully) and gets
involved in various gunfights (forcefully), among other things.

Land fluctuations, sea creatures in the forest, and whispering doors—it's a game more fantastic and more
eerie than the first.

Will our everywoman Alice be able to have a romantic relationship in a world devoid of common sense?

Alice in the Country of Clover
Character Information

Elliot March
VA: Tsuguo Mogami

Blood's right-hand man has a criminal past... and a temperamental present. But he's not as bad as he used to be, so that's something. Joining Blood has been good(?) for him.

Blood Dupre
VA: Katsuyuki Konishi

The head of the mafia Hatter Family, Blood is a cunning yet moody puppet-master. Alice now has the pleasure of having him for a landlord.

Alice Liddell
VA: Rie Kugimiya

A normal girl with a bit of a chip on her shoulder. Deciding to stay in the Wonderland she was carried to, she's adapted to her strange new lifestyle.

Vivaldi
VA: Yuuko Kaida

The beautiful Queen of Hearts has an unrivaled temper—which is really saying something in Wonderland. Although a picture-perfect Mad Queen, she cares for Alice as if Alice were her little sister...or a very interesting plaything.

Tweedle Dum
VA: Jun Fukuyama

The second "Bloody Twin" is equally cute and equally scary. In *Clover*, Dum can also turn into an adult.

Tweedle Dee
VA: Jun Fukuyama

One of the "Bloody Twin" gatekeepers of the Hatter territory, Dee can be cute when he's not being terrifying. In *Clover*, he sometimes turns into an adult.

Boris Airay
VA: Noriaki Sugiyama

This riddle-loving cat has a signature smirk—and in *Clover*, a new toy. One of his favorite pastimes is giving the Sleepy Mouse a hard time.

Ace
VA: Daisuke Hirakawa

The unlucky knight of Hearts was a former subordinate of Vivaldi and is perpetually lost. Even though he's depressed to be separated from his friend and boss Julius, he stays positive and tries to overcome it with a smile. He seems like a classic nice guy... or is he?

Peter White
VA: Kouki Miyata

The Prime Minister of Heart Castle—who has rabbit ears growing out of his head—invited (kidnapped) Alice to Wonderland. He loves Alice and hates everything else. His cruel, irrational actions are disturbing, but he acts like a completely different person (rabbit?) when in the throes of his love for Alice.

Gray Ringmarc
VA: Kazuya Nakai

Nightmare's subordinate in *Clover*. He used to have strong social ambition and considered assassinating Nightmare... but since Nightmare was such a useless boss, Gray couldn't help but feel sorry for him and ended up a dedicated assistant. He's a sound thinker with a strong work ethic. He's also highly skilled with his blades, rivaling even Ace.

Nightmare Gottschalk
VA: Tomokazu Sugita

A sickly nightmare who hates the hospital and needles. He has the power to read people's thoughts and enter dreams. Even though he likes to shut himself away in dreams, Gray drags him out to sulk from time to time. He technically holds a high position and has many subordinates, but since he can't even take care of his own health, he leaves most things to Gray.

Pierce Villiers
VA: Souichirou Hoshi

New to *Clover*, Pierce is an insomniac mouse who drinks too much coffee. He loves Nightmare (who can help him sleep) and hates Boris (who terrifies him). He dislikes Blood and Vivaldi for discarding coffee in favor of tea. He likes Elliot and Peter well enough, since rabbits aren't natural predators of mice.

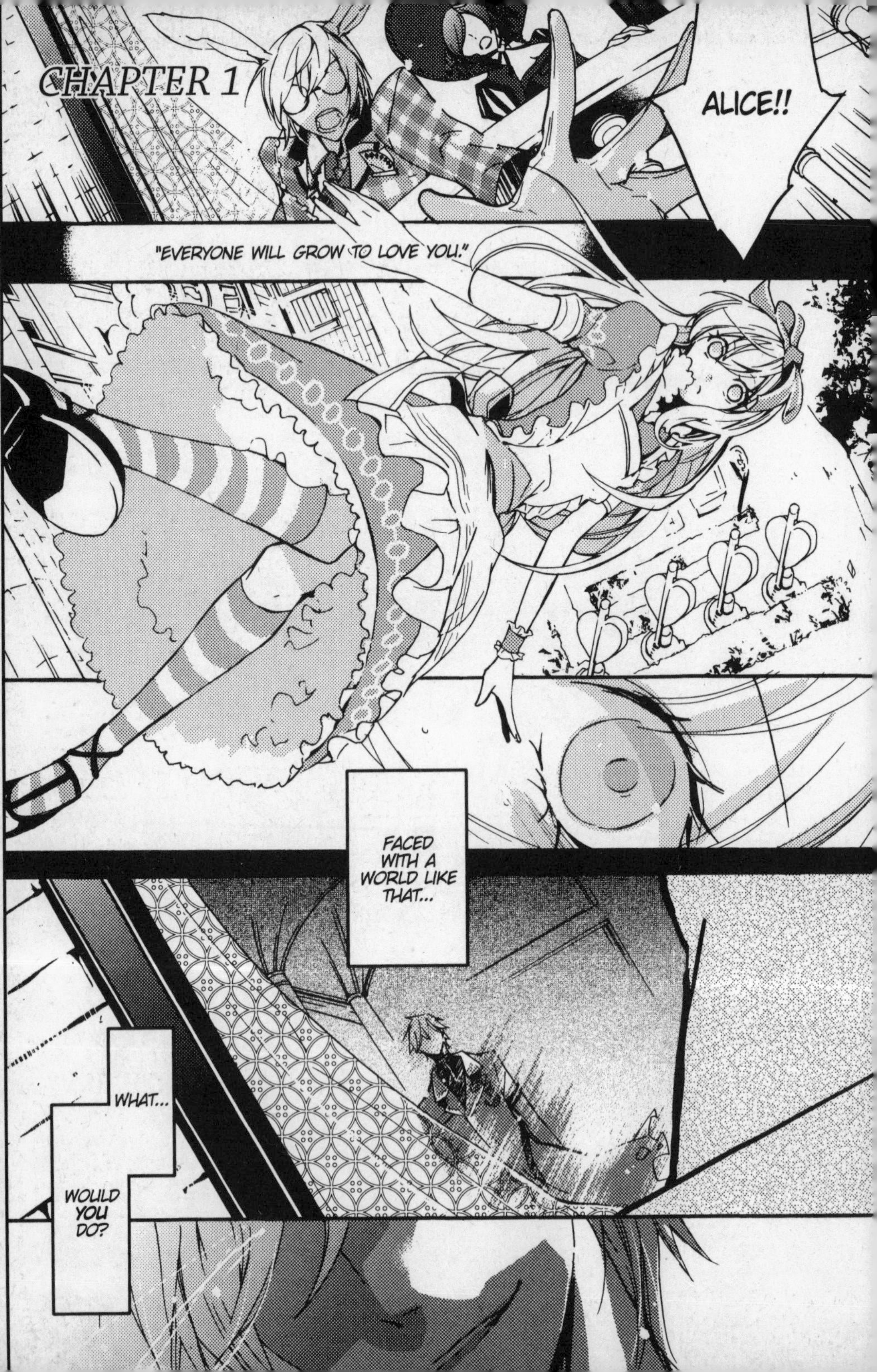
ALICE!!
CHAPTER 1
"EVERYONE WILL GROW TO LOVE YOU."
FACED WITH A WORLD LIKE THAT...
WHAT...
WOULD YOU DO?

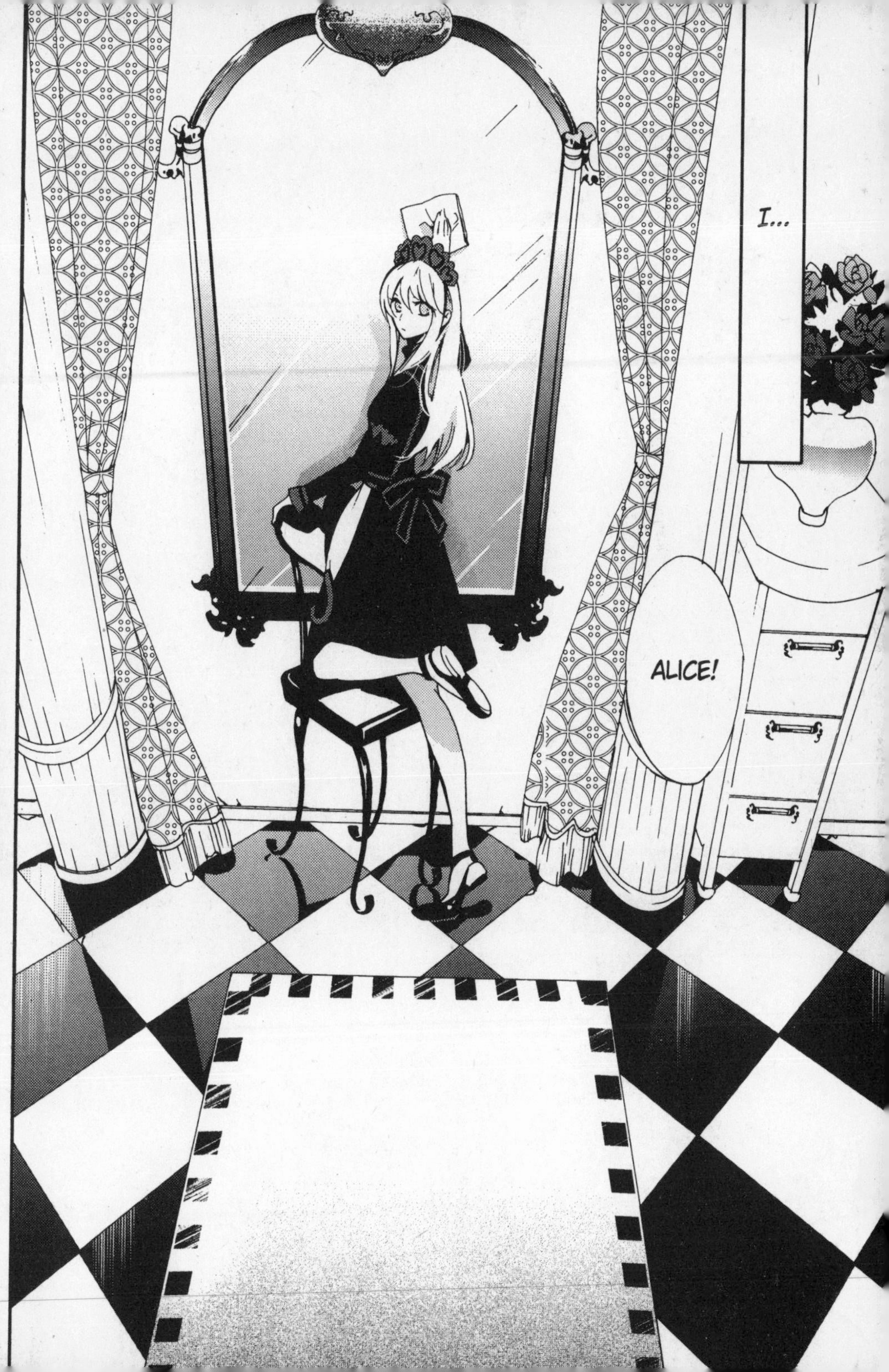
I...
ALICE!

Description:
The gang's adventures continue as a game of musical chairs turns nasty, Nano battles a fry thief, a bizarre body-swap situation occurs in the Shinonome household, Yuuko displays a talent for naming things, and Mio reveals her dream job.

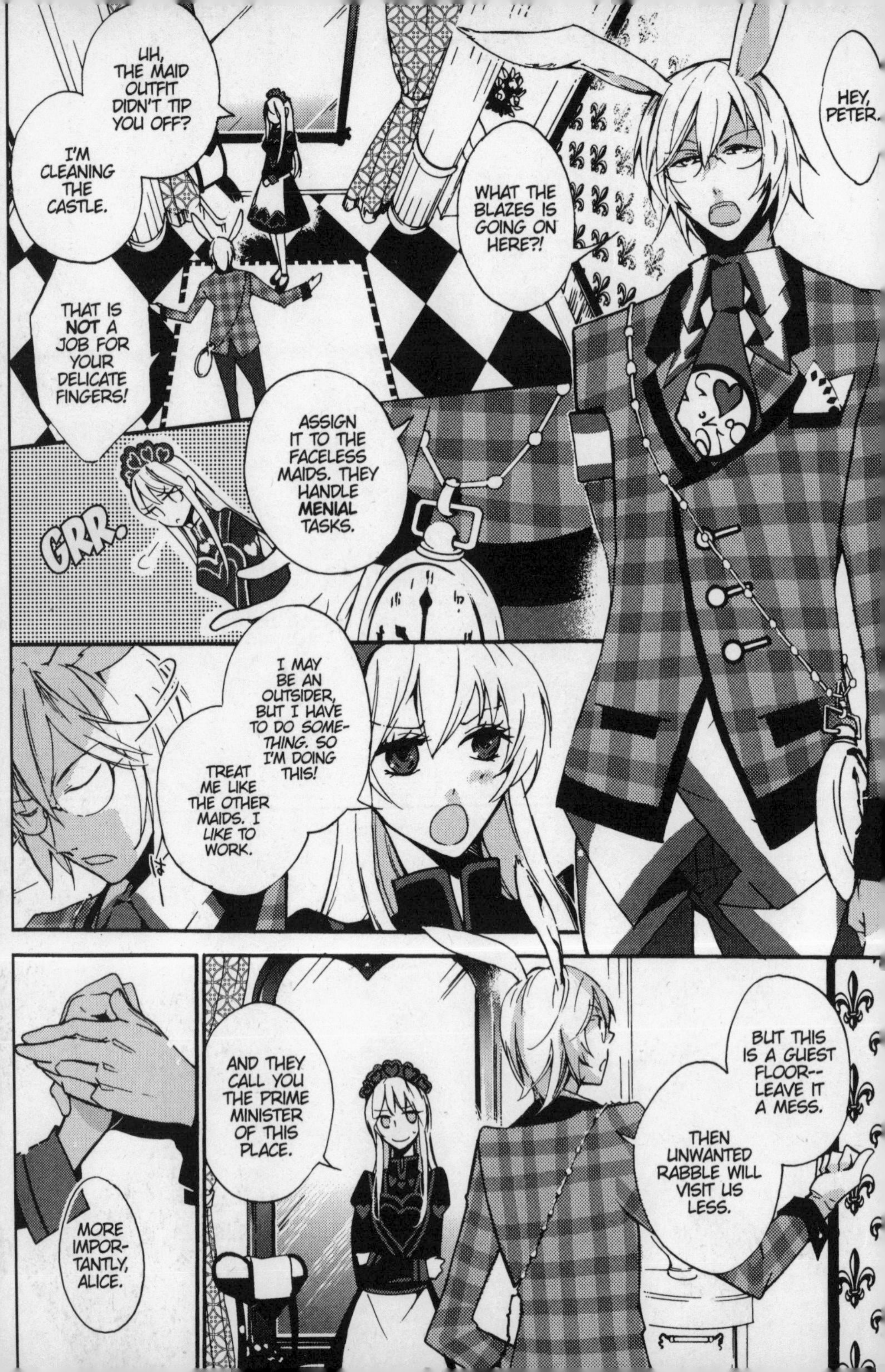
HEY, PETER.
WHAT THE BLAZES IS GOING ON HERE?!
UH, THE MAID OUTFIT DIDN'T TIP YOU OFF?
I'M CLEANING THE CASTLE.
THAT IS NOT A JOB FOR YOUR DELICATE FINGERS!
ASSIGN IT TO THE FACELESS MAIDS. THEY HANDLE MENIAL TASKS.
GRR.
I MAY BE AN OUTSIDER, BUT I HAVE TO DO SOME-THING. SO I'M DOING THIS!
TREAT ME LIKE THE OTHER MAIDS. I LIKE TO WORK.
BUT THIS IS A GUEST FLOOR--LEAVE IT A MESS.
THEN UNWANTED RABBLE WILL VISIT US LESS.
AND THEY CALL YOU THE PRIME MINISTER OF THIS PLACE.
MORE IMPOR-TANTLY, ALICE.

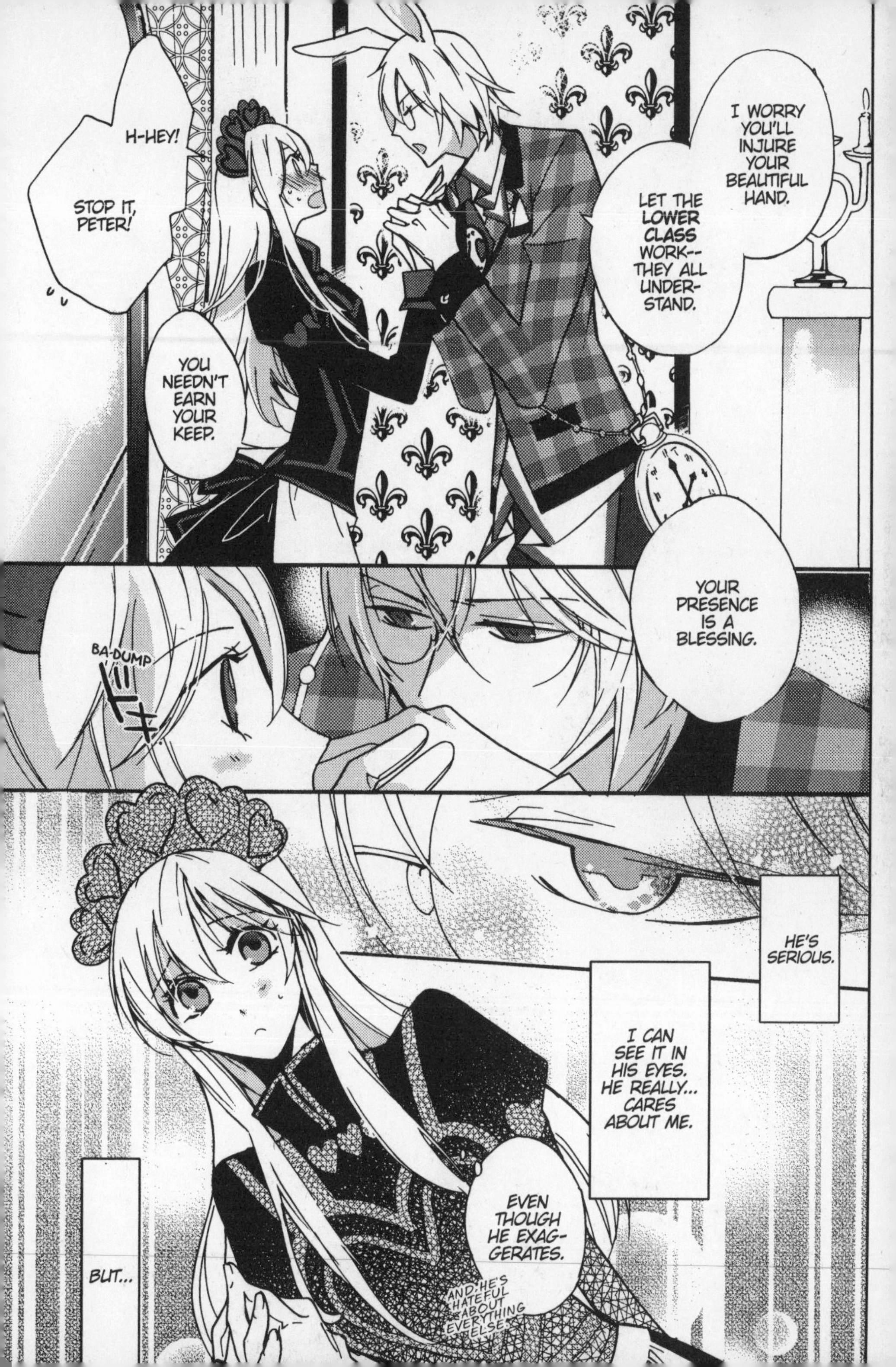
I WORRY YOU'LL INJURE YOUR BEAUTIFUL HAND.
LET THE LOWER CLASS WORK-- THEY ALL UNDERSTAND.
YOU NEEDN'T EARN YOUR KEEP.
H-HEY! STOP IT, PETER!
YOUR PRESENCE IS A BLESSING.
BA-DUMP
HE'S SERIOUS.
I CAN SEE IT IN HIS EYES. HE REALLY... CARES ABOUT ME.
EVEN THOUGH HE EXAG-GERATES.
AND HE'S HATEFUL ABOUT EVERYTHING ELSE.
BUT...

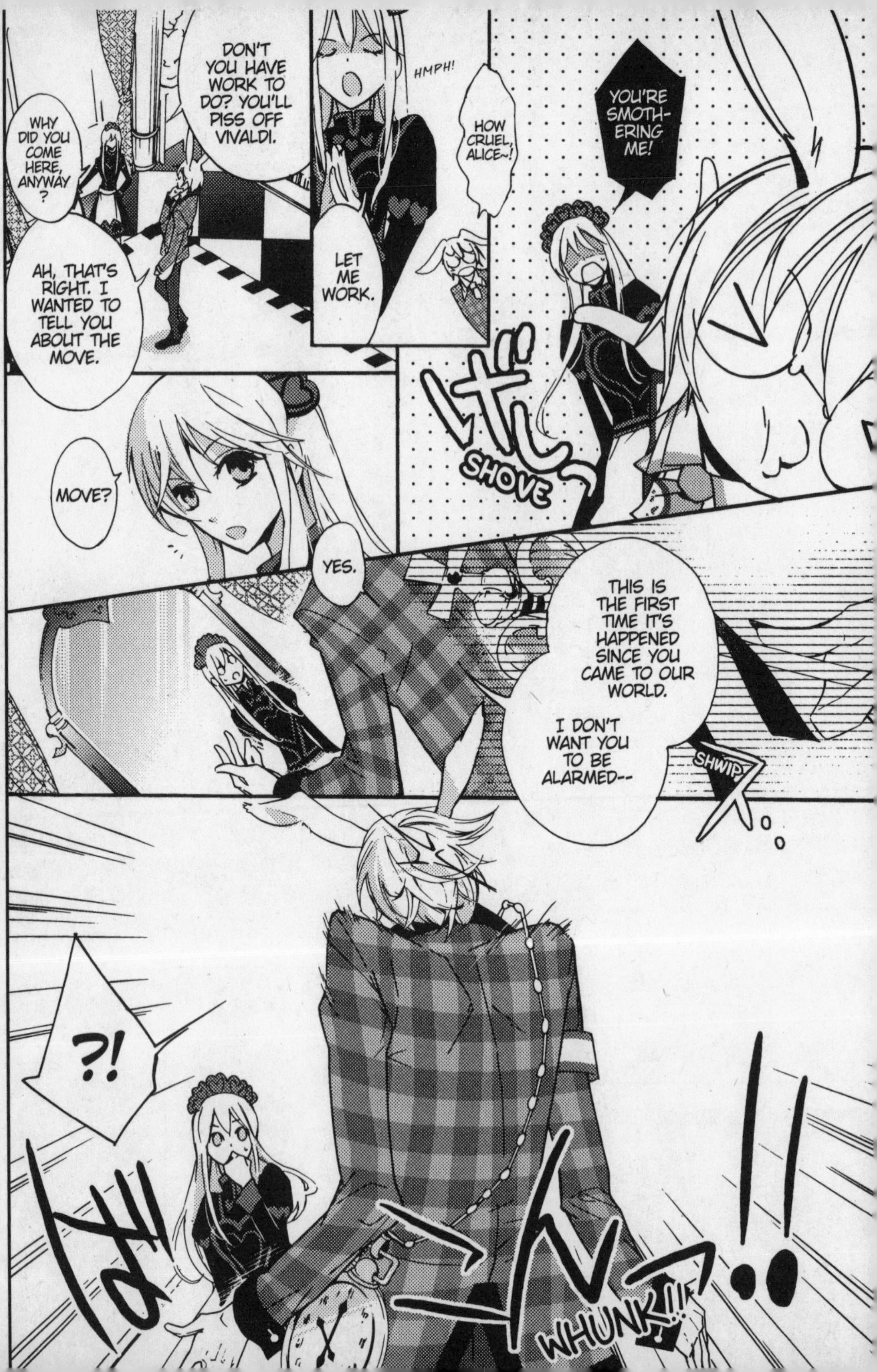
YOU'RE SMOTHERING ME!
SHOVE
HMPH!
HOW CRUEL, ALICE~!
DON'T YOU HAVE WORK TO DO? YOU'LL PISS OFF VIVALDI.
LET ME WORK.
WHY DID YOU COME HERE, ANYWAY?
AH, THAT'S RIGHT. I WANTED TO TELL YOU ABOUT THE MOVE.
MOVE?
YES.
THIS IS THE FIRST TIME IT'S HAPPENED SINCE YOU CAME TO OUR WORLD.
I DON'T WANT YOU TO BE ALARMED--
SHWIP
?!
!!
WHUNK!!

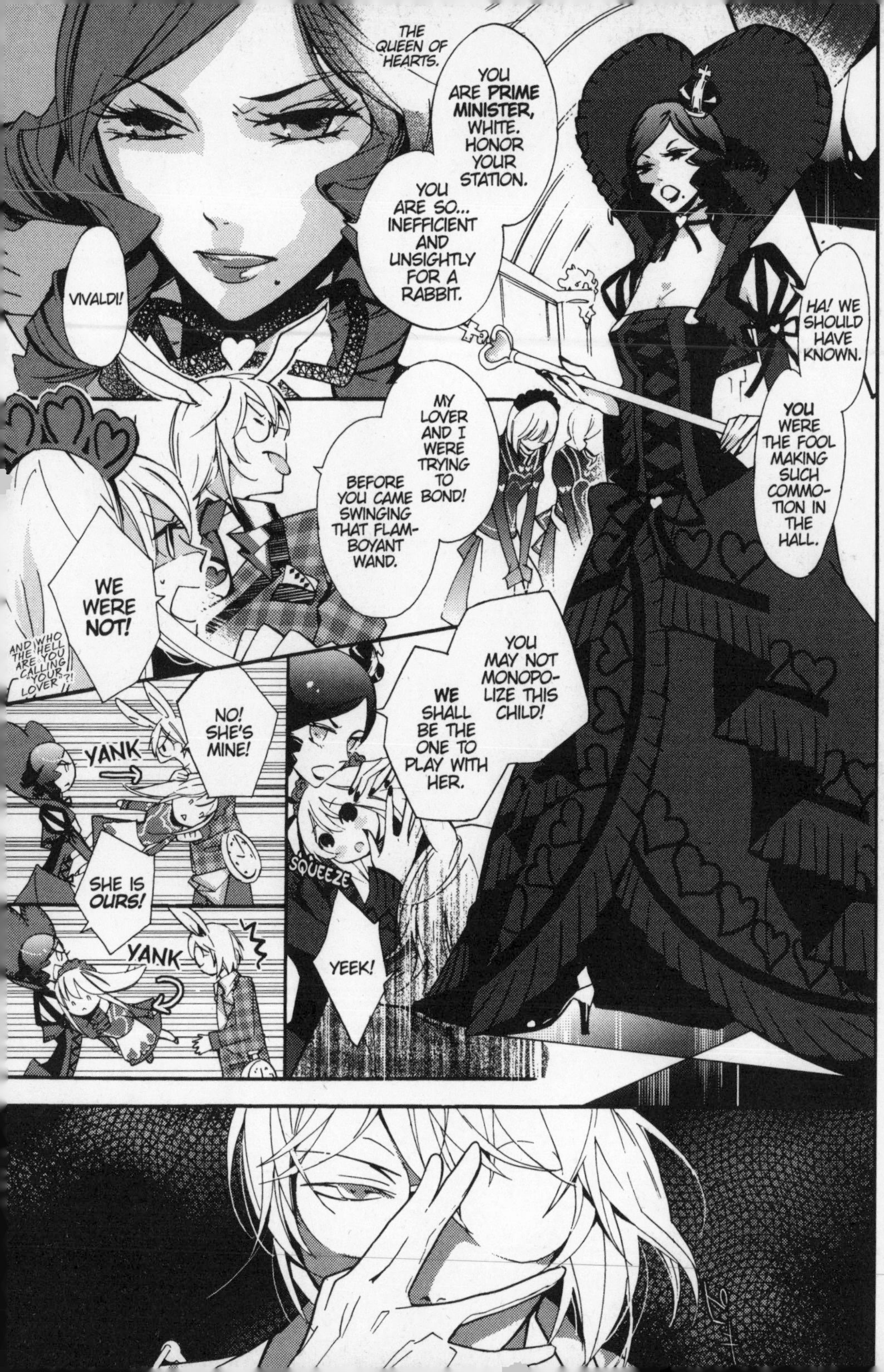
THE QUEEN OF HEARTS.
YOU ARE PRIME MINISTER, WHITE. HONOR YOUR STATION.
YOU ARE SO... INEFFICIENT AND UNSIGHTLY FOR A RABBIT.
VIVALDI!
HA! WE SHOULD HAVE KNOWN.
YOU WERE THE FOOL MAKING SUCH COMMOTION IN THE HALL.
MY LOVER AND I WERE TRYING TO BOND!
BEFORE YOU CAME SWINGING THAT FLAMBOYANT WAND.
WE WERE NOT!
AND WHO THE HELL ARE YOU CALLING "YOUR LOVER"?!
YOU MAY NOT MONOPOLIZE THIS CHILD!
WE SHALL BE THE ONE TO PLAY WITH HER.
SQUEEZE
YEEK!
NO! SHE'S MINE!
YANK
SHE IS OURS!
YANK

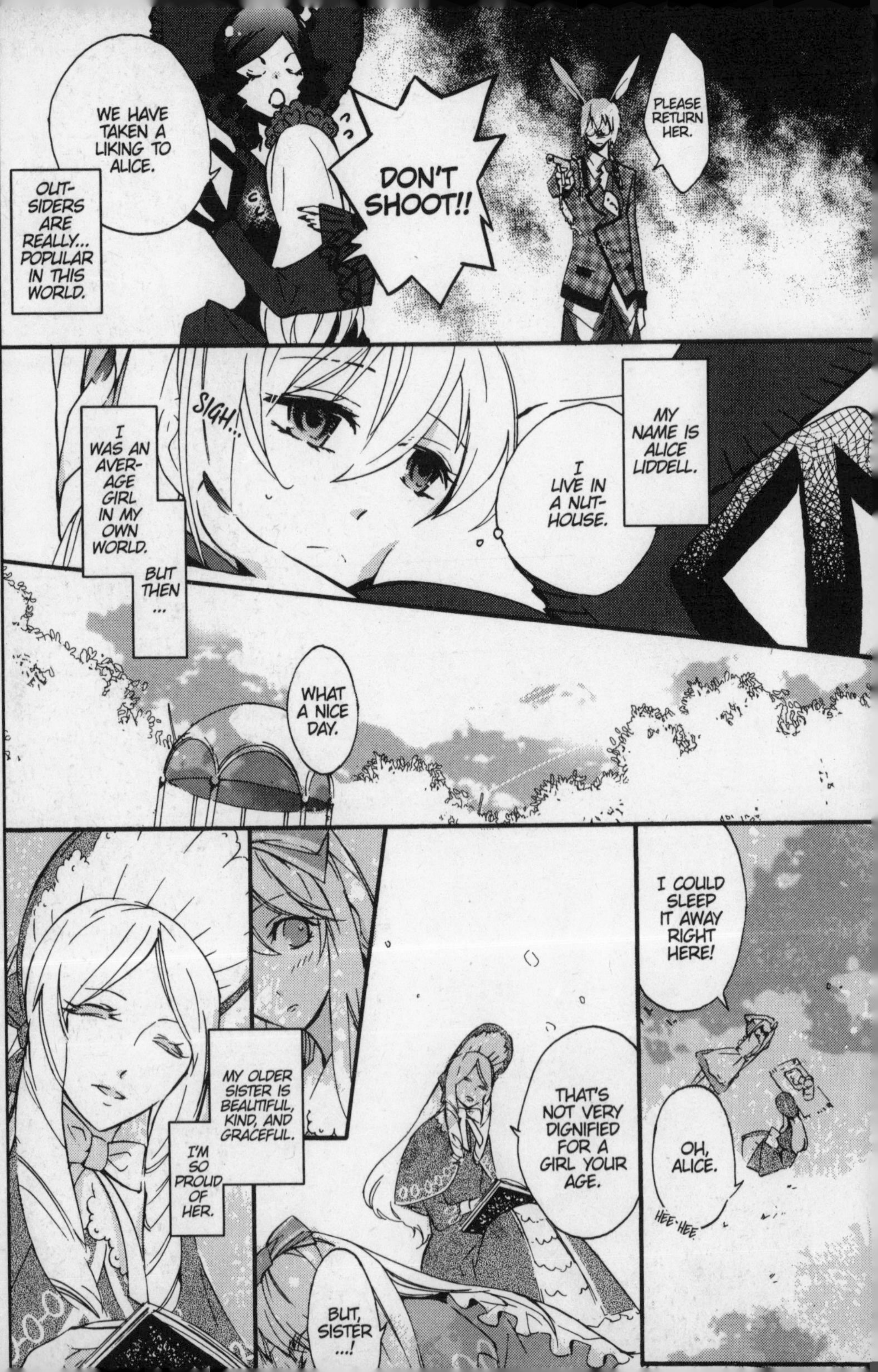
PLEASE RETURN HER.
DON'T SHOOT!!
WE HAVE TAKEN A LIKING TO ALICE.
OUT-SIDERS ARE REALLY... POPULAR IN THIS WORLD.
MY NAME IS ALICE LIDDELL.
I LIVE IN A NUT-HOUSE.
SIGH...
I WAS AN AVER-AGE GIRL IN MY OWN WORLD.
BUT THEN ...
WHAT A NICE DAY.
I COULD SLEEP IT AWAY RIGHT HERE!
OH, ALICE.
HEE-HEE
THAT'S NOT VERY DIGNIFIED FOR A GIRL YOUR AGE.
MY OLDER SISTER IS BEAUTIFUL, KIND, AND GRACEFUL.
I'M SO PROUD OF HER.
BUT, SISTER ...!

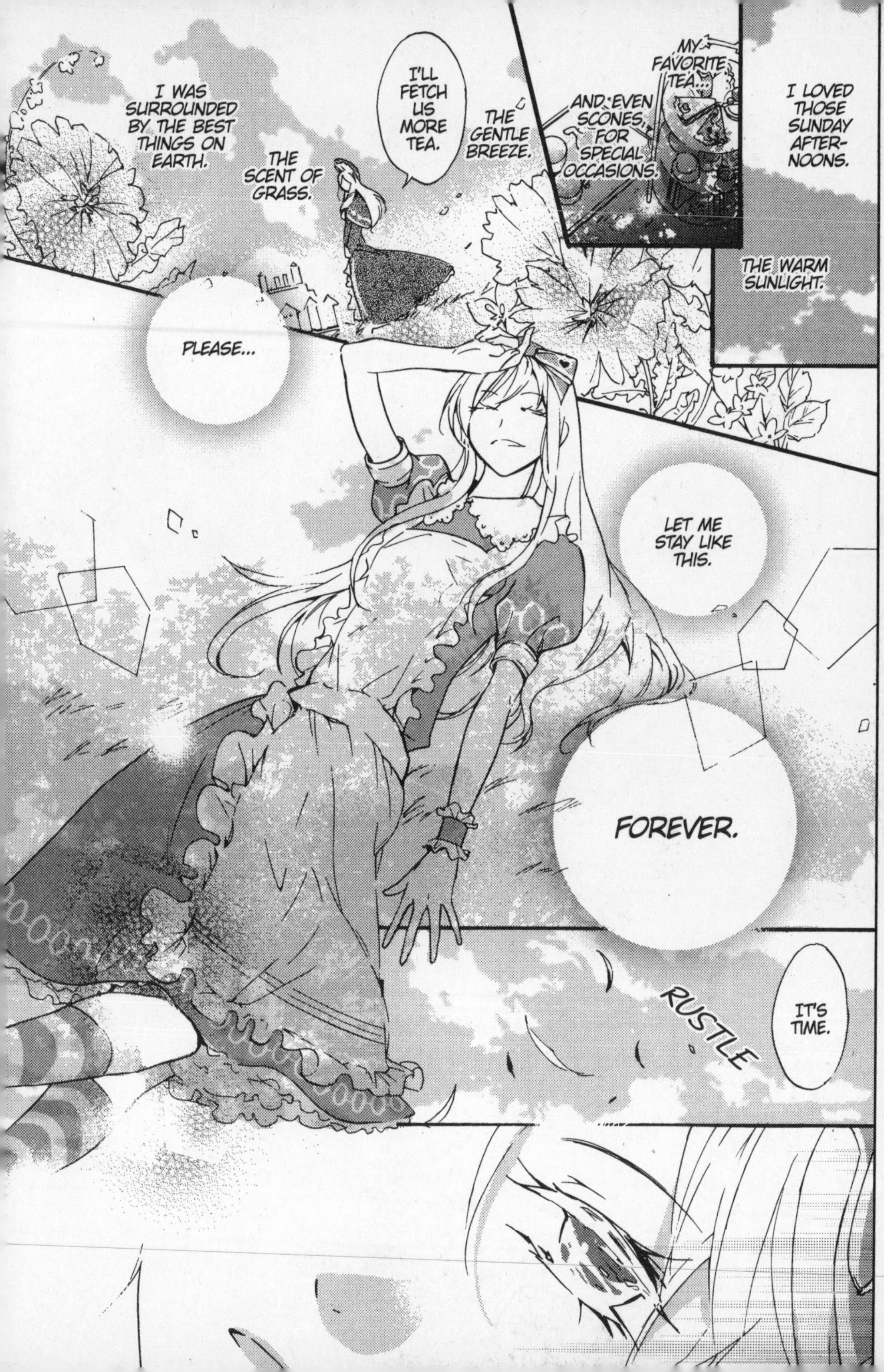
I LOVED THOSE SUNDAY AFTERNOONS.
THE WARM SUNLIGHT.
MY FAVORITE TEA...
AND EVEN SCONES, FOR SPECIAL OCCASIONS.
THE GENTLE BREEZE.
I'LL FETCH US MORE TEA.
THE SCENT OF GRASS.
I WAS SURROUNDED BY THE BEST THINGS ON EARTH.
PLEASE...
LET ME STAY LIKE THIS.
FOREVER.
IT'S TIME.
RUSTLE

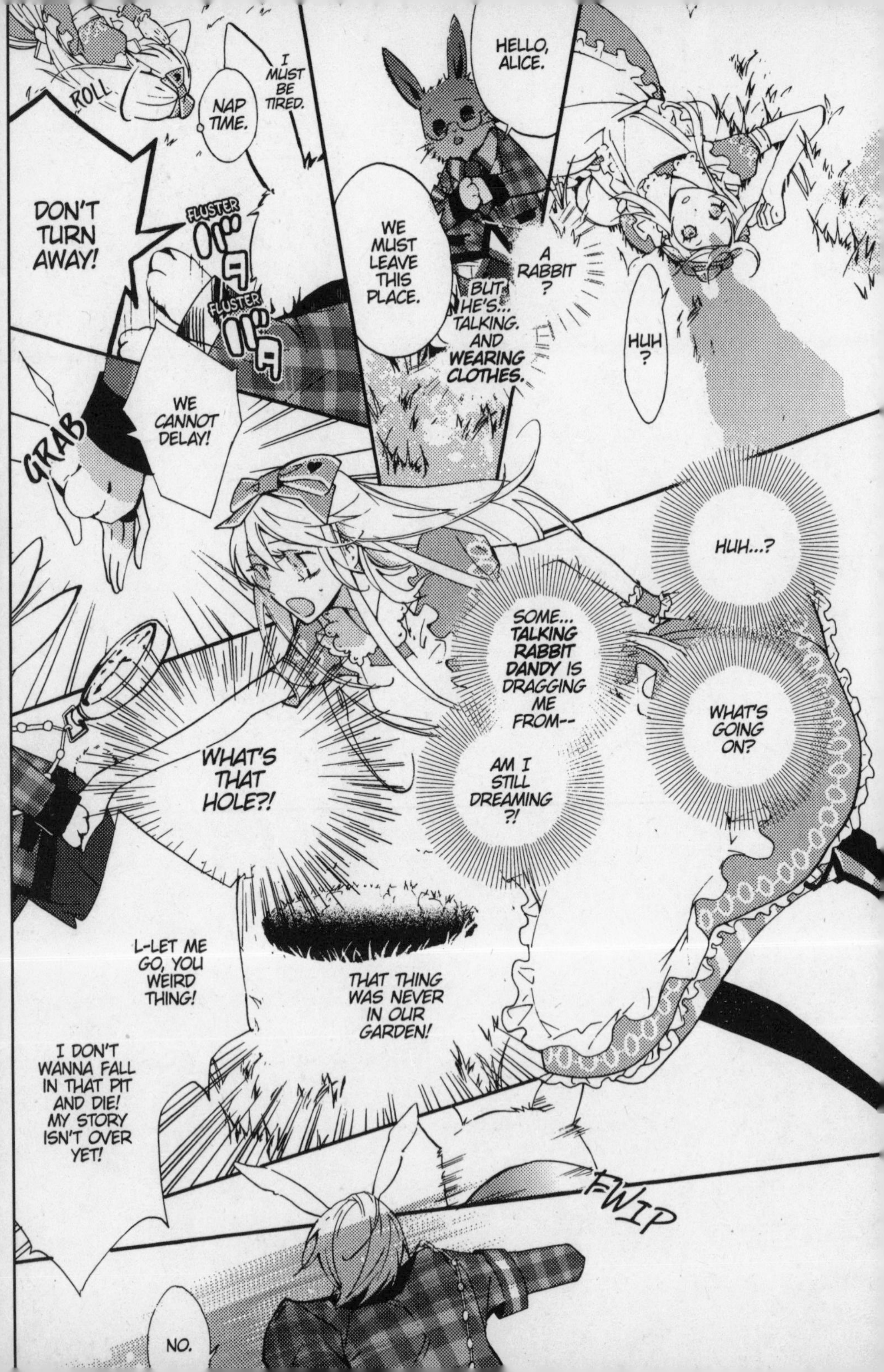
HELLO, ALICE.
HUH?
A RABBIT?
BUT HE'S... TALKING. AND WEARING CLOTHES.
WE MUST LEAVE THIS PLACE.
I MUST BE TIRED.
NAP TIME.
ROLL
DON'T TURN AWAY!
FLUSTER
FLUSTER
WE CANNOT DELAY!
GRAB
HUH...?
WHAT'S GOING ON?
SOME... TALKING RABBIT DANDY IS DRAGGING ME FROM--
AM I STILL DREAMING?!
WHAT'S THAT HOLE?!
THAT THING WAS NEVER IN OUR GARDEN!
L-LET ME GO, YOU WEIRD THING!
I DON'T WANNA FALL IN THAT PIT AND DIE! MY STORY ISN'T OVER YET!
FWIP
NO.

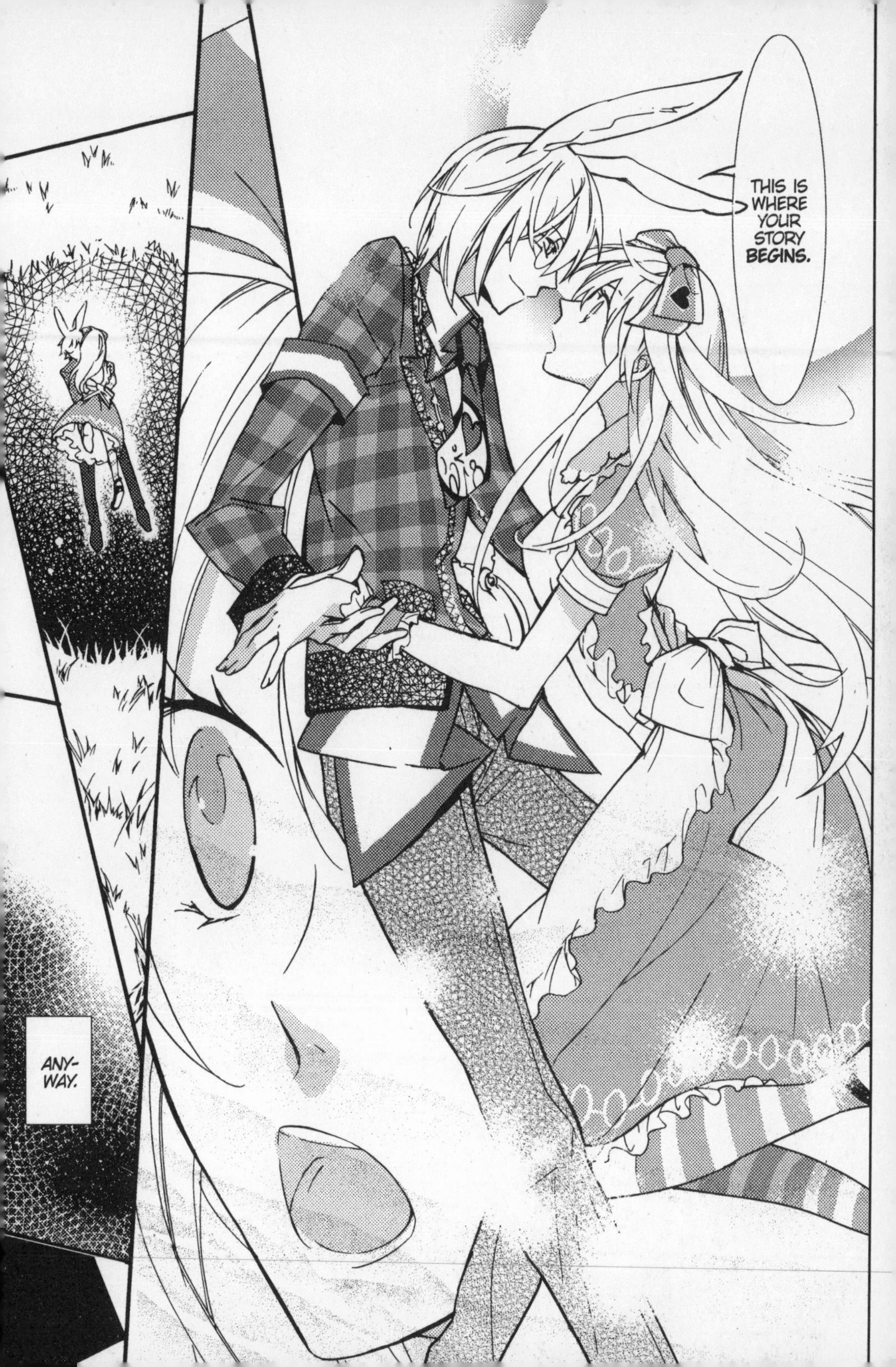
THIS IS WHERE YOUR STORY BEGINS.
ANY-WAY.

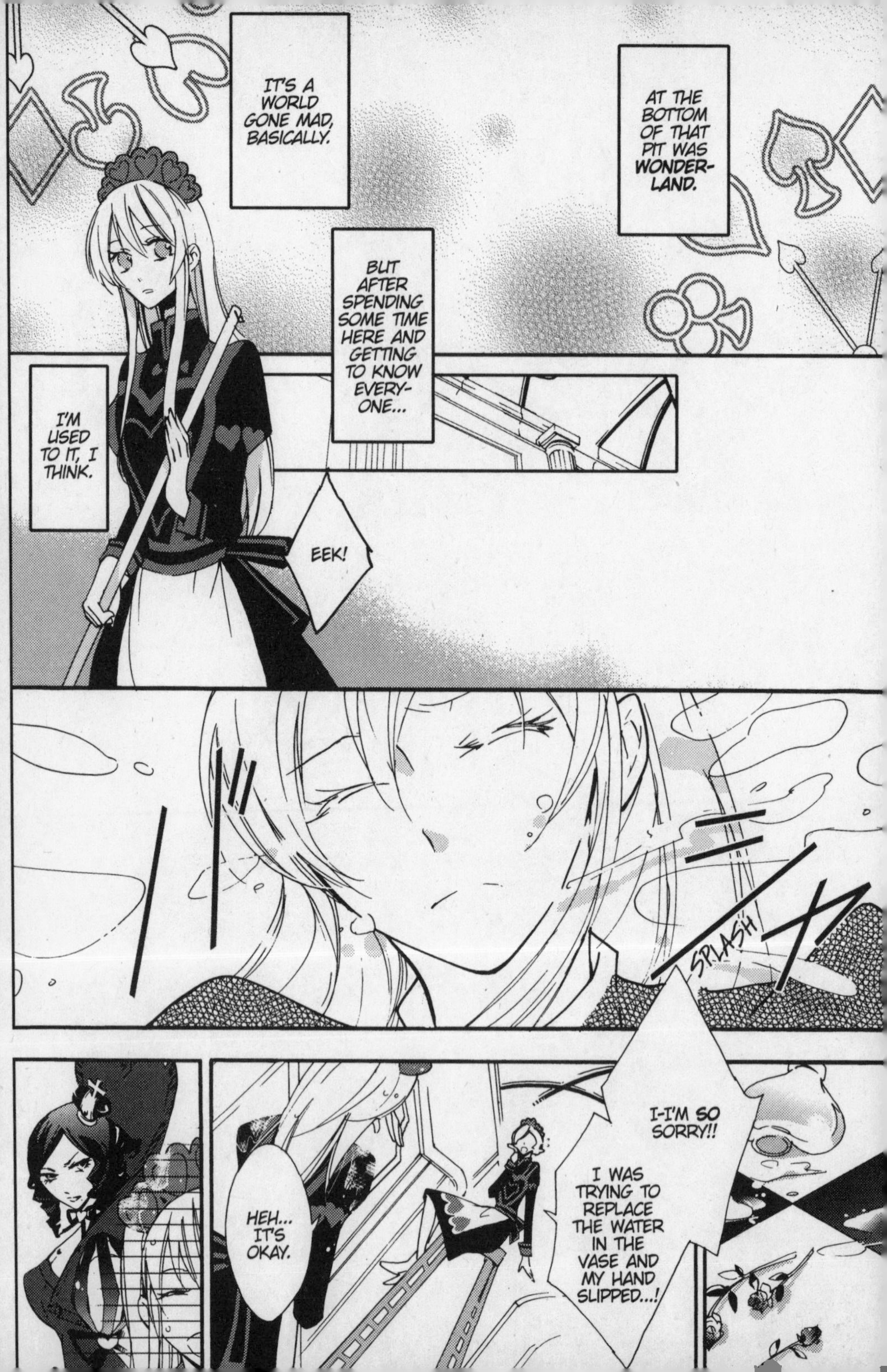
AT THE BOTTOM OF THAT PIT WAS WONDERLAND.
IT'S A WORLD GONE MAD, BASICALLY.
BUT AFTER SPENDING SOME TIME HERE AND GETTING TO KNOW EVERYONE...
I'M USED TO IT, I THINK.
EEK!
SPLASH
I-I'M SO SORRY!!
I WAS TRYING TO REPLACE THE WATER IN THE VASE AND MY HAND SLIPPED...!
HEH... IT'S OKAY.

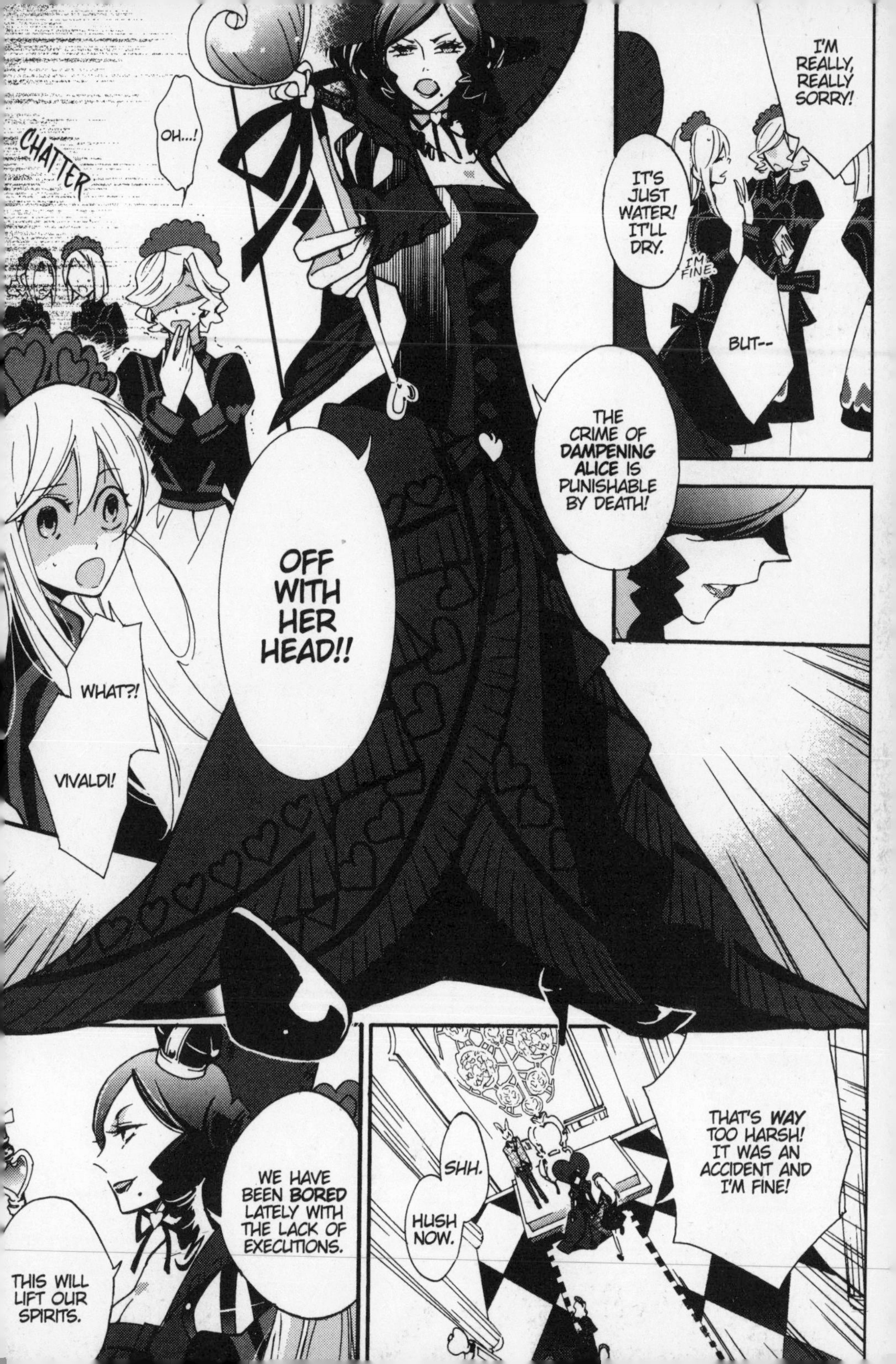
I'M REALLY, REALLY SORRY!
IT'S JUST WATER! IT'LL DRY.
I'M FINE.
BUT--
THE CRIME OF DAMPENING ALICE IS PUNISHABLE BY DEATH!
OH...!
CHATTER
OFF WITH HER HEAD!!
WHAT?!
VIVALDI!
THAT'S WAY TOO HARSH! IT WAS AN ACCIDENT AND I'M FINE!
SHH.
HUSH NOW.
WE HAVE BEEN BORED LATELY WITH THE LACK OF EXECUTIONS.
THIS WILL LIFT OUR SPIRITS.

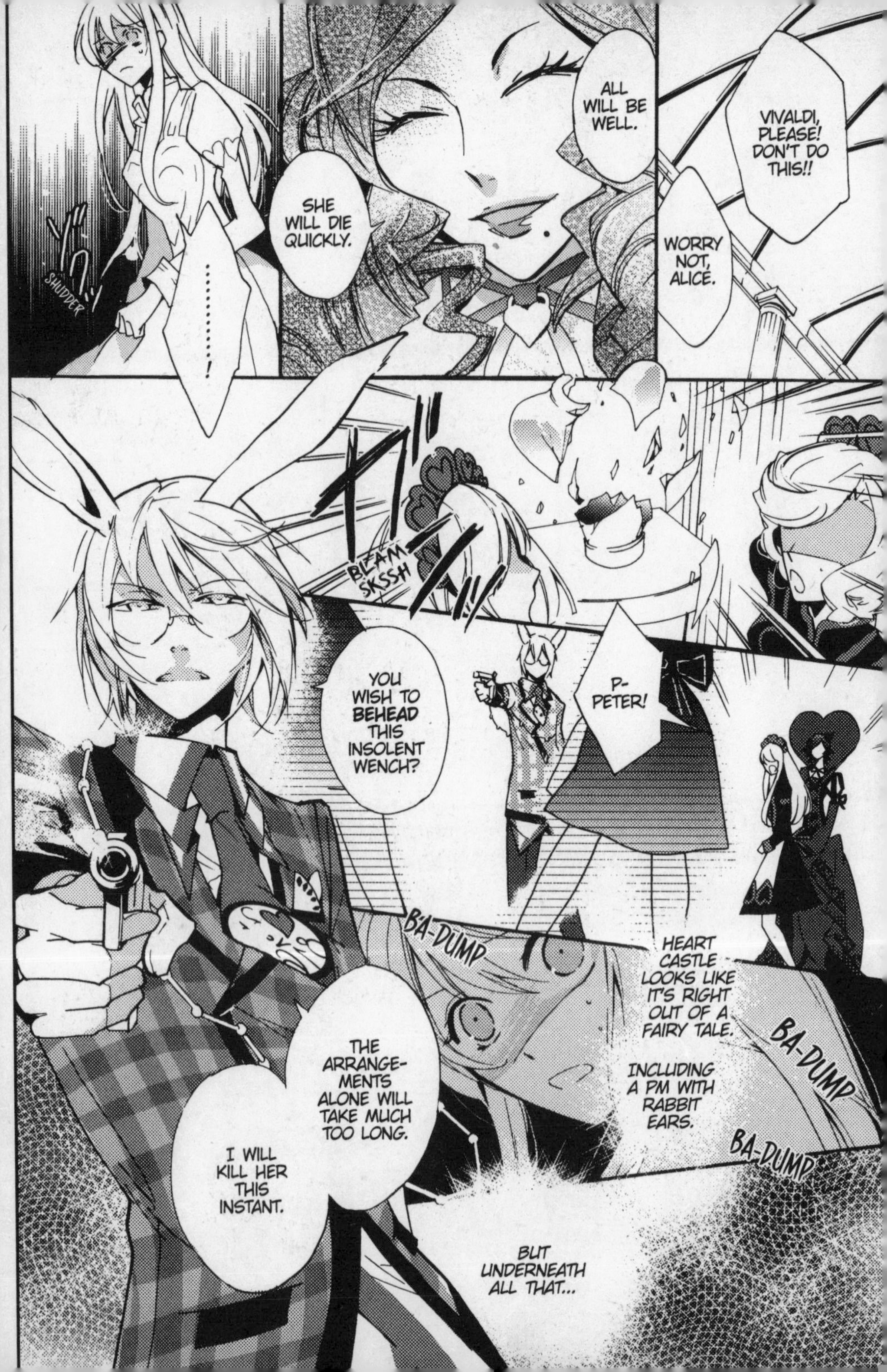
VIVALDI, PLEASE! DON'T DO THIS!!
WORRY NOT, ALICE.
ALL WILL BE WELL.
SHE WILL DIE QUICKLY.
SHUDDER
......!
BLAM
SKSSH
P-PETER!
YOU WISH TO BEHEAD THIS INSOLENT WENCH?
HEART CASTLE LOOKS LIKE IT'S RIGHT OUT OF A FAIRY TALE.
INCLUDING A PM WITH RABBIT EARS.
BA-DUMP
BA-DUMP
BA-DUMP
THE ARRANGE-MENTS ALONE WILL TAKE MUCH TOO LONG.
I WILL KILL HER THIS INSTANT.
BUT UNDERNEATH ALL THAT...

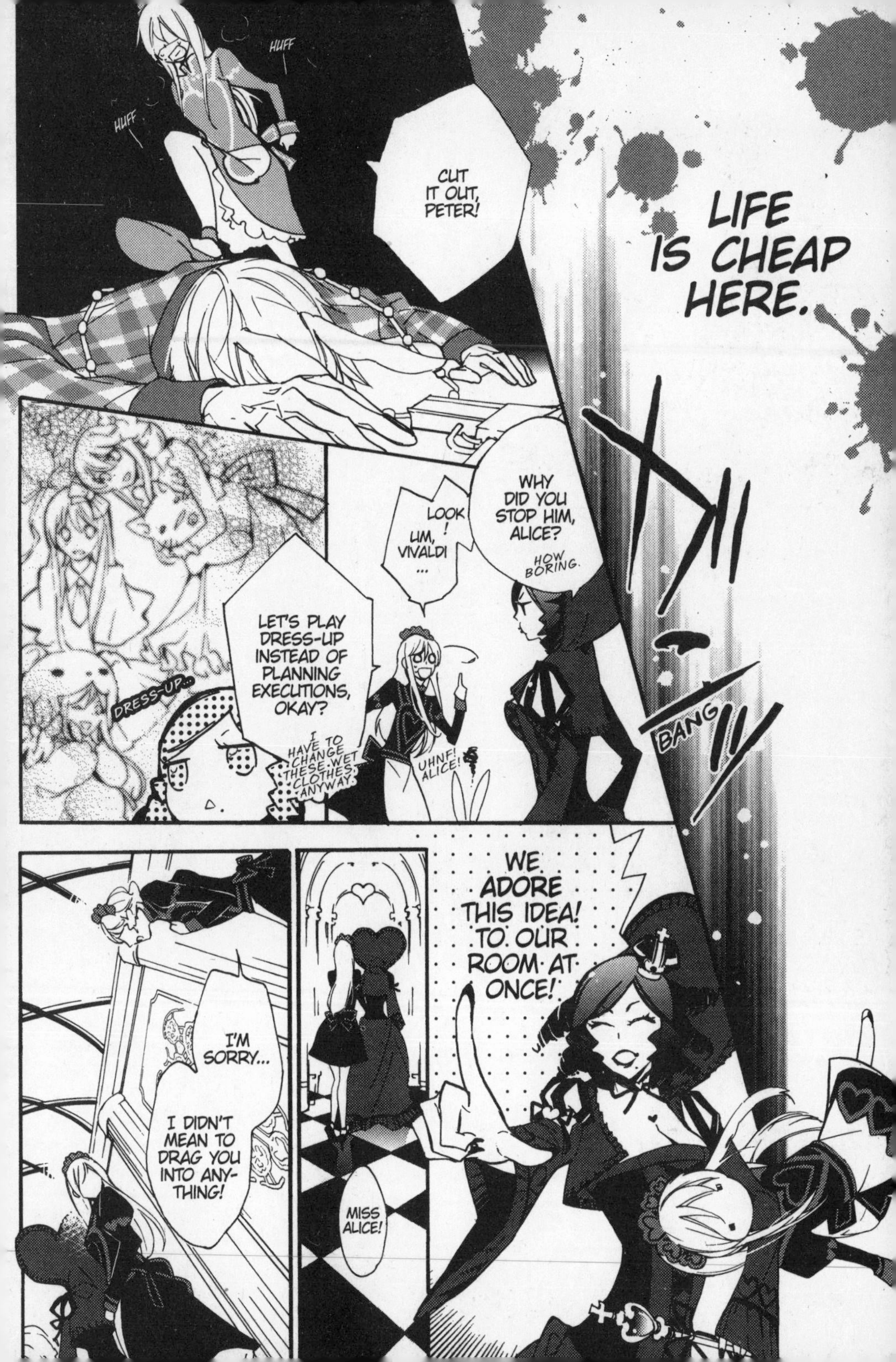

BANG
LIFE IS CHEAP HERE.
HUFF
HUFF
CUT IT OUT, PETER!
WHY DID YOU STOP HIM, ALICE?
HOW BORING.
LOOK! UM, VIVALDI...
LET'S PLAY DRESS-UP INSTEAD OF PLANNING EXECUTIONS, OKAY?
I HAVE TO CHANGE THESE WET CLOTHES ANYWAY.
UHNF! ALICE!
DRESS-UP...
WE ADORE THIS IDEA! TO OUR ROOM AT ONCE!
MISS ALICE!
I'M SORRY...
I DIDN'T MEAN TO DRAG YOU INTO ANYTHING!

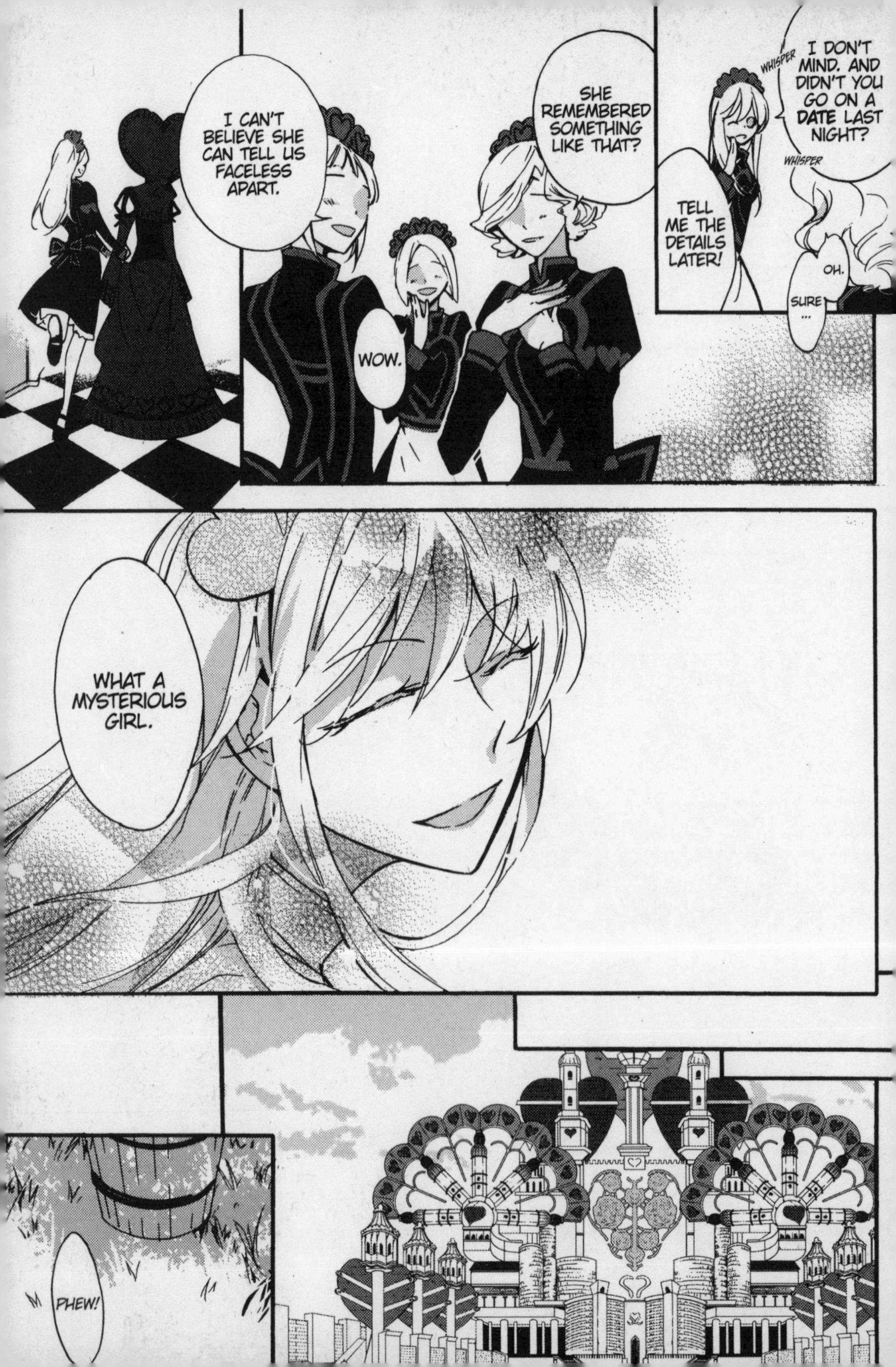
WHISPER
I DON'T MIND. AND DIDN'T YOU GO ON A DATE LAST NIGHT?
WHISPER
TELL ME THE DETAILS LATER!
OH.
SURE...
SHE REMEMBERED SOMETHING LIKE THAT?
I CAN'T BELIEVE SHE CAN TELL US FACELESS APART.
WOW.
WHAT A MYSTERIOUS GIRL.
PHEW!

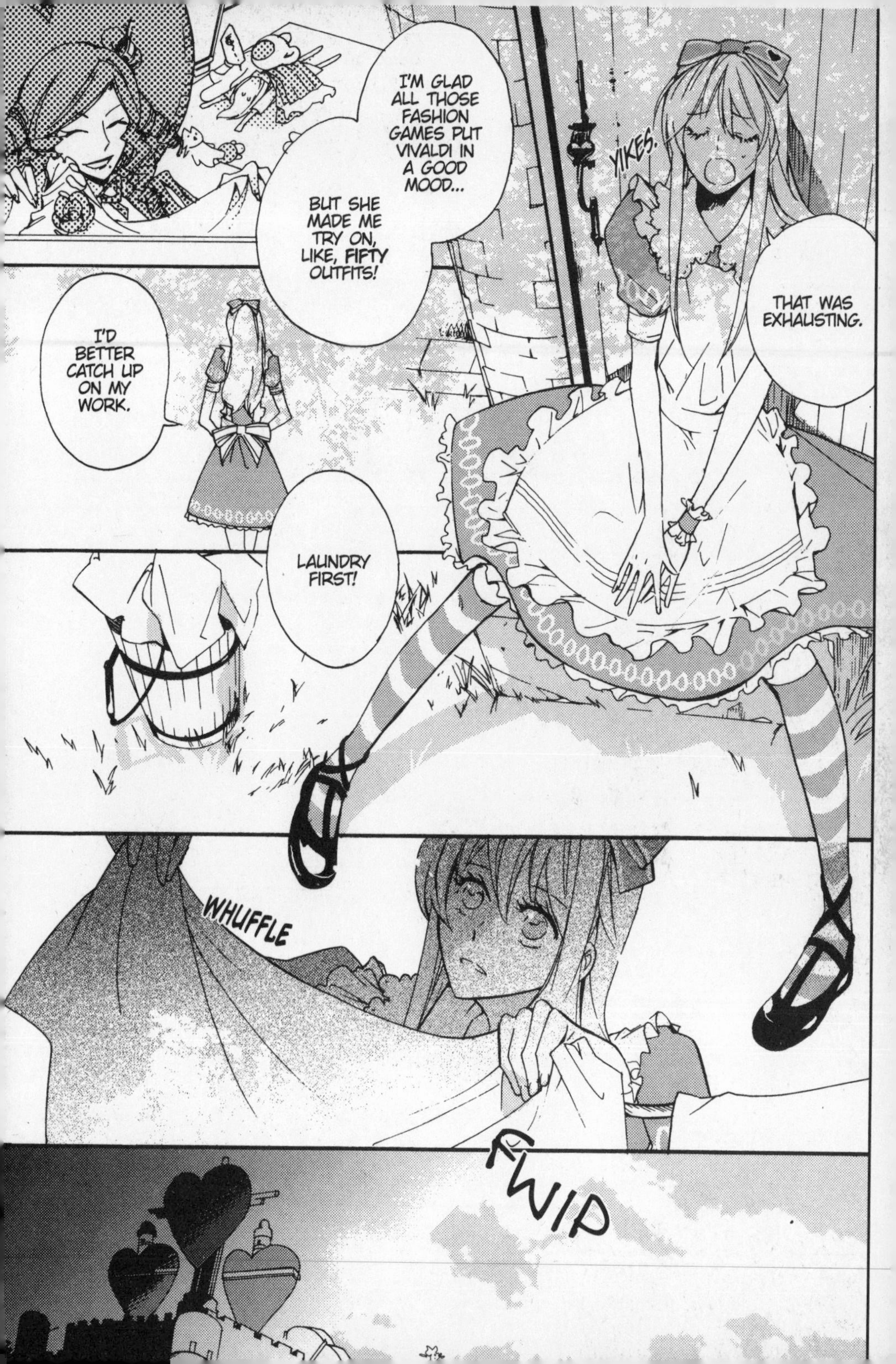
I'M GLAD ALL THOSE FASHION GAMES PUT VIVALDI IN A GOOD MOOD...
BUT SHE MADE ME TRY ON, LIKE, FIFTY OUTFITS!
YIKES.
THAT WAS EXHAUSTING.
I'D BETTER CATCH UP ON MY WORK.
LAUNDRY FIRST!
WHUFFLE
FWIP

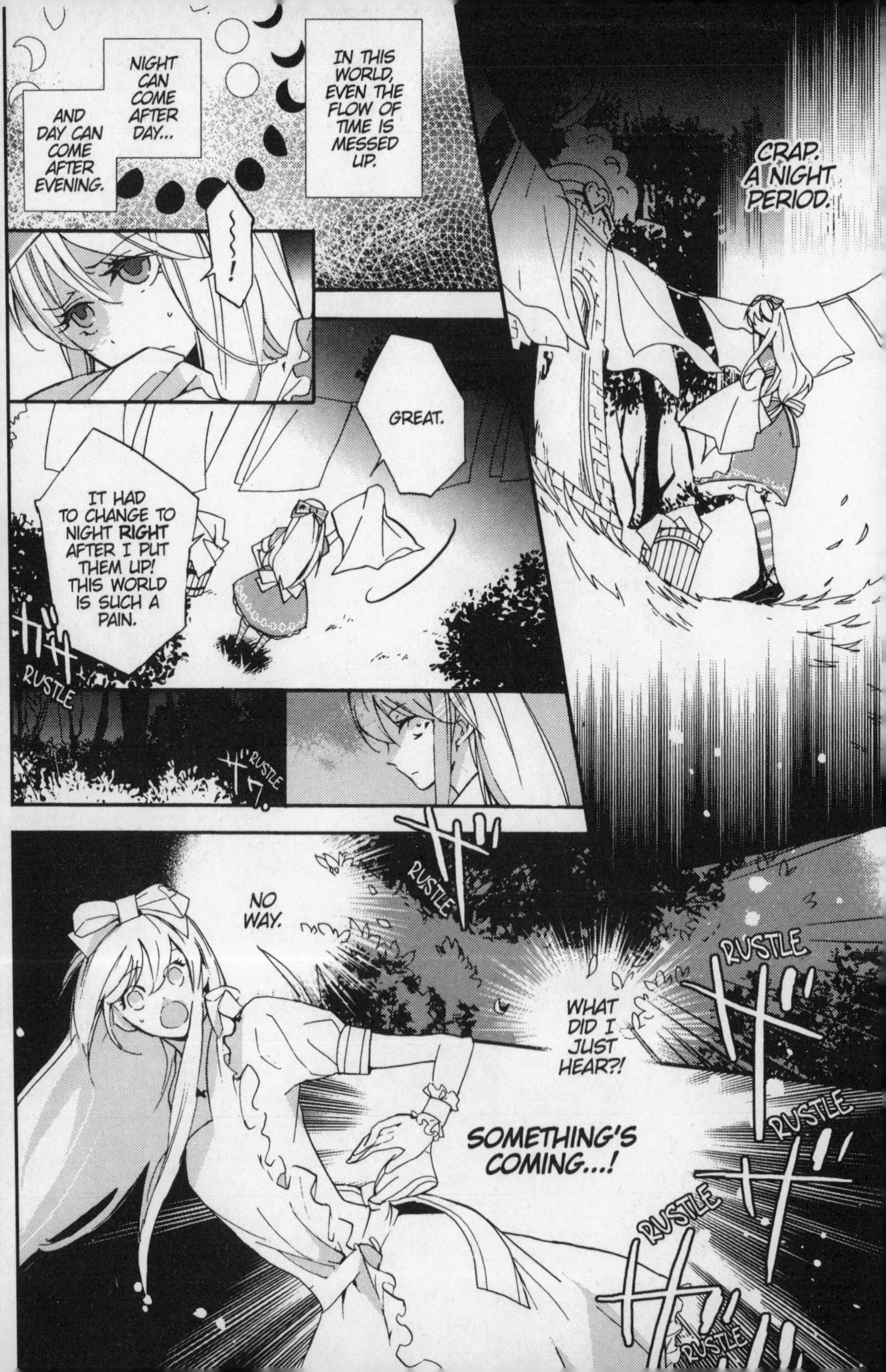
CRAP. A NIGHT PERIOD.
IN THIS WORLD, EVEN THE FLOW OF TIME IS MESSED UP.
NIGHT CAN COME AFTER DAY...
AND DAY CAN COME AFTER EVENING.
~~~!
GREAT.
IT HAD TO CHANGE TO NIGHT **RIGHT** AFTER I PUT THEM UP! THIS WORLD IS SUCH A PAIN.
RUSTLE
RUSTLE
RUSTLE
RUSTLE
WHAT DID I JUST HEAR?!
RUSTLE
SOMETHING'S COMING...!
RUSTLE
RUSTLE
NO WAY.
~~~

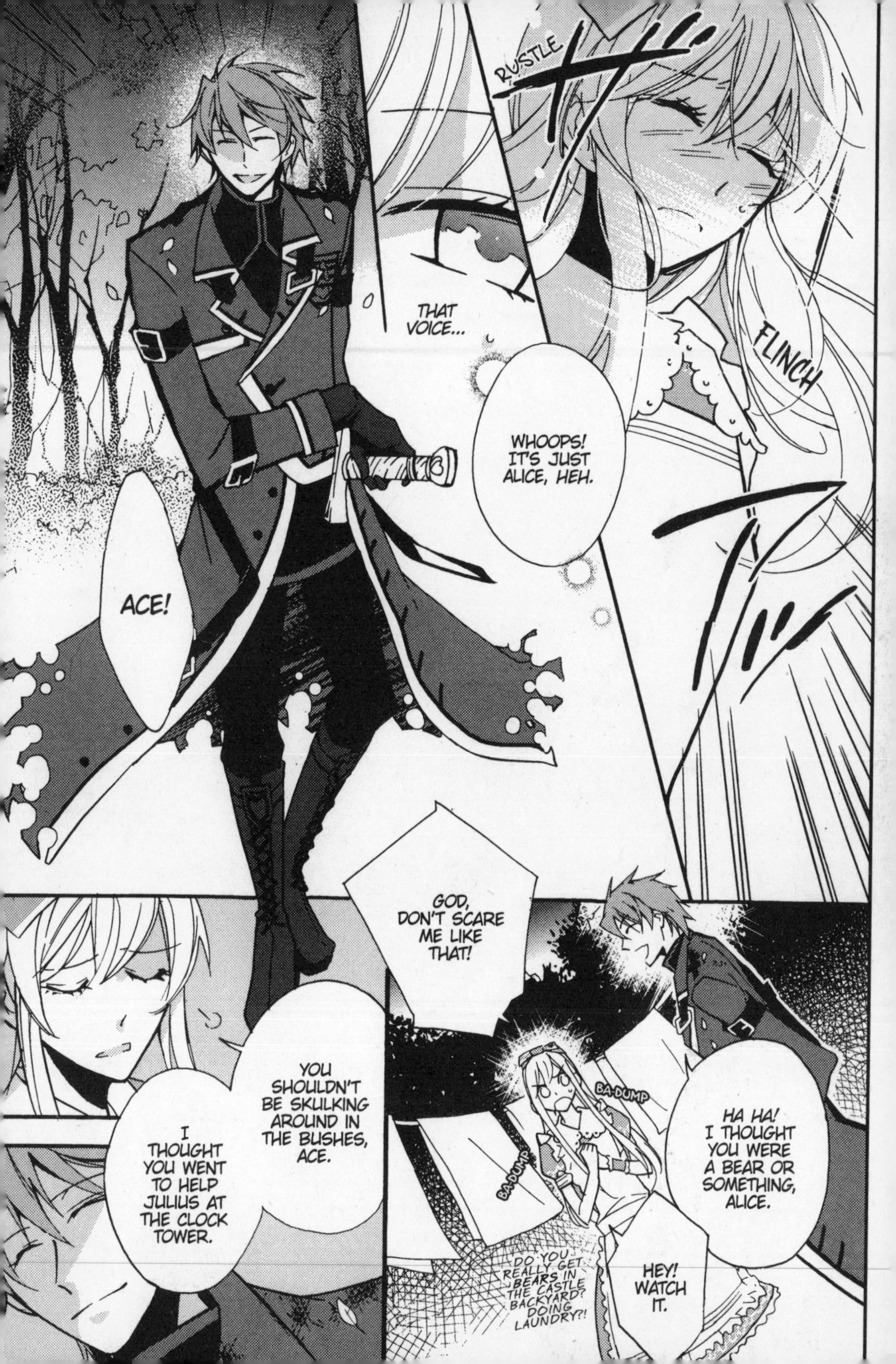
RUSTLE
FLINCH
THAT VOICE...
WHOOPS! IT'S JUST ALICE, HEH.
ACE!
GOD, DON'T SCARE ME LIKE THAT!
HA HA! I THOUGHT YOU WERE A BEAR OR SOMETHING, ALICE.
BA-DUMP
BA-DUMP
HEY! WATCH IT.
DO YOU REALLY GET BEARS IN THE CASTLE BACKYARD? DOING LAUNDRY?!
YOU SHOULDN'T BE SKULKING AROUND IN THE BUSHES, ACE.
I THOUGHT YOU WENT TO HELP JULIUS AT THE CLOCK TOWER.

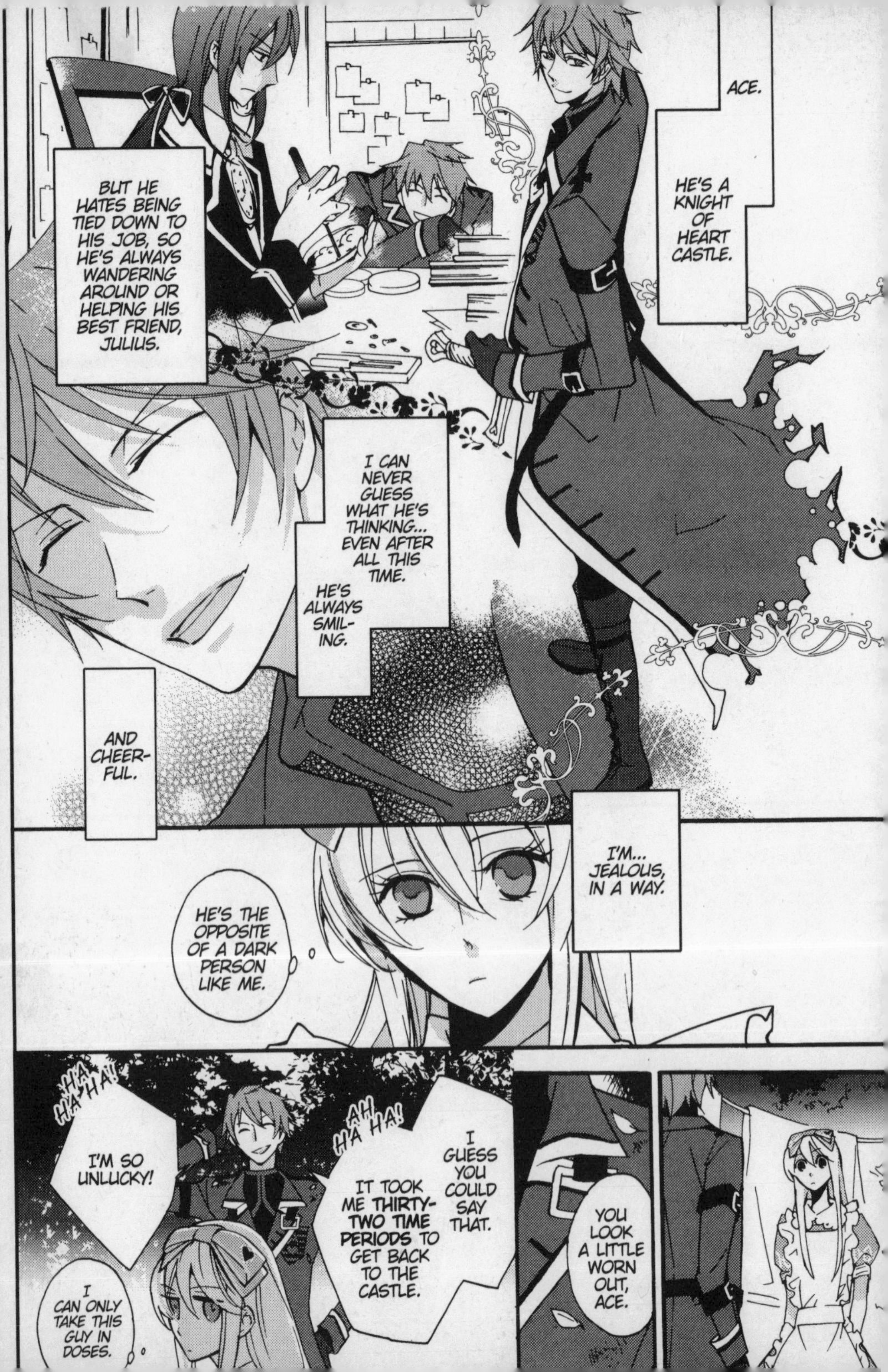
ACE.
HE'S A KNIGHT OF HEART CASTLE.
BUT HE HATES BEING TIED DOWN TO HIS JOB, SO HE'S ALWAYS WANDERING AROUND OR HELPING HIS BEST FRIEND, JULIUS.
I CAN NEVER GUESS WHAT HE'S THINKING... EVEN AFTER ALL THIS TIME.
HE'S ALWAYS SMILING.
AND CHEERFUL.
I'M... JEALOUS, IN A WAY.
HE'S THE OPPOSITE OF A DARK PERSON LIKE ME.
YOU LOOK A LITTLE WORN OUT, ACE.
I GUESS YOU COULD SAY THAT.
AH HA HA!
IT TOOK ME **THIRTY-TWO TIME PERIODS** TO GET BACK TO THE CASTLE.
HA HA!
I'M SO UNLUCKY!
I CAN ONLY TAKE THIS GUY IN DOSES.

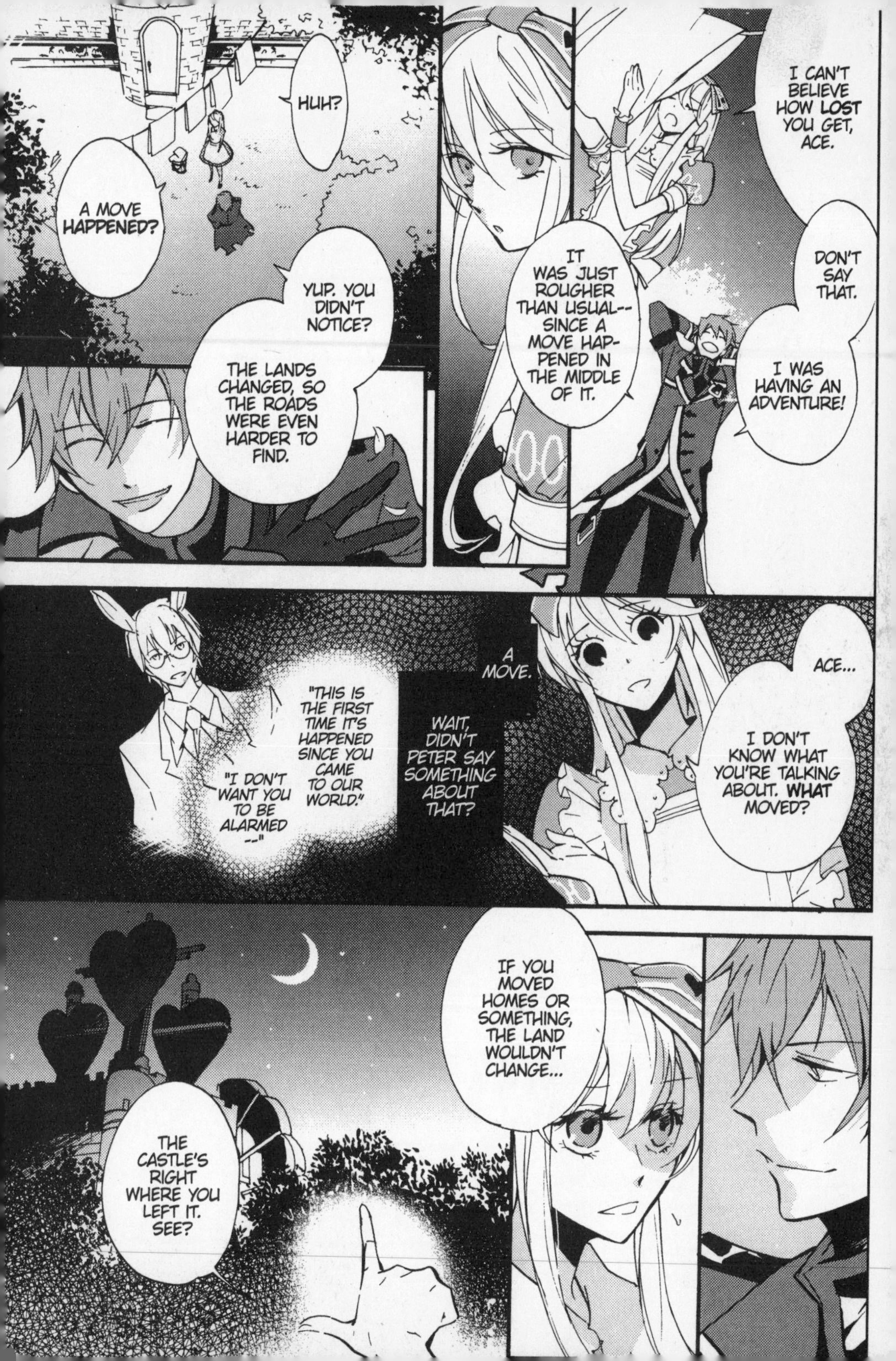
I CAN'T BELIEVE HOW LOST YOU GET, ACE.
DON'T SAY THAT.
I WAS HAVING AN ADVENTURE!
IT WAS JUST ROUGHER THAN USUAL-- SINCE A MOVE HAPPENED IN THE MIDDLE OF IT.
HUH?
A MOVE HAPPENED?
YUP. YOU DIDN'T NOTICE?
THE LANDS CHANGED, SO THE ROADS WERE EVEN HARDER TO FIND.
ACE...
I DON'T KNOW WHAT YOU'RE TALKING ABOUT. WHAT MOVED?
A MOVE.
WAIT, DIDN'T PETER SAY SOMETHING ABOUT THAT?
"THIS IS THE FIRST TIME IT'S HAPPENED SINCE YOU CAME TO OUR WORLD."
"I DON'T WANT YOU TO BE ALARMED --"
IF YOU MOVED HOMES OR SOMETHING, THE LAND WOULDN'T CHANGE...
THE CASTLE'S RIGHT WHERE YOU LEFT IT. SEE?

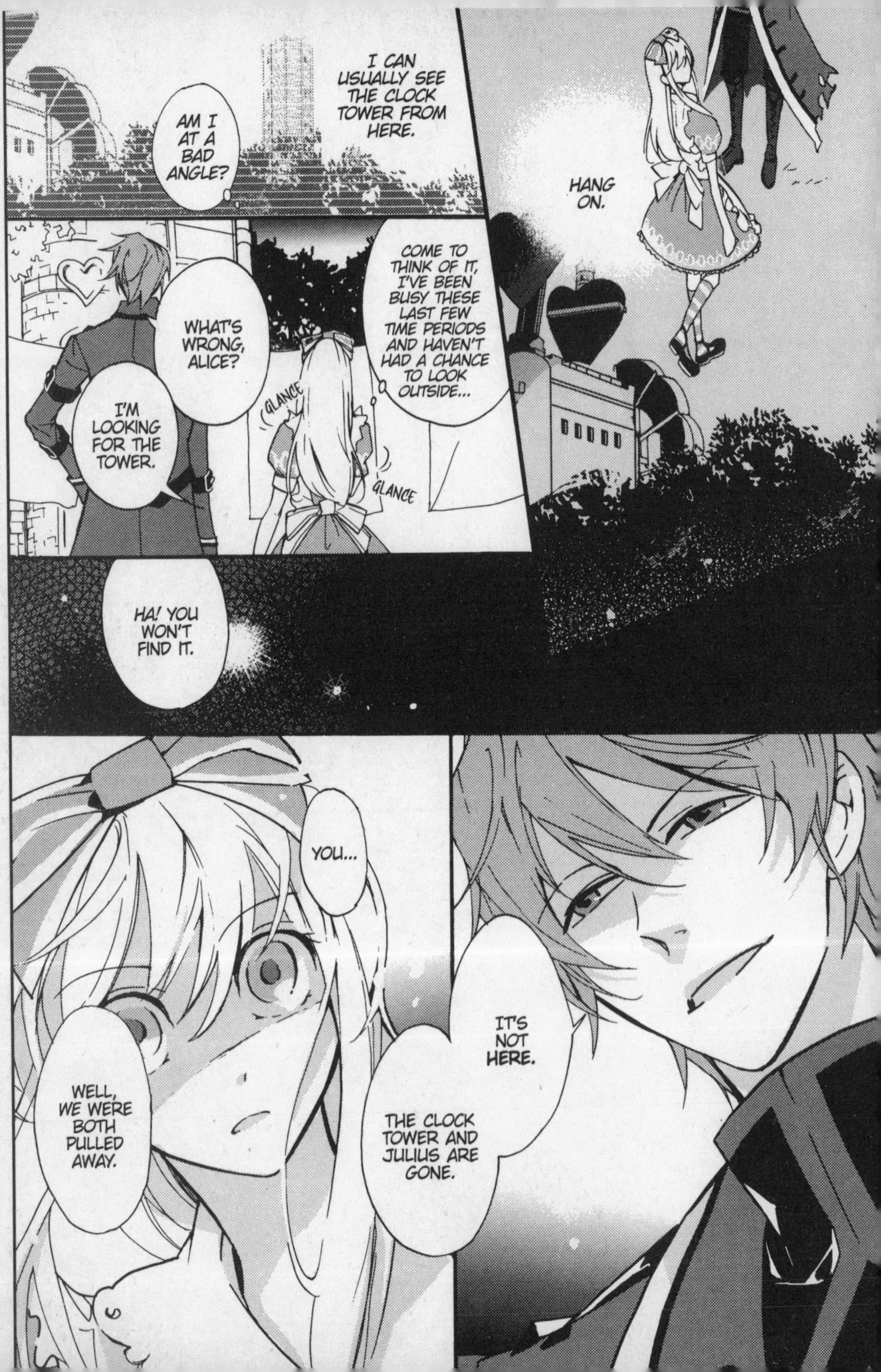
HANG ON.
I CAN USUALLY SEE THE CLOCK TOWER FROM HERE.
AM I AT A BAD ANGLE?
COME TO THINK OF IT, I'VE BEEN BUSY THESE LAST FEW TIME PERIODS AND HAVEN'T HAD A CHANCE TO LOOK OUTSIDE...
GLANCE
GLANCE
WHAT'S WRONG, ALICE?
I'M LOOKING FOR THE TOWER.
HA! YOU WON'T FIND IT.
IT'S NOT HERE.
THE CLOCK TOWER AND JULIUS ARE GONE.
YOU...
WELL, WE WERE BOTH PULLED AWAY.

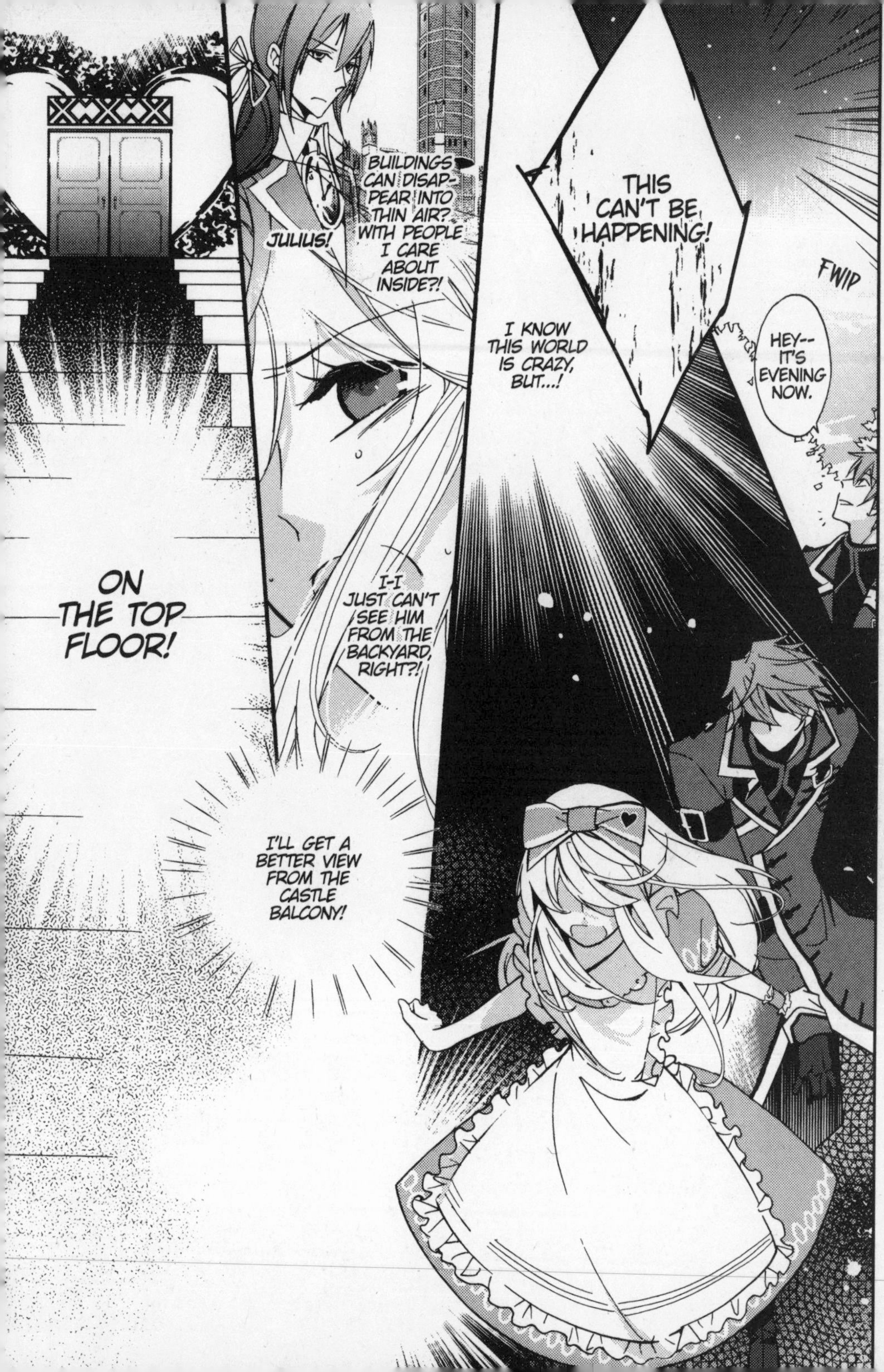
THIS CAN'T BE HAPPENING!
FWIP
HEY-- IT'S EVENING NOW.
I KNOW THIS WORLD IS CRAZY, BUT...!
BUILDINGS CAN DISAP-PEAR INTO THIN AIR? WITH PEOPLE I CARE ABOUT INSIDE?!
JULIUS!
I-I JUST CAN'T SEE HIM FROM THE BACKYARD, RIGHT?!
I'LL GET A BETTER VIEW FROM THE CASTLE BALCONY!
ON THE TOP FLOOR!

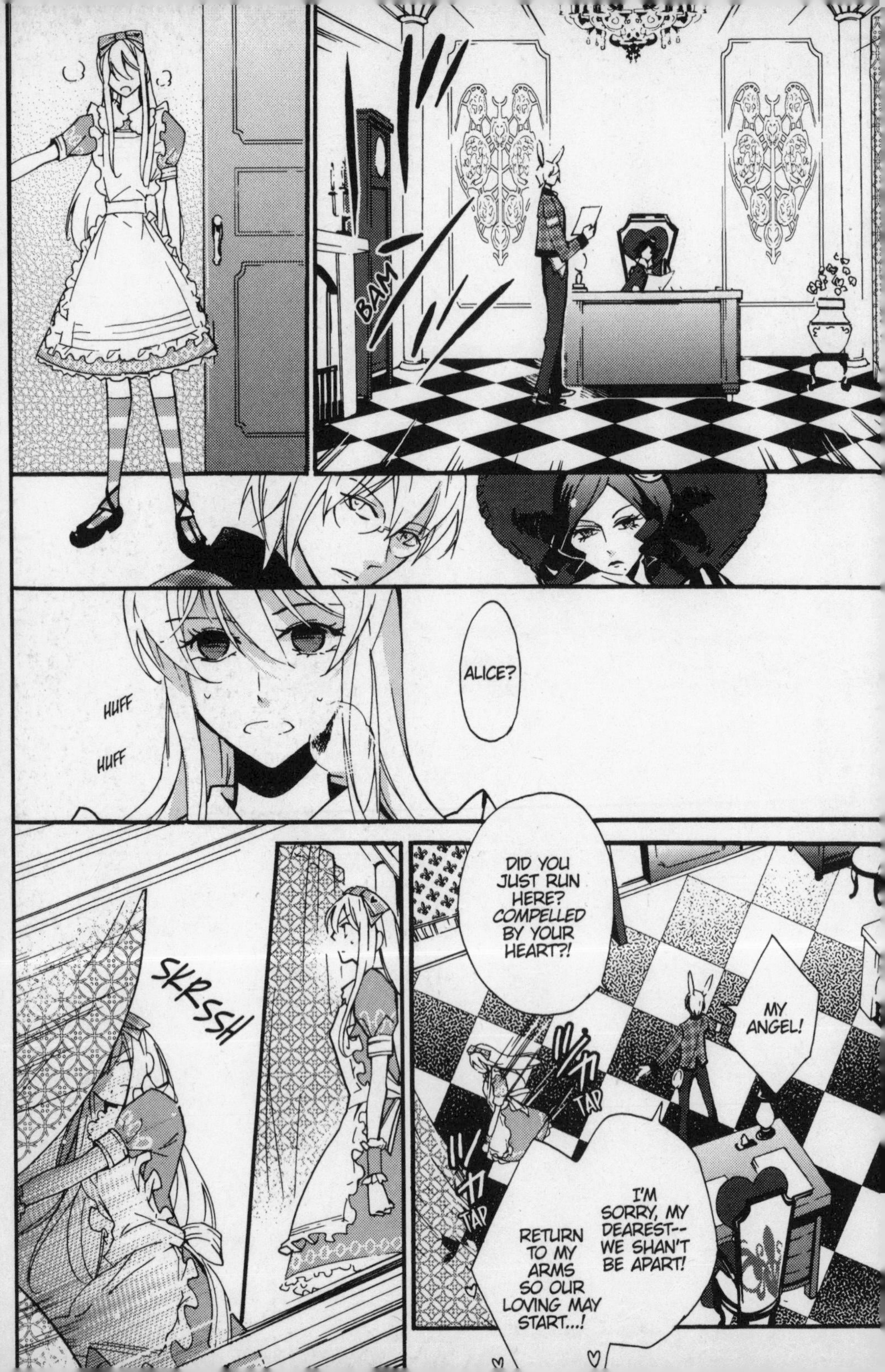
BAM
ALICE?
HUFF
HUFF
DID YOU JUST RUN HERE? COMPELLED BY YOUR HEART?!
MY ANGEL!
TAP
TAP
I'M SORRY, MY DEAREST-- WE SHAN'T BE APART!
RETURN TO MY ARMS SO OUR LOVING MAY START...!
SKRSSH

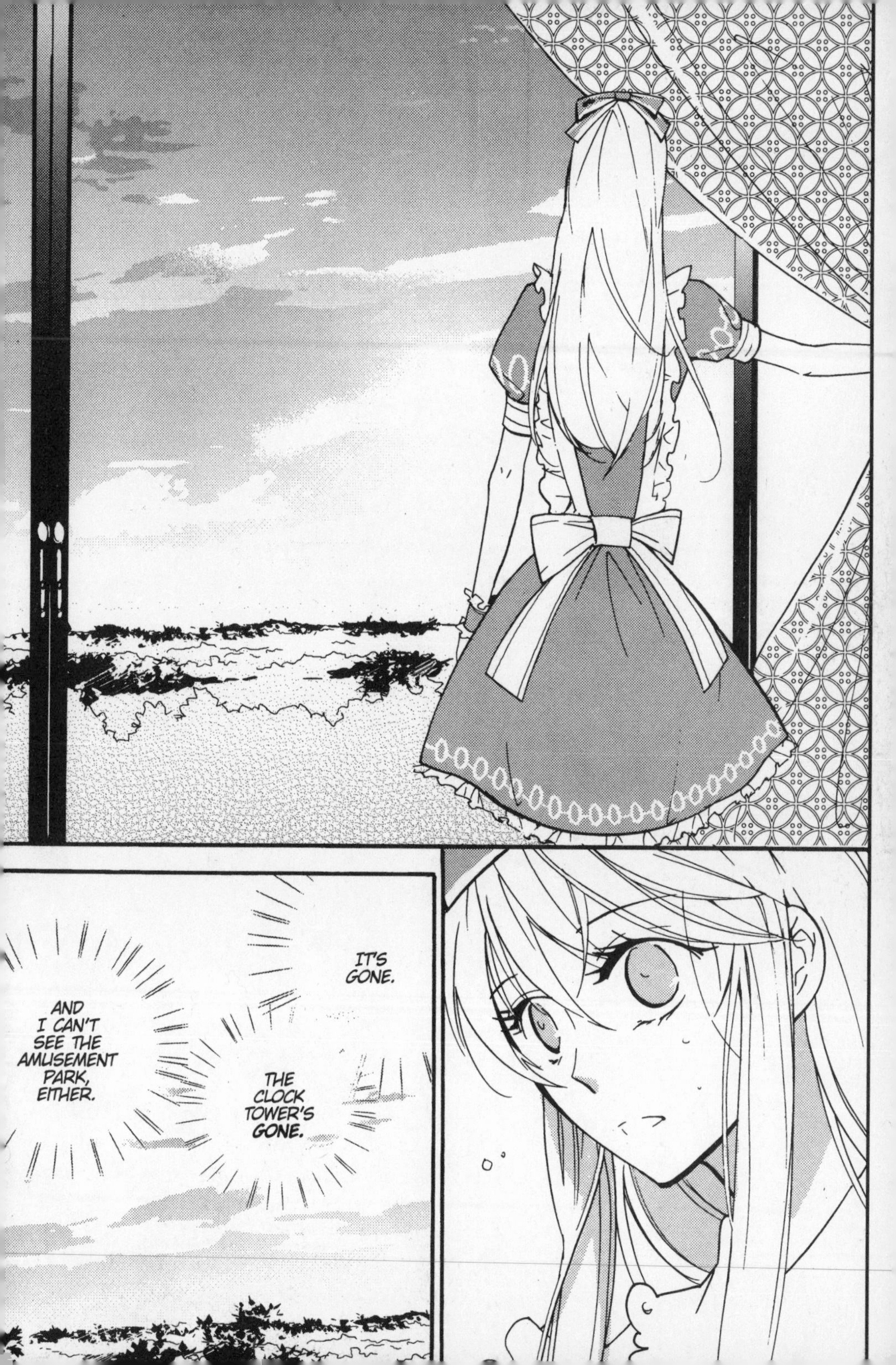
IT'S GONE.
THE CLOCK TOWER'S GONE.
AND I CAN'T SEE THE AMUSEMENT PARK, EITHER.

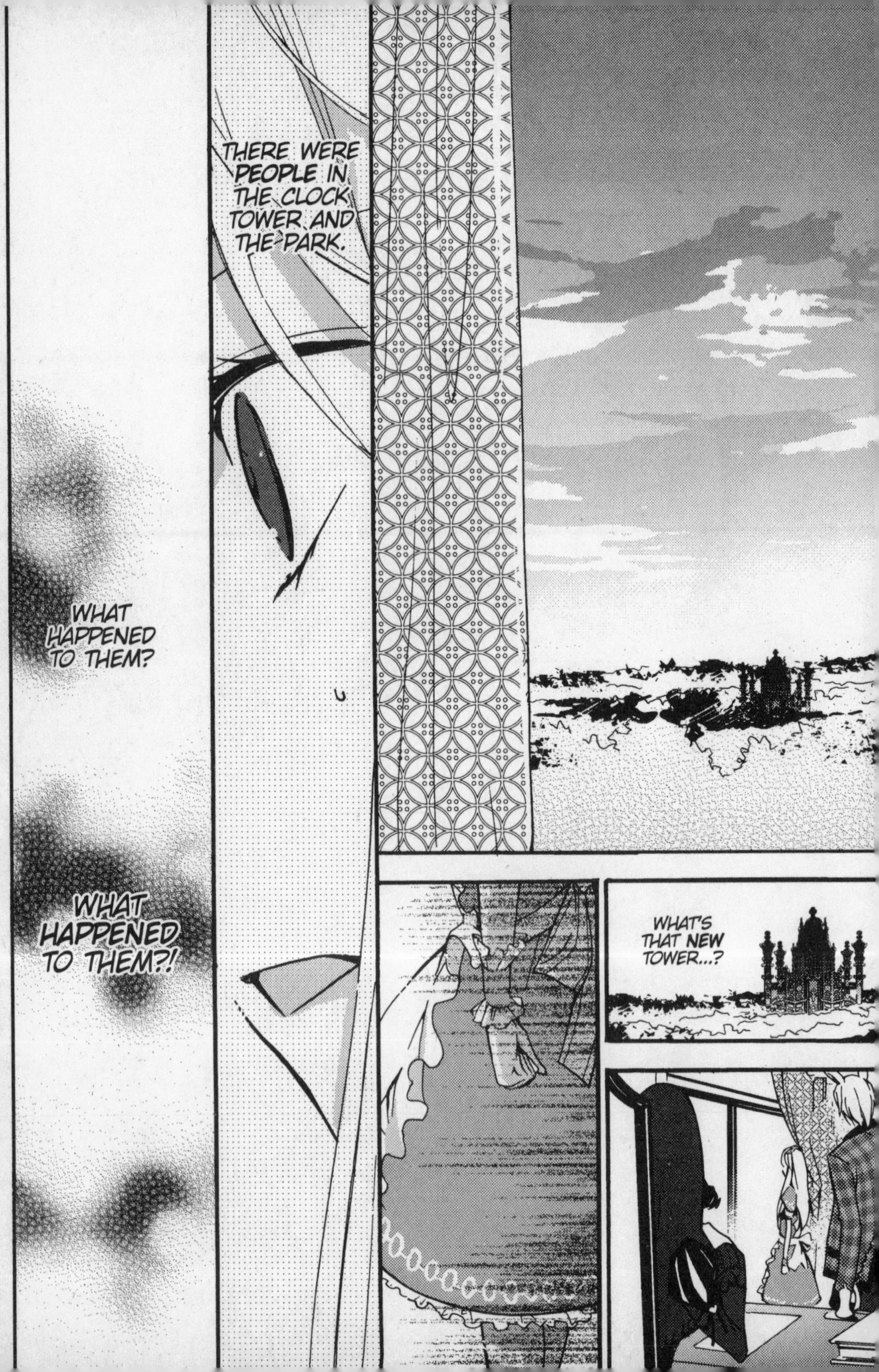
WHAT'S THAT NEW TOWER...?
THERE WERE PEOPLE IN THE CLOCK TOWER AND THE PARK.
WHAT HAPPENED TO THEM?
WHAT HAPPENED TO THEM?!

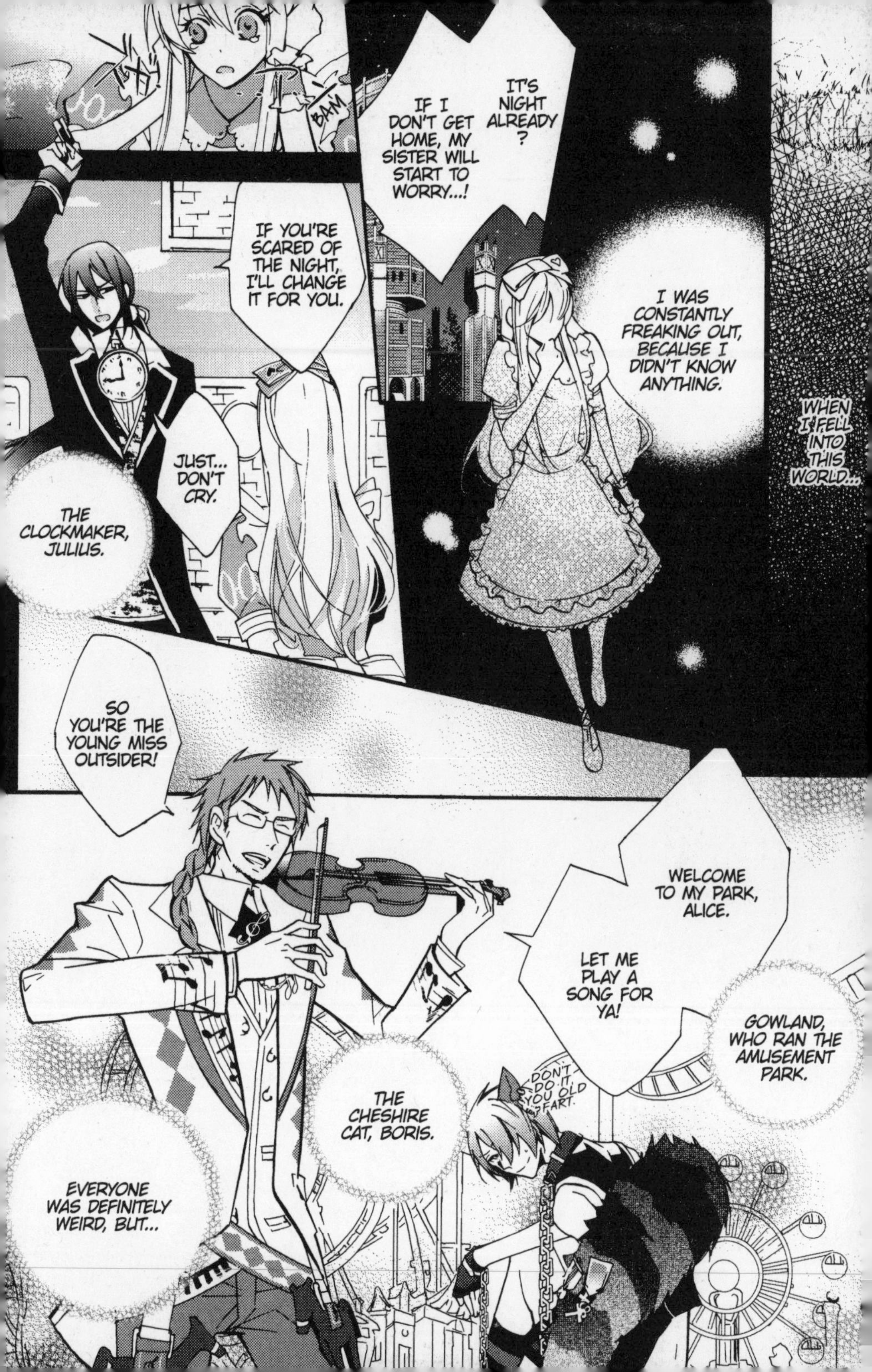
WHEN I FELL INTO THIS WORLD...
IT'S NIGHT ALREADY?
IF I DON'T GET HOME, MY SISTER WILL START TO WORRY...!
I WAS CONSTANTLY FREAKING OUT, BECAUSE I DIDN'T KNOW ANYTHING.
BAM
IF YOU'RE SCARED OF THE NIGHT, I'LL CHANGE IT FOR YOU.
JUST... DON'T CRY.
THE CLOCKMAKER, JULIUS.
WELCOME TO MY PARK, ALICE.
LET ME PLAY A SONG FOR YA!
GOWLAND, WHO RAN THE AMUSEMENT PARK.
SO YOU'RE THE YOUNG MISS OUTSIDER!
DON'T DO IT, YOU OLD FART.
THE CHESHIRE CAT, BORIS.
EVERYONE WAS DEFINITELY WEIRD, BUT...

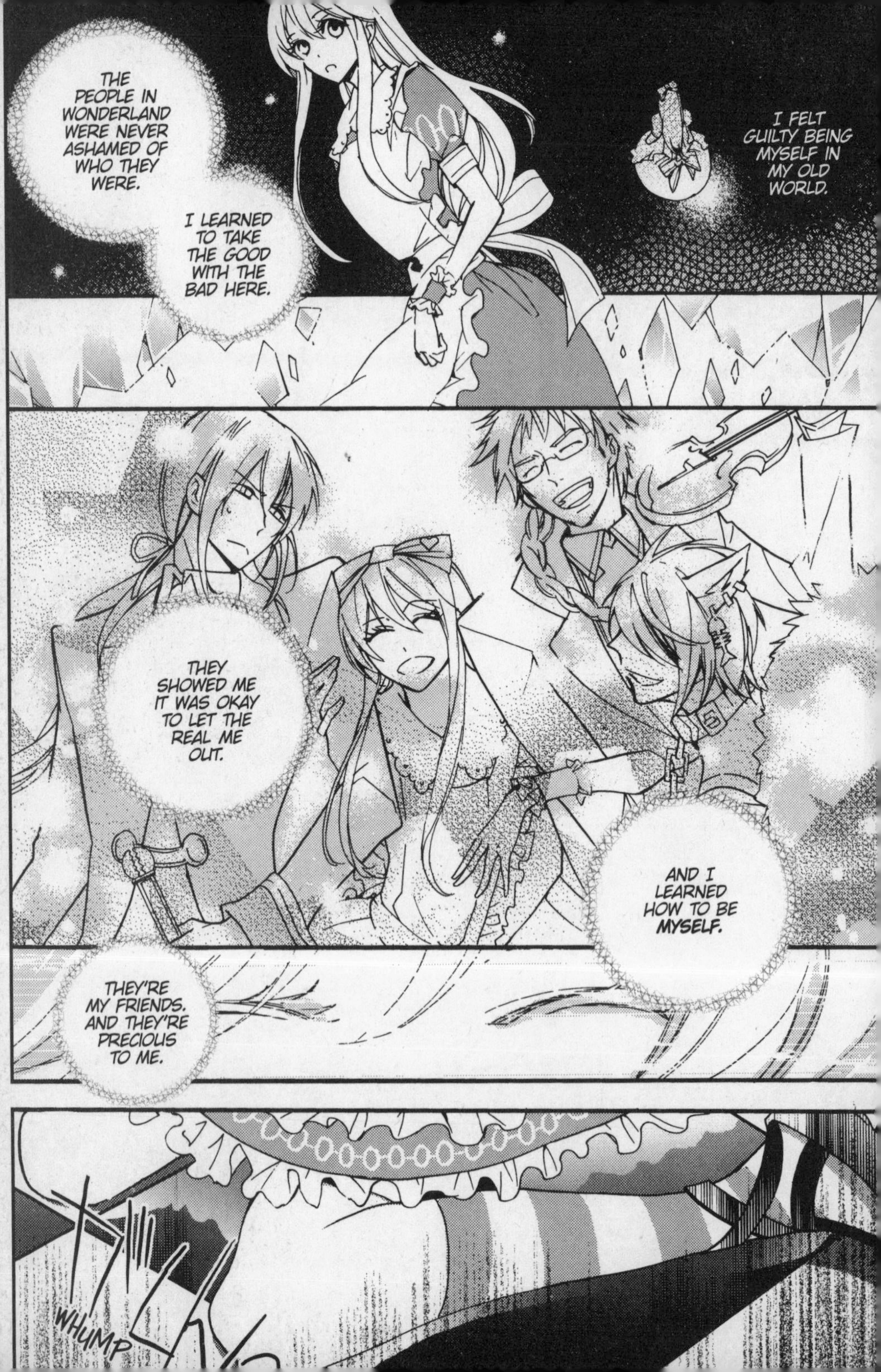

I FELT GUILTY BEING MYSELF IN MY OLD WORLD.
THE PEOPLE IN WONDERLAND WERE NEVER ASHAMED OF WHO THEY WERE.
I LEARNED TO TAKE THE GOOD WITH THE BAD HERE.
THEY SHOWED ME IT WAS OKAY TO LET THE REAL ME OUT.
AND I LEARNED HOW TO BE **MYSELF**.
THEY'RE MY FRIENDS. AND THEY'RE PRECIOUS TO ME.
WHUMP

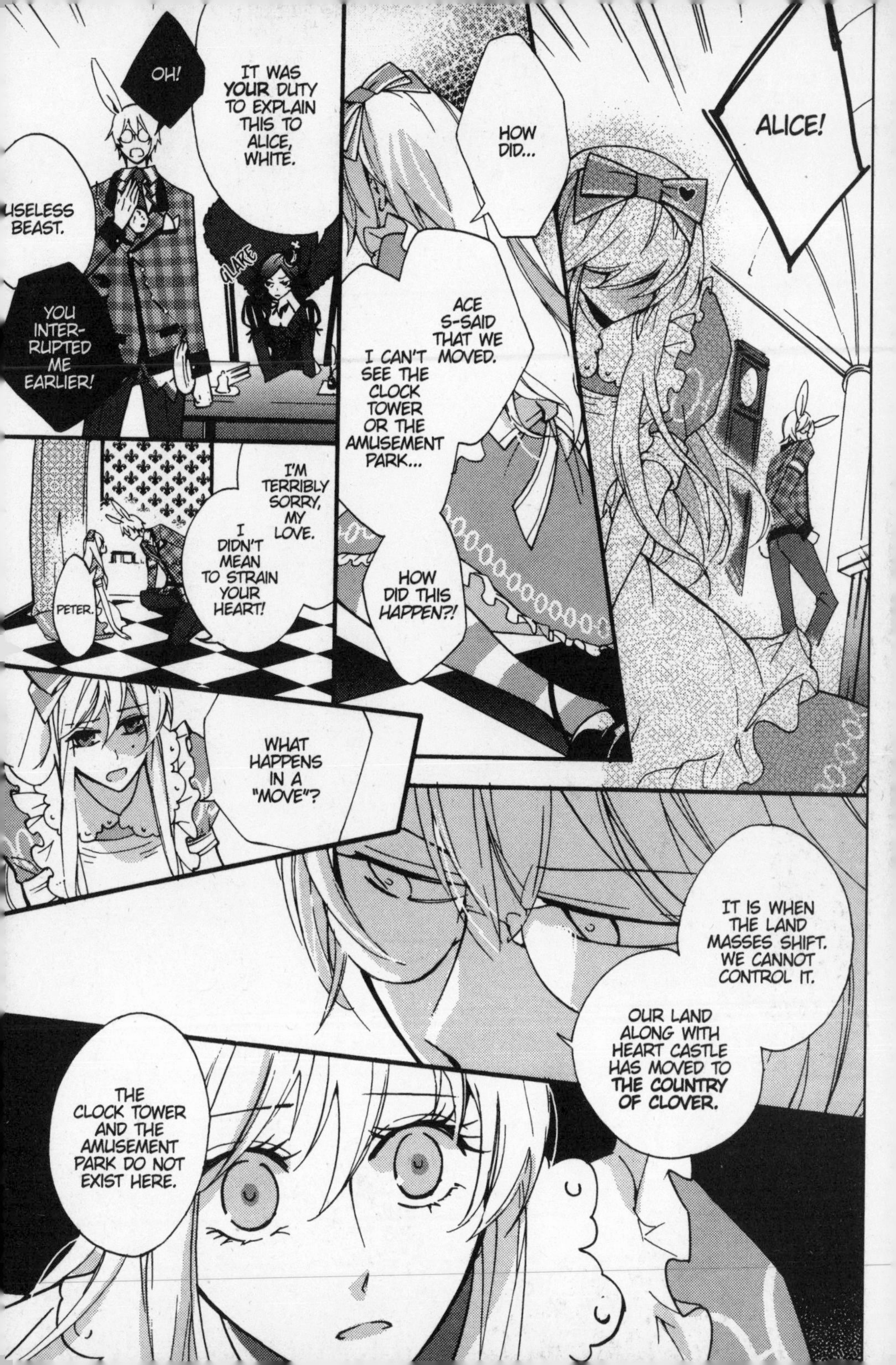

ALICE!
HOW DID...
ACE S-SAID THAT WE MOVED.
I CAN'T SEE THE CLOCK TOWER OR THE AMUSEMENT PARK...
HOW DID THIS HAPPEN?!
IT WAS YOUR DUTY TO EXPLAIN THIS TO ALICE, WHITE.
OH!
GLARE
USELESS BEAST.
YOU INTER-RUPTED ME EARLIER!
I'M TERRIBLY SORRY, MY LOVE.
I DIDN'T MEAN TO STRAIN YOUR HEART!
PETER.
WHAT HAPPENS IN A "MOVE"?
IT IS WHEN THE LAND MASSES SHIFT. WE CANNOT CONTROL IT.
OUR LAND ALONG WITH HEART CASTLE HAS MOVED TO THE COUNTRY OF CLOVER.
THE CLOCK TOWER AND THE AMUSEMENT PARK DO NOT EXIST HERE.

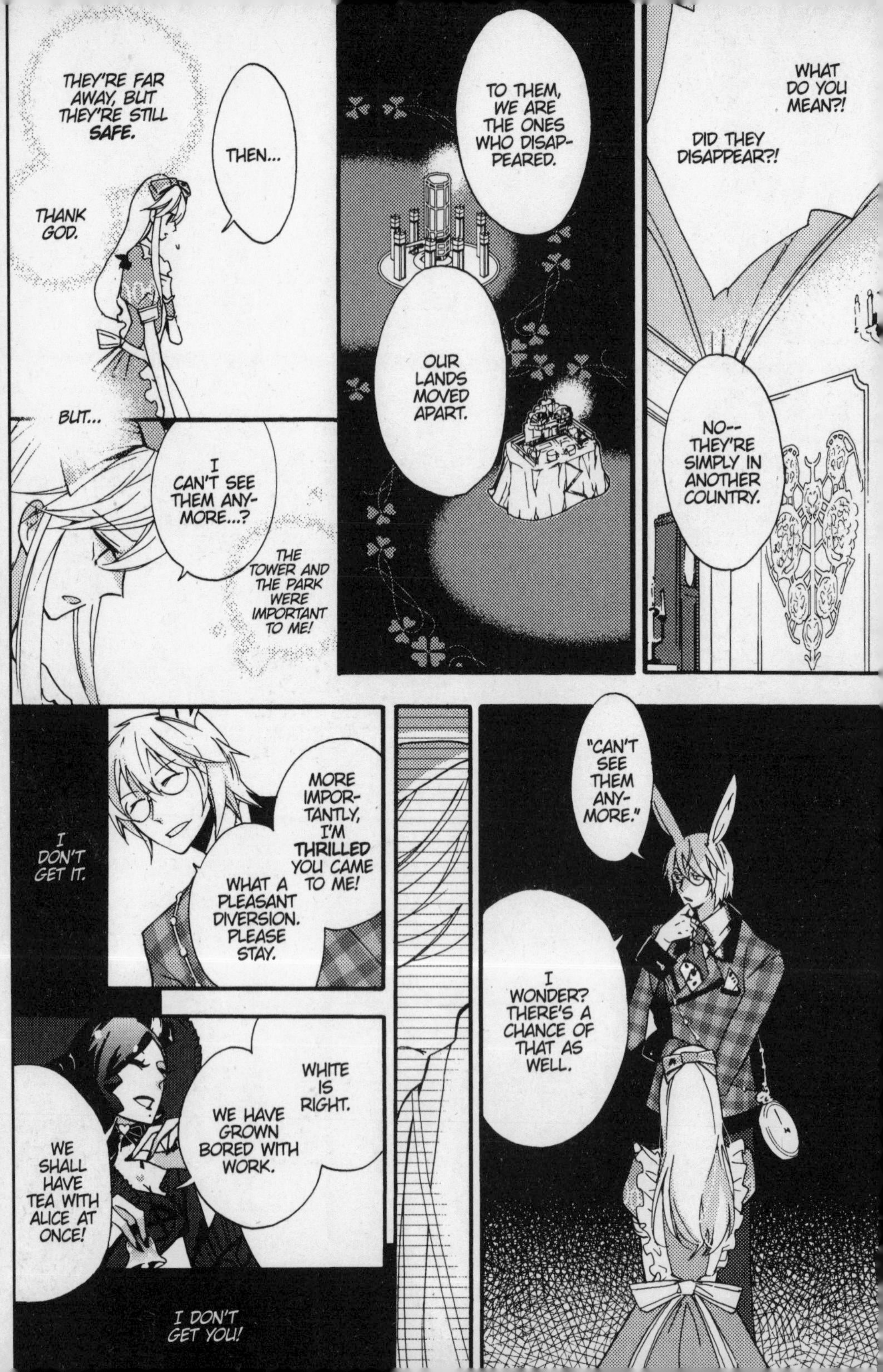
WHAT DO YOU MEAN?!
DID THEY DISAPPEAR?!
NO-- THEY'RE SIMPLY IN ANOTHER COUNTRY.
TO THEM, WE ARE THE ONES WHO DISAP-PEARED.
OUR LANDS MOVED APART.
THEY'RE FAR AWAY, BUT THEY'RE STILL SAFE.
THEN...
THANK GOD.
BUT...
I CAN'T SEE THEM ANY-MORE...?
THE TOWER AND THE PARK WERE IMPORTANT TO ME!
"CAN'T SEE THEM ANY-MORE."
I WONDER? THERE'S A CHANCE OF THAT AS WELL.
MORE IMPOR-TANTLY, I'M THRILLED YOU CAME TO ME!
WHAT A PLEASANT DIVERSION. PLEASE STAY.
I DON'T GET IT.
WHITE IS RIGHT.
WE HAVE GROWN BORED WITH WORK.
WE SHALL HAVE TEA WITH ALICE AT ONCE!
I DON'T GET YOU!

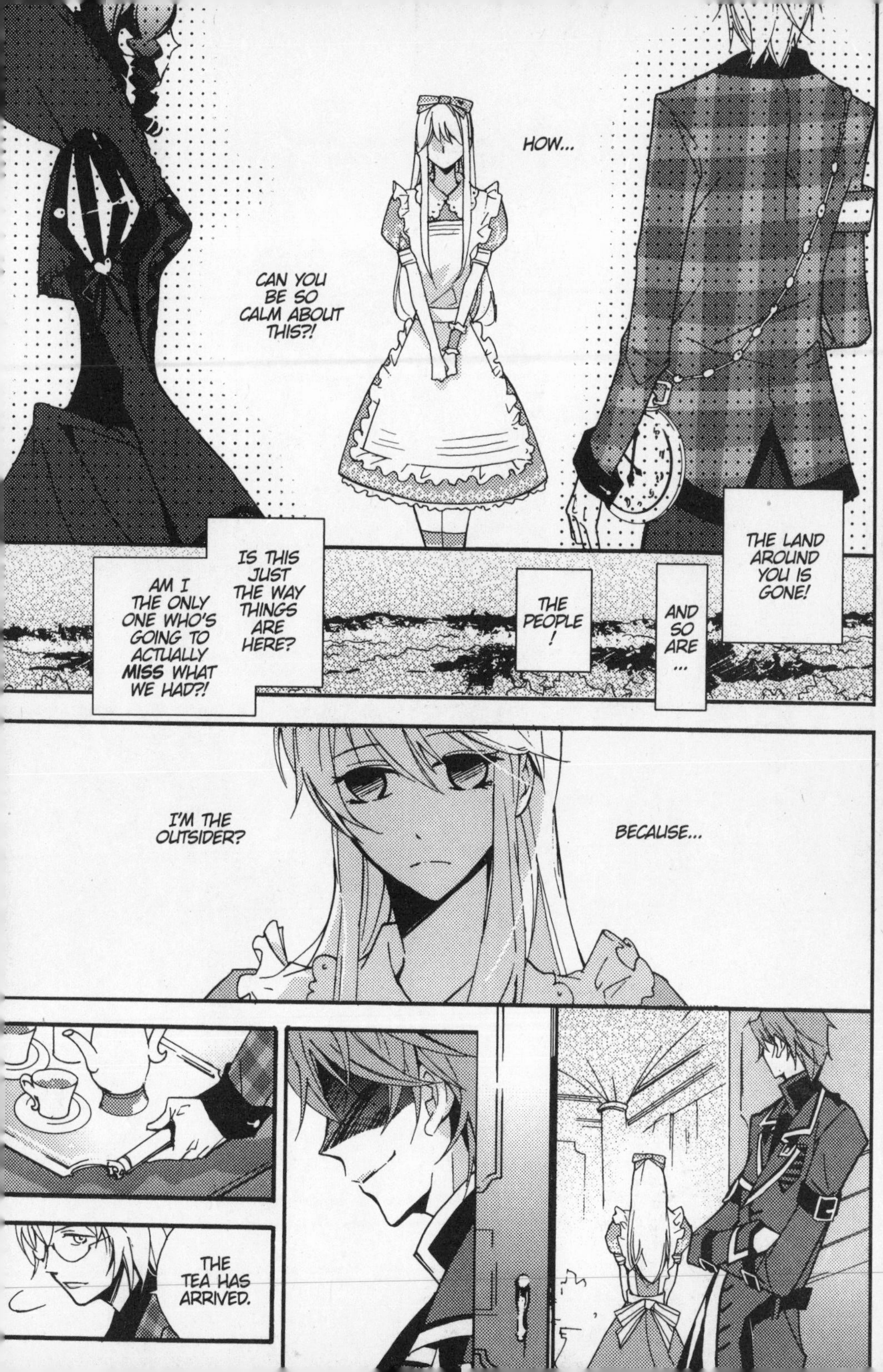
HOW...
CAN YOU BE SO CALM ABOUT THIS?!
THE LAND AROUND YOU IS GONE!
AND SO ARE ...
THE PEOPLE !
IS THIS JUST THE WAY THINGS ARE HERE?
AM I THE ONLY ONE WHO'S GOING TO ACTUALLY MISS WHAT WE HAD?!
BECAUSE...
I'M THE OUTSIDER?
THE TEA HAS ARRIVED.

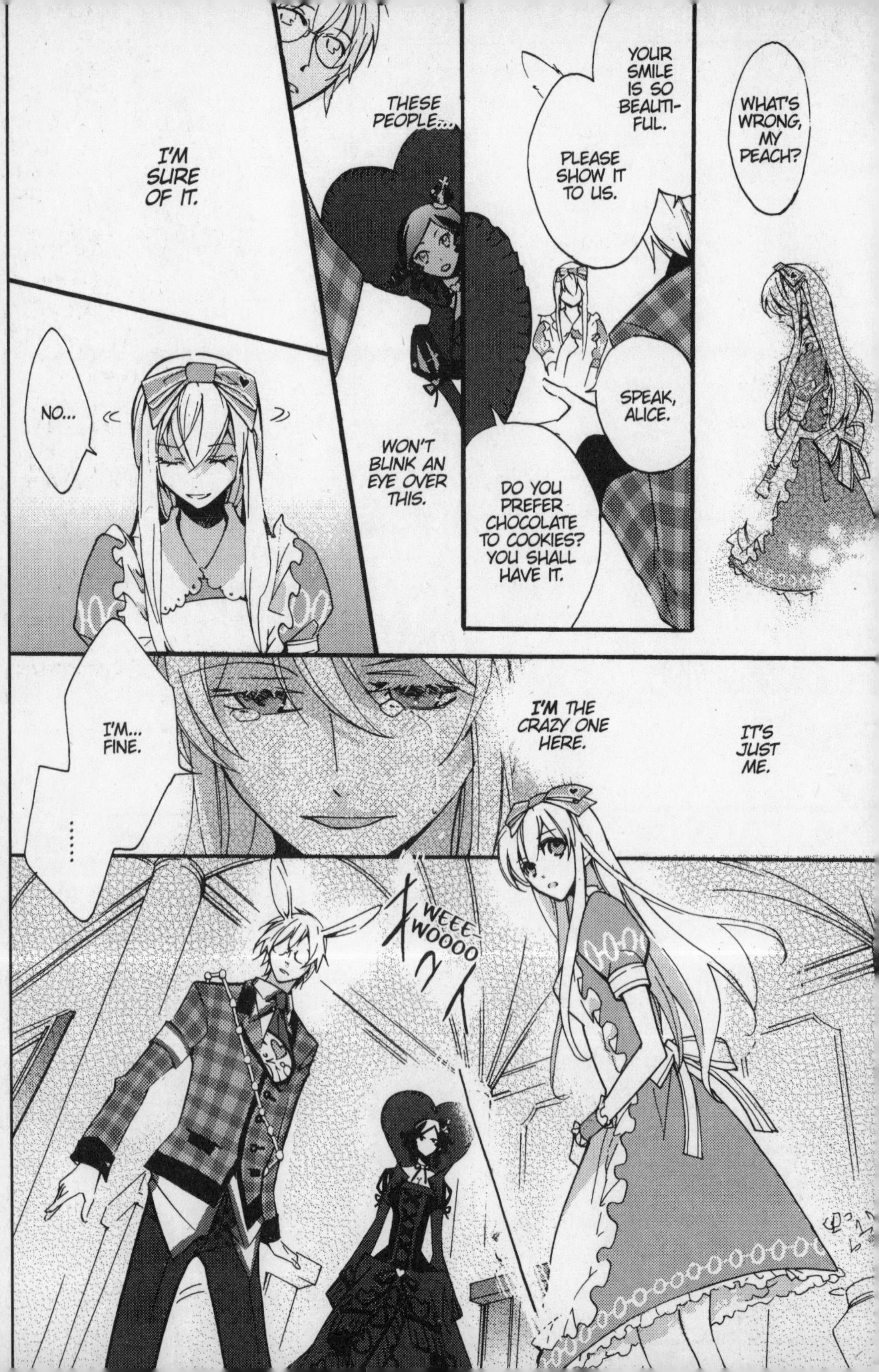
WHAT'S WRONG, MY PEACH?
YOUR SMILE IS SO BEAUTI-FUL.
PLEASE SHOW IT TO US.
SPEAK, ALICE.
DO YOU PREFER CHOCOLATE TO COOKIES? YOU SHALL HAVE IT.
THESE PEOPLE...
WON'T BLINK AN EYE OVER THIS.
I'M SURE OF IT.
NO...
IT'S JUST ME.
I'M THE CRAZY ONE HERE.
I'M... FINE.
......
WEEE WOOOO

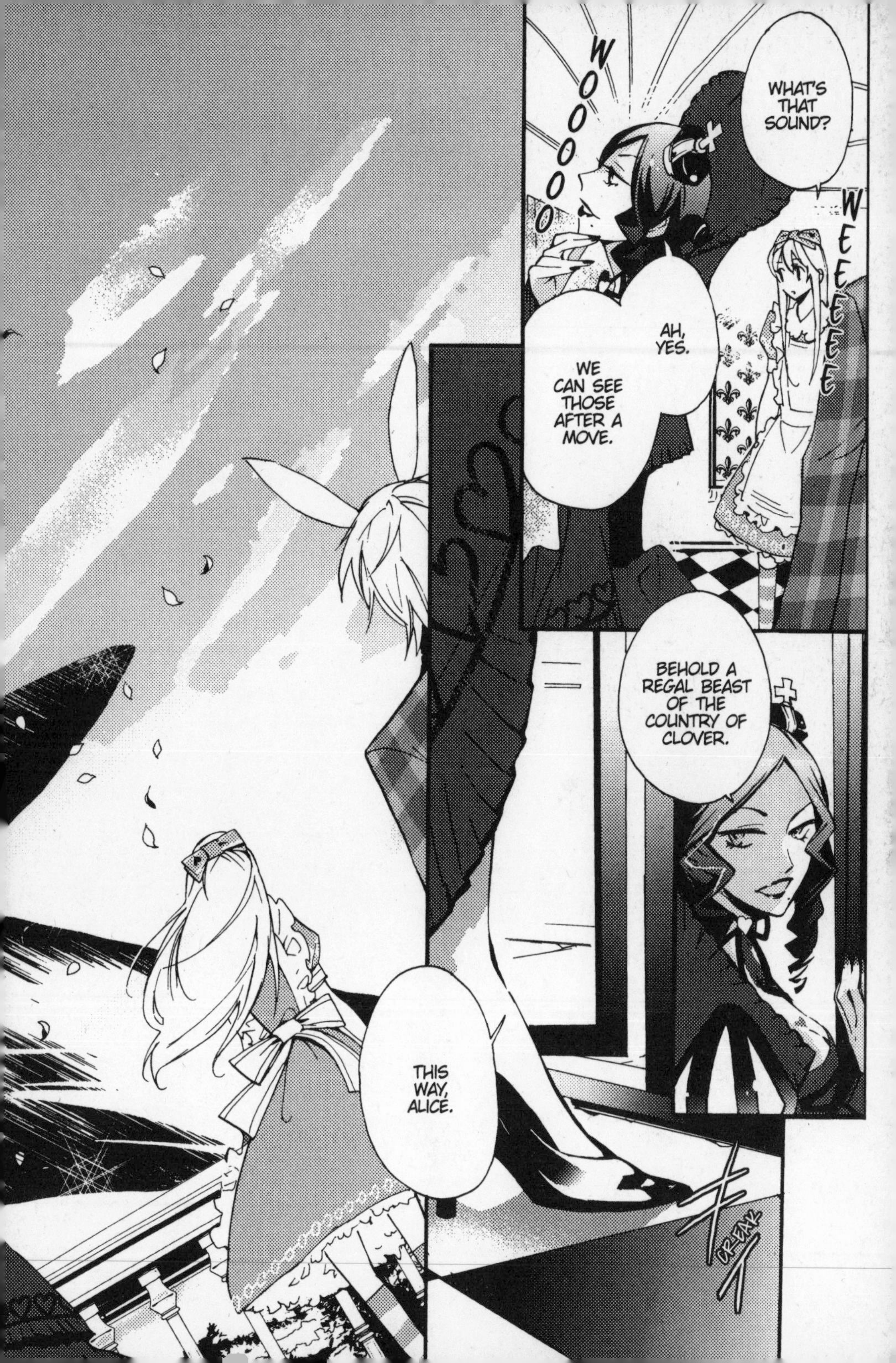
WHAT'S THAT SOUND?
WOOOOOO
WEEEEEE
AH, YES.
WE CAN SEE THOSE AFTER A MOVE.
BEHOLD A REGAL BEAST OF THE COUNTRY OF CLOVER.
CREAK
THIS WAY, ALICE.

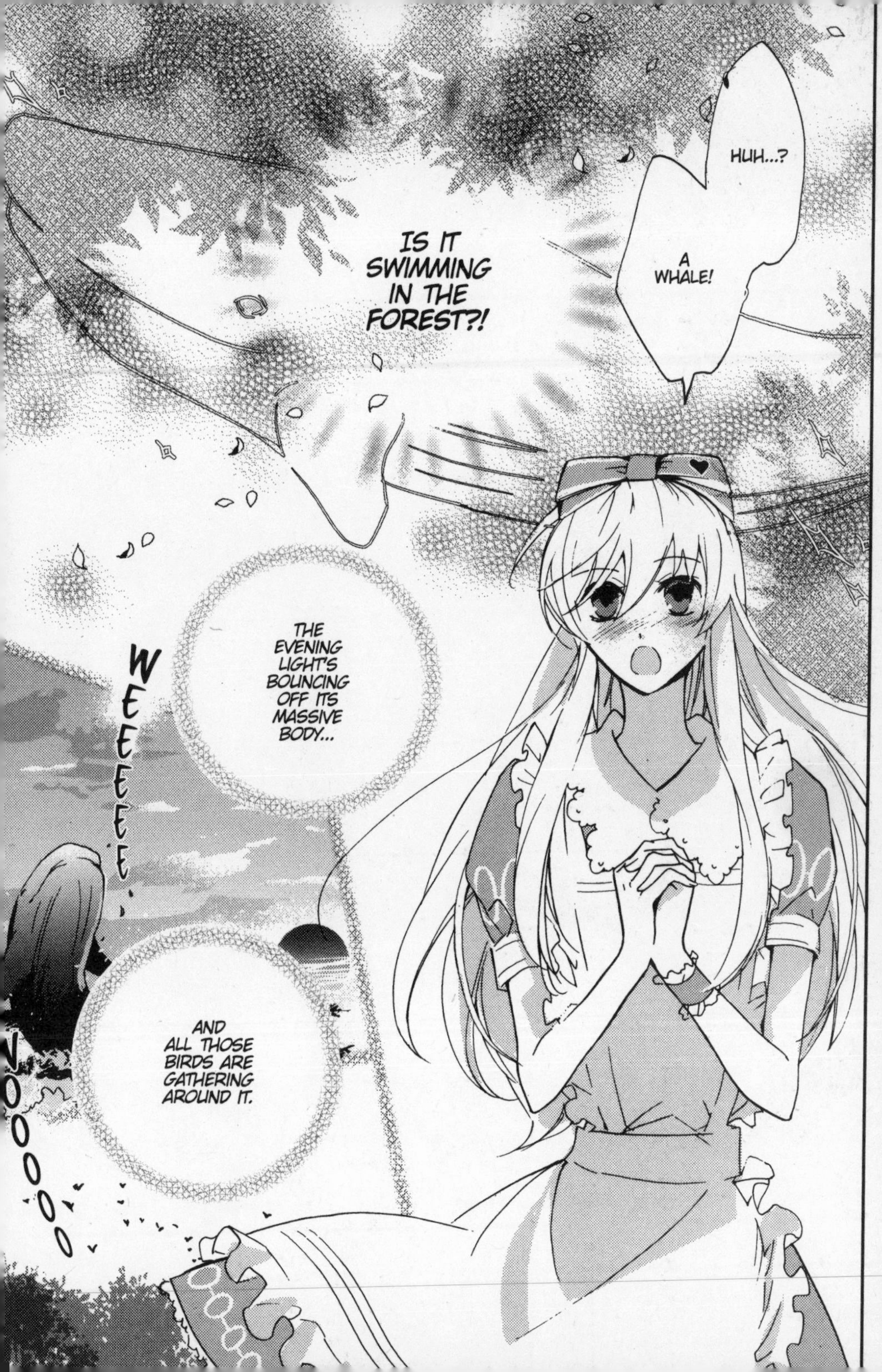
HUH...?
A WHALE!
IS IT SWIMMING IN THE FOREST?!
THE EVENING LIGHT'S BOUNCING OFF ITS MASSIVE BODY...
AND ALL THOSE BIRDS ARE GATHERING AROUND IT.
WEEEEEEE..
VOOOOOO

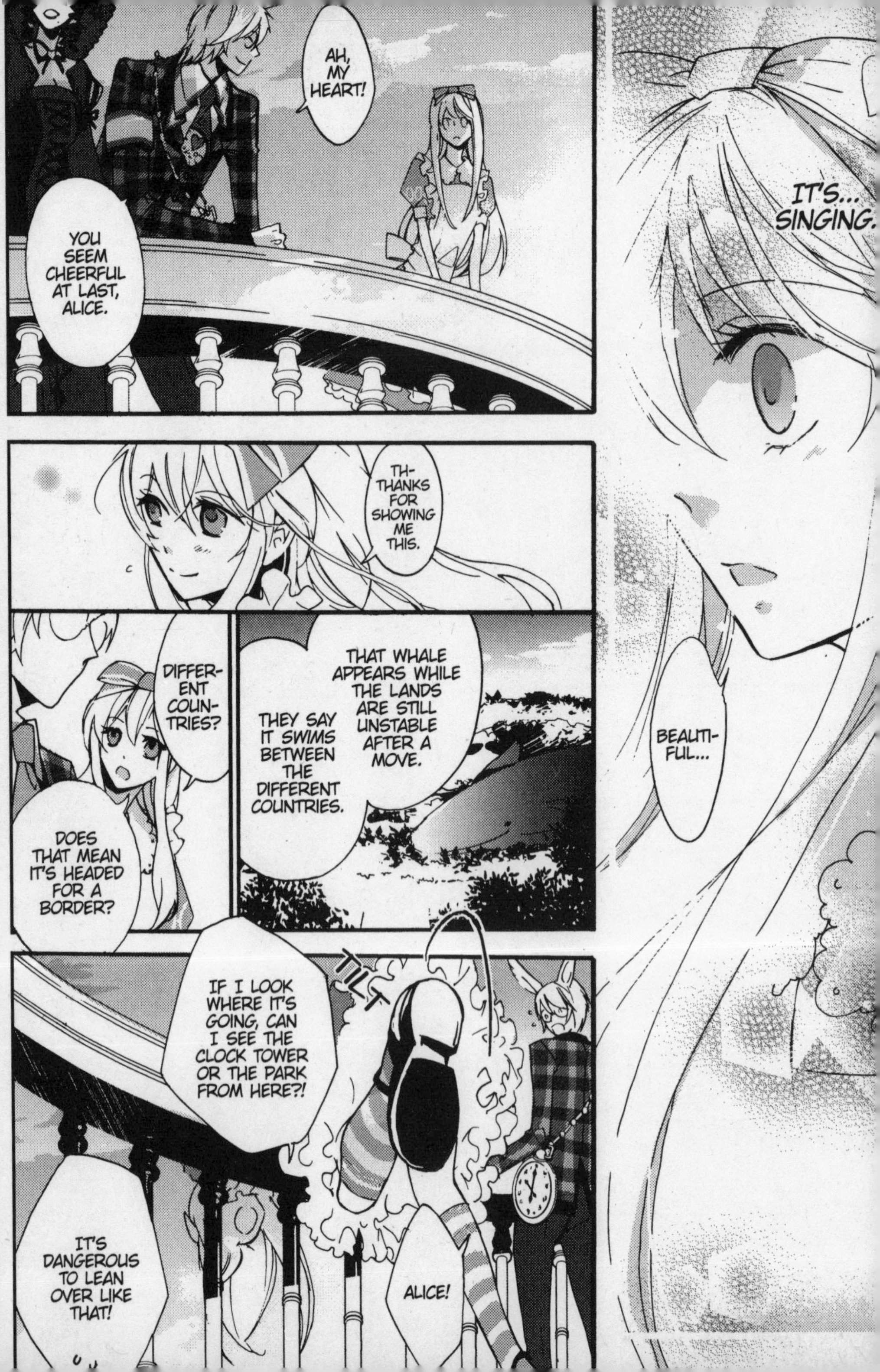
IT'S... SINGING.
BEAUTI-FUL...
AH, MY HEART!
YOU SEEM CHEERFUL AT LAST, ALICE.
TH-THANKS FOR SHOWING ME THIS.
THAT WHALE APPEARS WHILE THE LANDS ARE STILL UNSTABLE AFTER A MOVE.
THEY SAY IT SWIMS BETWEEN THE DIFFERENT COUNTRIES.
DIFFER-ENT COUN-TRIES?
DOES THAT MEAN IT'S HEADED FOR A BORDER?
IF I LOOK WHERE IT'S GOING, CAN I SEE THE CLOCK TOWER OR THE PARK FROM HERE?!
TILT
ALICE!
IT'S DANGEROUS TO LEAN OVER LIKE THAT!

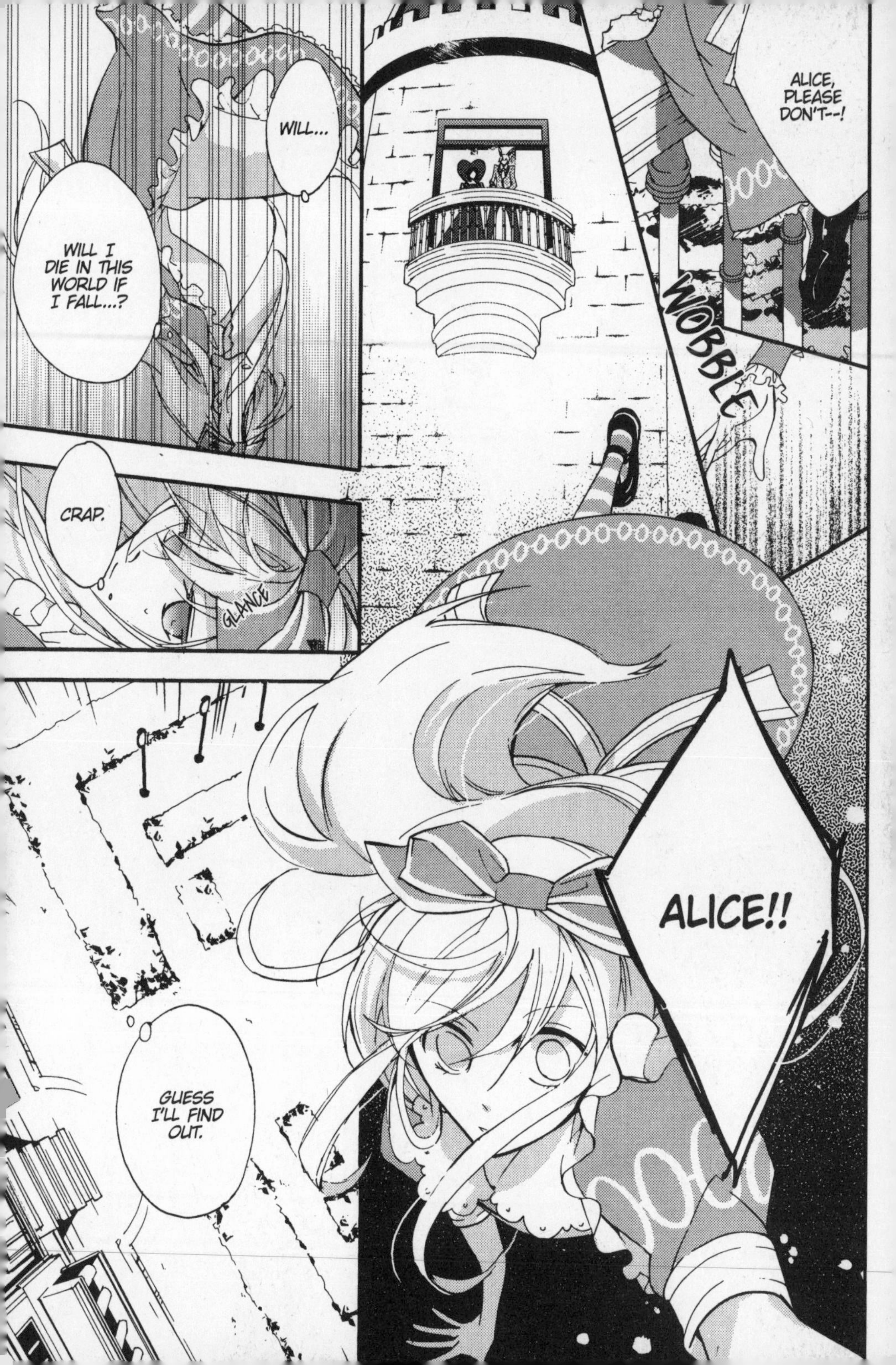
ALICE, PLEASE DON'T--!
WOBBLE
WILL...
WILL I DIE IN THIS WORLD IF I FALL...?
CRAP.
GLANCE
ALICE!!
GUESS I'LL FIND OUT.

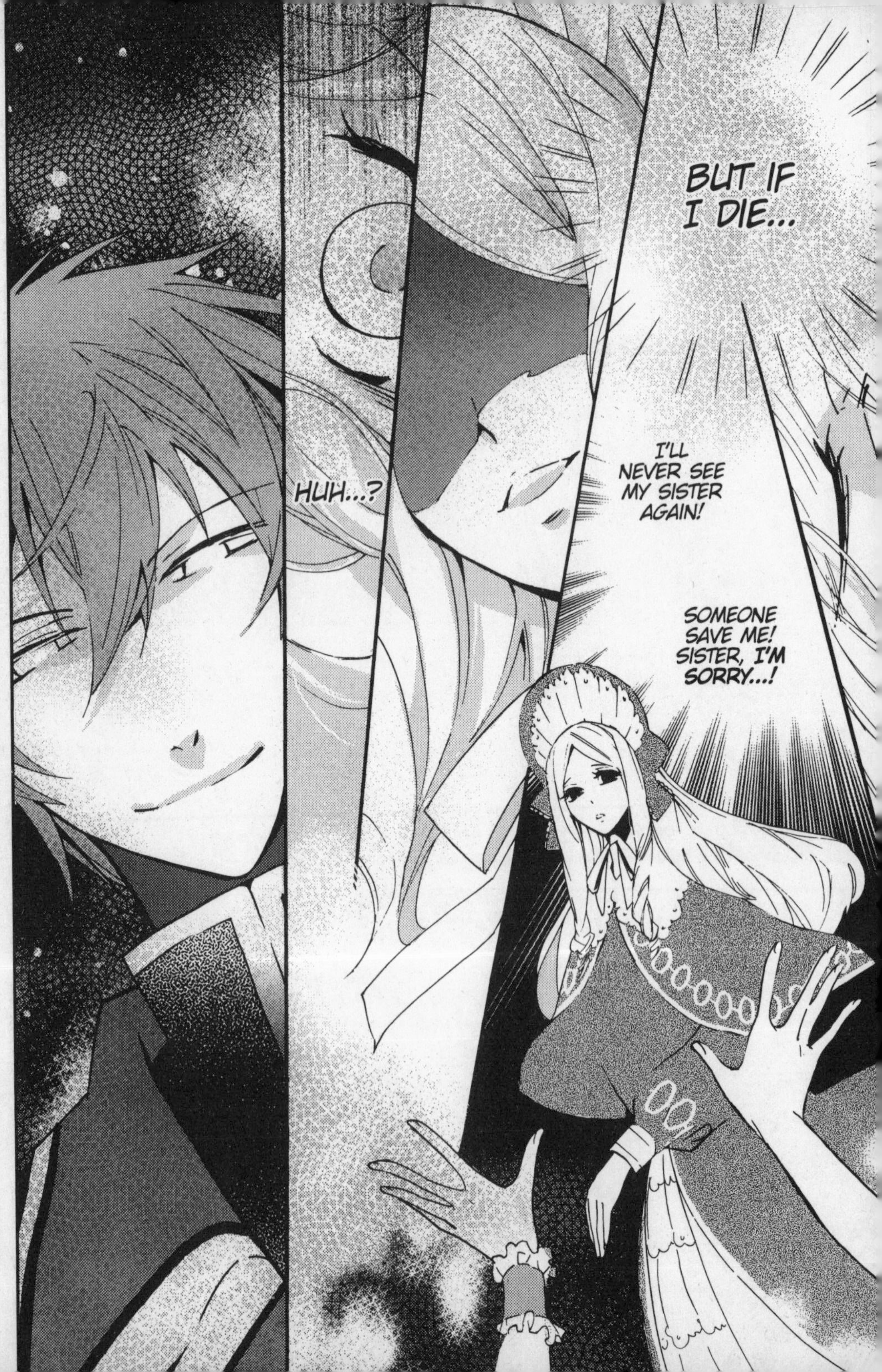
BUT IF I DIE...
I'LL NEVER SEE MY SISTER AGAIN!
SOMEONE SAVE ME! SISTER, I'M SORRY...!
HUH...?

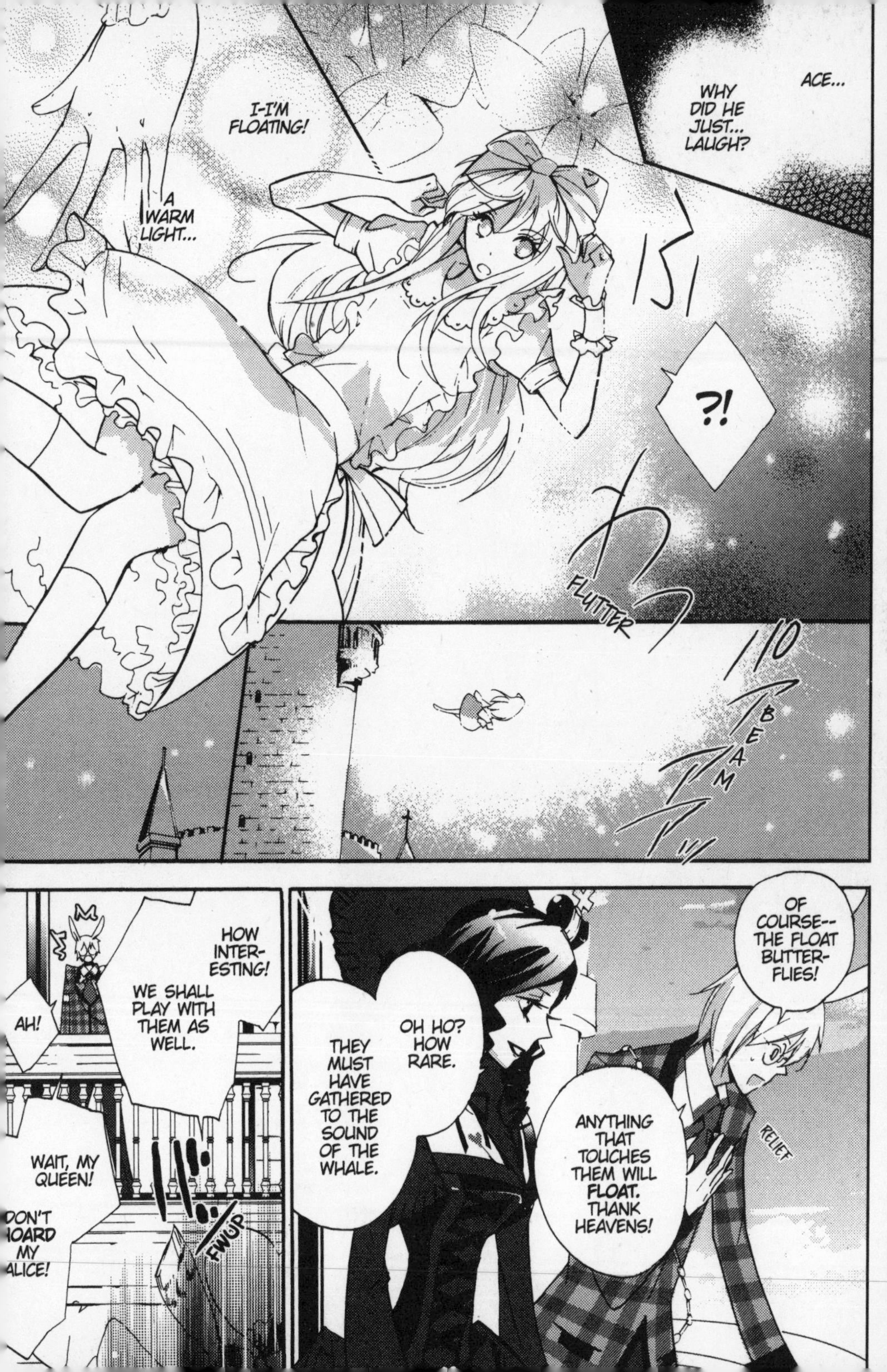
ACE...
WHY DID HE JUST... LAUGH?
?!
I-I'M FLOATING!
A WARM LIGHT...
FLUTTER
BEAM
OF COURSE-- THE FLOAT BUTTER-FLIES!
RELIEF
ANYTHING THAT TOUCHES THEM WILL FLOAT. THANK HEAVENS!
OH HO? HOW RARE.
THEY MUST HAVE GATHERED TO THE SOUND OF THE WHALE.
HOW INTER-ESTING!
WE SHALL PLAY WITH THEM AS WELL.
AH!
WAIT, MY QUEEN!
DON'T HOARD MY ALICE!
FWUP

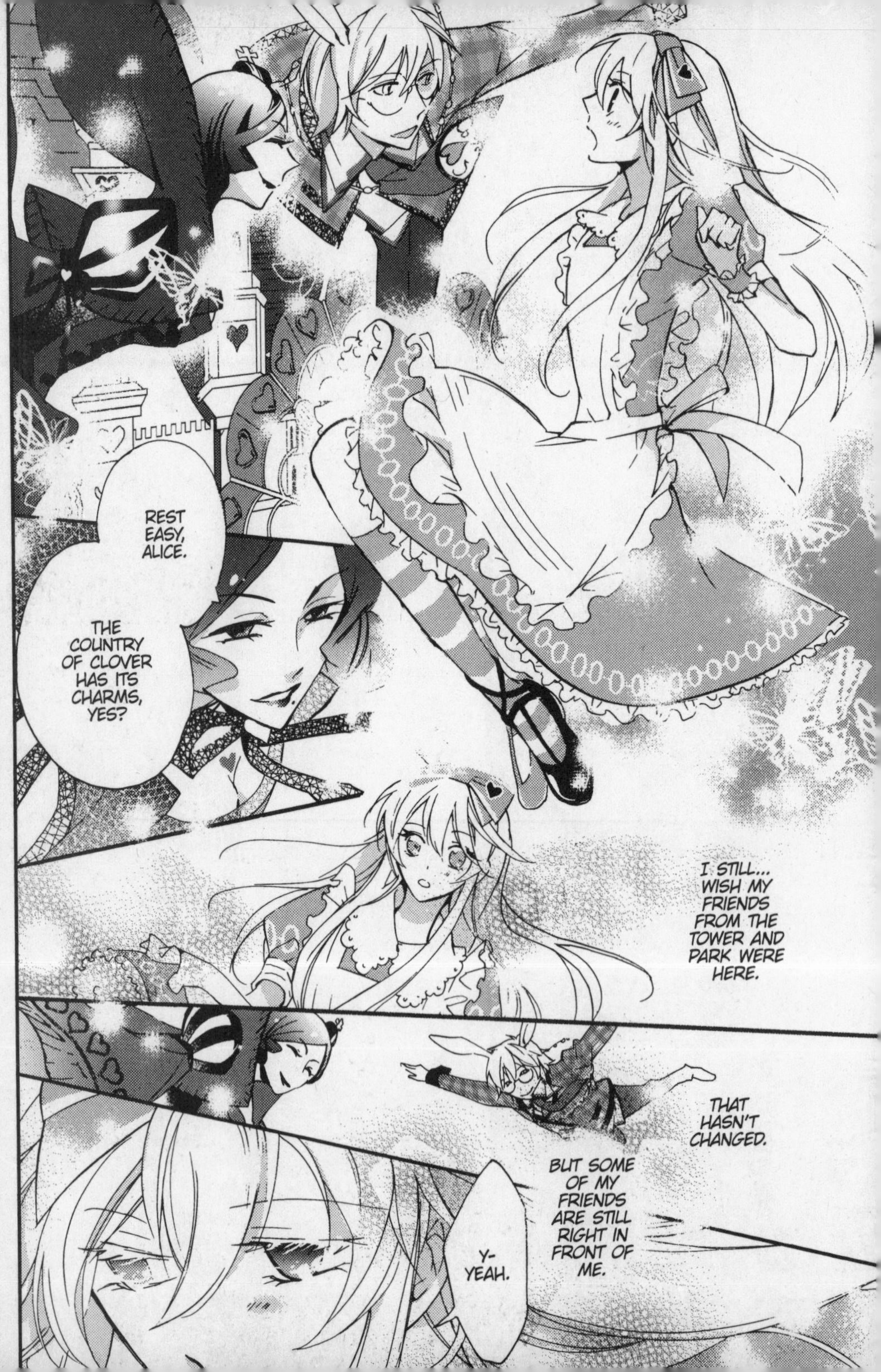
REST EASY, ALICE.
THE COUNTRY OF CLOVER HAS ITS CHARMS, YES?
I STILL... WISH MY FRIENDS FROM THE TOWER AND PARK WERE HERE.
THAT HASN'T CHANGED.
BUT SOME OF MY FRIENDS ARE STILL RIGHT IN FRONT OF ME.
Y-YEAH.

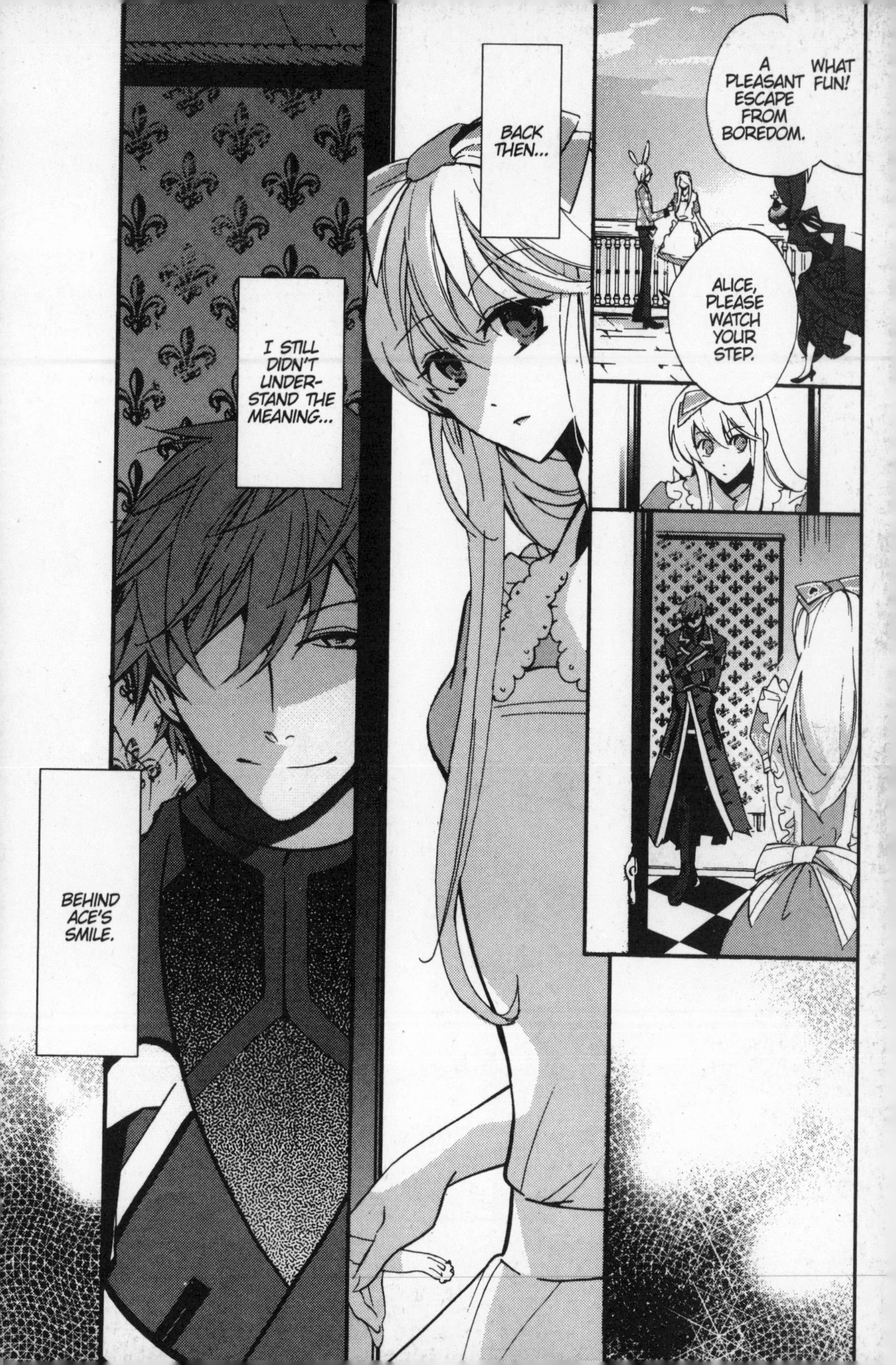
WHAT FUN! A PLEASANT ESCAPE FROM BOREDOM.
ALICE, PLEASE WATCH YOUR STEP.
BACK THEN...
I STILL DIDN'T UNDER-STAND THE MEANING...
BEHIND ACE'S SMILE.

I'M ALONE HERE.
IN DARKNESS.
CHAPTER 2
JULIUS?
GOWLAND?
BORIS?
ANSWER ME!
WHERE DID YOU ALL GO?!
WH...
ACE! YOU'RE STILL HERE!

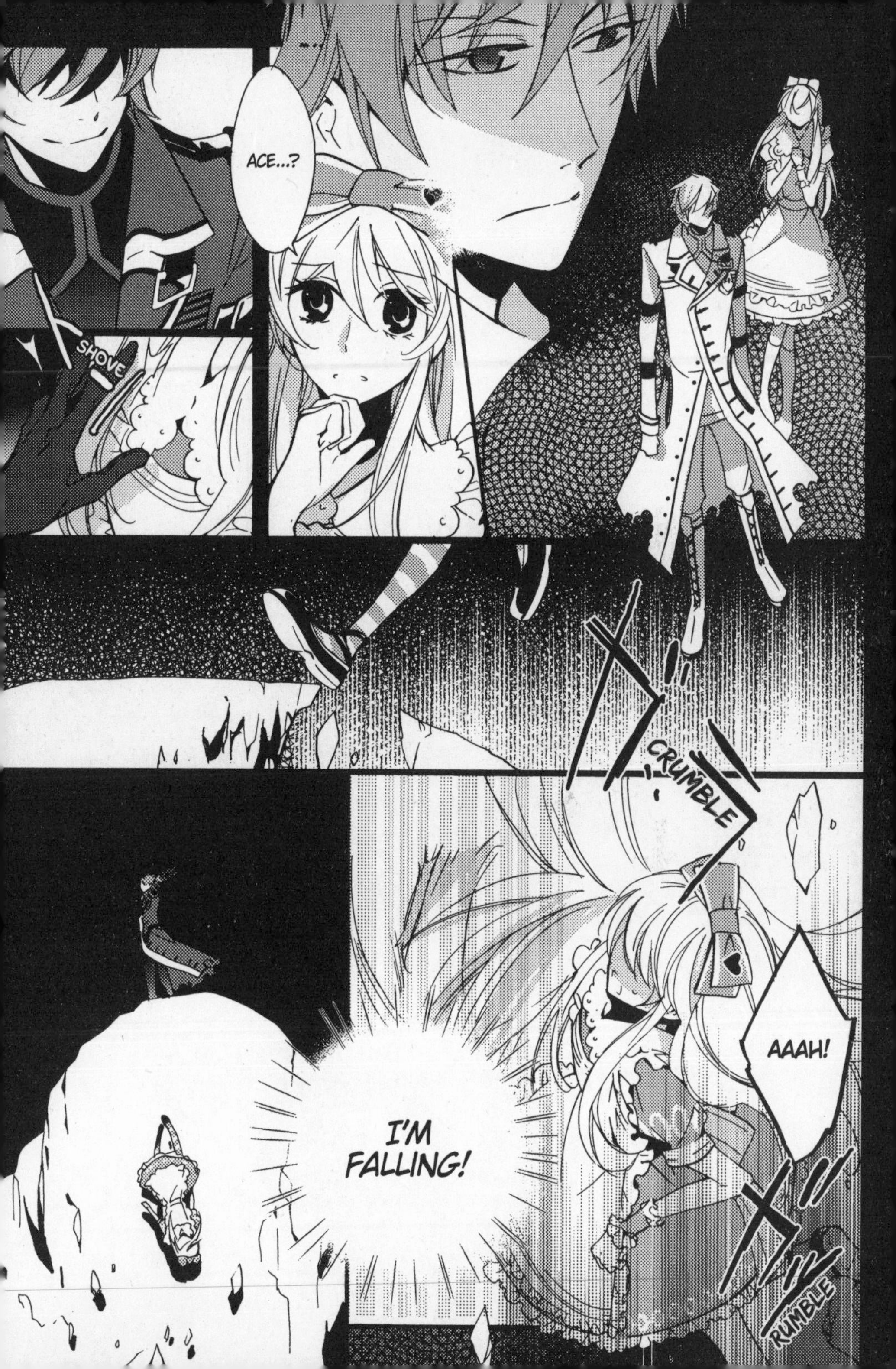
ACE...?
SHOVE
CRUMBLE
AAAH!
RUMBLE
I'M FALLING!

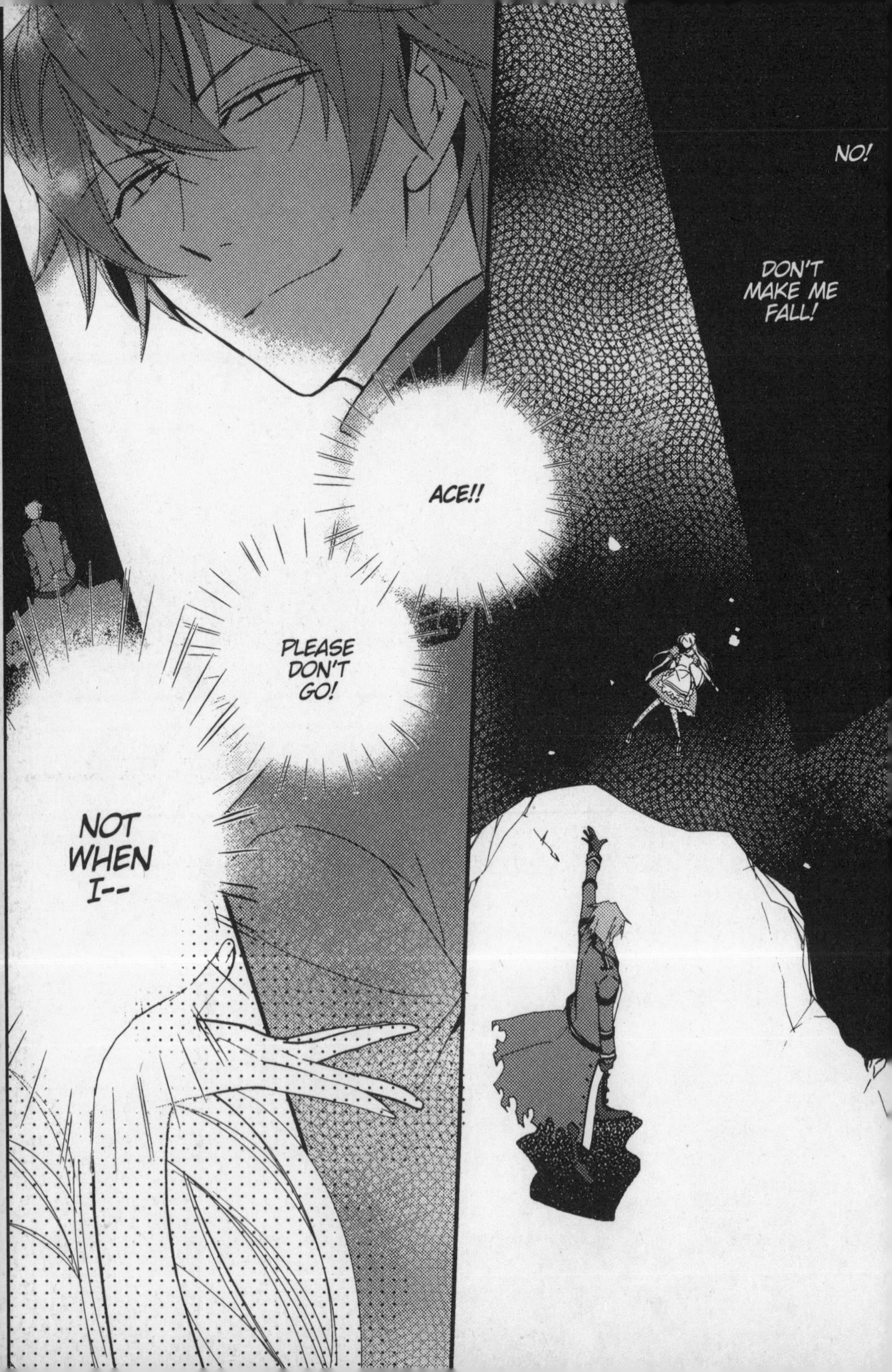
NO!
DON'T MAKE ME FALL!
ACE!!
PLEASE DON'T GO!
NOT WHEN I--

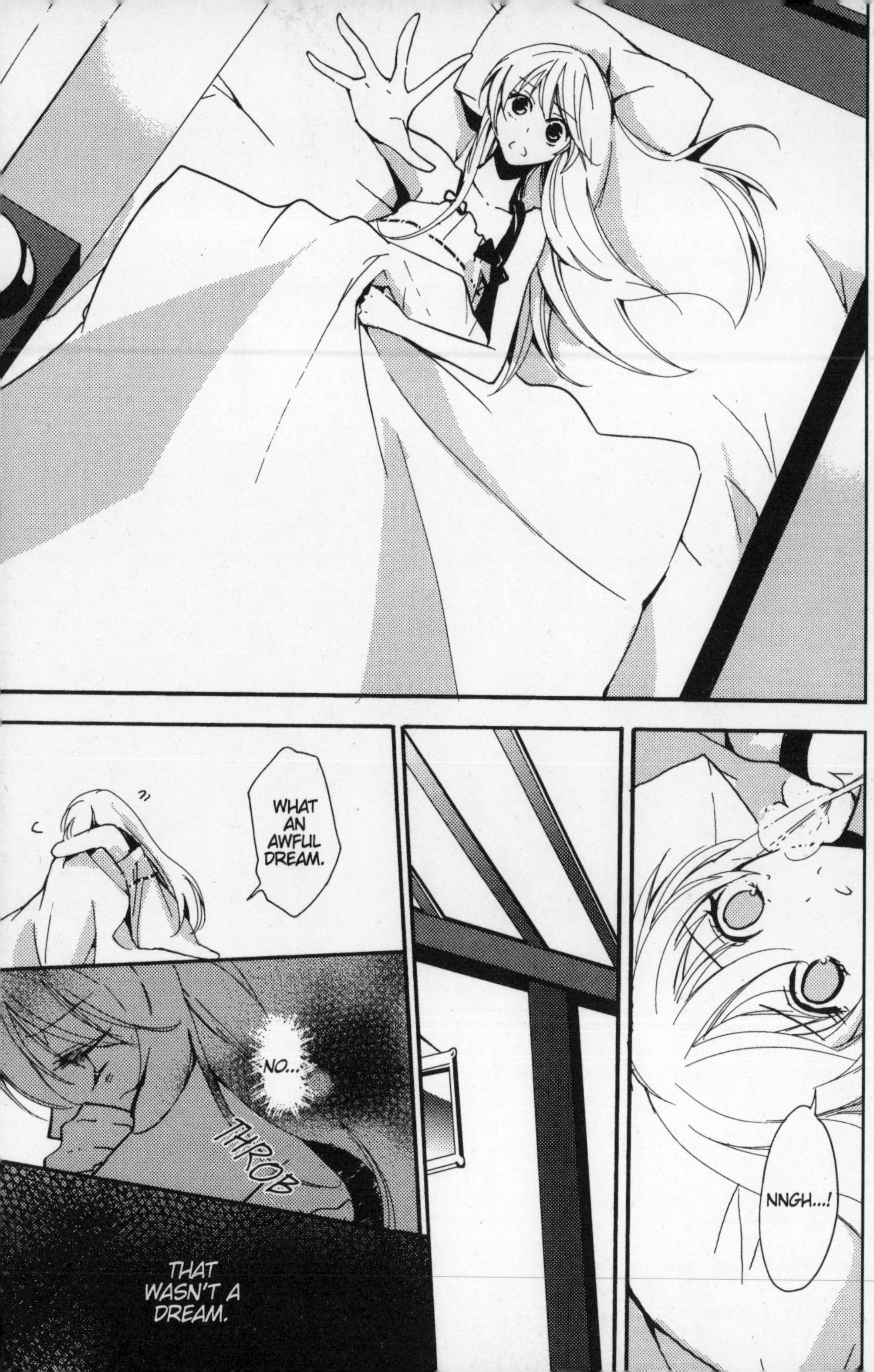
NNGH...!
WHAT AN AWFUL DREAM.
NO...
THROB
THAT WASN'T A DREAM.

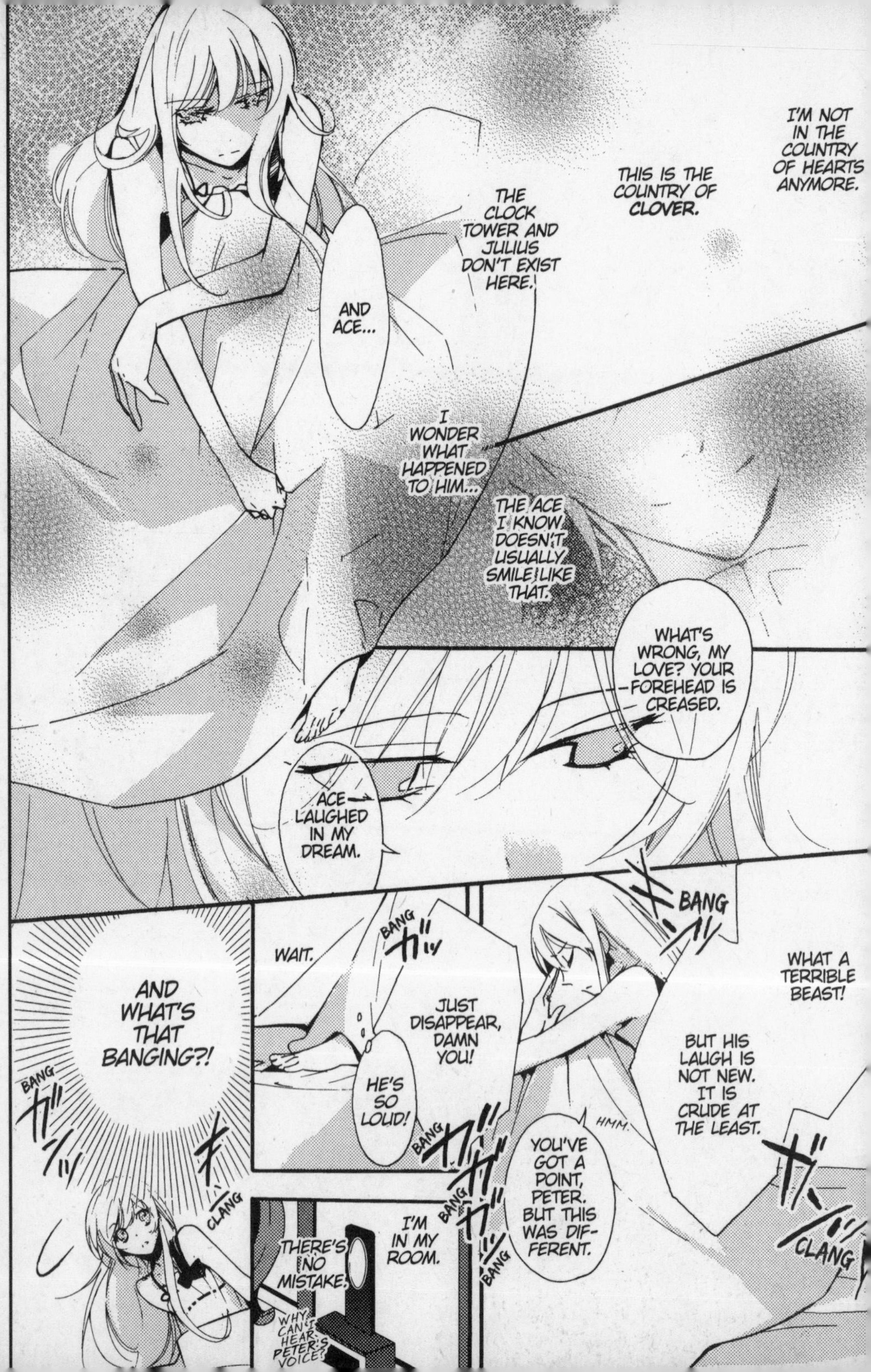
I'M NOT IN THE COUNTRY OF HEARTS ANYMORE.
THIS IS THE COUNTRY OF CLOVER.
THE CLOCK TOWER AND JULIUS DON'T EXIST HERE.
AND ACE...
I WONDER WHAT HAPPENED TO HIM...
THE ACE I KNOW DOESN'T USUALLY SMILE LIKE THAT.
WHAT'S WRONG, MY LOVE? YOUR FOREHEAD IS CREASED.
ACE LAUGHED IN MY DREAM.
BANG
WHAT A TERRIBLE BEAST!
BUT HIS LAUGH IS NOT NEW. IT IS CRUDE AT THE LEAST.
CLANG
HMM.
YOU'VE GOT A POINT, PETER. BUT THIS WAS DIFFERENT.
BANG
BANG
BANG
WAIT.
BANG
JUST DISAPPEAR, DAMN YOU!
HE'S SO LOUD!
BANG
I'M IN MY ROOM.
THERE'S NO MISTAKE.
WHY CAN I HEAR PETER'S VOICE?
AND WHAT'S THAT BANGING?!
BANG
CLANG

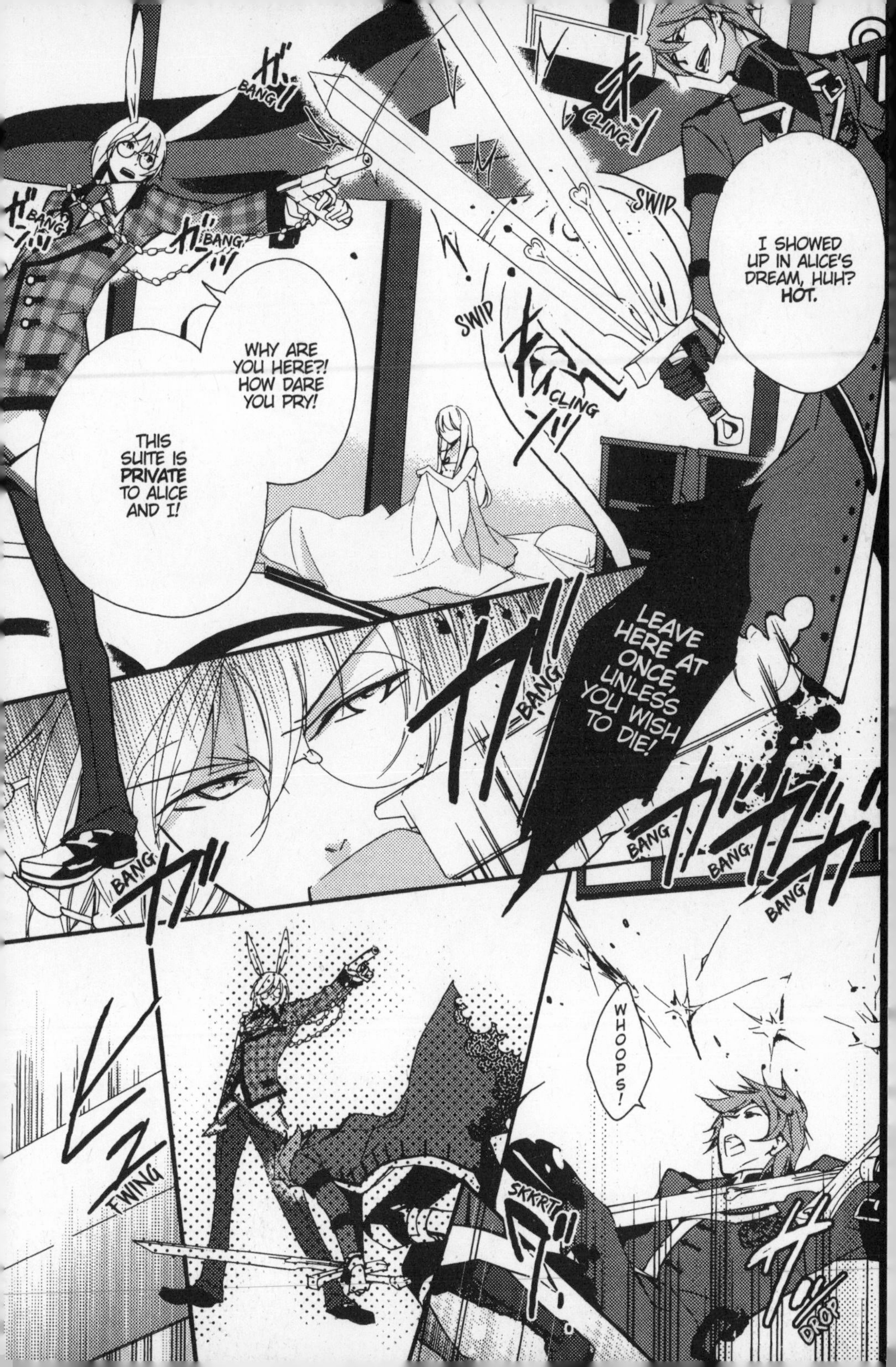
CLING
SWIP
I SHOWED UP IN ALICE'S DREAM, HUH? HOT.
BANG
BANG
BANG
SWIP
CLING
WHY ARE YOU HERE?! HOW DARE YOU PRY!
THIS SUITE IS PRIVATE TO ALICE AND I!
BANG
BANG
BANG
BANG
LEAVE HERE AT ONCE, UNLESS YOU WISH TO DIE!
BANG
WHOOPS!
SKKRT
DROP
FWING

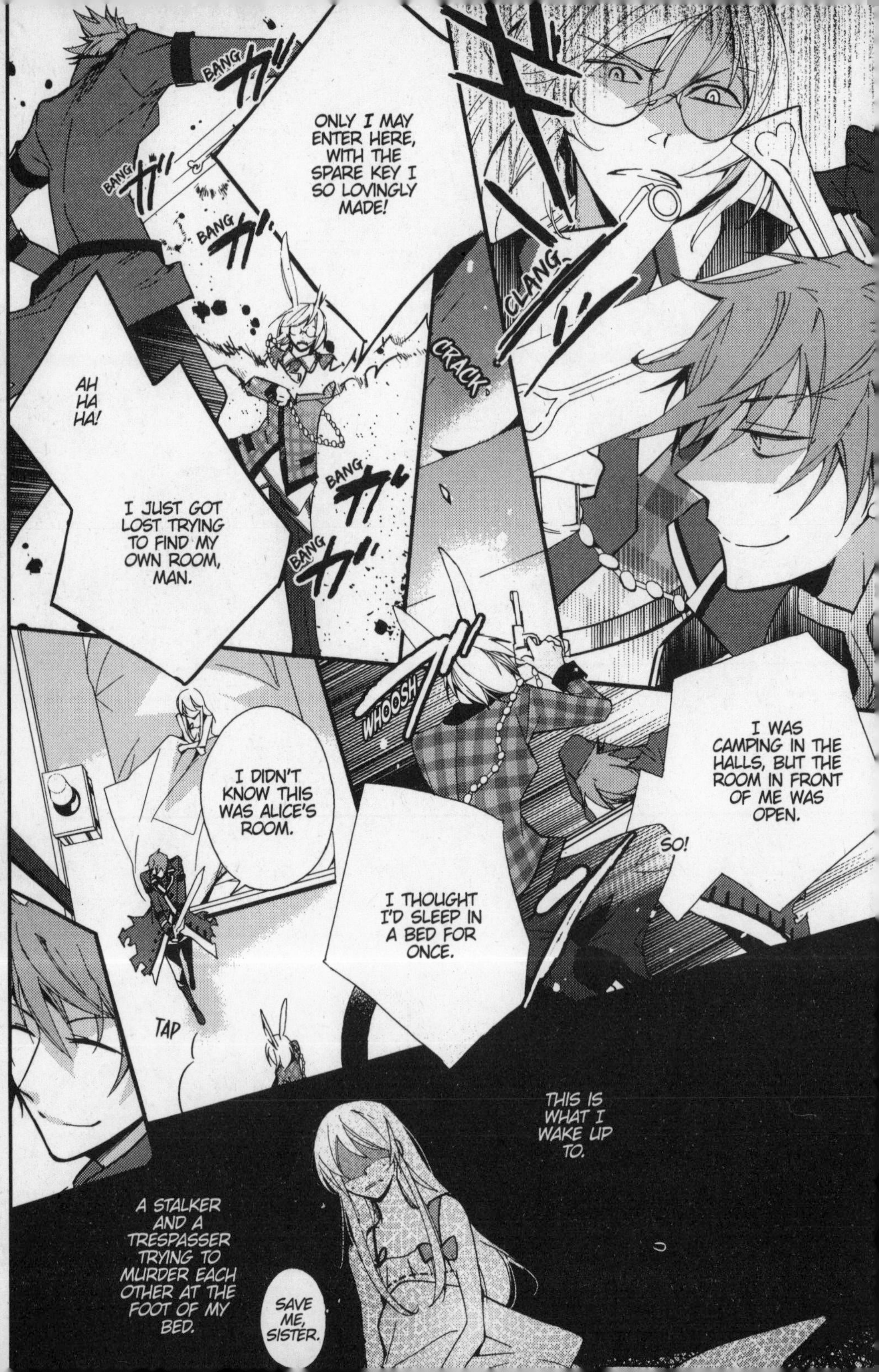
ONLY I MAY ENTER HERE, WITH THE SPARE KEY I SO LOVINGLY MADE!
CLANG
BANG
BANG
BANG
CRACK
AH HA HA!
BANG
BANG
I JUST GOT LOST TRYING TO FIND MY OWN ROOM, MAN.
I WAS CAMPING IN THE HALLS, BUT THE ROOM IN FRONT OF ME WAS OPEN.
SO!
I THOUGHT I'D SLEEP IN A BED FOR ONCE.
WHOOSH
I DIDN'T KNOW THIS WAS ALICE'S ROOM.
TAP
THIS IS WHAT I WAKE UP TO.
A STALKER AND A TRESPASSER TRYING TO MURDER EACH OTHER AT THE FOOT OF MY BED.
SAVE ME, SISTER.

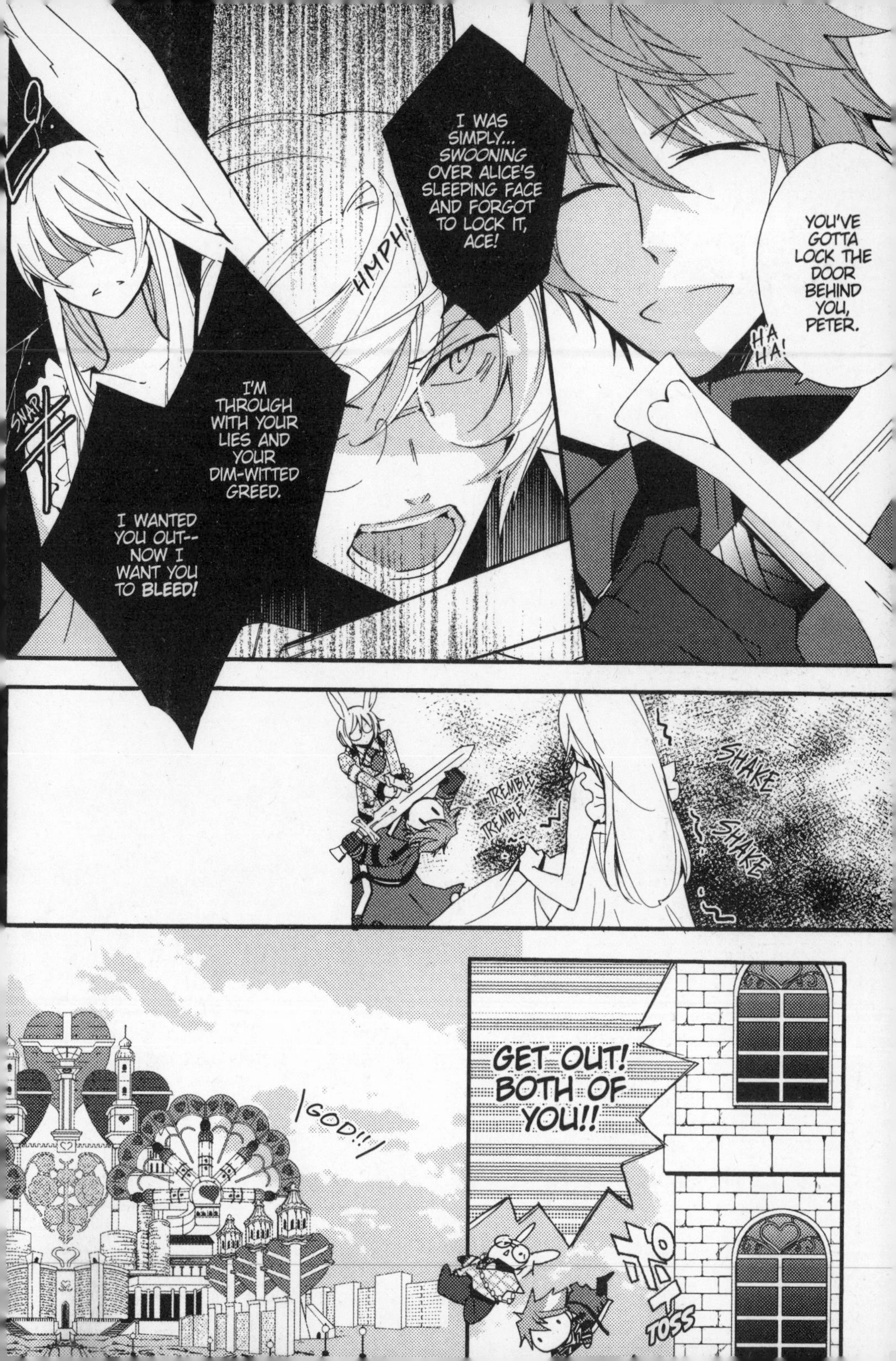
YOU'VE GOTTA LOCK THE DOOR BEHIND YOU, PETER.
HA HA!
I WAS SIMPLY... SWOONING OVER ALICE'S SLEEPING FACE AND FORGOT TO LOCK IT, ACE!
HMPH!
I'M THROUGH WITH YOUR LIES AND YOUR DIM-WITTED GREED.
I WANTED YOU OUT--NOW I WANT YOU TO BLEED!
SNAP
SHAKE
SHAKE
TREMBLE
TREMBLE
GET OUT! BOTH OF YOU!!
TOSS
GOD!!

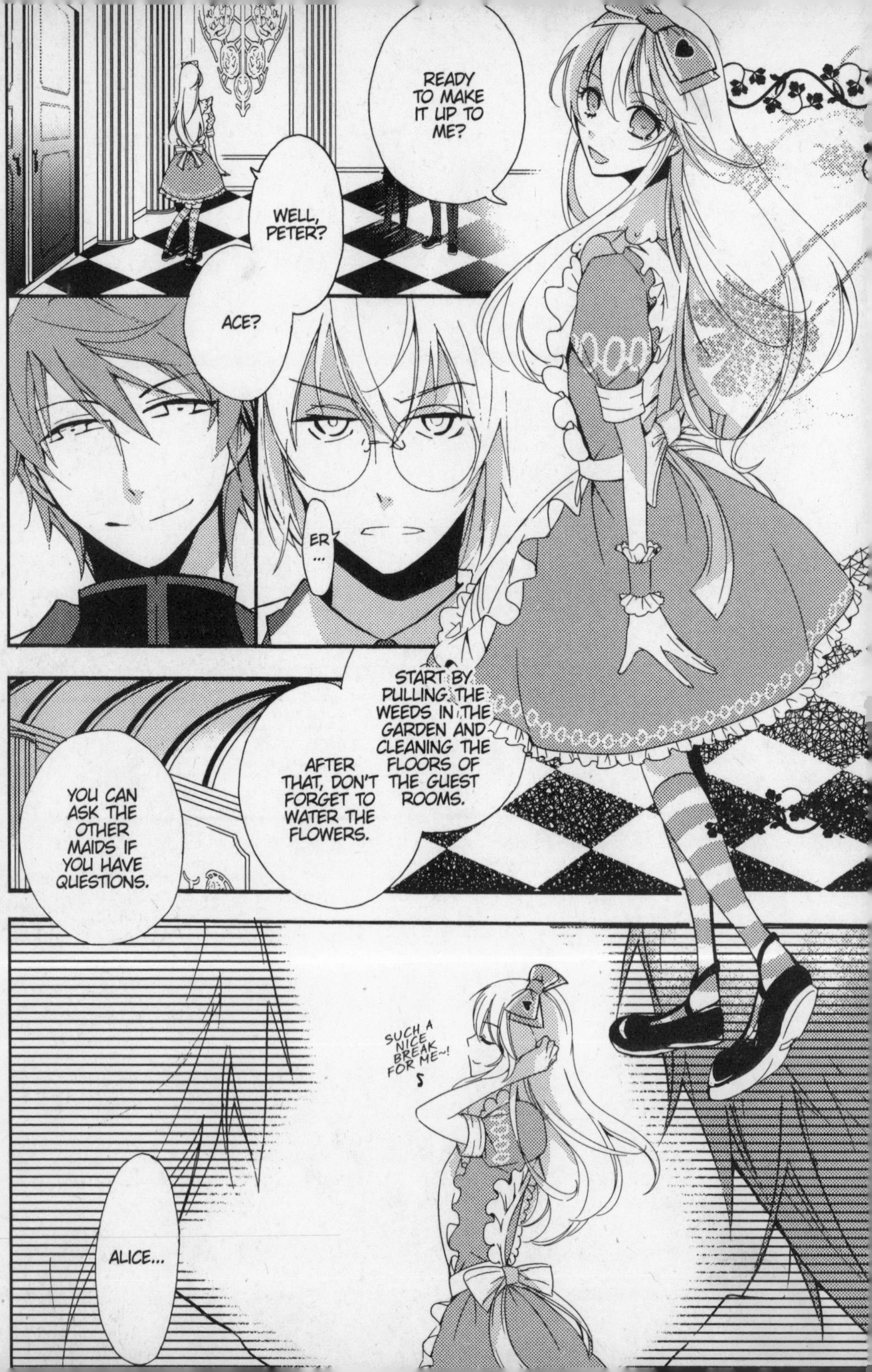

READY TO MAKE IT UP TO ME?
WELL, PETER?
ACE?
ER ...
START BY PULLING THE WEEDS IN THE GARDEN AND CLEANING THE FLOORS OF THE GUEST ROOMS.
AFTER THAT, DON'T FORGET TO WATER THE FLOWERS.
YOU CAN ASK THE OTHER MAIDS IF YOU HAVE QUESTIONS.
SUCH A NICE BREAK FOR ME~!
ALICE...

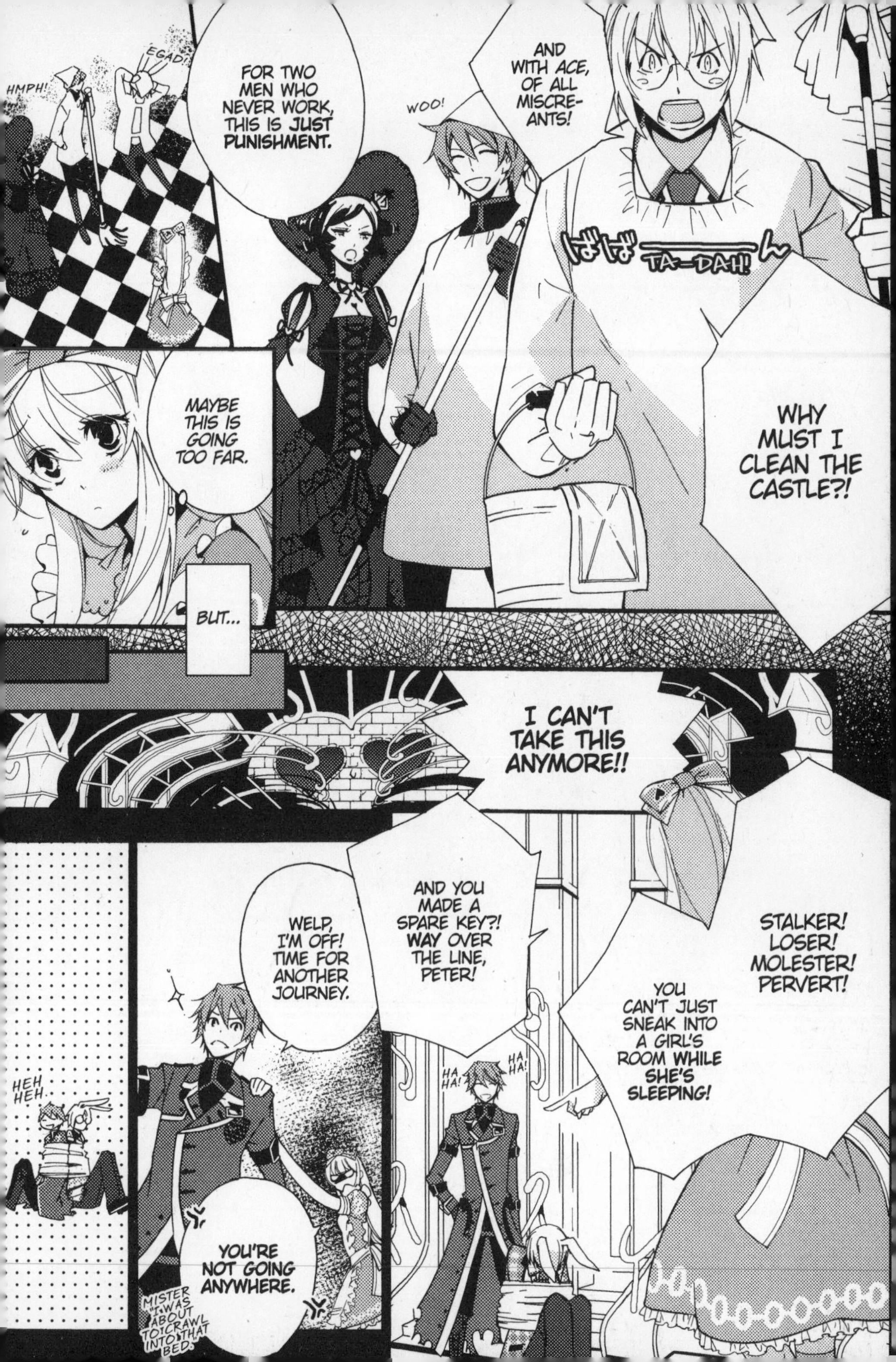
ばば——ん
TA-DAH!
AND WITH ACE, OF ALL MISCREANTS!
WHY MUST I CLEAN THE CASTLE?!
WOO!
FOR TWO MEN WHO NEVER WORK, THIS IS JUST PUNISHMENT.
EGAD!
HMPH!
MAYBE THIS IS GOING TOO FAR.
BUT...
I CAN'T TAKE THIS ANYMORE!!
STALKER! LOSER! MOLESTER! PERVERT!
YOU CAN'T JUST SNEAK INTO A GIRL'S ROOM WHILE SHE'S SLEEPING!
AND YOU MADE A SPARE KEY?! WAY OVER THE LINE, PETER!
HA HA!
HA HA!
WELP, I'M OFF! TIME FOR ANOTHER JOURNEY.
YOU'RE NOT GOING ANYWHERE.
HEH HEH.
MISTER "I WAS ABOUT TO CRAWL INTO THAT BED."

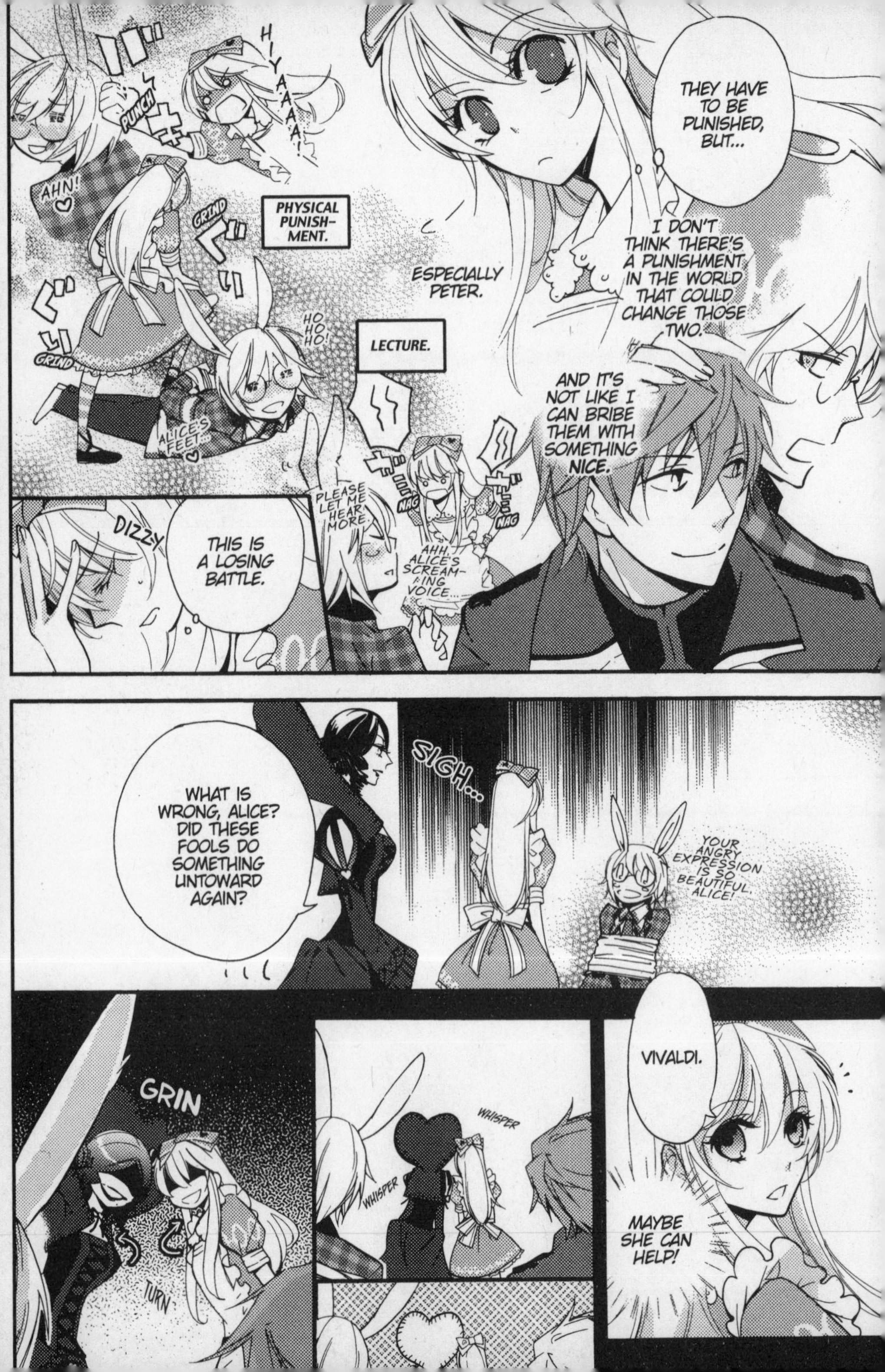
THEY HAVE TO BE PUNISHED, BUT...
I DON'T THINK THERE'S A PUNISHMENT IN THE WORLD THAT COULD CHANGE THOSE TWO.
ESPECIALLY PETER.
PHYSICAL PUNISH-MENT.
HIYAAAAA!
PUNCH
AHN!
GRIND
GRIND
HO HO HO!
ALICE'S FEET...
LECTURE.
NAG
NAG
PLEASE LET ME HEAR MORE.
AHH, ALICE'S SCREAM-ING VOICE...
AND IT'S NOT LIKE I CAN BRIBE THEM WITH SOMETHING NICE.
DIZZY
THIS IS A LOSING BATTLE.
SIGH...
YOUR ANGRY EXPRESSION IS SO BEAUTIFUL, ALICE!
WHAT IS WRONG, ALICE? DID THESE FOOLS DO SOMETHING UNTOWARD AGAIN?
VIVALDI.
MAYBE SHE CAN HELP!
WHISPER
WHISPER
GRIN
TURN

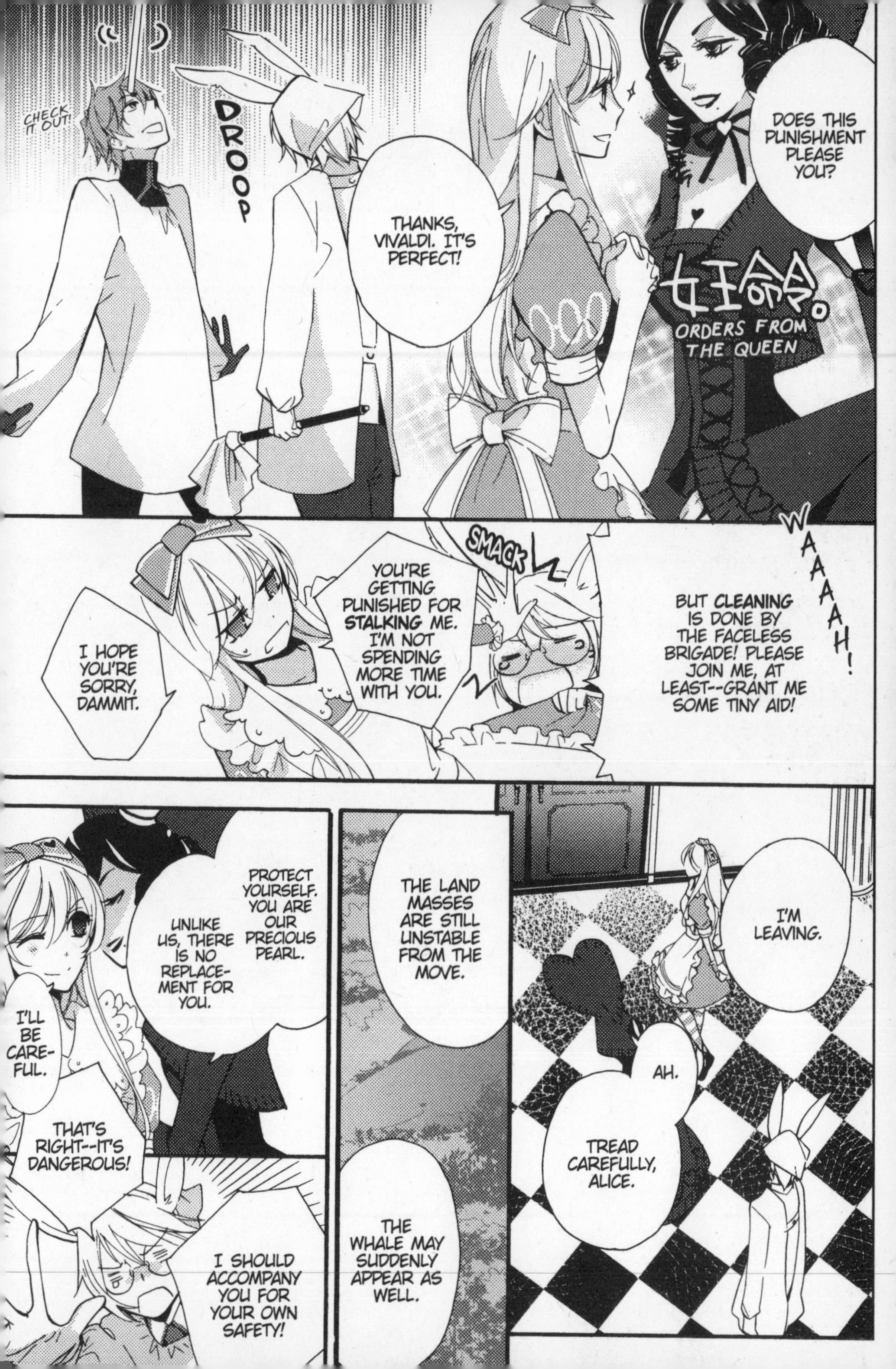
DOES THIS PUNISHMENT PLEASE YOU?
ORDERS FROM THE QUEEN
THANKS, VIVALDI. IT'S PERFECT!
DROOP
CHECK IT OUT!
WAAAAAH!
BUT CLEANING IS DONE BY THE FACELESS BRIGADE! PLEASE JOIN ME, AT LEAST--GRANT ME SOME TINY AID!
SMACK
YOU'RE GETTING PUNISHED FOR STALKING ME. I'M NOT SPENDING MORE TIME WITH YOU.
I HOPE YOU'RE SORRY, DAMMIT.
I'M LEAVING.
AH.
TREAD CAREFULLY, ALICE.
THE LAND MASSES ARE STILL UNSTABLE FROM THE MOVE.
THE WHALE MAY SUDDENLY APPEAR AS WELL.
PROTECT YOURSELF. YOU ARE OUR PRECIOUS PEARL.
UNLIKE US, THERE IS NO REPLACEMENT FOR YOU.
I'LL BE CAREFUL.
THAT'S RIGHT--IT'S DANGEROUS!
I SHOULD ACCOMPANY YOU FOR YOUR OWN SAFETY!

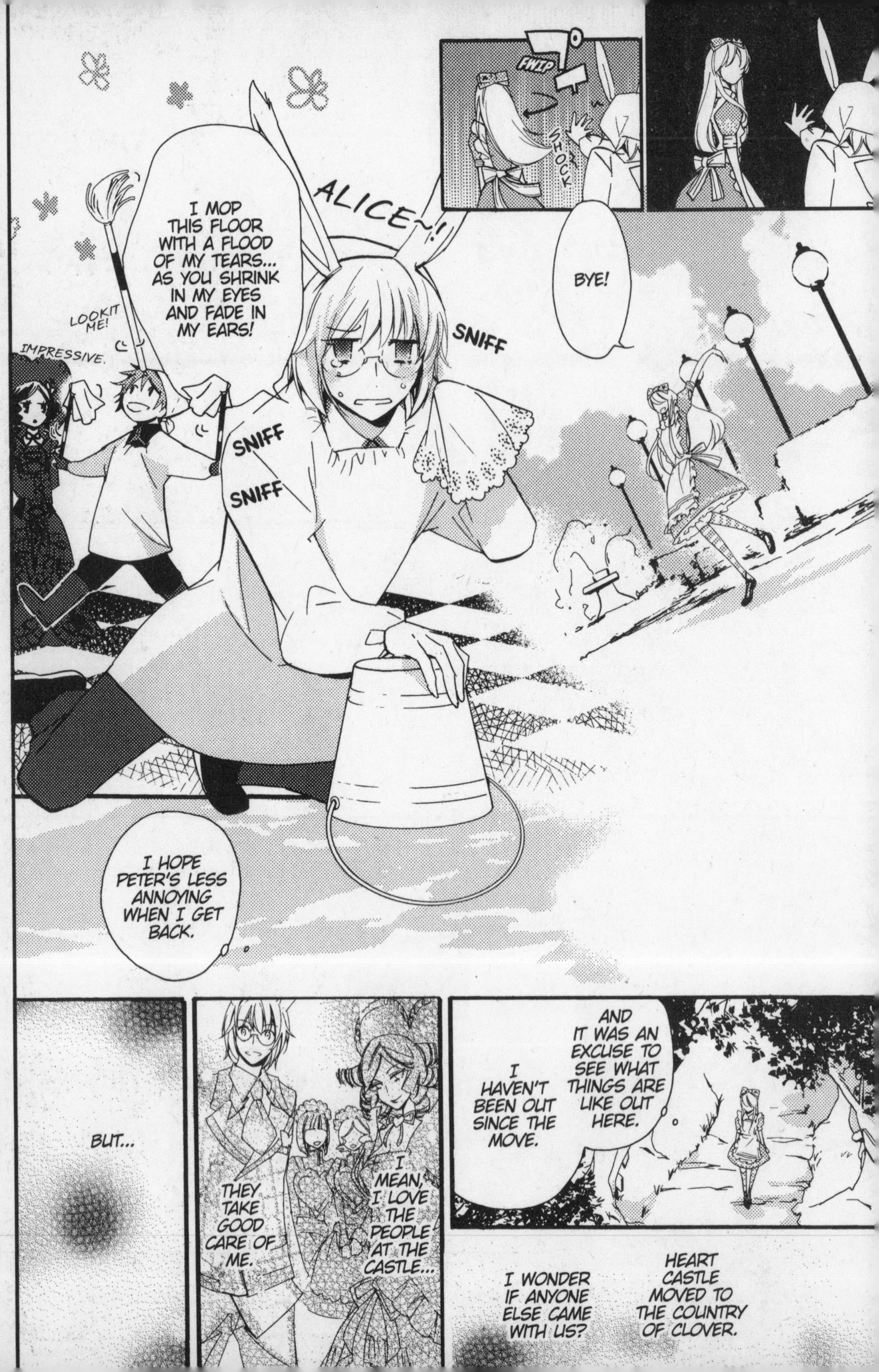
FWIP
SHOCK
ALICE~!
BYE!
SNIFF
I MOP THIS FLOOR WITH A FLOOD OF MY TEARS... AS YOU SHRINK IN MY EYES AND FADE IN MY EARS!
LOOKIT ME!
IMPRESSIVE.
SNIFF
SNIFF
I HOPE PETER'S LESS ANNOYING WHEN I GET BACK.
AND IT WAS AN EXCUSE TO SEE WHAT THINGS ARE LIKE OUT HERE.
I HAVEN'T BEEN OUT SINCE THE MOVE.
I MEAN, I LOVE THE PEOPLE AT THE CASTLE...
THEY TAKE GOOD CARE OF ME.
BUT...
HEART CASTLE MOVED TO THE COUNTRY OF CLOVER.
I WONDER IF ANYONE ELSE CAME WITH US?

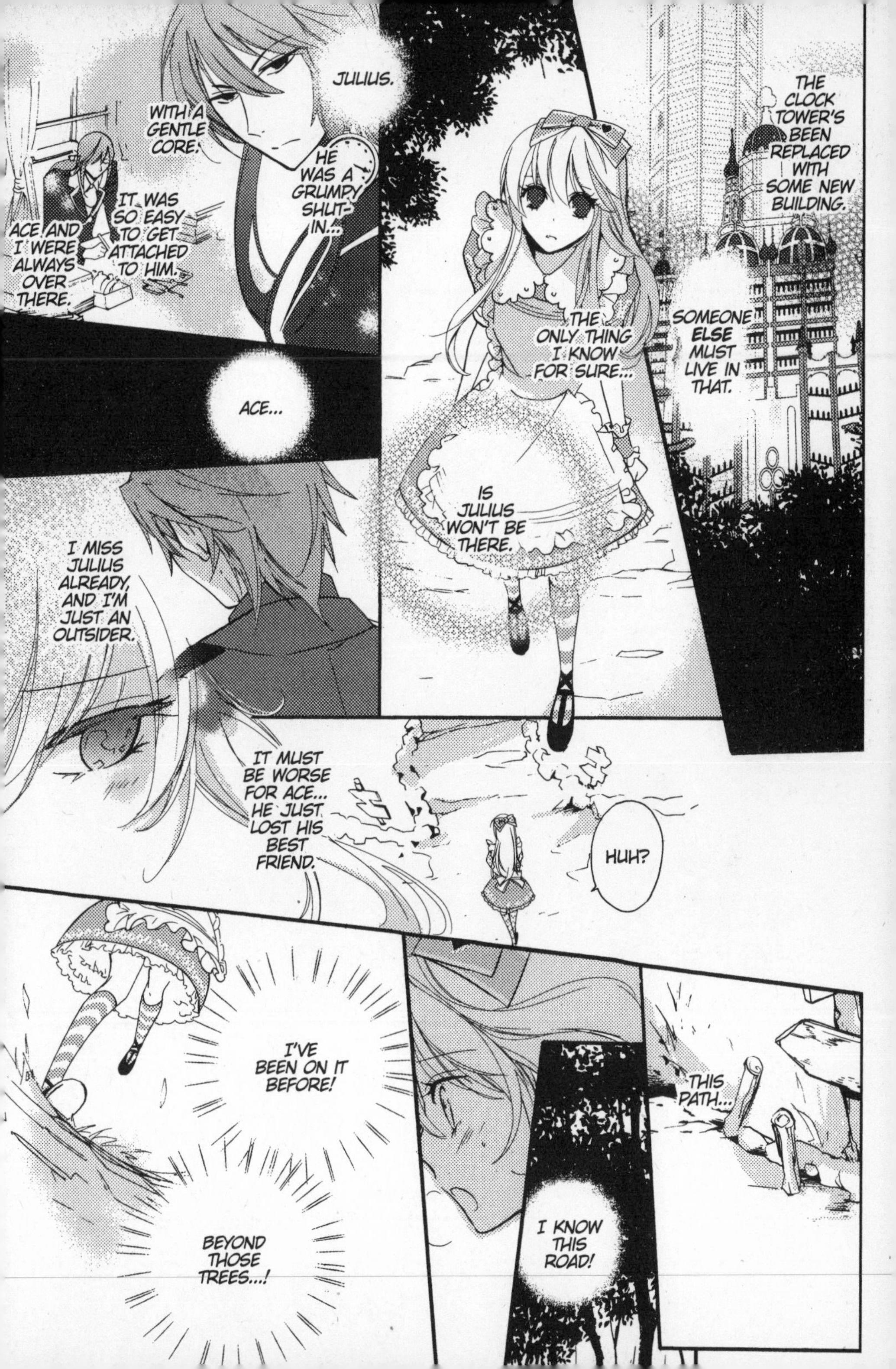
THE CLOCK TOWER'S BEEN REPLACED WITH SOME NEW BUILDING.
SOMEONE ELSE MUST LIVE IN THAT.
THE ONLY THING I KNOW FOR SURE...
IS JULIUS WON'T BE THERE.
JULIUS.
HE WAS A GRUMPY SHUT-IN...
WITH A GENTLE CORE.
IT WAS SO EASY TO GET ATTACHED TO HIM.
ACE AND I WERE ALWAYS OVER THERE.
ACE...
I MISS JULIUS ALREADY, AND I'M JUST AN OUTSIDER.
IT MUST BE WORSE FOR ACE... HE JUST LOST HIS BEST FRIEND.
HUH?
THIS PATH...
I KNOW THIS ROAD!
I'VE BEEN ON IT BEFORE!
BEYOND THOSE TREES...!

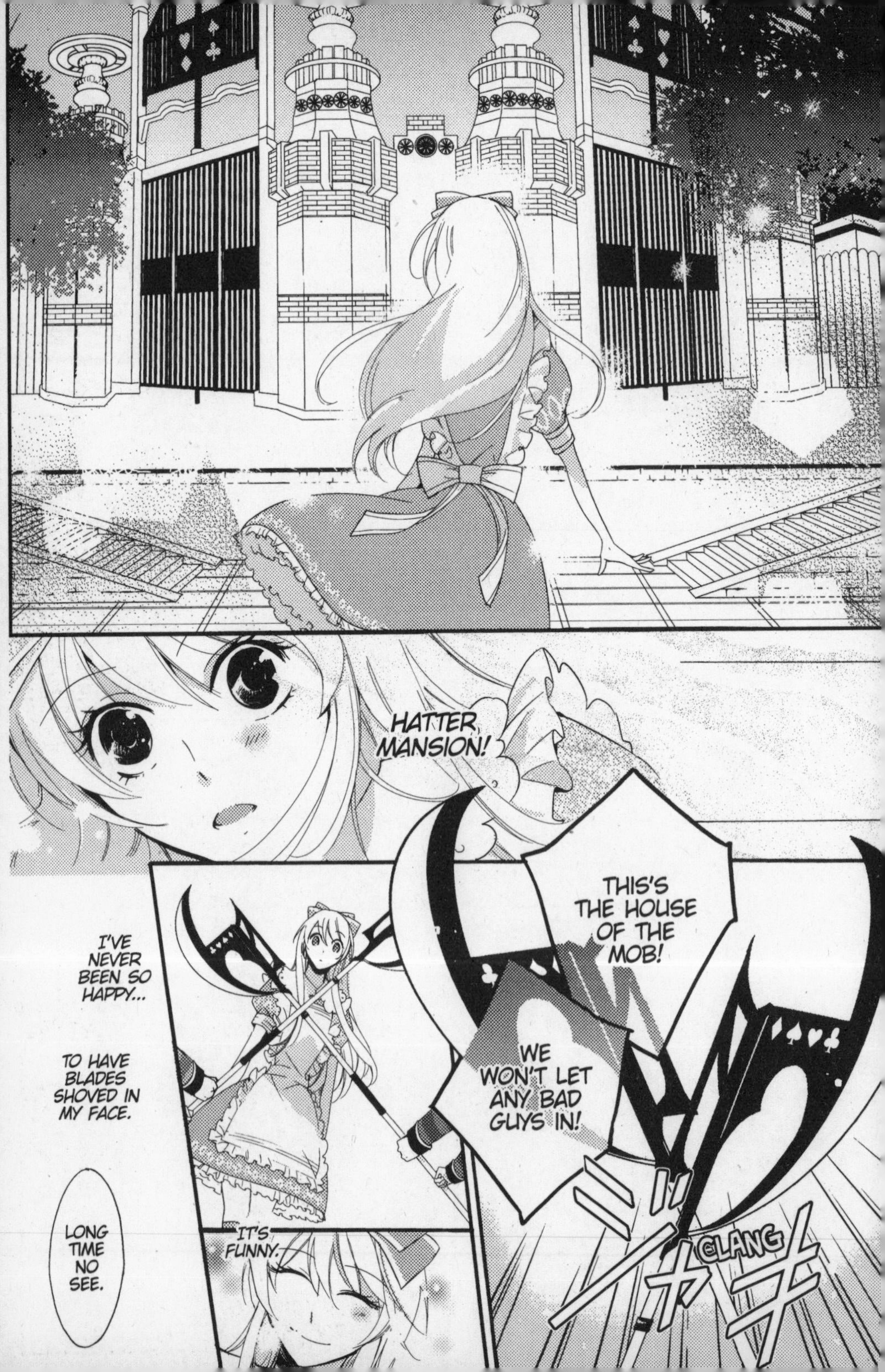
HATTER MANSION!
THIS'S THE HOUSE OF THE MOB!
WE WON'T LET ANY BAD GUYS IN!
CLANG
I'VE NEVER BEEN SO HAPPY...
TO HAVE BLADES SHOVED IN MY FACE.
IT'S FUNNY.
LONG TIME NO SEE.

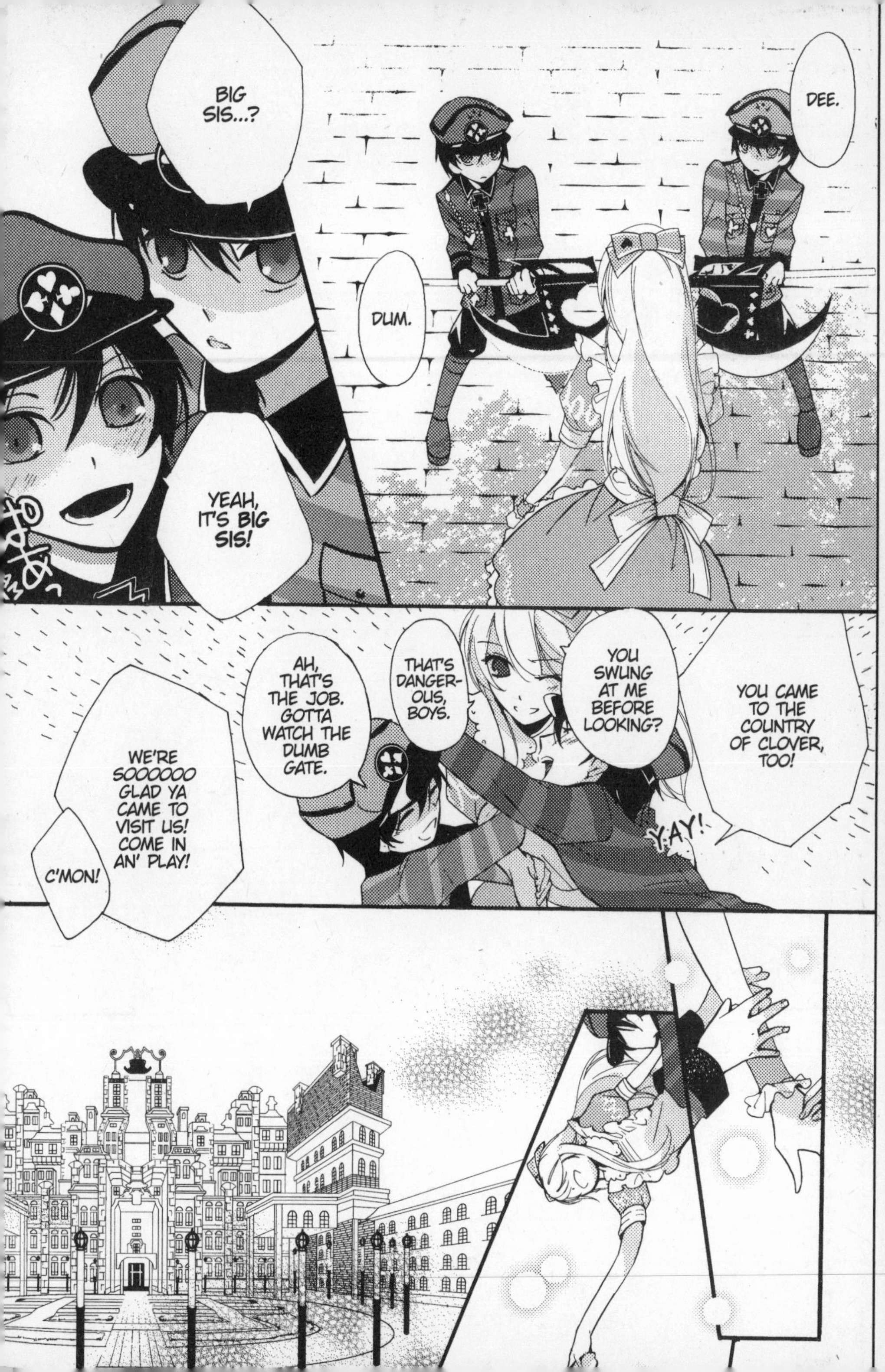
DEE.
DUM.
BIG SIS...?
YEAH, IT'S BIG SIS!
YOU CAME TO THE COUNTRY OF CLOVER, TOO!
YAY!
YOU SWUNG AT ME BEFORE LOOKING?
THAT'S DANGER-OUS, BOYS.
AH, THAT'S THE JOB. GOTTA WATCH THE DUMB GATE.
WE'RE SOOOOOO GLAD YA CAME TO VISIT US! COME IN AN' PLAY!
C'MON!

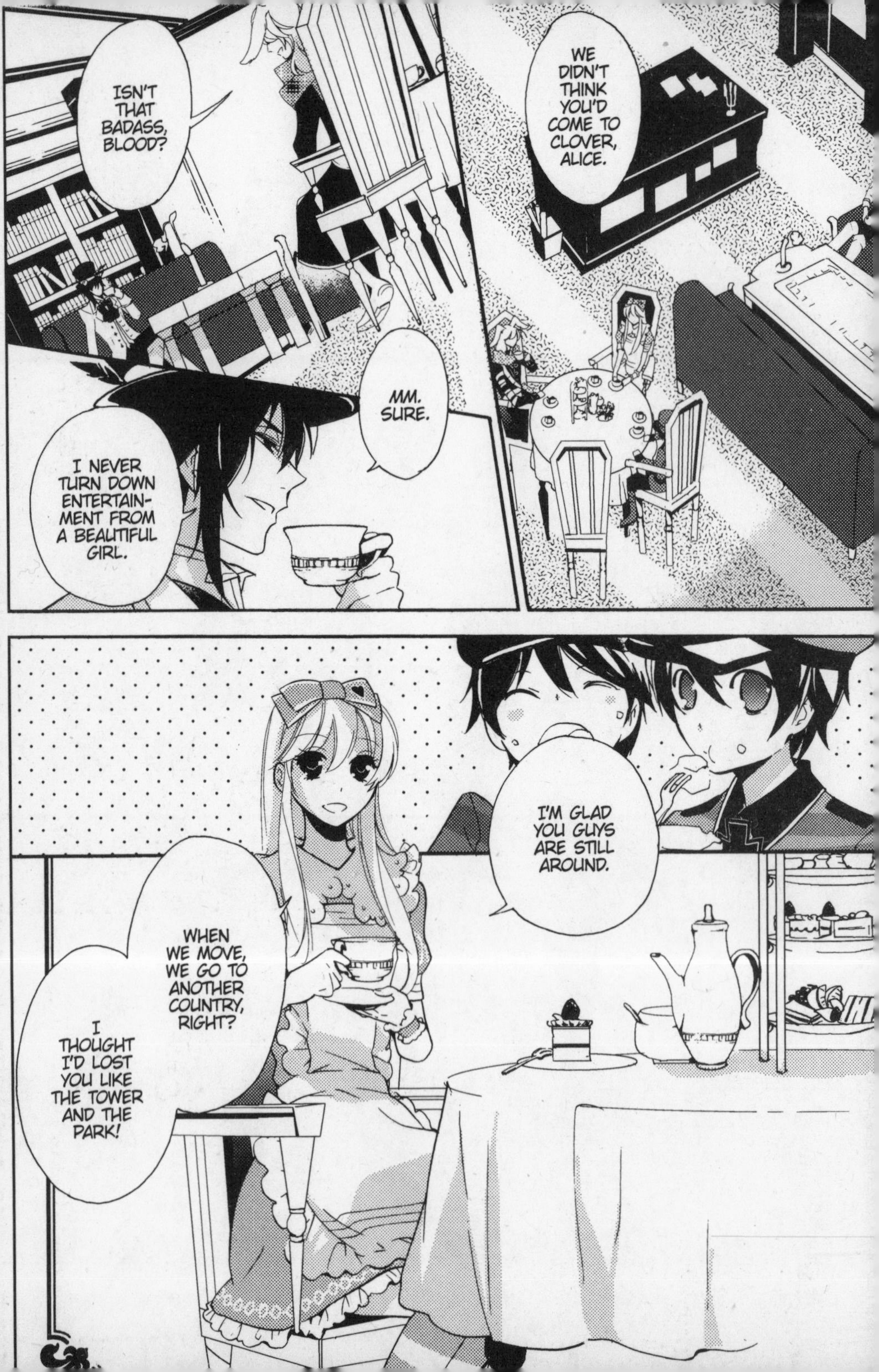
WE DIDN'T THINK YOU'D COME TO CLOVER, ALICE.
ISN'T THAT BADASS, BLOOD?
MM. SURE.
I NEVER TURN DOWN ENTERTAIN-MENT FROM A BEAUTIFUL GIRL.
I'M GLAD YOU GUYS ARE STILL AROUND.
WHEN WE MOVE, WE GO TO ANOTHER COUNTRY, RIGHT?
I THOUGHT I'D LOST YOU LIKE THE TOWER AND THE PARK!

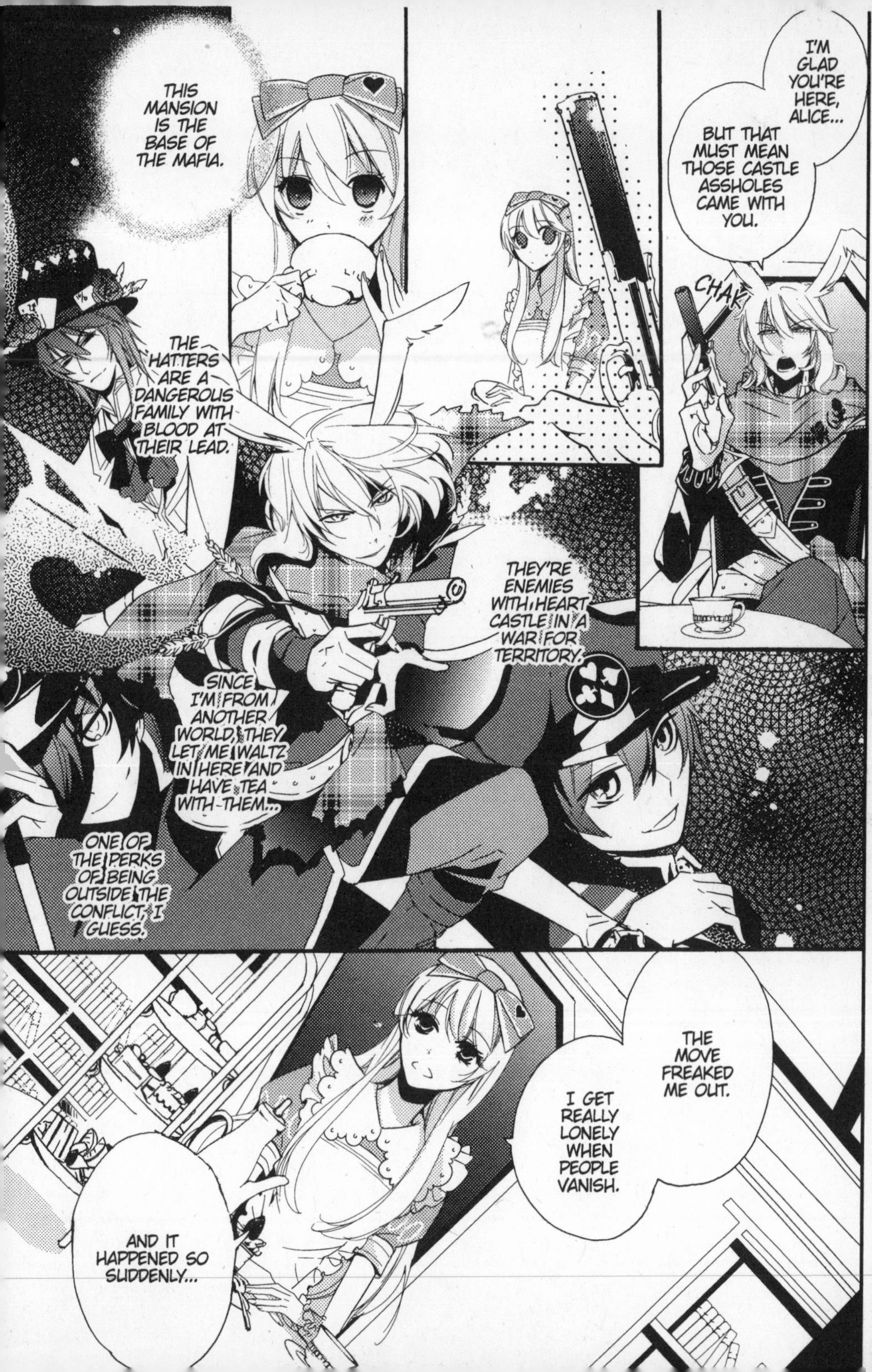

I'M GLAD YOU'RE HERE, ALICE...
BUT THAT MUST MEAN THOSE CASTLE ASSHOLES CAME WITH YOU.
CHAK
THIS MANSION IS THE BASE OF THE MAFIA.
THE HATTERS ARE A DANGEROUS FAMILY WITH BLOOD AT THEIR LEAD.
THEY'RE ENEMIES WITH HEART CASTLE IN A WAR FOR TERRITORY.
SINCE I'M FROM ANOTHER WORLD, THEY LET ME WALTZ IN HERE AND HAVE TEA WITH THEM...
ONE OF THE PERKS OF BEING OUTSIDE THE CONFLICT, I GUESS.
THE MOVE FREAKED ME OUT.
I GET REALLY LONELY WHEN PEOPLE VANISH.
AND IT HAPPENED SO SUDDENLY...

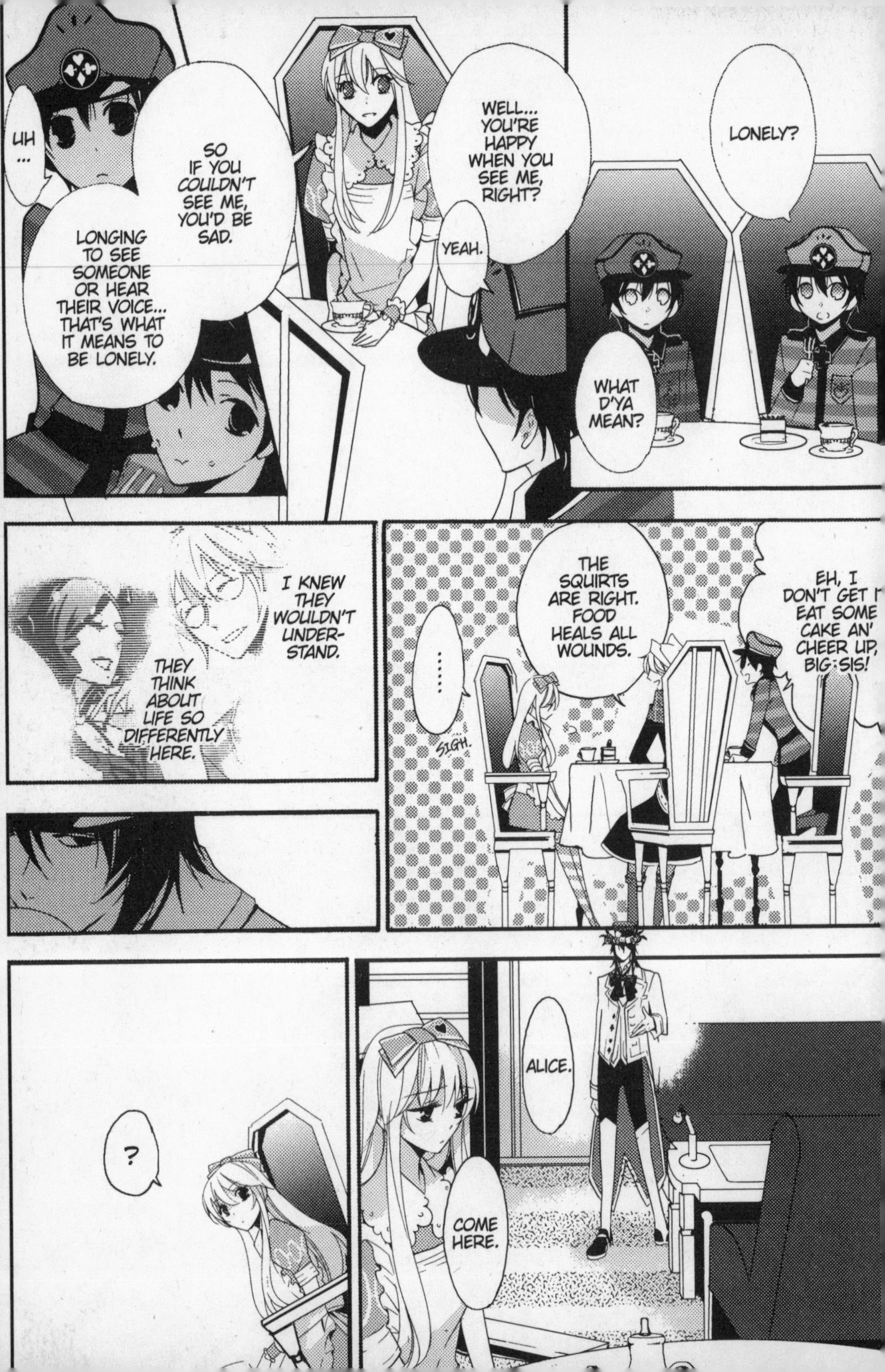
LONELY?
WHAT D'YA MEAN?
WELL... YOU'RE HAPPY WHEN YOU SEE ME, RIGHT?
YEAH.
SO IF YOU COULDN'T SEE ME, YOU'D BE SAD.
UH ...
LONGING TO SEE SOMEONE OR HEAR THEIR VOICE... THAT'S WHAT IT MEANS TO BE LONELY.
EH, I DON'T GET I EAT SOME CAKE AN' CHEER UP, BIG SIS!
THE SQUIRTS ARE RIGHT. FOOD HEALS ALL WOUNDS.
......
SIGH.
I KNEW THEY WOULDN'T UNDER-STAND.
THEY THINK ABOUT LIFE SO DIFFERENTLY HERE.
ALICE.
COME HERE.
?

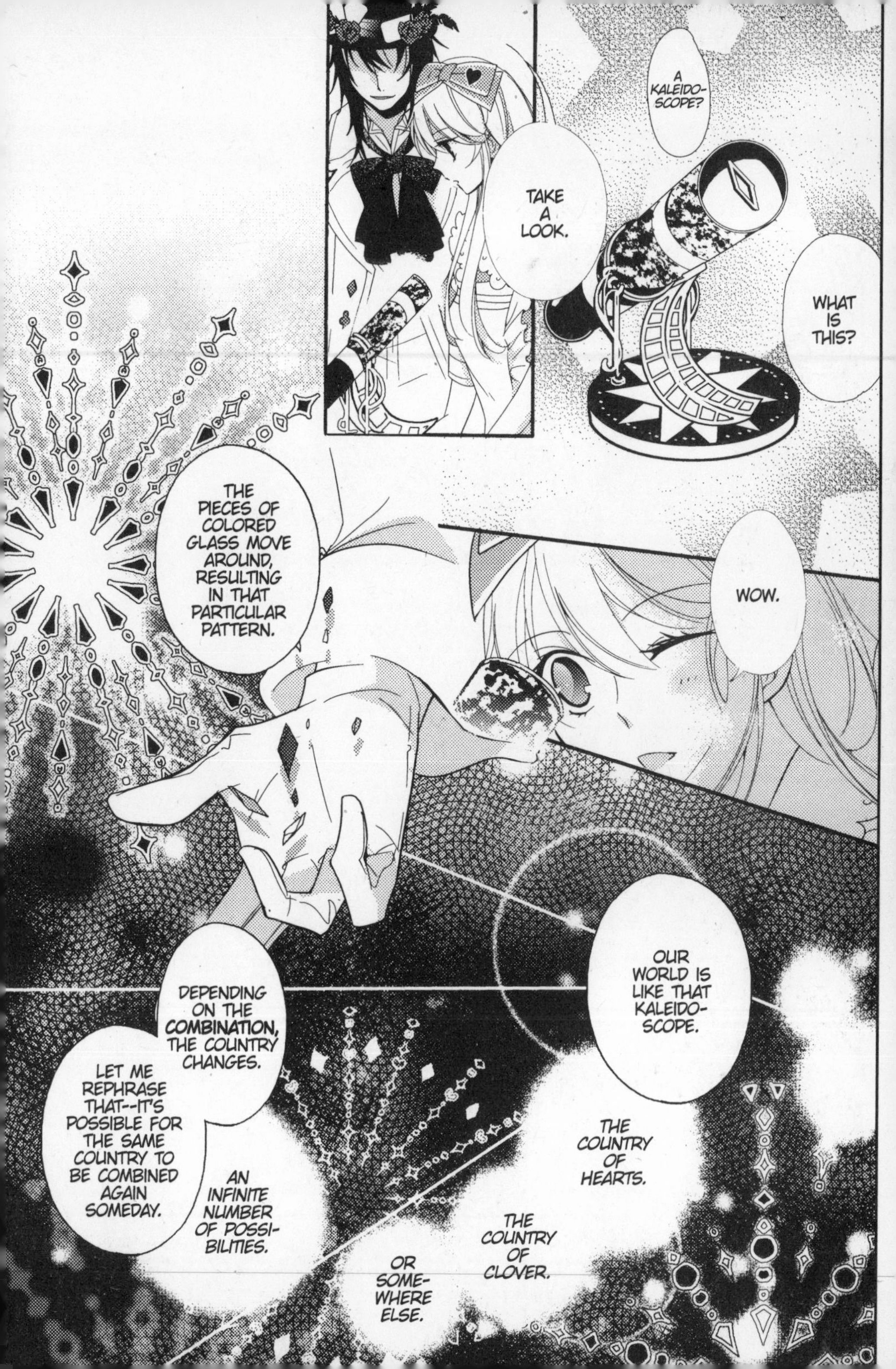
WHAT IS THIS?
A KALEIDO-SCOPE?
TAKE A LOOK.
WOW.
THE PIECES OF COLORED GLASS MOVE AROUND, RESULTING IN THAT PARTICULAR PATTERN.
OUR WORLD IS LIKE THAT KALEIDO-SCOPE.
DEPENDING ON THE COMBINATION, THE COUNTRY CHANGES.
LET ME REPHRASE THAT--IT'S POSSIBLE FOR THE SAME COUNTRY TO BE COMBINED AGAIN SOMEDAY.
THE COUNTRY OF HEARTS.
THE COUNTRY OF CLOVER.
OR SOME-WHERE ELSE.
AN INFINITE NUMBER OF POSSI-BILITIES.

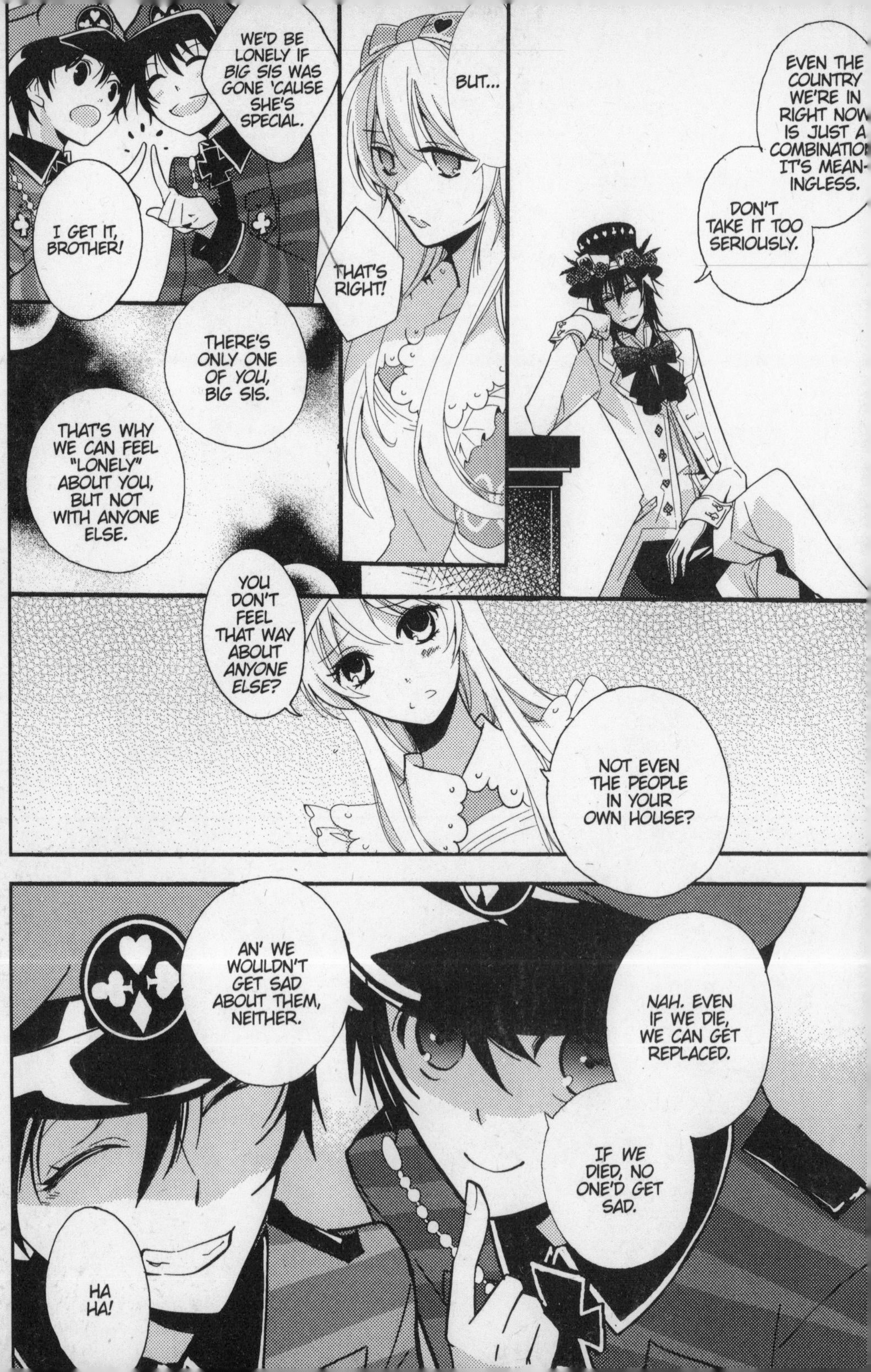

EVEN THE COUNTRY WE'RE IN RIGHT NOW IS JUST A COMBINATION. IT'S MEAN-INGLESS.
DON'T TAKE IT TOO SERIOUSLY.
BUT...
WE'D BE LONELY IF BIG SIS WAS GONE 'CAUSE SHE'S SPECIAL.
I GET IT, BROTHER!
THAT'S RIGHT!
THERE'S ONLY ONE OF YOU, BIG SIS.
THAT'S WHY WE CAN FEEL "LONELY" ABOUT YOU, BUT NOT WITH ANYONE ELSE.
YOU DON'T FEEL THAT WAY ABOUT ANYONE ELSE?
NOT EVEN THE PEOPLE IN YOUR OWN HOUSE?
NAH. EVEN IF WE DIE, WE CAN GET REPLACED.
AN' WE WOULDN'T GET SAD ABOUT THEM, NEITHER.
IF WE DIED, NO ONE'D GET SAD.
HA HA!

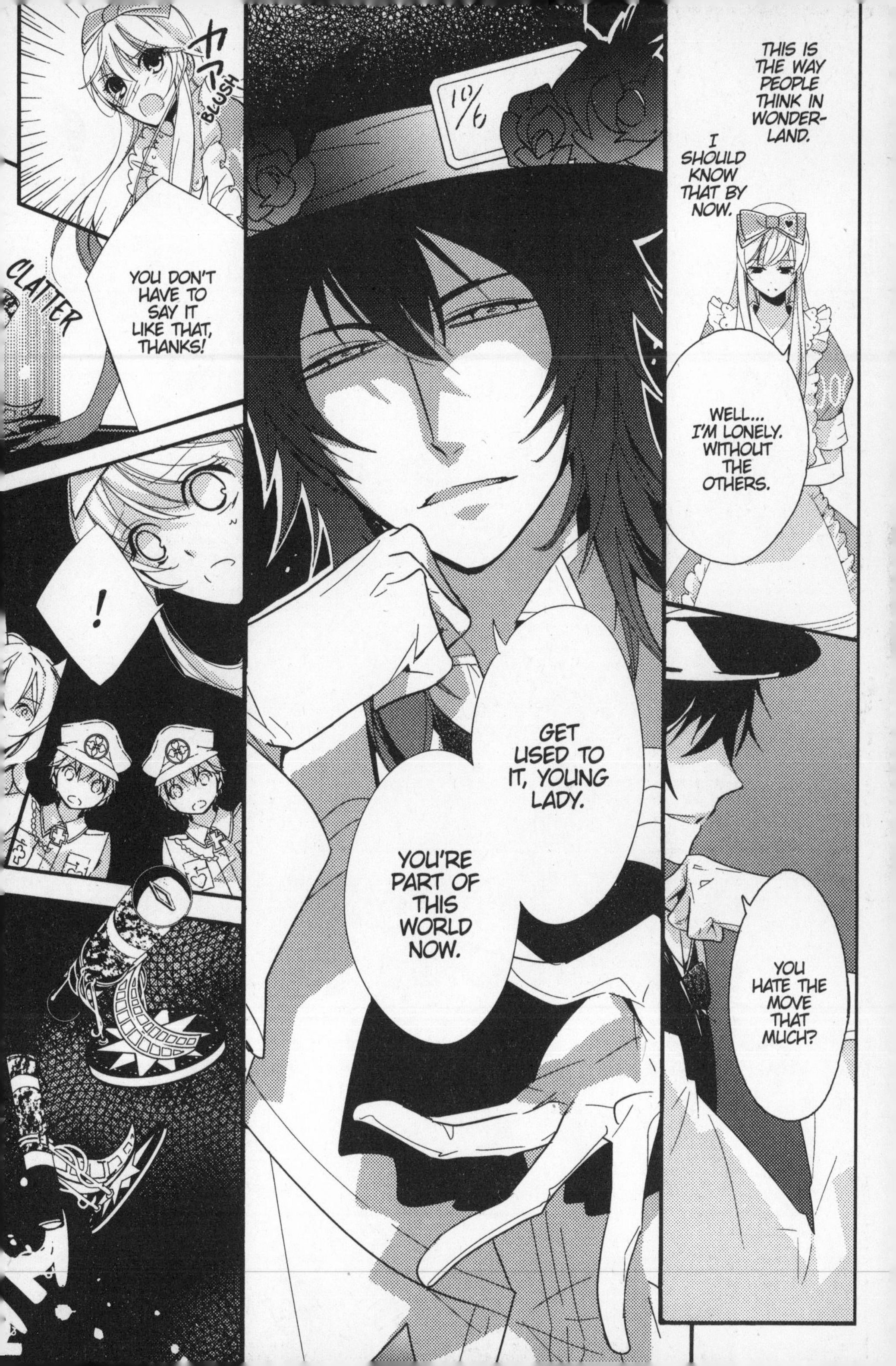
THIS IS THE WAY PEOPLE THINK IN WONDER-LAND.
I SHOULD KNOW THAT BY NOW.
WELL... I'M LONELY. WITHOUT THE OTHERS.
YOU HATE THE MOVE THAT MUCH?
GET USED TO IT, YOUNG LADY.
YOU'RE PART OF THIS WORLD NOW.
カァ
BLUSH
YOU DON'T HAVE TO SAY IT LIKE THAT, THANKS!
CLATTER
!

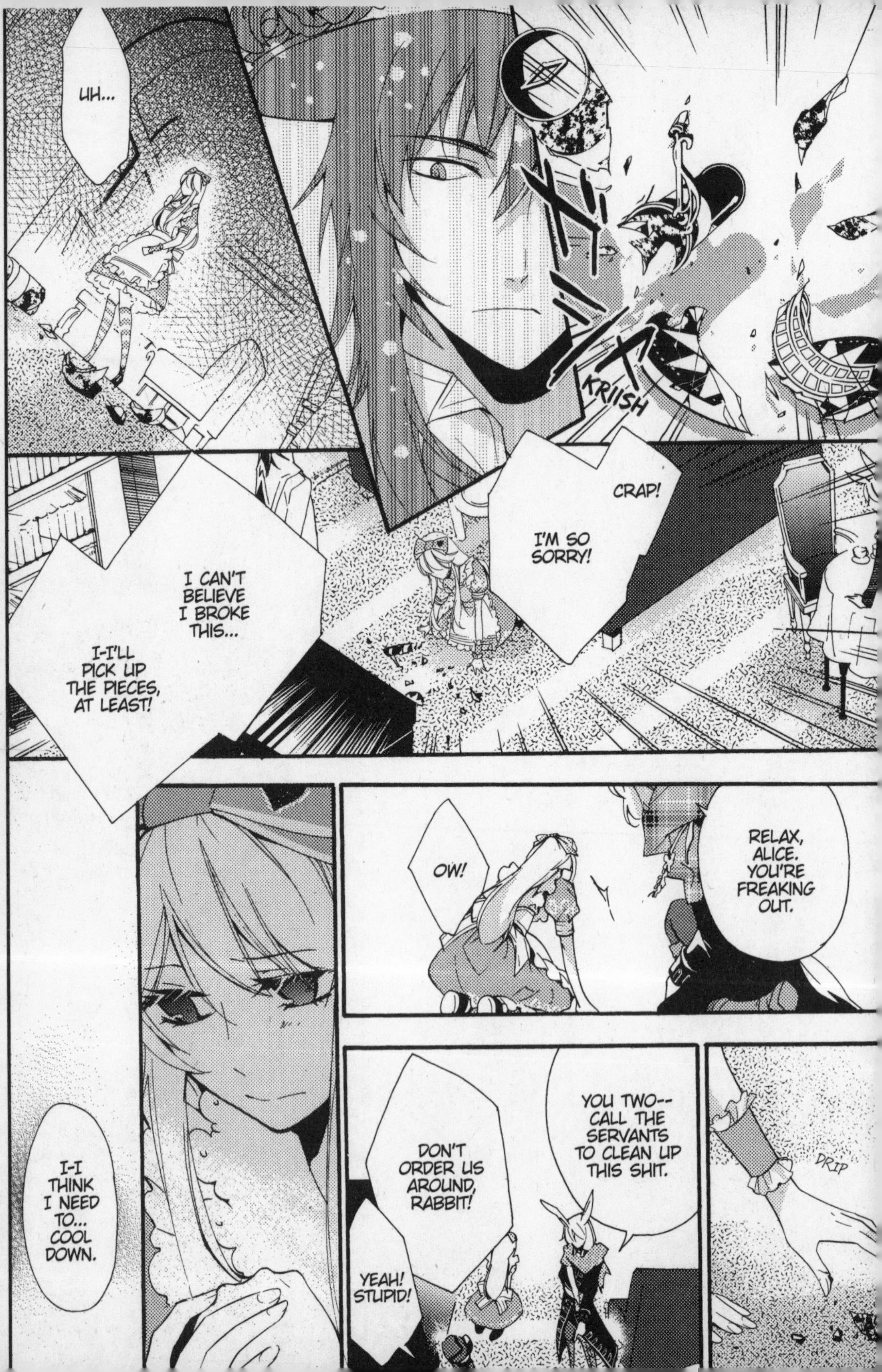
KRIISH
UH...
CRAP!
I'M SO SORRY!
I CAN'T BELIEVE I BROKE THIS...
I-I'LL PICK UP THE PIECES, AT LEAST!
RELAX, ALICE. YOU'RE FREAKING OUT.
OW!
DRIP
YOU TWO-- CALL THE SERVANTS TO CLEAN UP THIS SHIT.
DON'T ORDER US AROUND, RABBIT!
YEAH! STUPID!
I-I THINK I NEED TO... COOL DOWN.

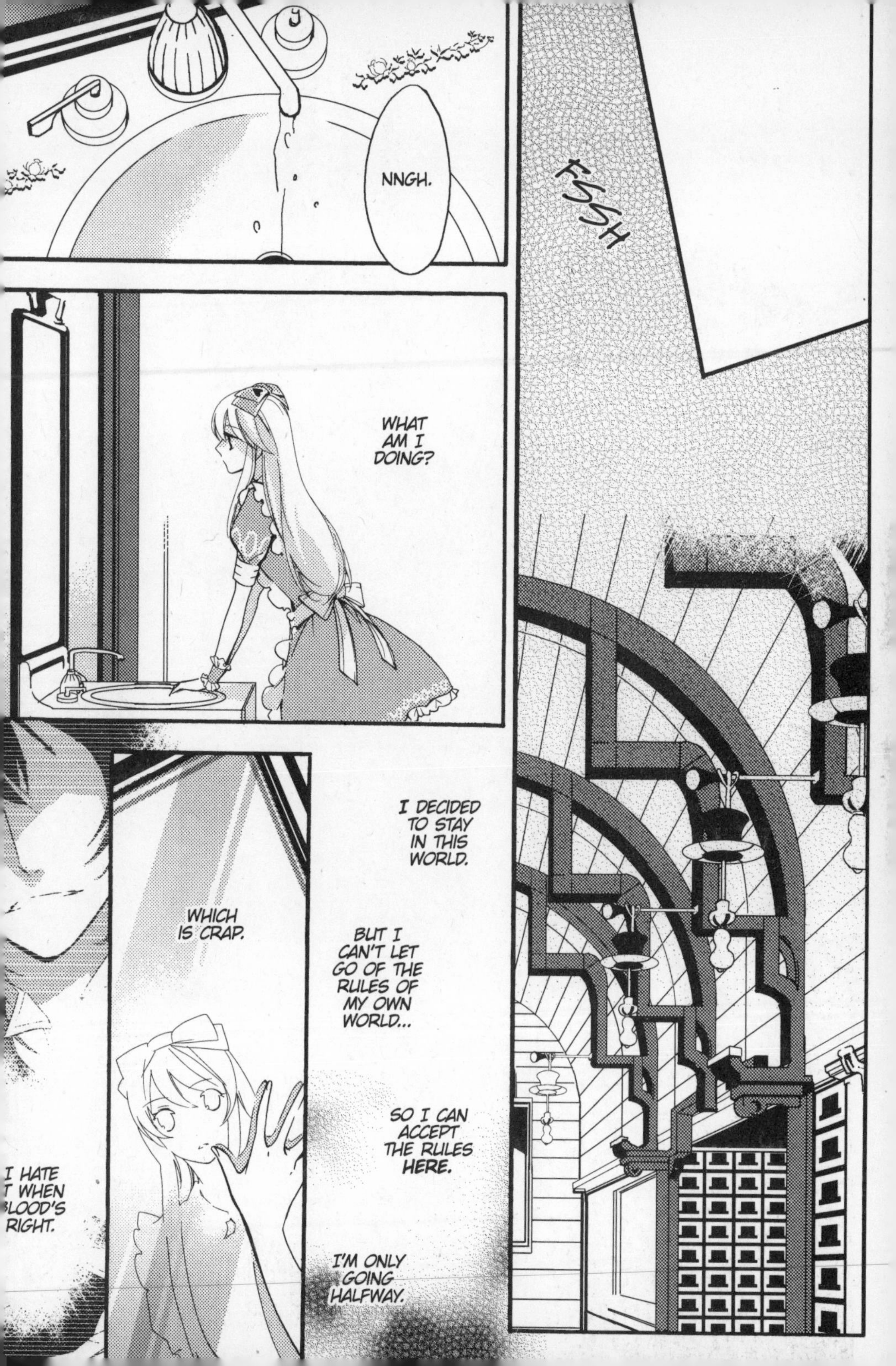
FSSH
NNGH.
WHAT AM I DOING?
I DECIDED TO STAY IN THIS WORLD.
BUT I CAN'T LET GO OF THE RULES OF MY OWN WORLD...
SO I CAN ACCEPT THE RULES HERE.
I'M ONLY GOING HALFWAY.
WHICH IS CRAP.
I HATE T WHEN LOOD'S RIGHT.

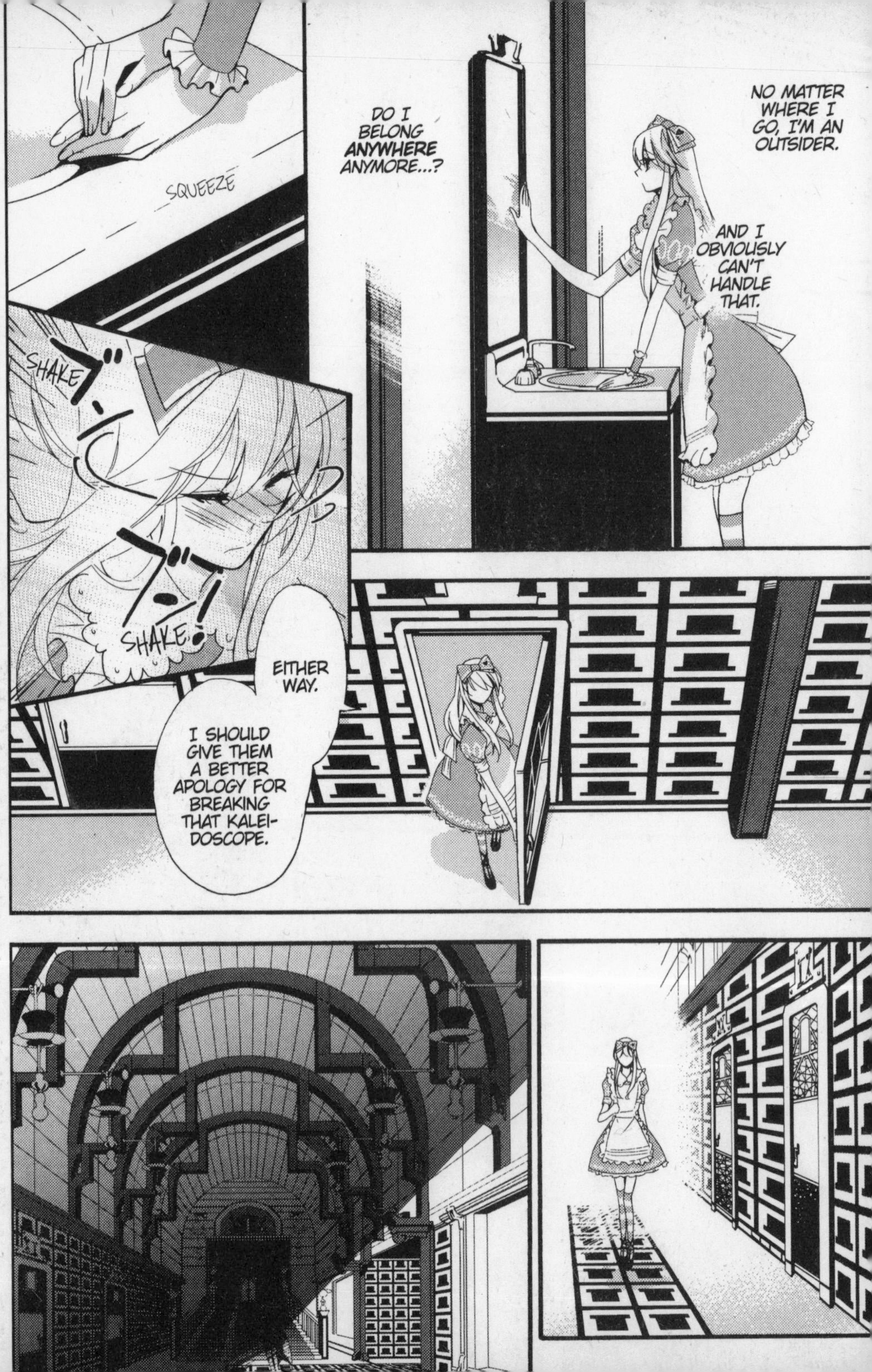
NO MATTER WHERE I GO, I'M AN OUTSIDER.
AND I OBVIOUSLY CAN'T HANDLE THAT.
DO I BELONG **ANYWHERE** ANYMORE...?
SQUEEZE
SHAKE
SHAKE
EITHER WAY.
I SHOULD GIVE THEM A BETTER APOLOGY FOR BREAKING THAT KALEI-DOSCOPE.

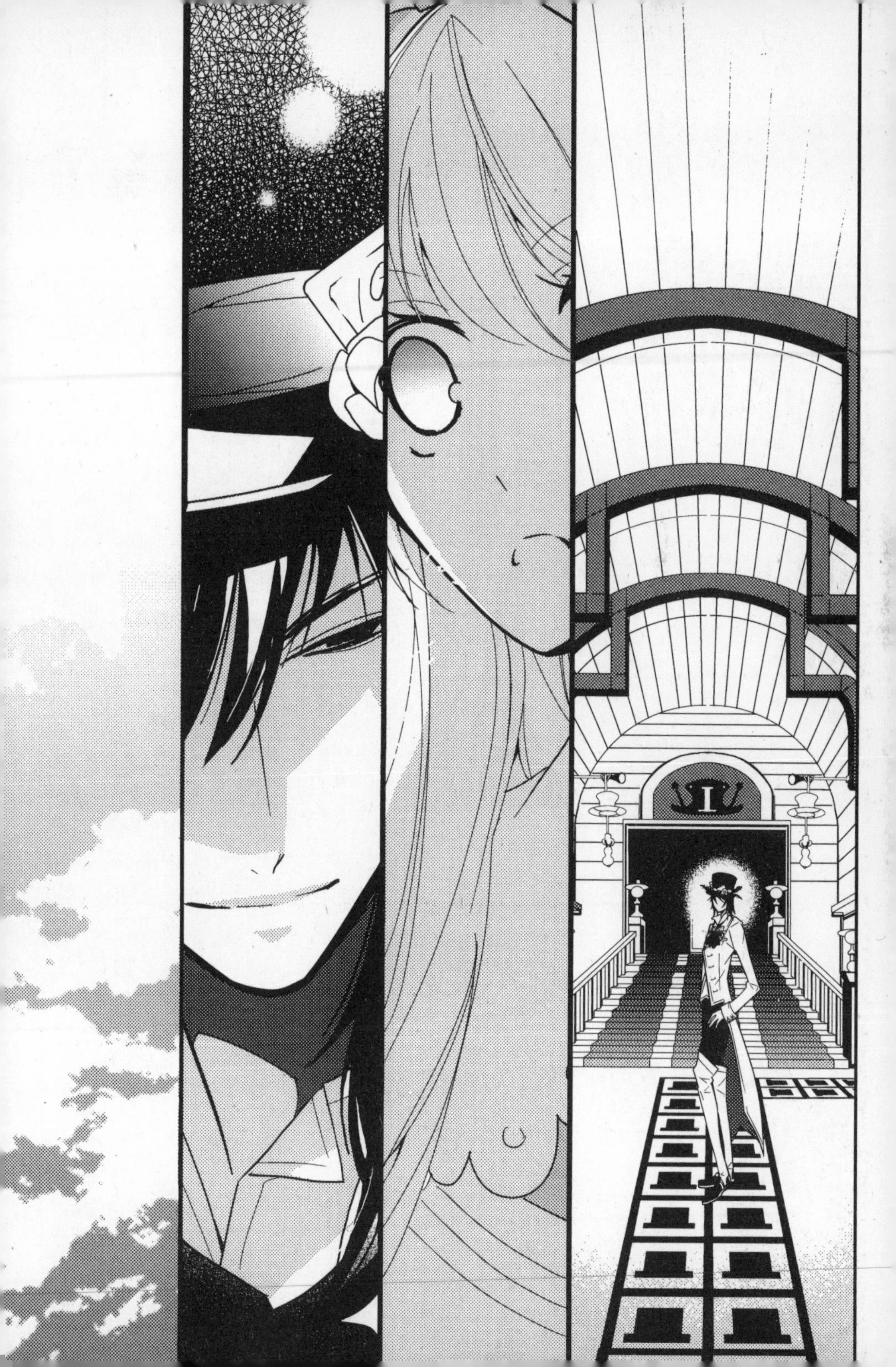

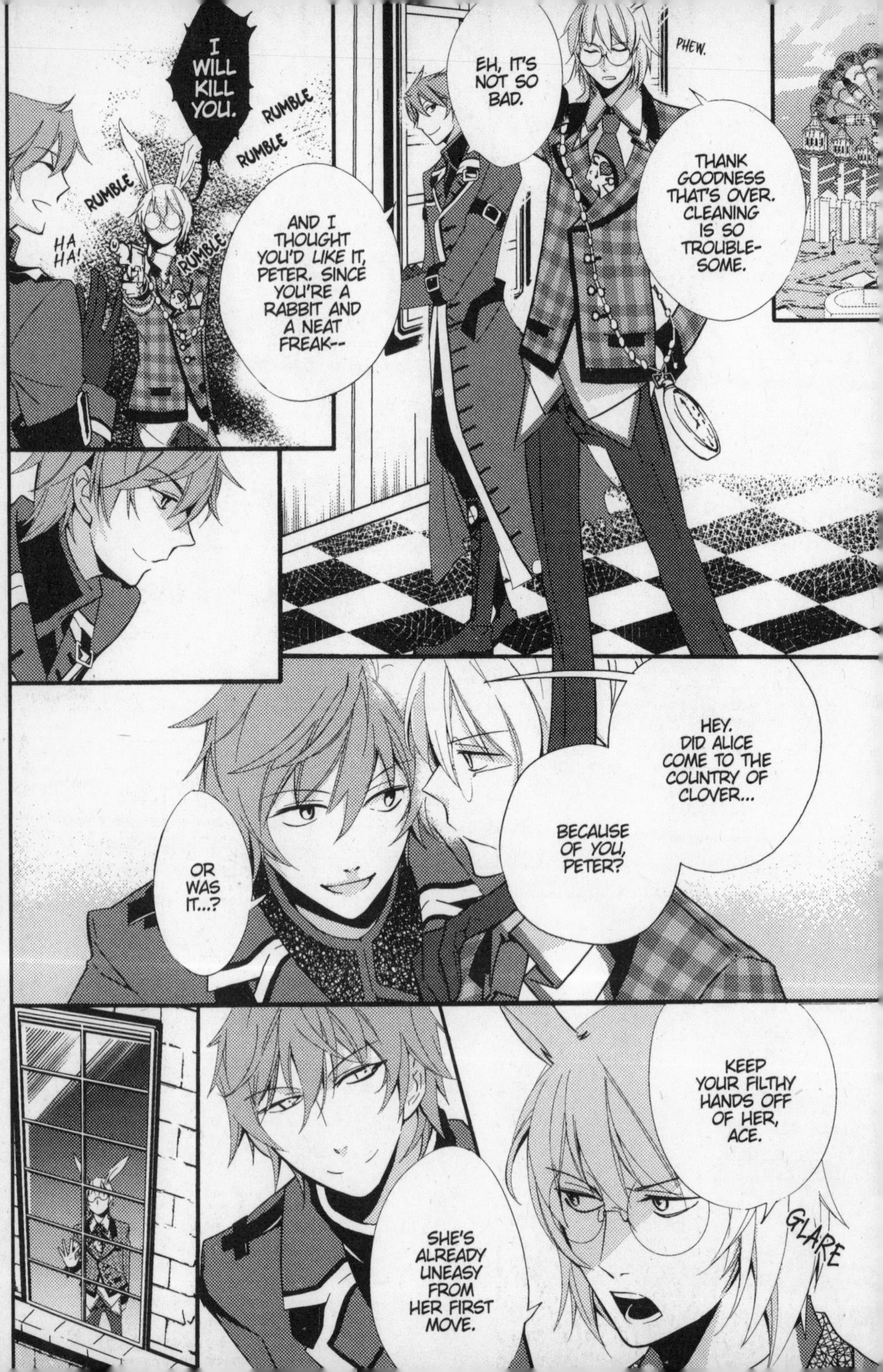
PHEW.
THANK GOODNESS THAT'S OVER. CLEANING IS SO TROUBLE-SOME.
EH, IT'S NOT SO BAD.
AND I THOUGHT YOU'D LIKE IT, PETER. SINCE YOU'RE A RABBIT AND A NEAT FREAK--
I WILL KILL YOU.
RUMBLE
RUMBLE
RUMBLE
RUMBLE
HA HA!
HEY. DID ALICE COME TO THE COUNTRY OF CLOVER...
BECAUSE OF YOU, PETER?
OR WAS IT...?
KEEP YOUR FILTHY HANDS OFF OF HER, ACE.
GLARE
SHE'S ALREADY UNEASY FROM HER FIRST MOVE.

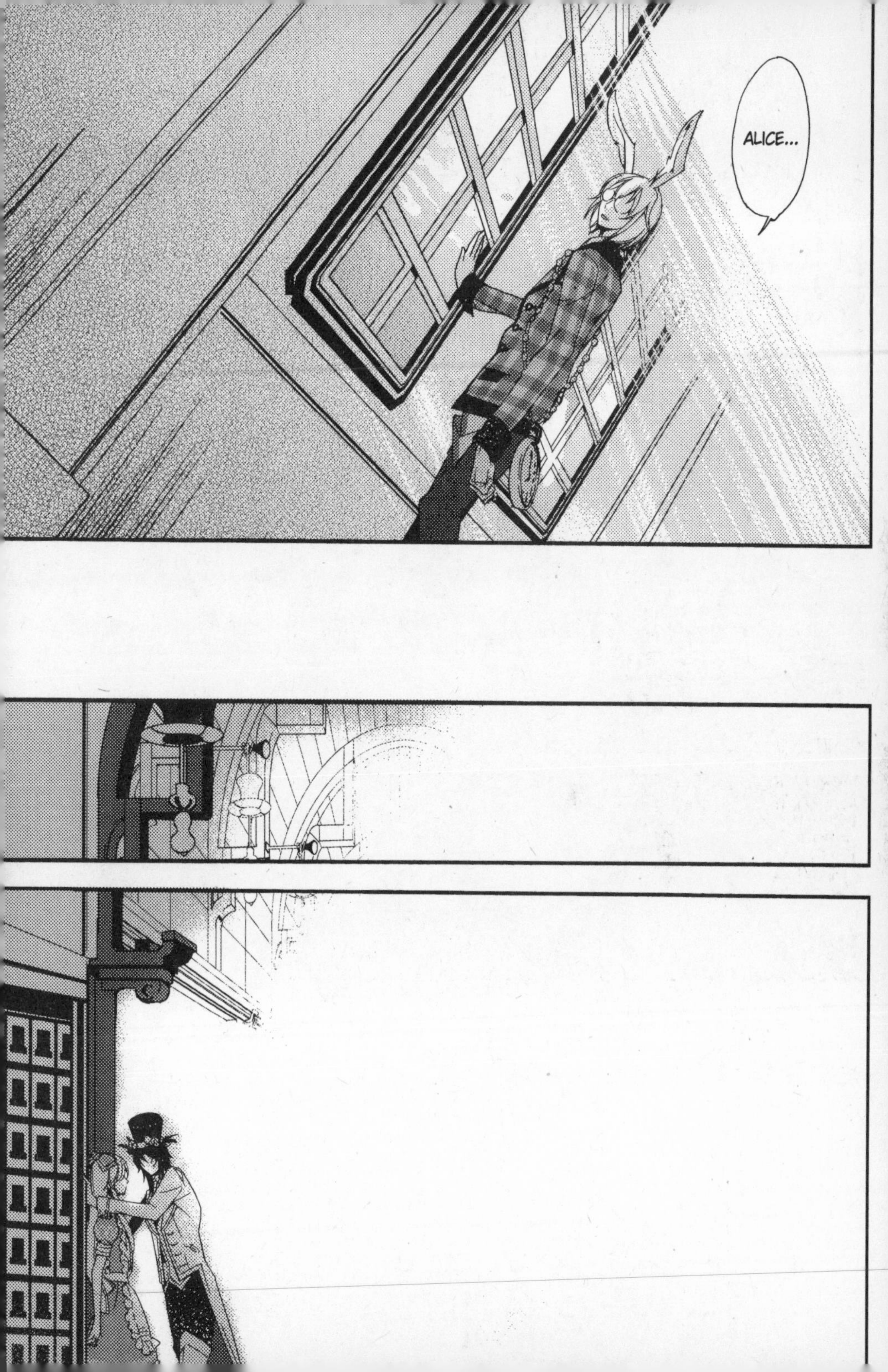
ALICE...

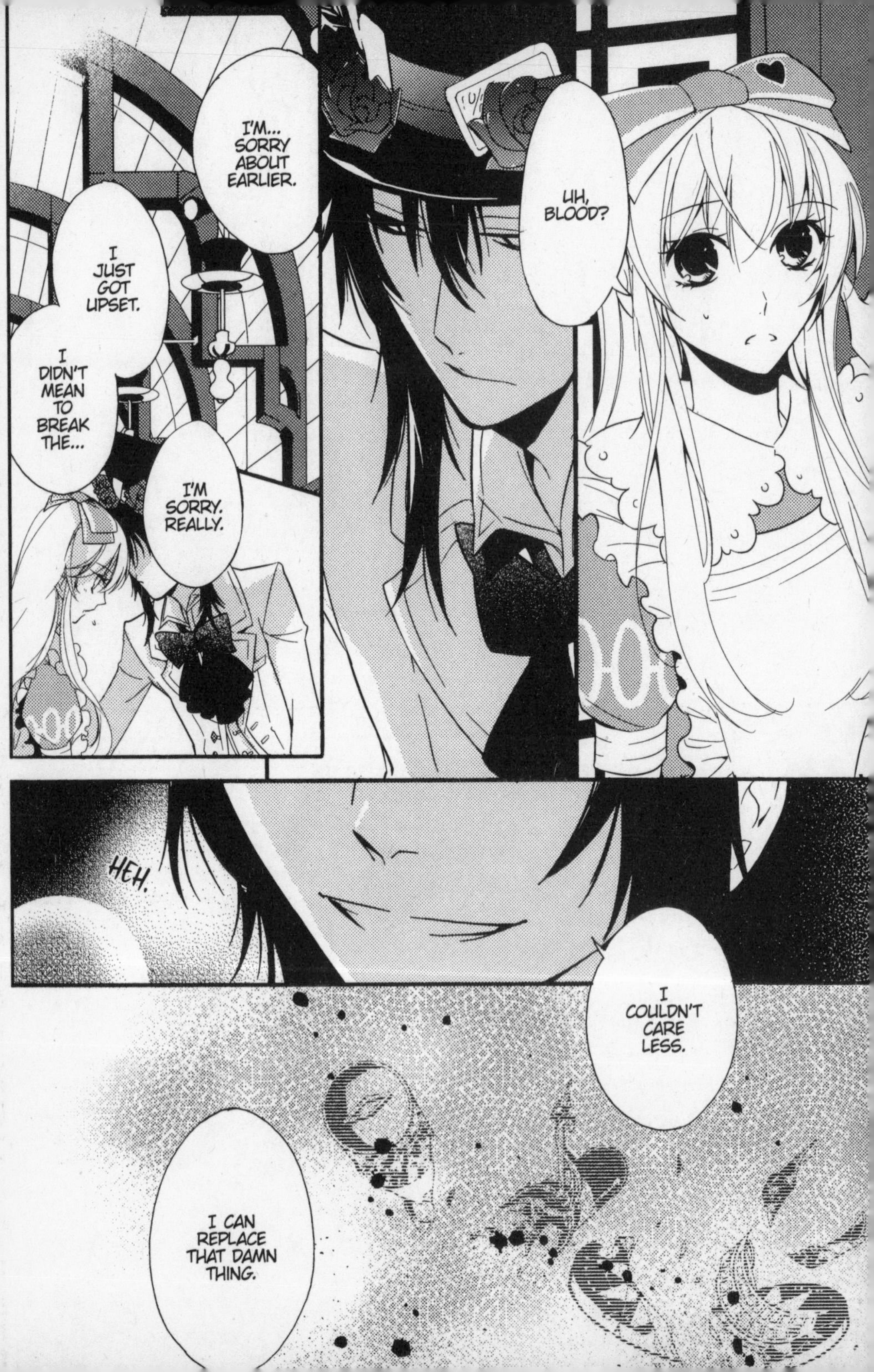
UH, BLOOD?
I'M... SORRY ABOUT EARLIER.
I JUST GOT UPSET.
I DIDN'T MEAN TO BREAK THE...
I'M SORRY. REALLY.
HEH.
I COULDN'T CARE LESS.
I CAN REPLACE THAT DAMN THING.

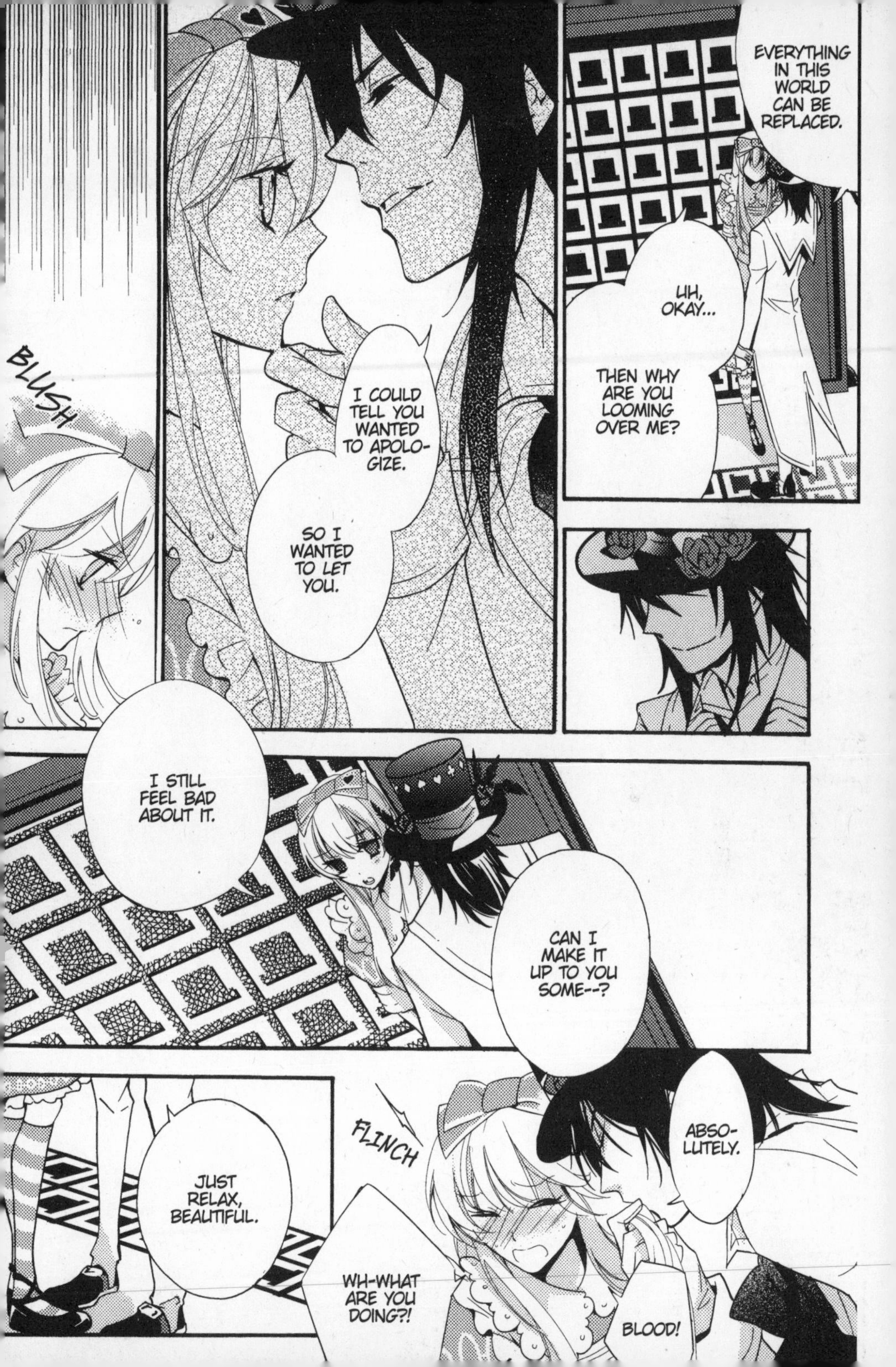
EVERYTHING IN THIS WORLD CAN BE REPLACED.
UH, OKAY...
THEN WHY ARE YOU LOOMING OVER ME?
I COULD TELL YOU WANTED TO APOLOGIZE.
SO I WANTED TO LET YOU.
BLUSH
I STILL FEEL BAD ABOUT IT.
CAN I MAKE IT UP TO YOU SOME--?
ABSOLUTELY.
FLINCH
BLOOD!
WH-WHAT ARE YOU DOING?!
JUST RELAX, BEAUTIFUL.

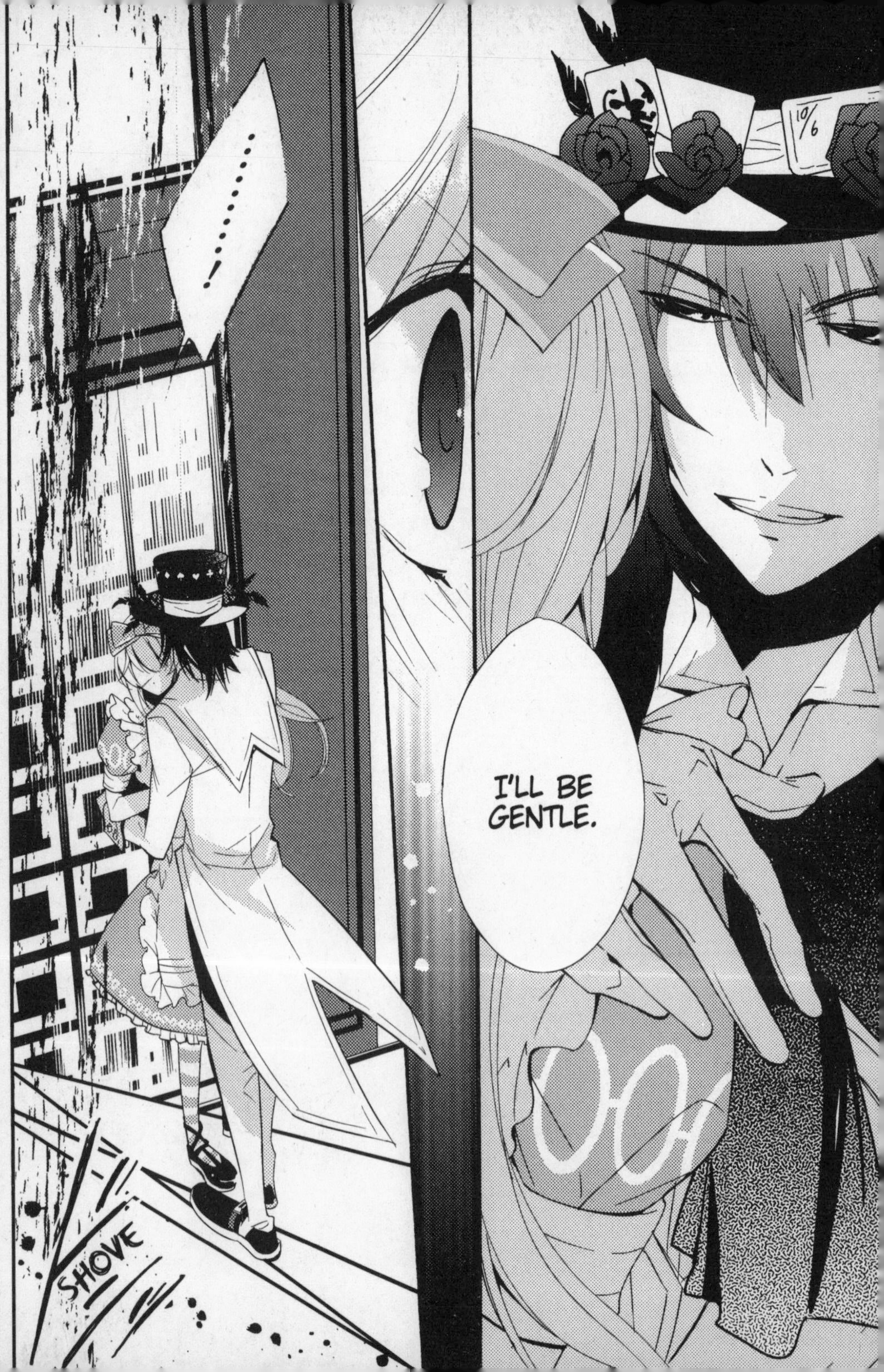
I'LL BE GENTLE.
......!
SHOVE

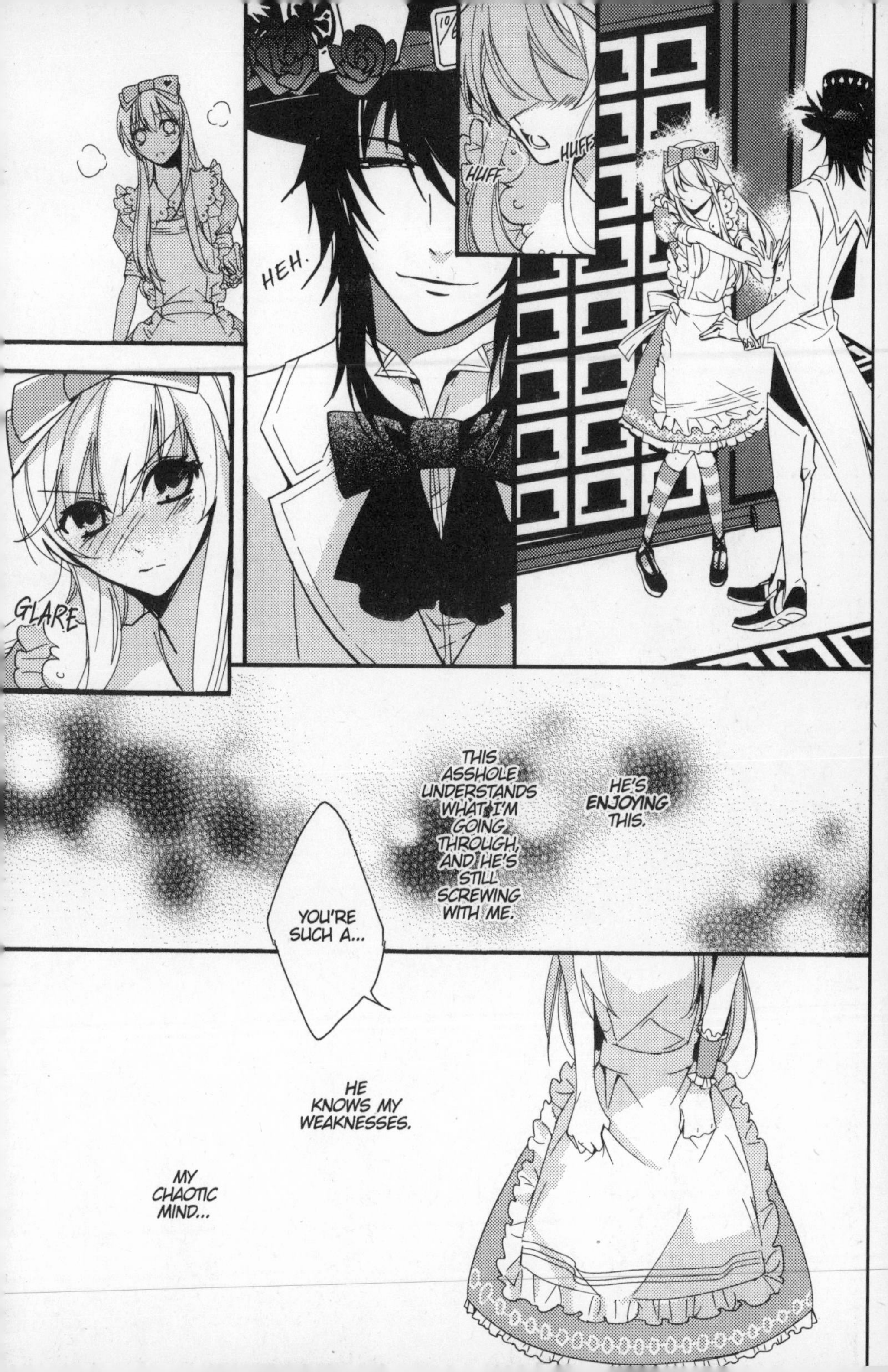
HUFF
HUFF
HEH.
GLARE
HE'S ENJOYING THIS.
THIS ASSHOLE UNDERSTANDS WHAT I'M GOING THROUGH, AND HE'S STILL SCREWING WITH ME.
YOU'RE SUCH A...
HE KNOWS MY WEAKNESSES.
MY CHAOTIC MIND...

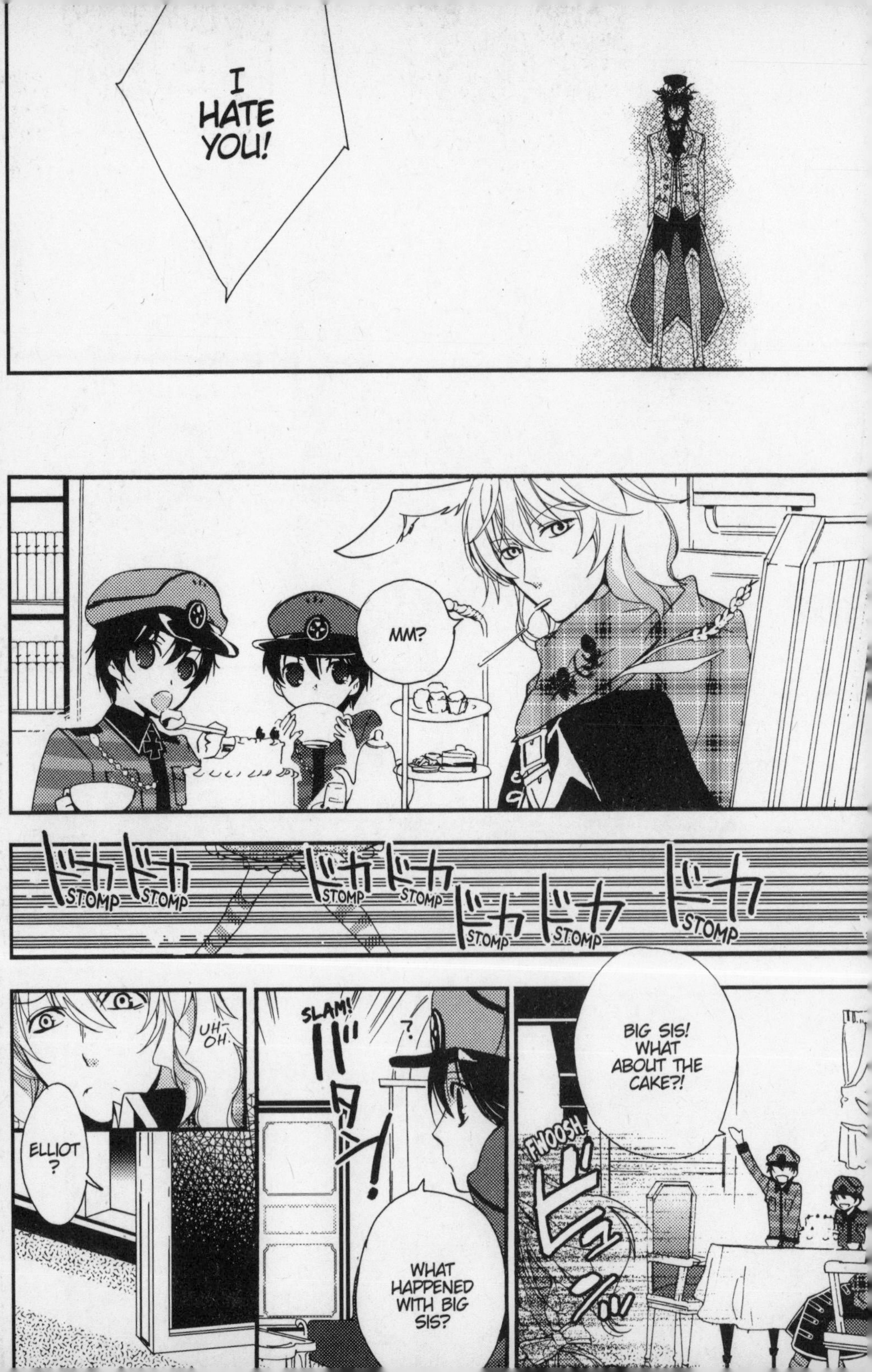
I HATE YOU!
MM?
STOMP STOMP STOMP STOMP STOMP STOMP STOMP STOMP
BIG SIS! WHAT ABOUT THE CAKE?!
FWOOSH
SLAM!
?
WHAT HAPPENED WITH BIG SIS?
UH-OH.
ELLIOT?

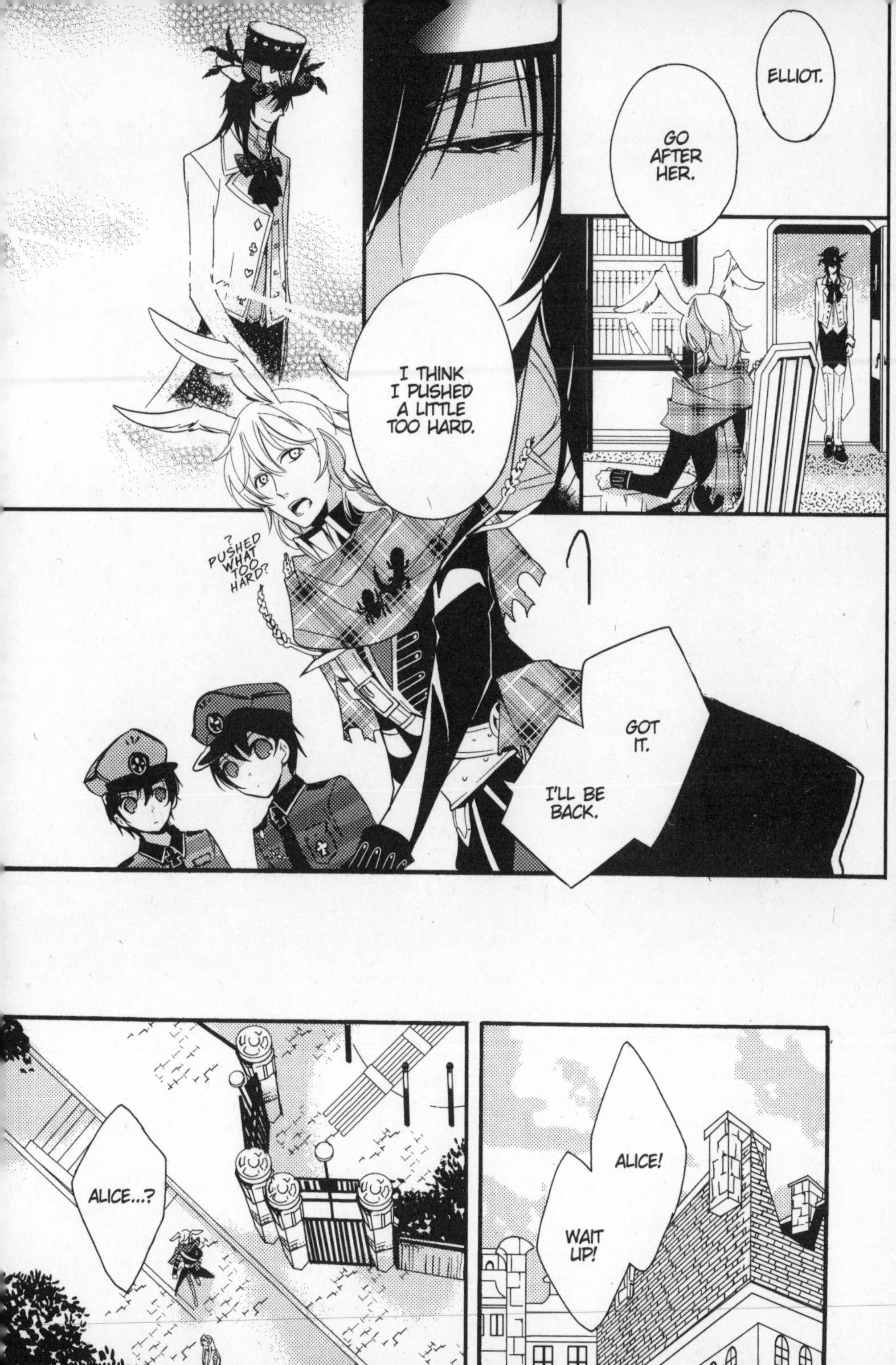
ELLIOT.
GO AFTER HER.
I THINK I PUSHED A LITTLE TOO HARD.
? PUSHED WHAT TOO HARD?
GOT IT.
I'LL BE BACK.
ALICE!
WAIT UP!
ALICE...?

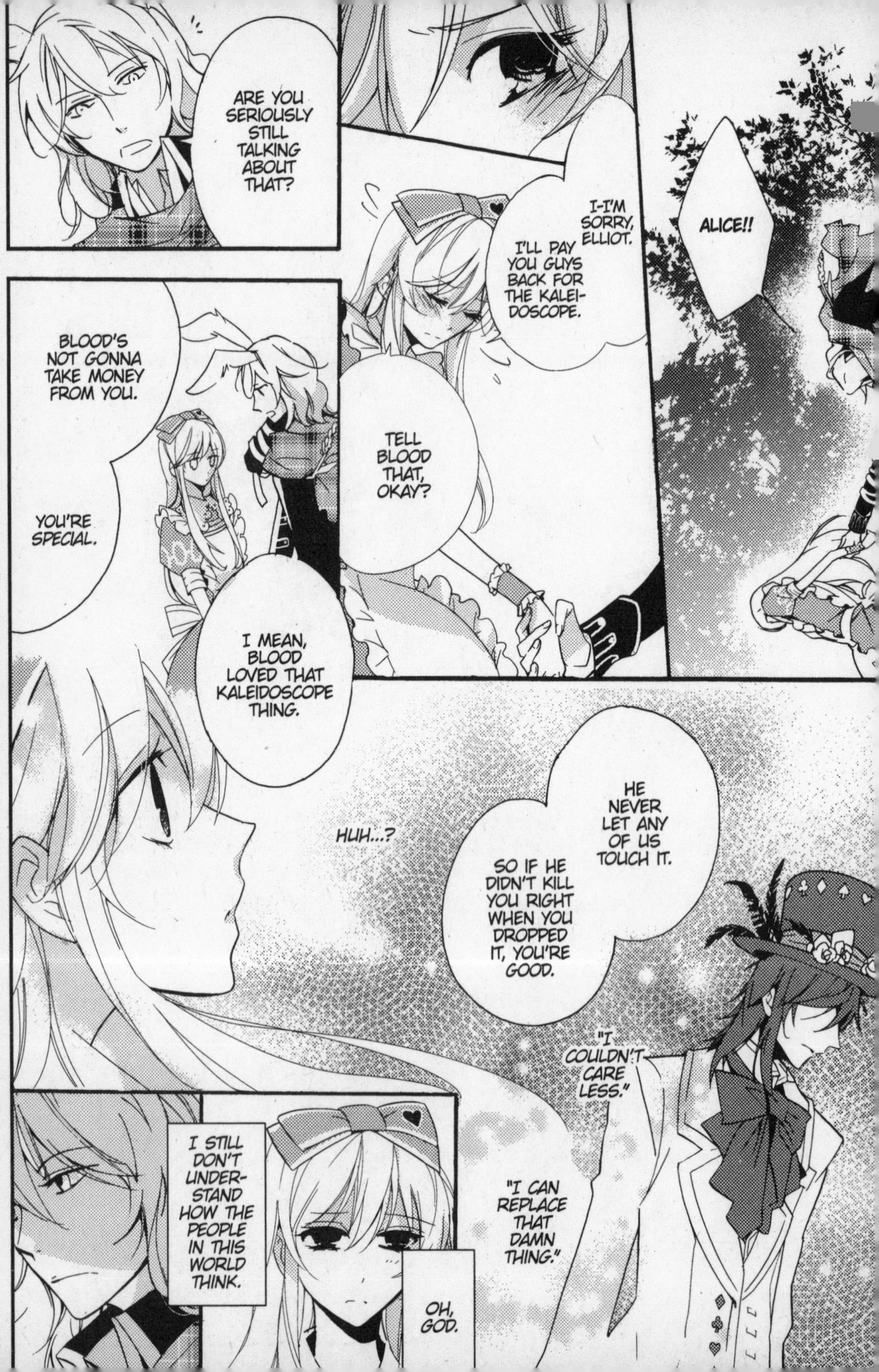
ALICE!!
I-I'M SORRY, ELLIOT.
I'LL PAY YOU GUYS BACK FOR THE KALEI-DOSCOPE.
TELL BLOOD THAT, OKAY?
ARE YOU SERIOUSLY STILL TALKING ABOUT THAT?
BLOOD'S NOT GONNA TAKE MONEY FROM YOU.
YOU'RE SPECIAL.
I MEAN, BLOOD LOVED THAT KALEIDOSCOPE THING.
HE NEVER LET ANY OF US TOUCH IT.
SO IF HE DIDN'T KILL YOU RIGHT WHEN YOU DROPPED IT, YOU'RE GOOD.
HUH...?
"I COULDN'T CARE LESS."
"I CAN REPLACE THAT DAMN THING."
I STILL DON'T UNDER-STAND HOW THE PEOPLE IN THIS WORLD THINK.
OH, GOD.

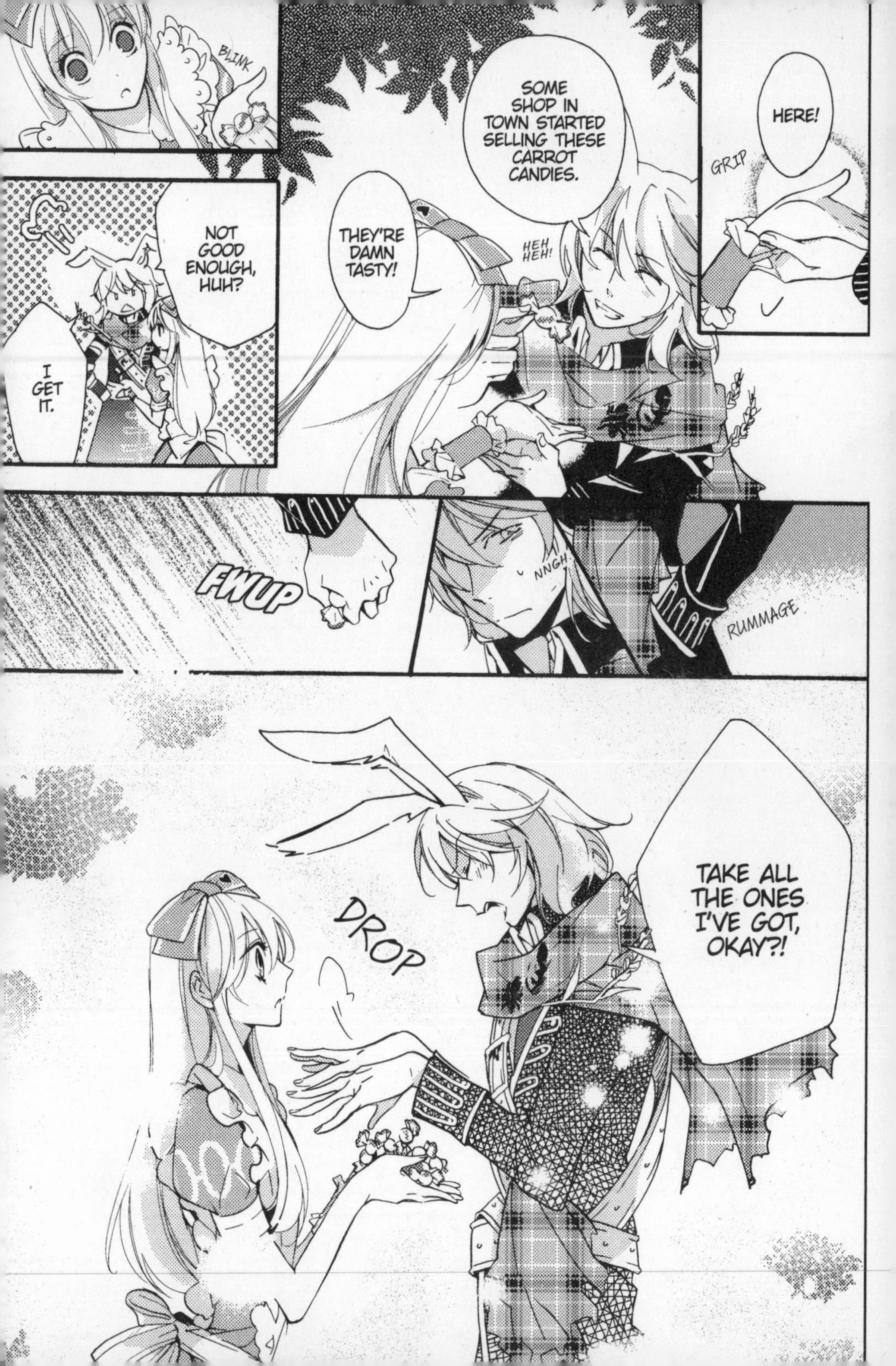
HERE!
GRIP
SOME SHOP IN TOWN STARTED SELLING THESE CARROT CANDIES.
HEH, HEH!
THEY'RE DAMN TASTY!
BLINK
NOT GOOD ENOUGH, HUH?
I GET IT.
RUMMAGE
NNGH.
FWUP
TAKE ALL THE ONES I'VE GOT, OKAY?!
DROP

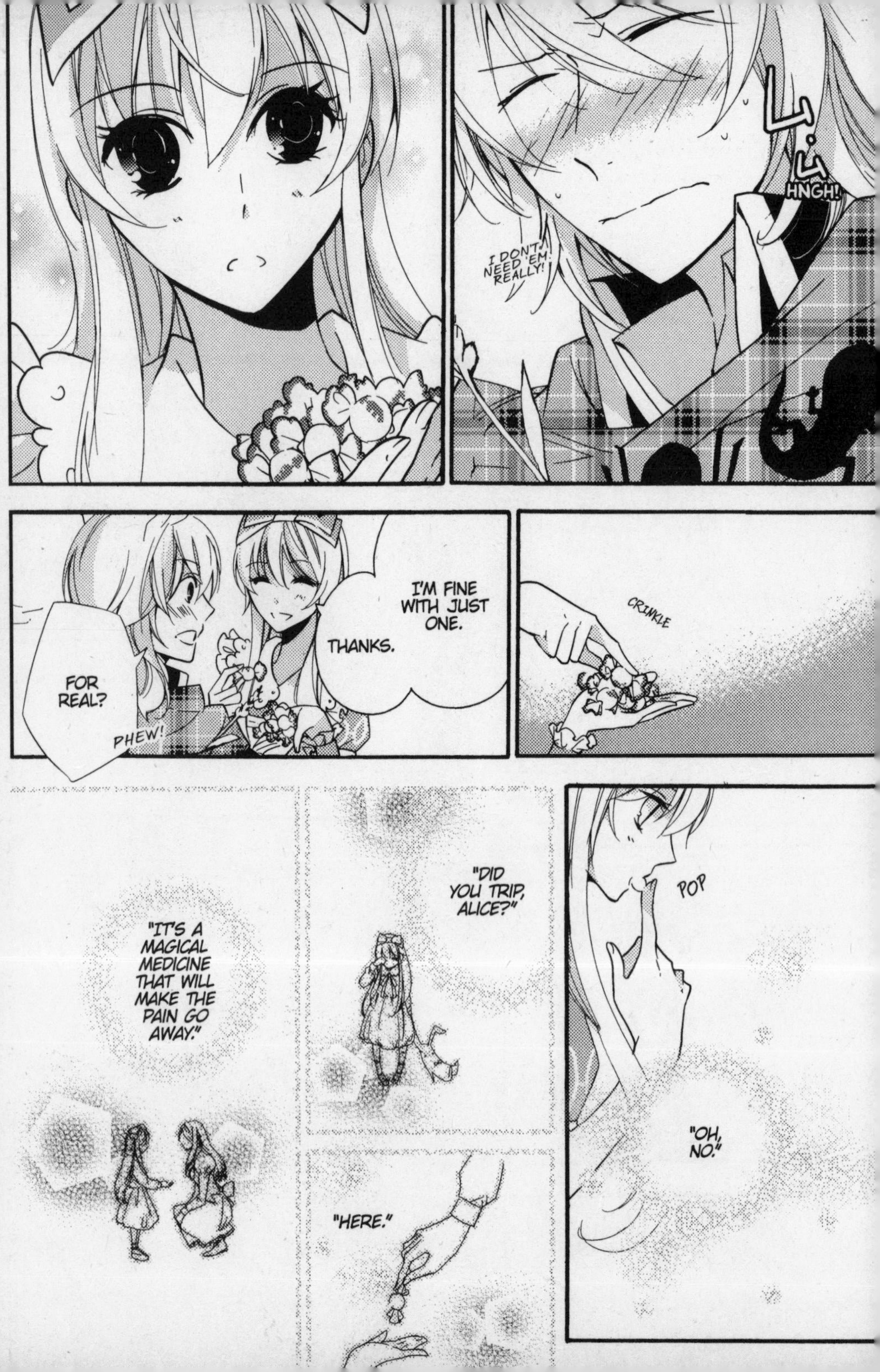
HNGH!
I DON'T NEED 'EM. REALLY!
CRINKLE
I'M FINE WITH JUST ONE.
THANKS.
FOR REAL?
PHEW!
POP
"OH, NO."
"DID YOU TRIP, ALICE?"
"HERE."
"IT'S A MAGICAL MEDICINE THAT WILL MAKE THE PAIN GO AWAY."

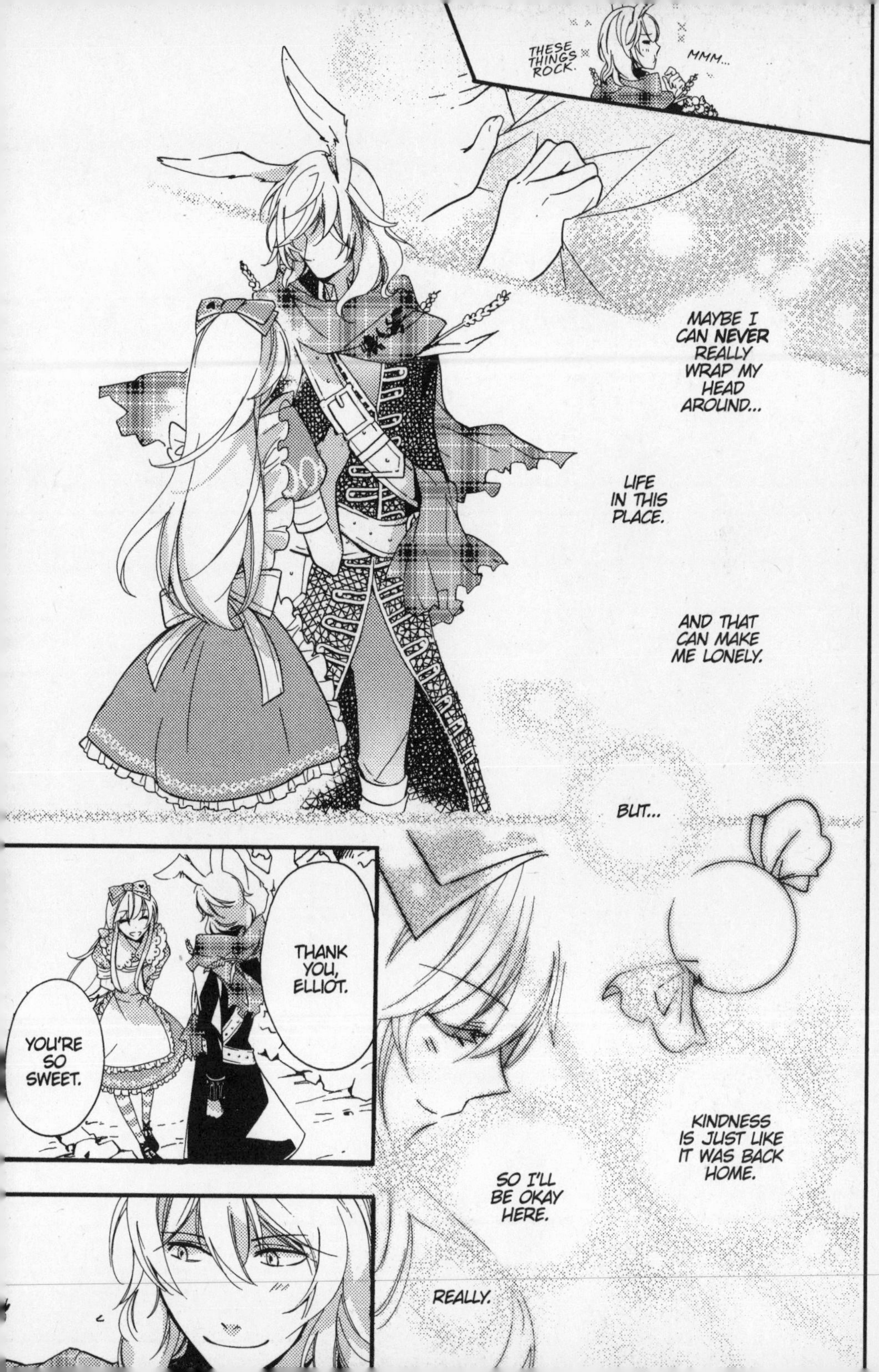
MMM...
THESE THINGS ROCK.
MAYBE I CAN NEVER REALLY WRAP MY HEAD AROUND...
LIFE IN THIS PLACE.
AND THAT CAN MAKE ME LONELY.
BUT...
KINDNESS IS JUST LIKE IT WAS BACK HOME.
SO I'LL BE OKAY HERE.
REALLY.
THANK YOU, ELLIOT.
YOU'RE SO SWEET.

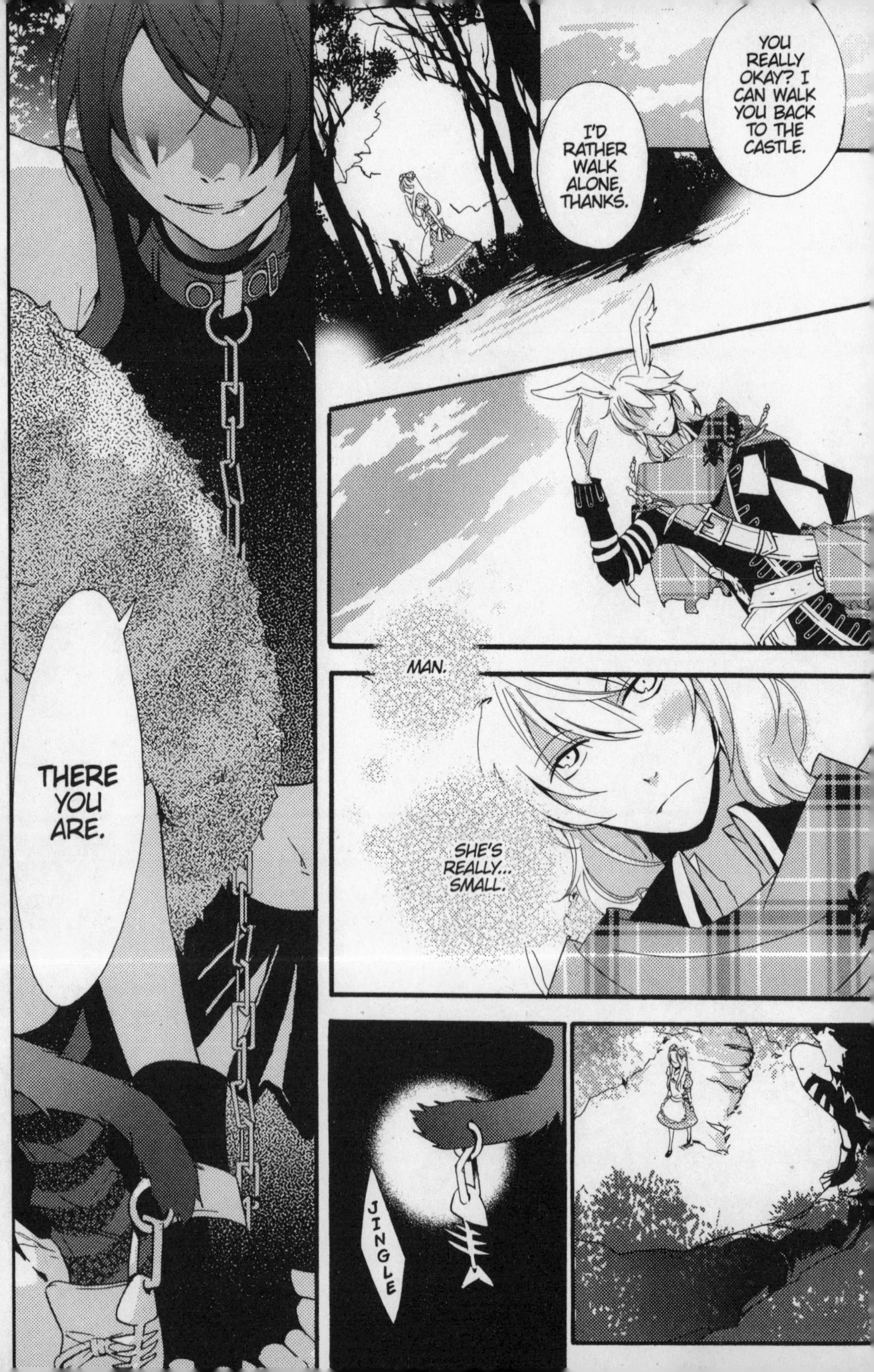
YOU REALLY OKAY? I CAN WALK YOU BACK TO THE CASTLE.
I'D RATHER WALK ALONE, THANKS.
MAN.
SHE'S REALLY... SMALL.
JINGLE
THERE YOU ARE.

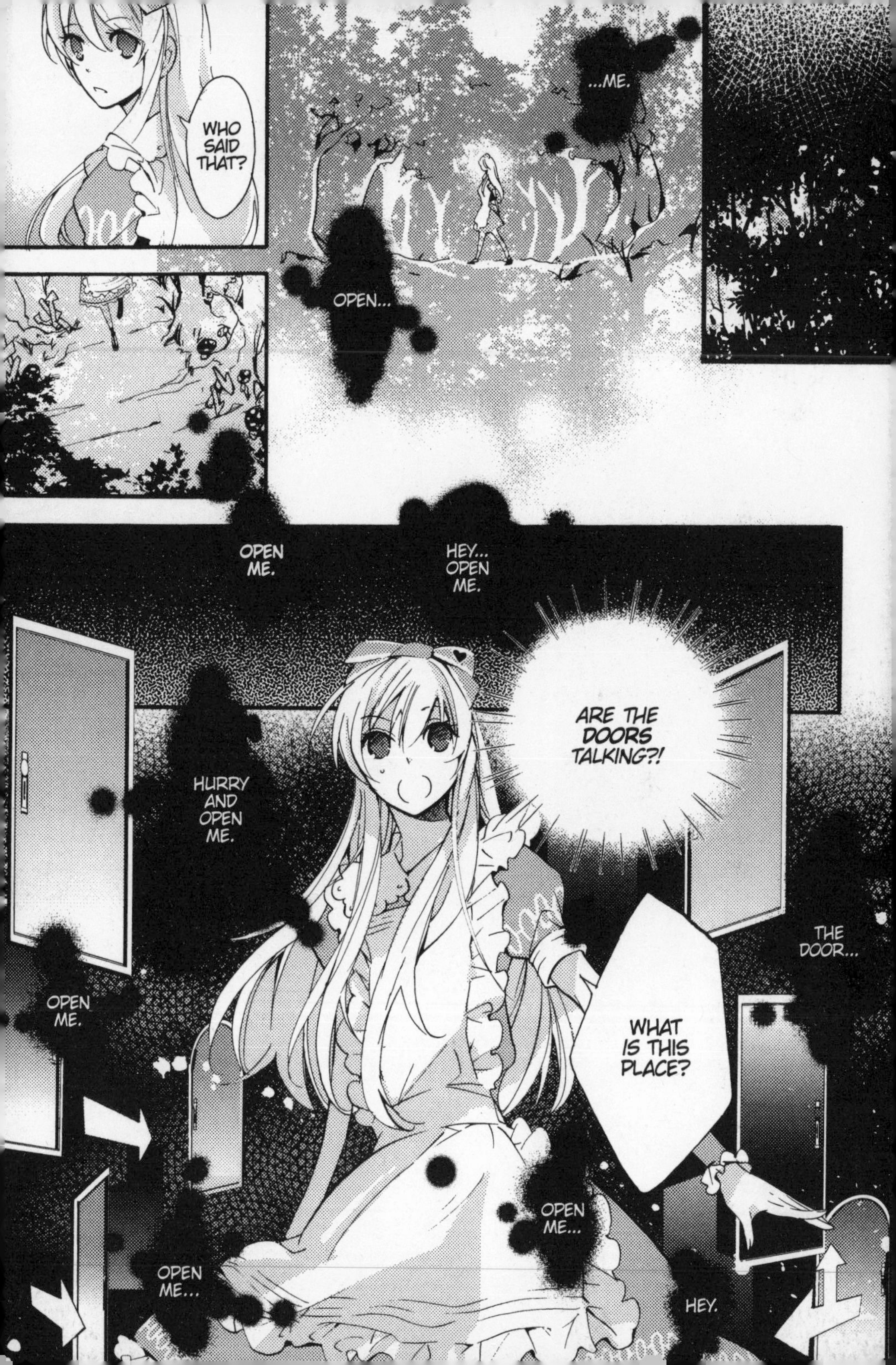
...ME.
OPEN...
WHO SAID THAT?
HEY... OPEN ME.
OPEN ME.
ARE THE DOORS TALKING?!
THE DOOR...
HURRY AND OPEN ME.
WHAT IS THIS PLACE?
OPEN ME.
OPEN ME...
HEY.
OPEN ME...

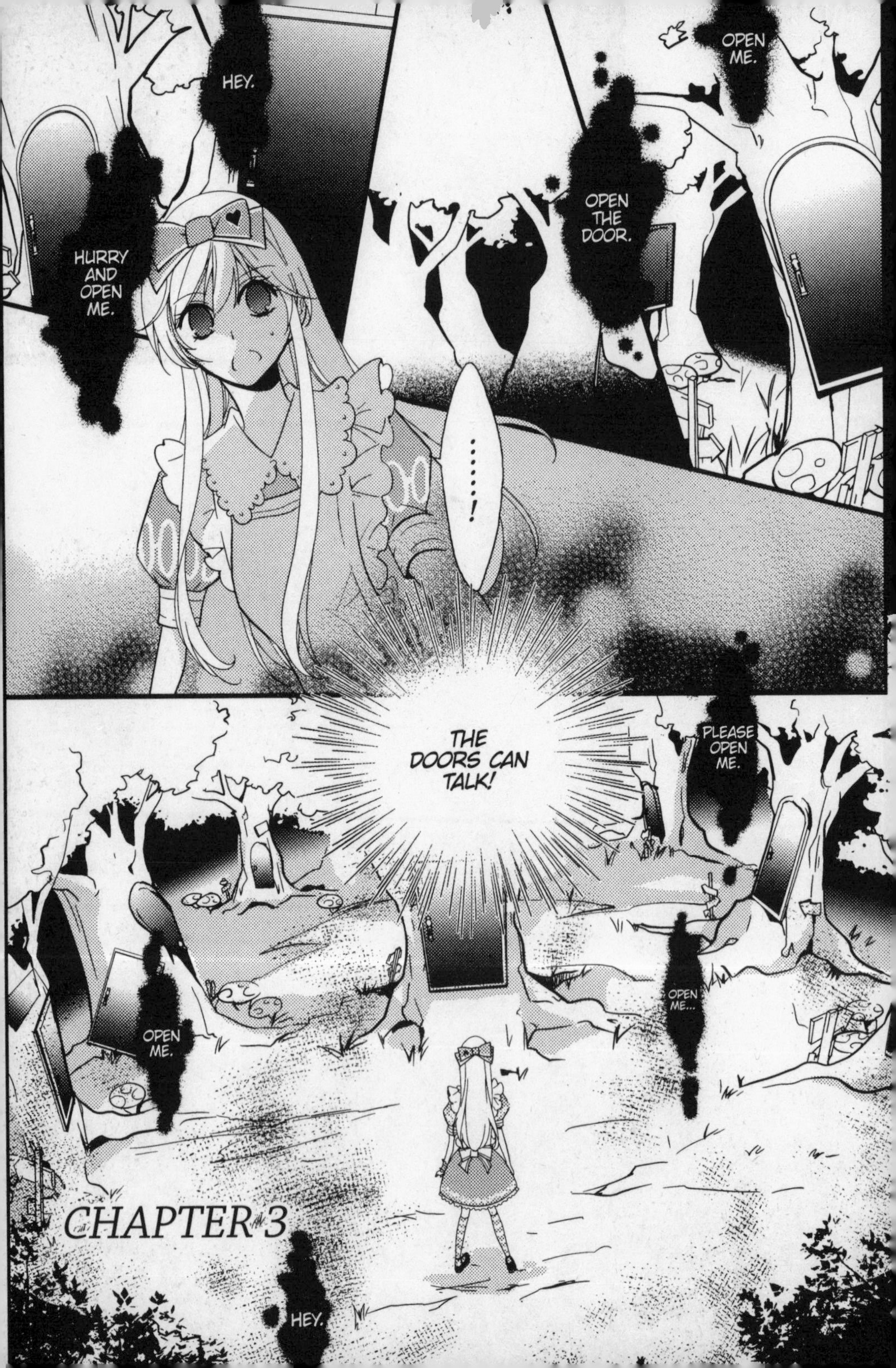
OPEN ME.
HEY.
OPEN THE DOOR.
HURRY AND OPEN ME.
......!
PLEASE OPEN ME.
THE DOORS CAN TALK!
OPEN ME...
OPEN ME.
CHAPTER 3
HEY.

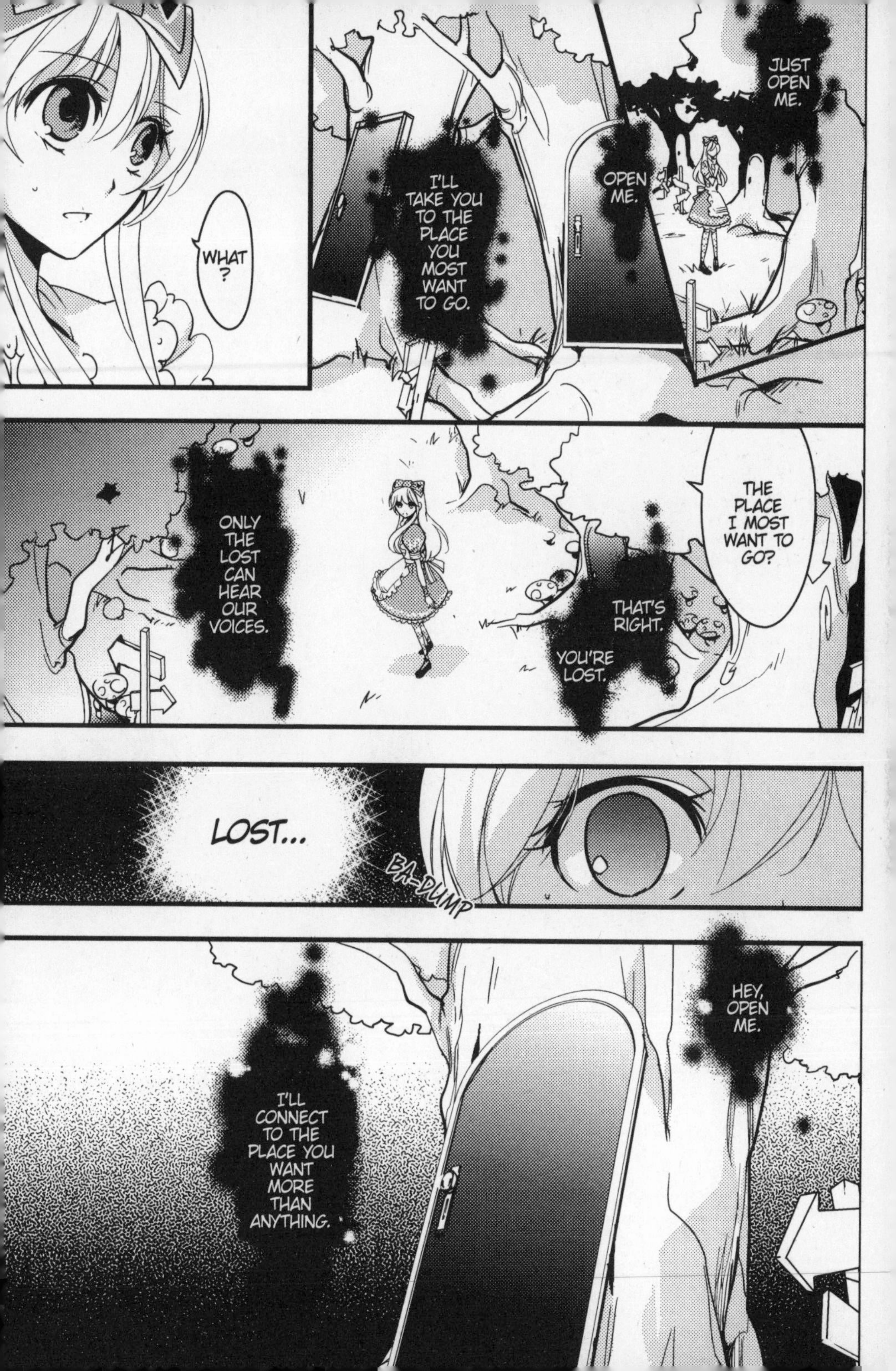
JUST OPEN ME.
OPEN ME.
I'LL TAKE YOU TO THE PLACE YOU MOST WANT TO GO.
WHAT?
THE PLACE I MOST WANT TO GO?
THAT'S RIGHT.
YOU'RE LOST.
ONLY THE LOST CAN HEAR OUR VOICES.
BA-DUMP
LOST...
HEY, OPEN ME.
I'LL CONNECT TO THE PLACE YOU WANT MORE THAN ANYTHING.

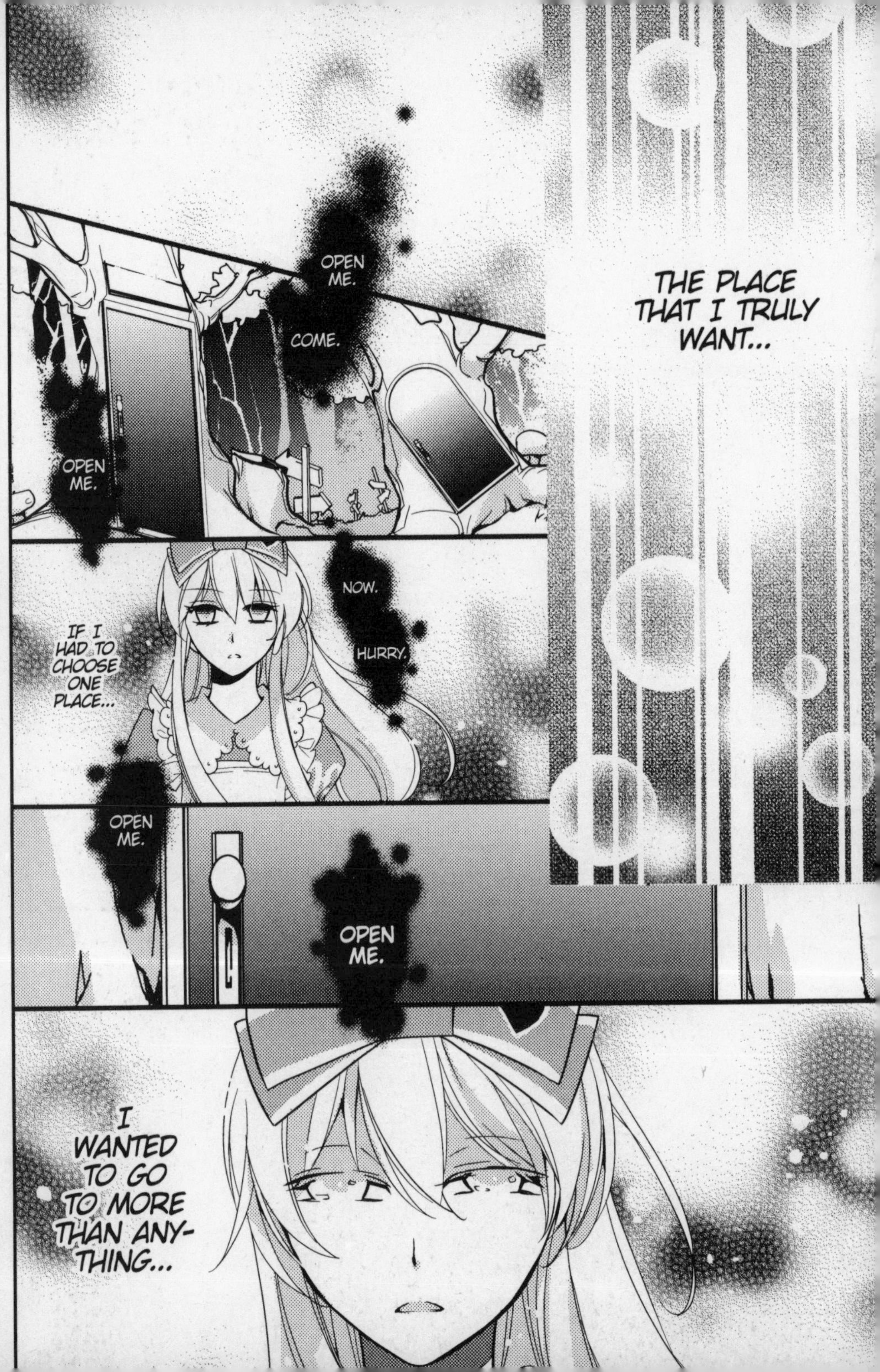

THE PLACE THAT I TRULY WANT...
OPEN ME.
COME.
OPEN ME.
NOW.
HURRY.
IF I HAD TO CHOOSE ONE PLACE...
OPEN ME.
OPEN ME.
I WANTED TO GO TO MORE THAN ANYTHING...

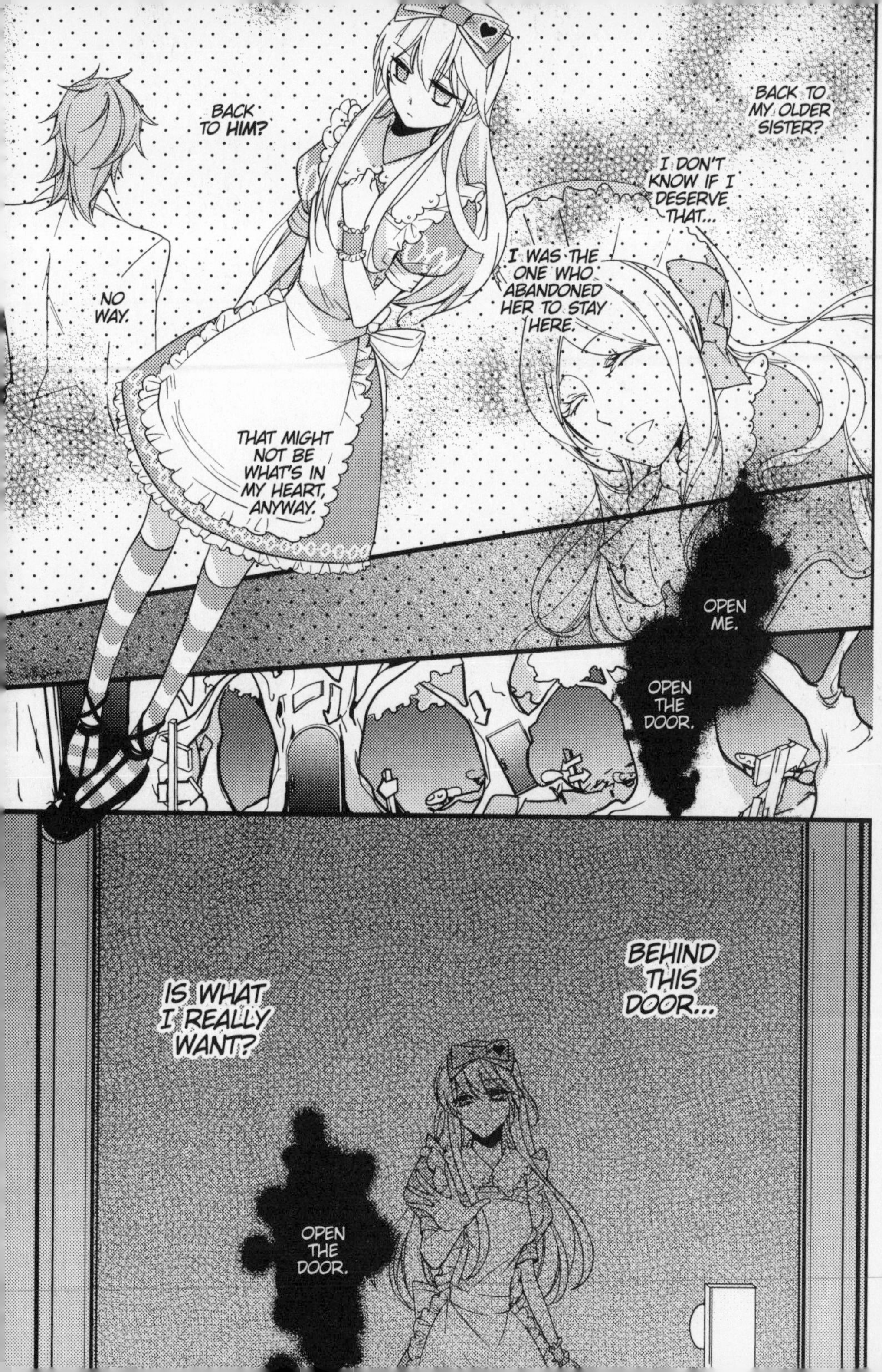
BACK TO MY OLDER SISTER?
I DON'T KNOW IF I DESERVE THAT...
I WAS THE ONE WHO ABANDONED HER TO STAY HERE.
BACK TO HIM?
NO WAY.
THAT MIGHT NOT BE WHAT'S IN MY HEART, ANYWAY.
OPEN ME.
OPEN THE DOOR.
BEHIND THIS DOOR...
IS WHAT I REALLY WANT?
OPEN THE DOOR.

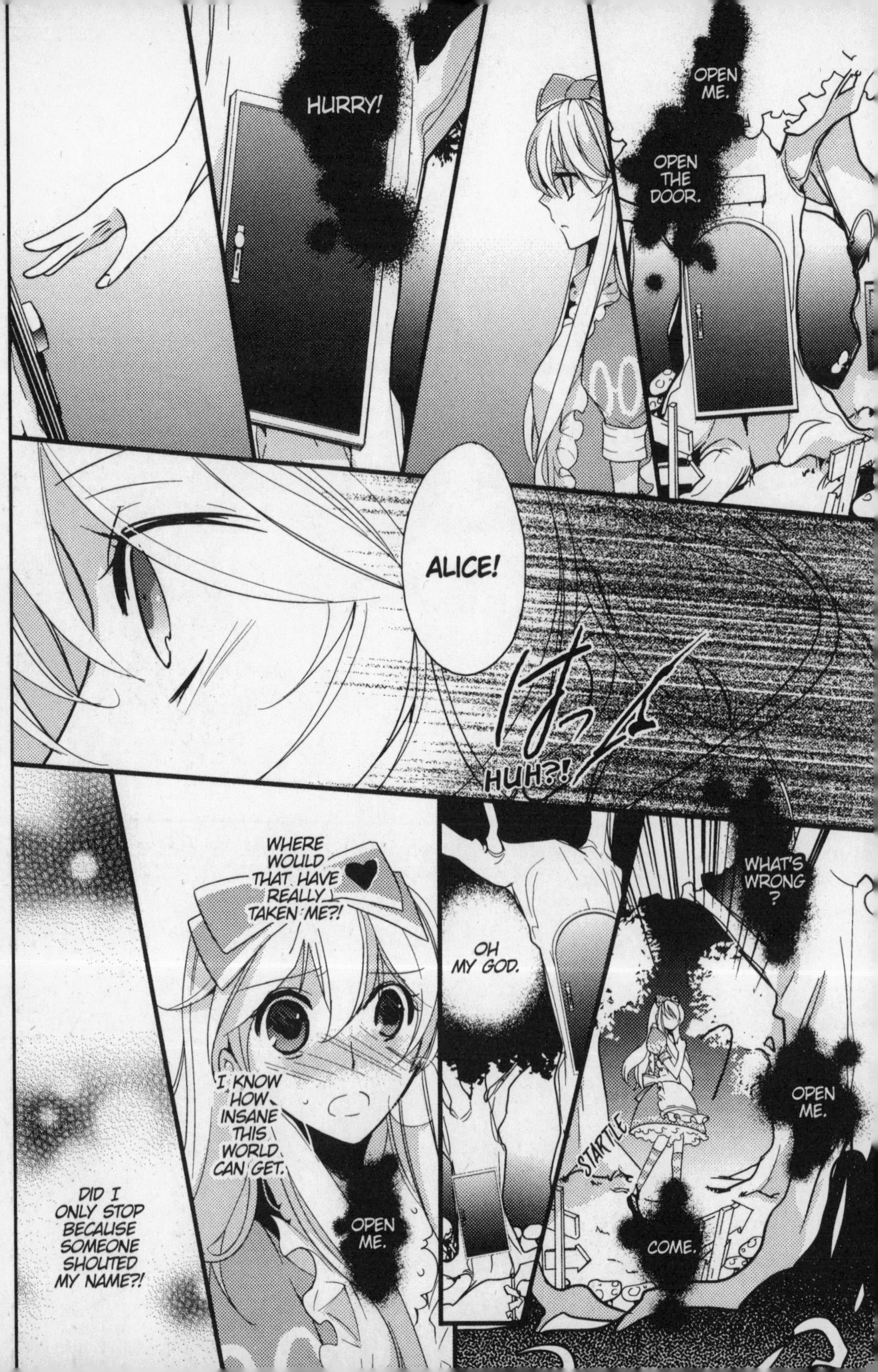
OPEN ME.
OPEN THE DOOR.
HURRY!
ALICE!
HUH?!
WHAT'S WRONG?
OH MY GOD.
OPEN ME.
STARTLE
COME.
WHERE WOULD THAT HAVE REALLY TAKEN ME?!
I KNOW HOW INSANE THIS WORLD CAN GET.
OPEN ME.
DID I ONLY STOP BECAUSE SOMEONE SHOUTED MY NAME?!

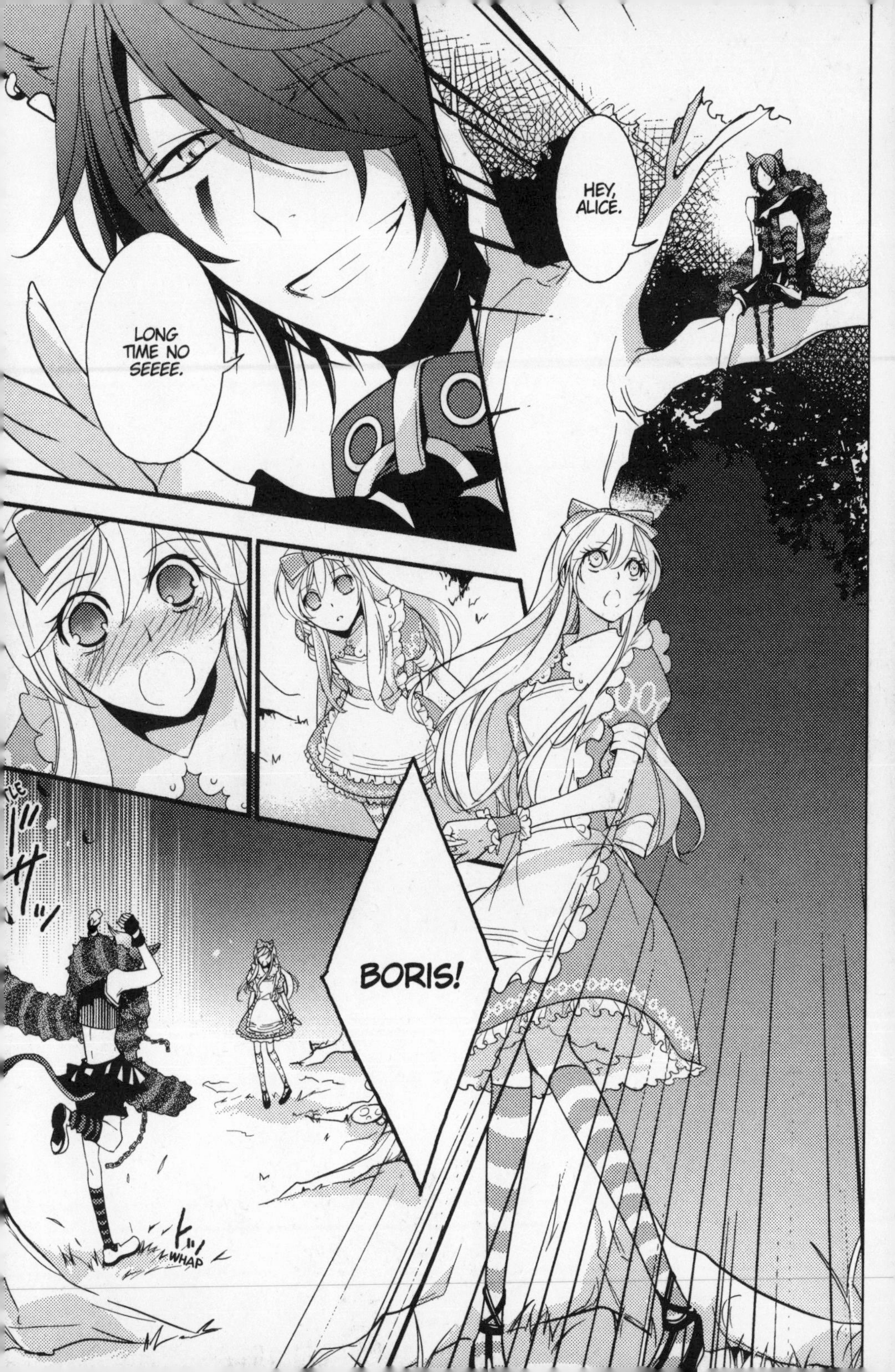
HEY, ALICE.
LONG TIME NO SEEEE.
BORIS!
WHAP

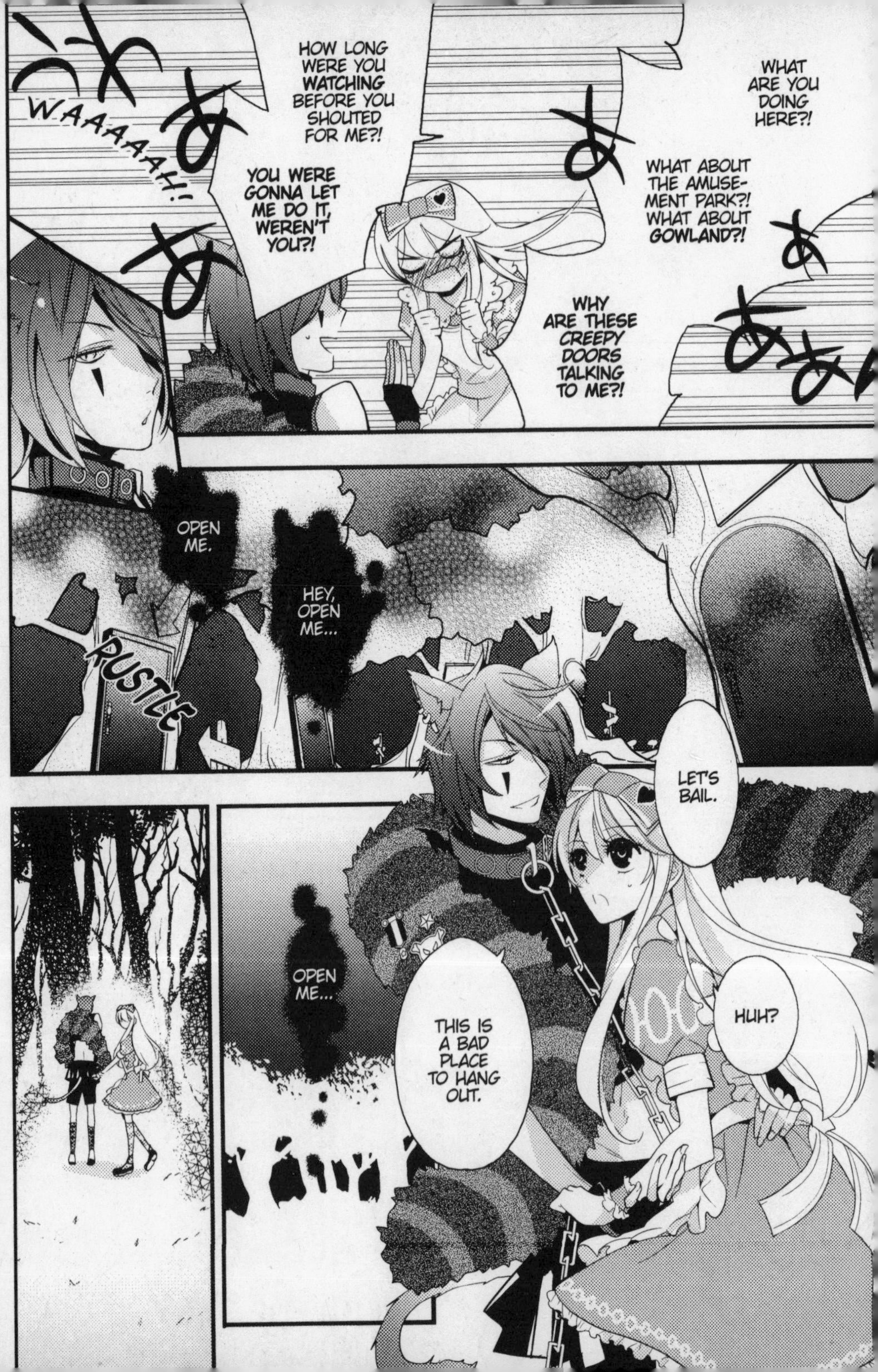
WHAT ARE YOU DOING HERE?!
WHAT ABOUT THE AMUSEMENT PARK?! WHAT ABOUT GOWLAND?!
WHY ARE THESE CREEPY DOORS TALKING TO ME?!
HOW LONG WERE YOU WATCHING BEFORE YOU SHOUTED FOR ME?!
YOU WERE GONNA LET ME DO IT, WEREN'T YOU?!
WAAAAAAH!
HEY, OPEN ME...
OPEN ME.
RUSTLE
LET'S BAIL.
HUH?
THIS IS A BAD PLACE TO HANG OUT.
OPEN ME...

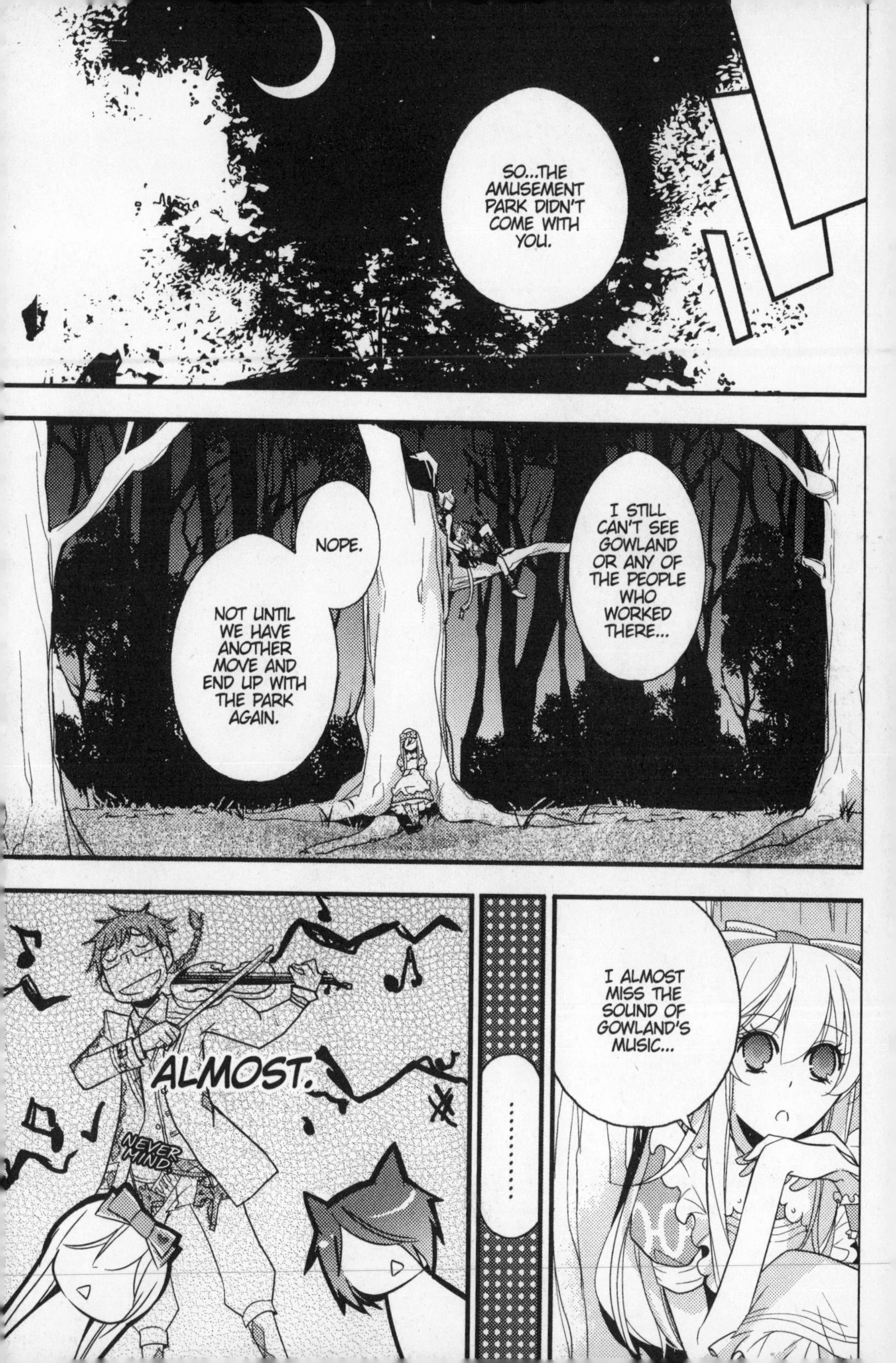
SO...THE AMUSEMENT PARK DIDN'T COME WITH YOU.
I STILL CAN'T SEE GOWLAND OR ANY OF THE PEOPLE WHO WORKED THERE...
NOPE.
NOT UNTIL WE HAVE ANOTHER MOVE AND END UP WITH THE PARK AGAIN.
I ALMOST MISS THE SOUND OF GOWLAND'S MUSIC...
......
ALMOST.
NEVER MIND

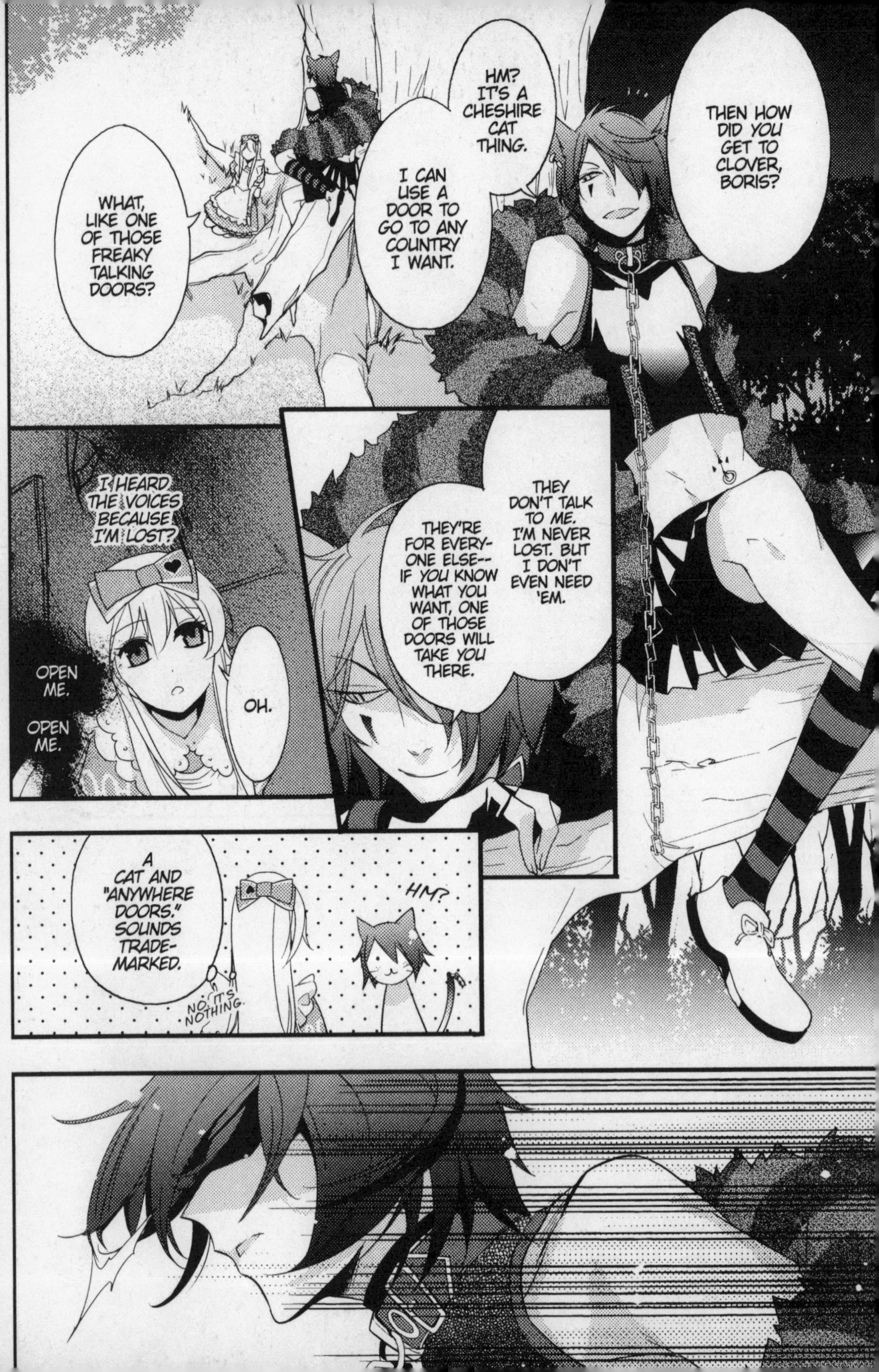
THEN HOW DID *YOU* GET TO CLOVER, BORIS?
HM? IT'S A CHESHIRE CAT THING.
I CAN USE A DOOR TO GO TO ANY COUNTRY I WANT.
WHAT, LIKE ONE OF THOSE FREAKY TALKING DOORS?
THEY DON'T TALK TO *ME*. I'M NEVER LOST. BUT I DON'T EVEN NEED 'EM.
THEY'RE FOR EVERY-ONE ELSE-- IF *YOU* KNOW WHAT YOU WANT, ONE OF THOSE DOORS WILL TAKE *YOU* THERE.
I HEARD THE VOICES BECAUSE I'M LOST?
OH.
OPEN ME.
OPEN ME.
A CAT AND "ANYWHERE DOORS." SOUNDS TRADE-MARKED.
HM?
NO, IT'S NOTHING.

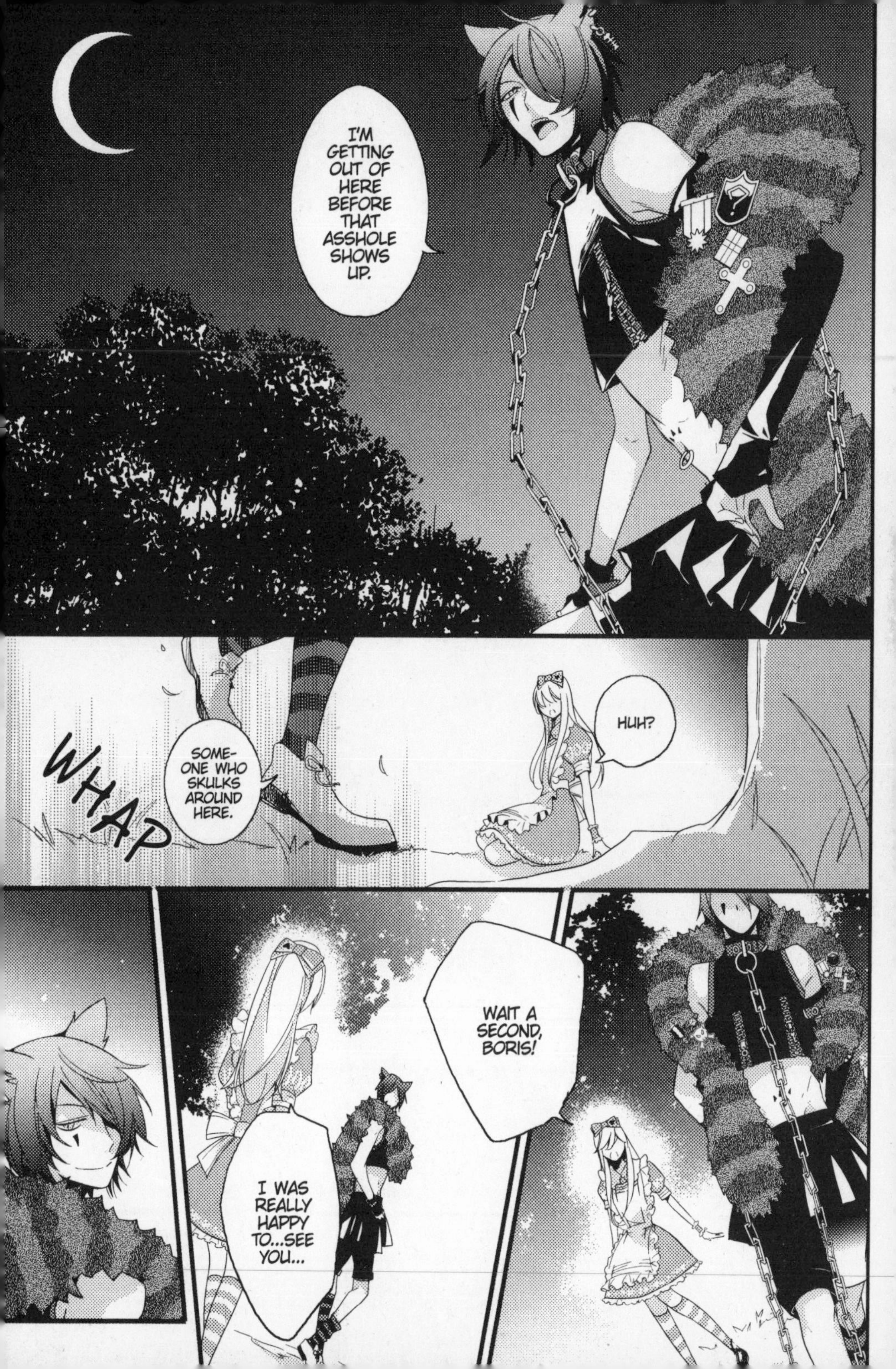
I'M GETTING OUT OF HERE BEFORE THAT ASSHOLE SHOWS UP.
HUH?
SOME-ONE WHO SKULKS AROUND HERE.
WHAP
WAIT A SECOND, BORIS!
I WAS REALLY HAPPY TO...SEE YOU...

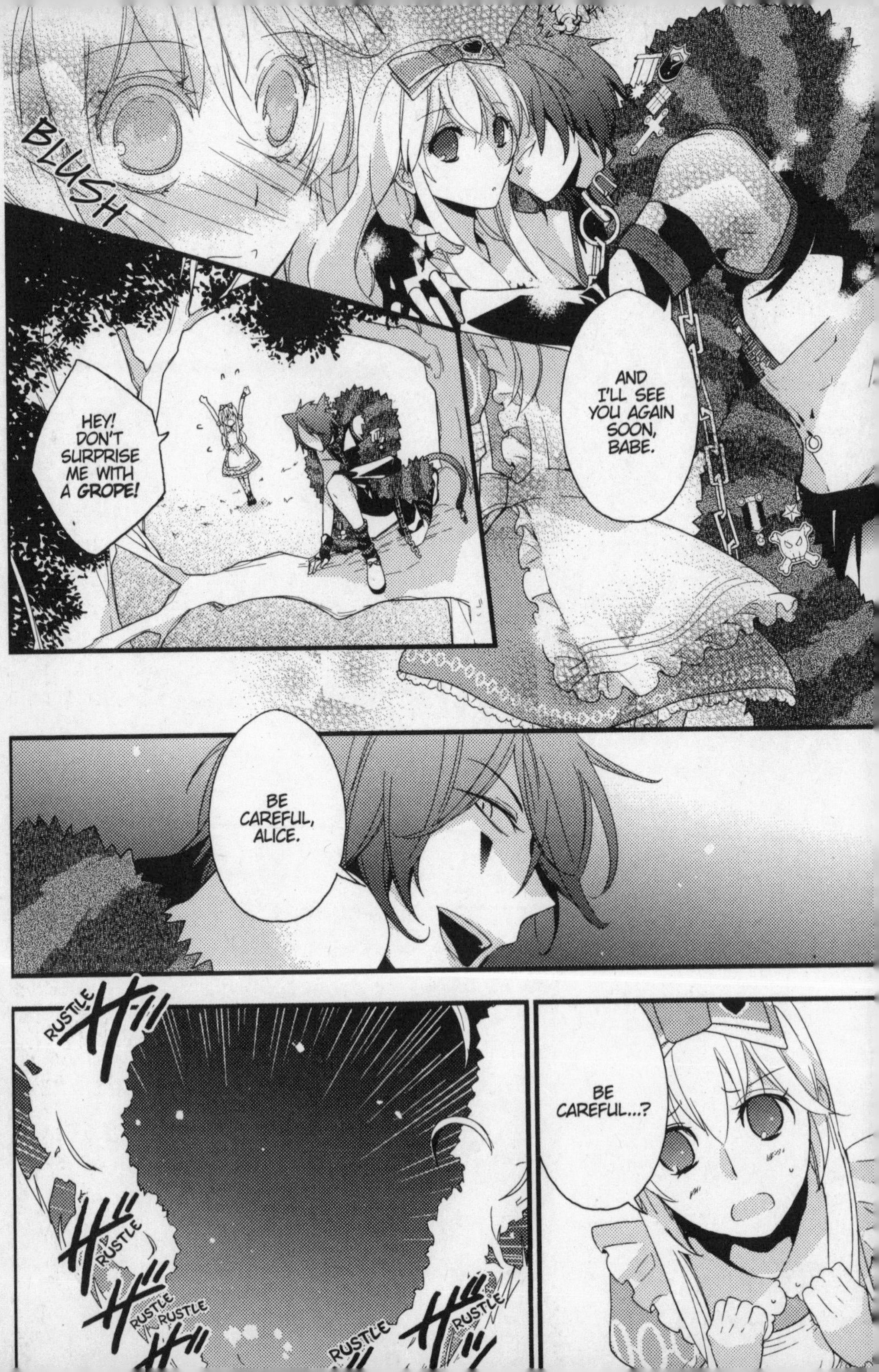
AND I'LL SEE YOU AGAIN SOON, BABE.
BLUSH
HEY! DON'T SURPRISE ME WITH A GROPE!
BE CAREFUL, ALICE.
BE CAREFUL...?
RUSTLE
RUSTLE
RUSTLE
RUSTLE
RUSTLE
RUSTLE

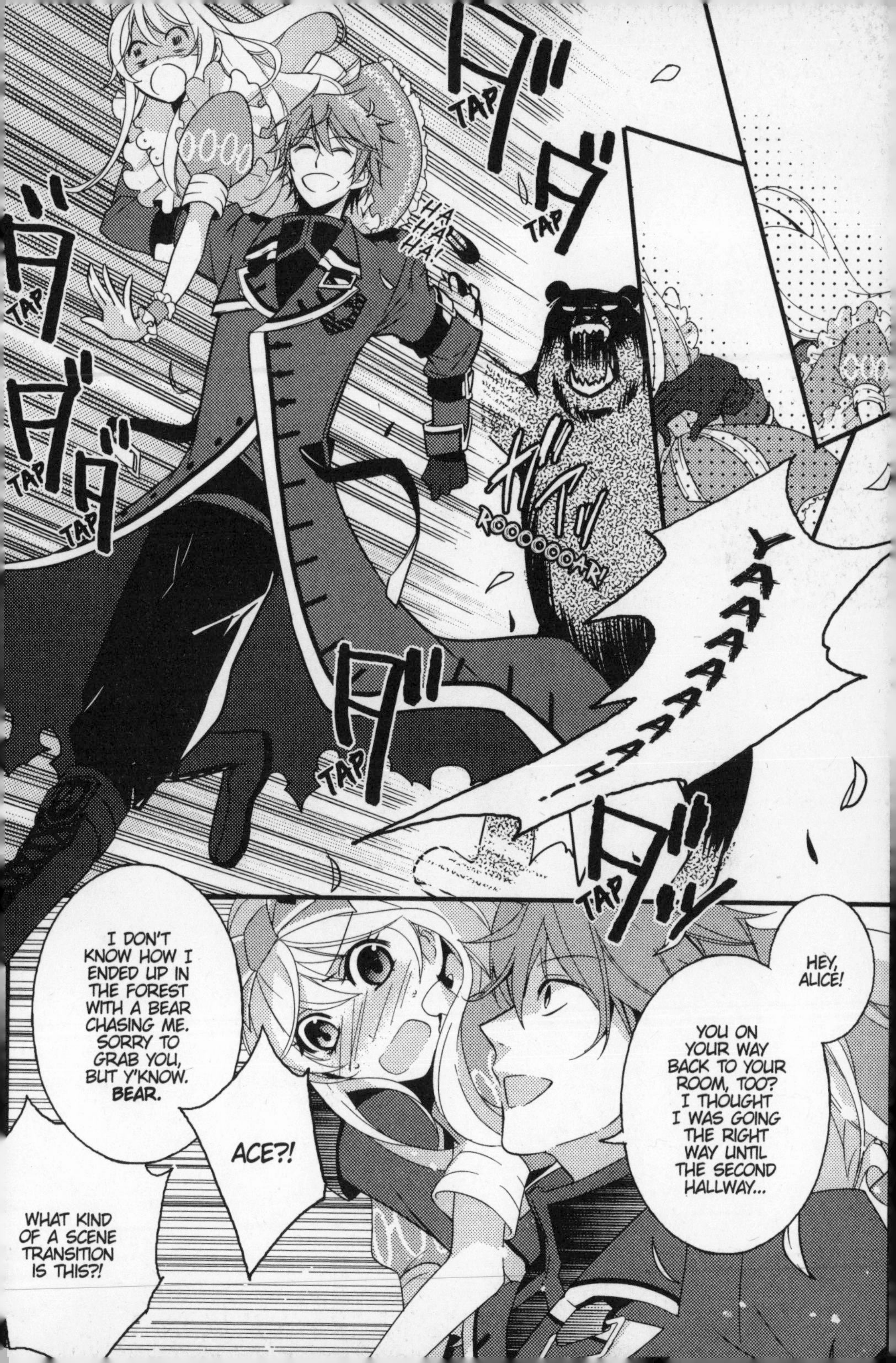
TAP
TAP
HA HA HA!
TAP
TAP
TAP
ROOOOOOAR!
YAAAAAAAAH!!
TAP
TAP
HEY, ALICE!
YOU ON YOUR WAY BACK TO YOUR ROOM, TOO? I THOUGHT I WAS GOING THE RIGHT WAY UNTIL THE SECOND HALLWAY...
I DON'T KNOW HOW I ENDED UP IN THE FOREST WITH A BEAR CHASING ME. SORRY TO GRAB YOU, BUT Y'KNOW. BEAR.
ACE?!
WHAT KIND OF A SCENE TRANSITION IS THIS?!

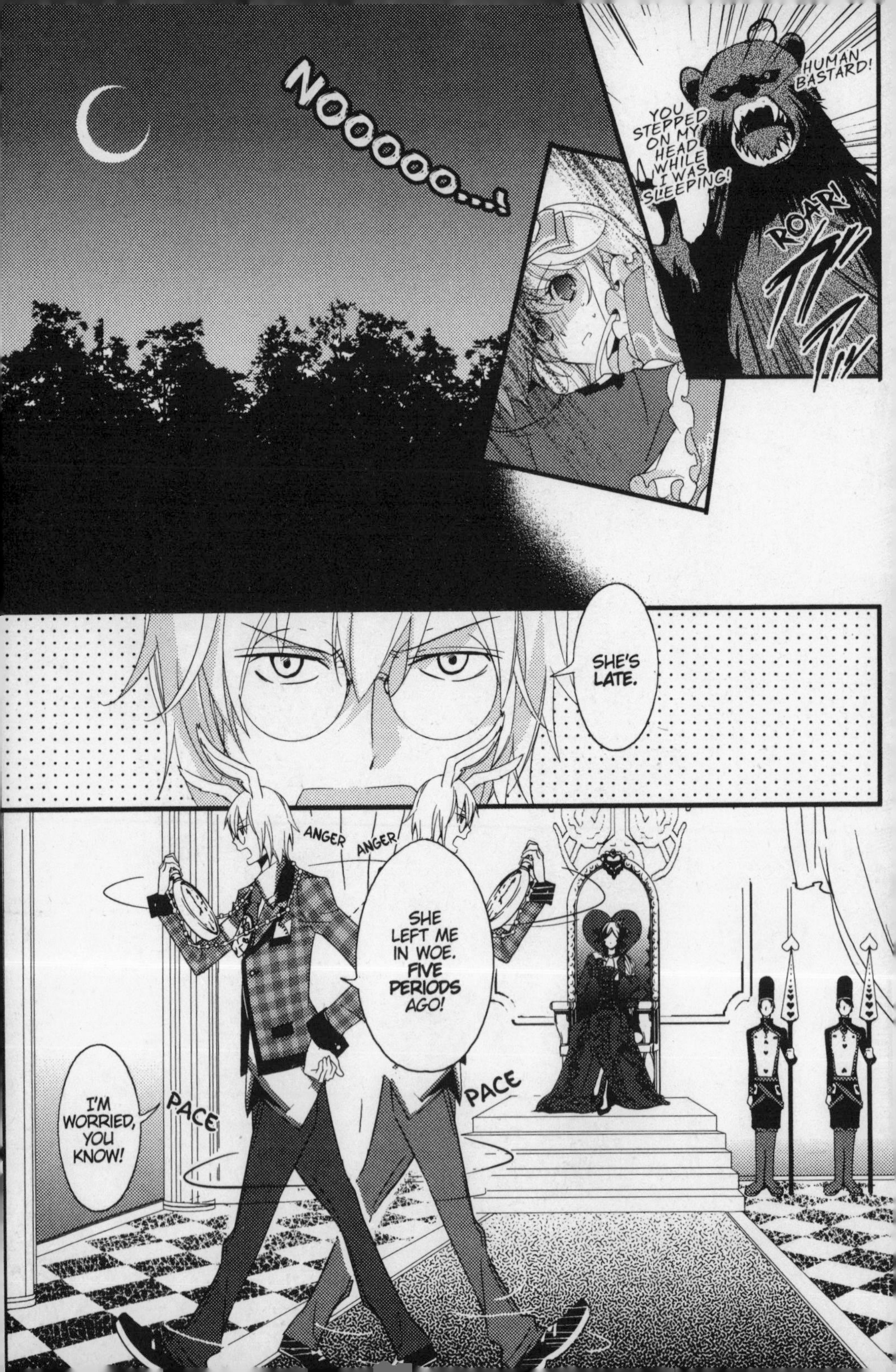
HUMAN BASTARD!
YOU STEPPED ON MY HEAD WHILE I WAS SLEEPING!
ROAR!
NOOOOOO...!
SHE'S LATE.
ANGER ANGER
SHE LEFT ME IN WOE. FIVE PERIODS AGO!
PACE
PACE
I'M WORRIED, YOU KNOW!

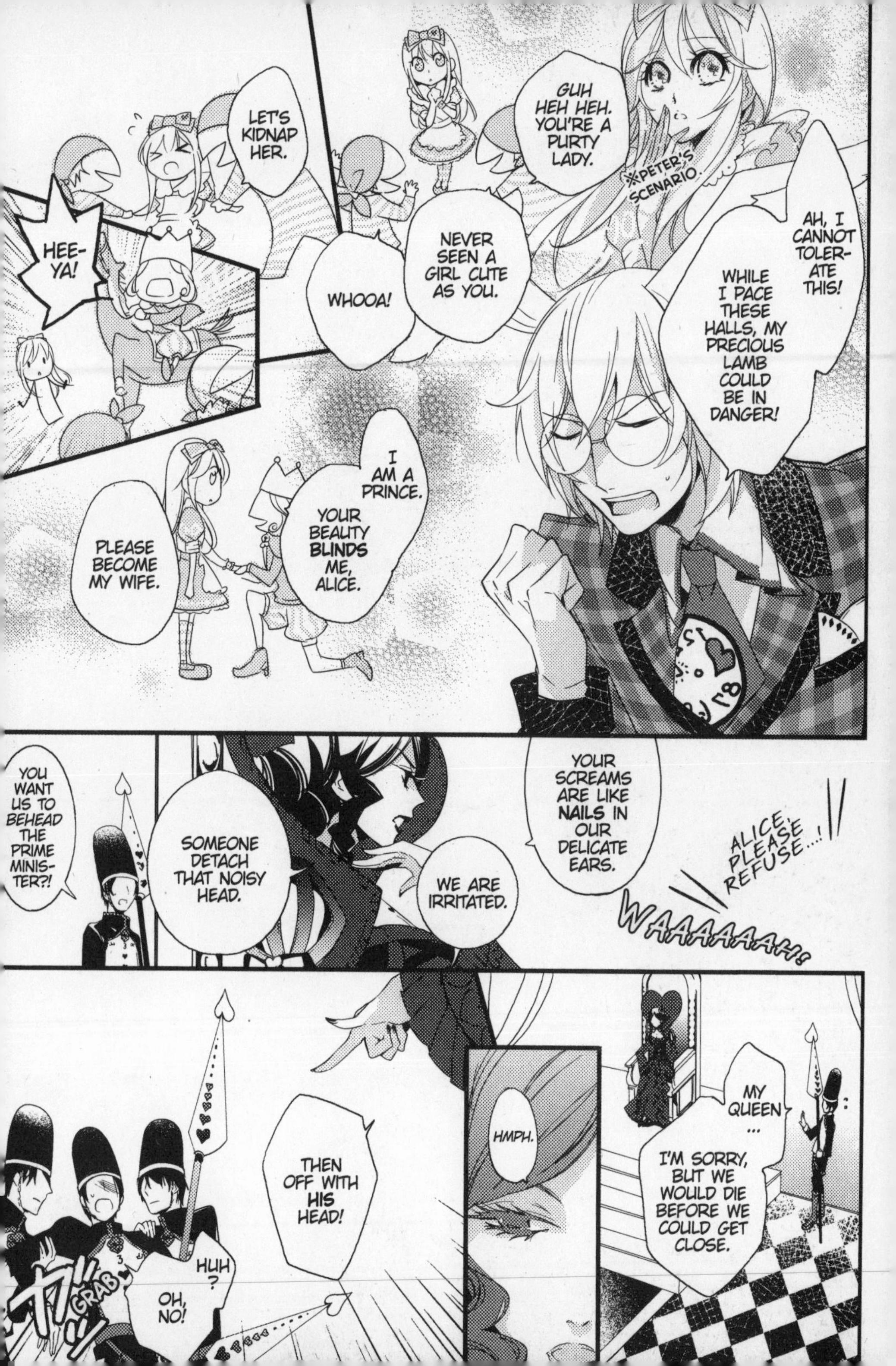
※PETER'S SCENARIO.
GUH HEH HEH. YOU'RE A PURTY LADY.
AH, I CANNOT TOLERATE THIS!
WHILE I PACE THESE HALLS, MY PRECIOUS LAMB COULD BE IN DANGER!
NEVER SEEN A GIRL CUTE AS YOU.
WHOOA!
LET'S KIDNAP HER.
HEE-YA!
I AM A PRINCE.
YOUR BEAUTY BLINDS ME, ALICE.
PLEASE BECOME MY WIFE.
ALICE, PLEASE REFUSE...!
WAAAAAAAH!
YOUR SCREAMS ARE LIKE NAILS IN OUR DELICATE EARS.
WE ARE IRRITATED.
SOMEONE DETACH THAT NOISY HEAD.
YOU WANT US TO BEHEAD THE PRIME MINISTER?!
MY QUEEN ...
I'M SORRY, BUT WE WOULD DIE BEFORE WE COULD GET CLOSE.
HMPH.
THEN OFF WITH HIS HEAD!
HUH?
OH, NO!
GRAB

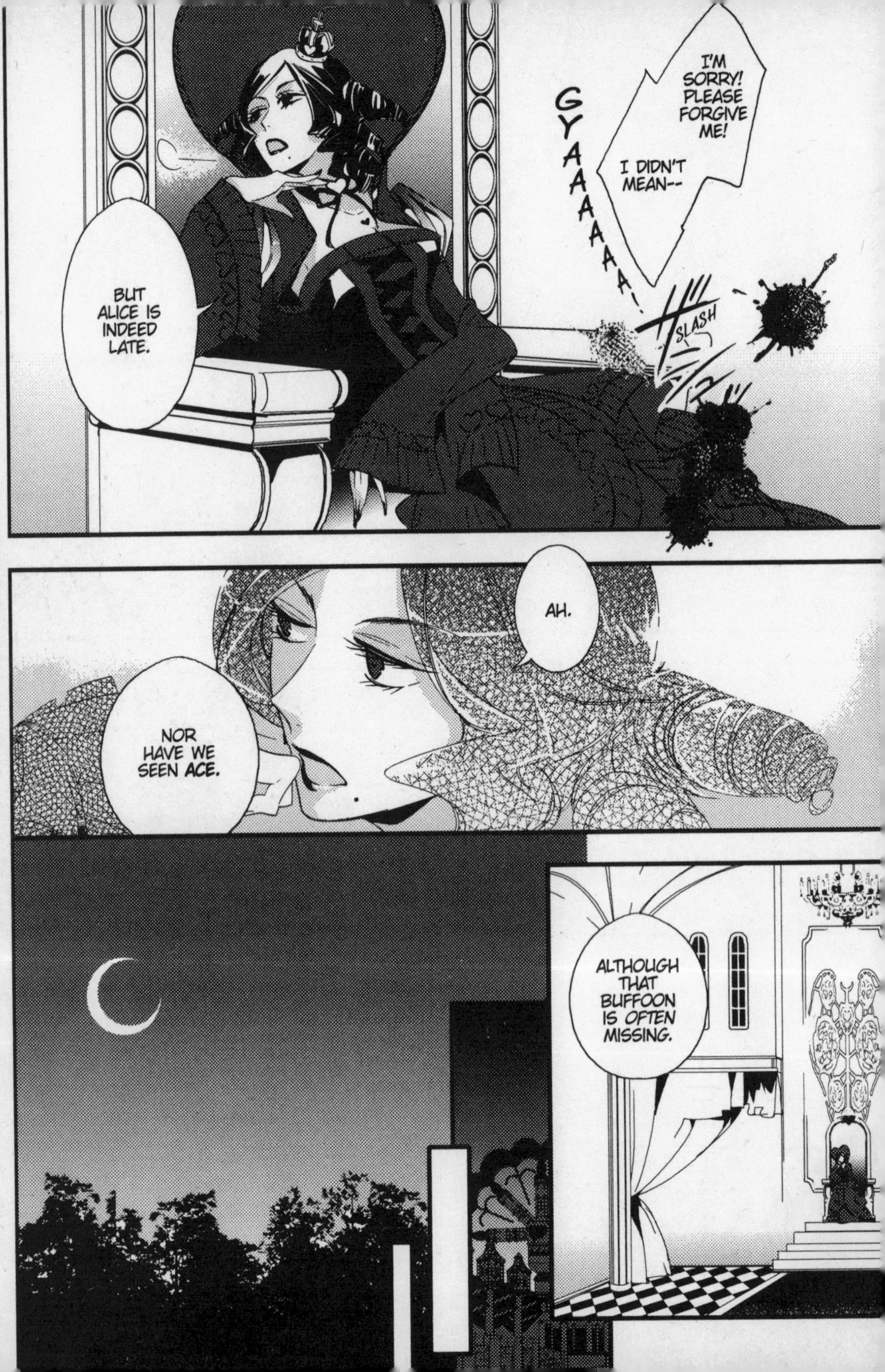
I'M SORRY! PLEASE FORGIVE ME!
I DIDN'T MEAN--
GYAAAAAA!
SLASH
BUT ALICE IS INDEED LATE.
AH.
NOR HAVE WE SEEN ACE.
ALTHOUGH THAT BUFFOON IS OFTEN MISSING.

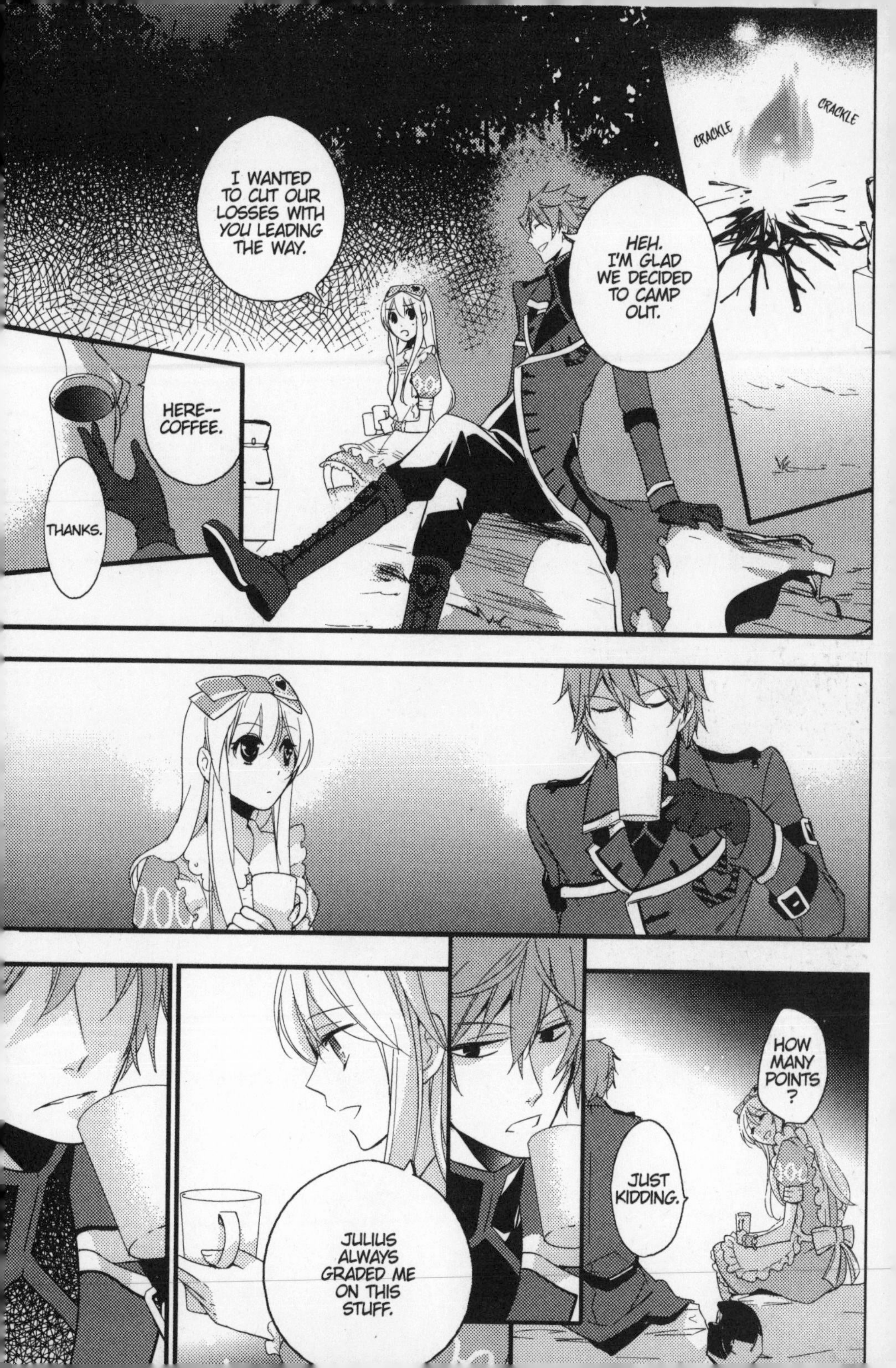
CRACKLE
CRACKLE
HEH. I'M GLAD WE DECIDED TO CAMP OUT.
I WANTED TO CUT OUR LOSSES WITH YOU LEADING THE WAY.
HERE-- COFFEE.
THANKS.
HOW MANY POINTS?
JUST KIDDING.
JULIUS ALWAYS GRADED ME ON THIS STUFF.

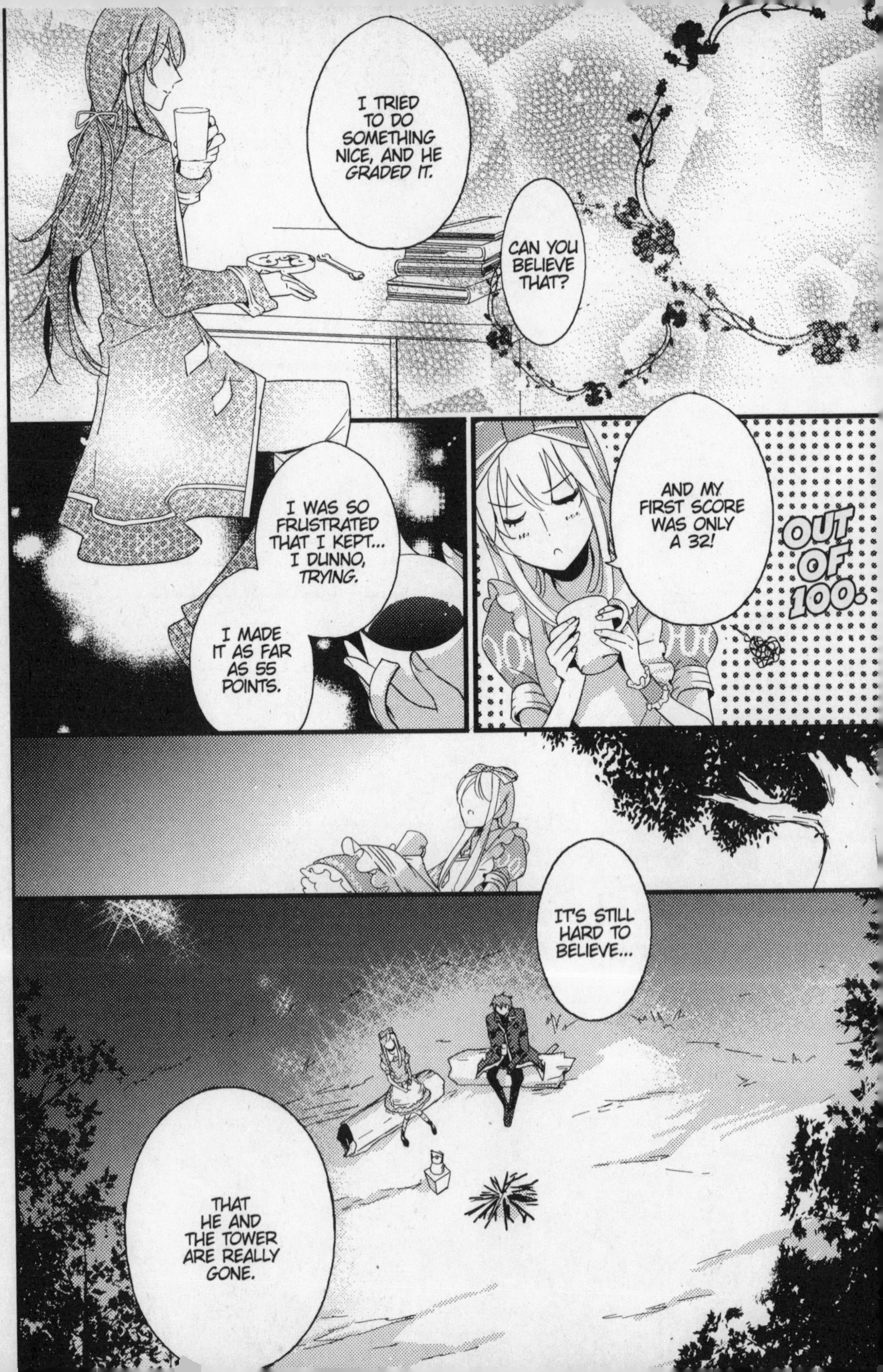
I TRIED TO DO SOMETHING NICE, AND HE GRADED IT.
CAN YOU BELIEVE THAT?
AND MY FIRST SCORE WAS ONLY A 32!
OUT OF 100.
I WAS SO FRUSTRATED THAT I KEPT... I DUNNO, TRYING.
I MADE IT AS FAR AS 55 POINTS.
IT'S STILL HARD TO BELIEVE...
THAT HE AND THE TOWER ARE REALLY GONE.

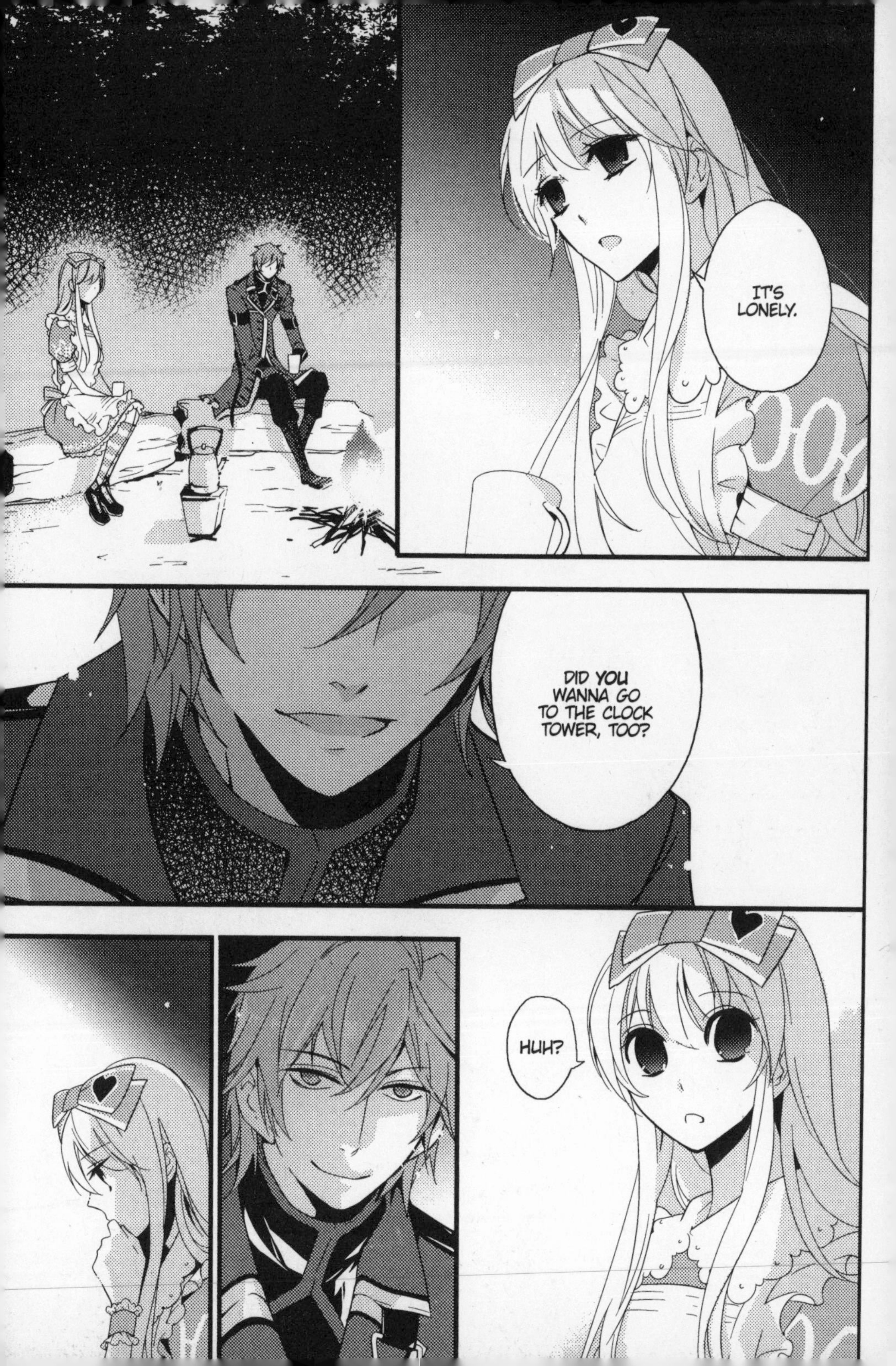
IT'S LONELY.
DID YOU WANNA GO TO THE CLOCK TOWER, TOO?
HUH?

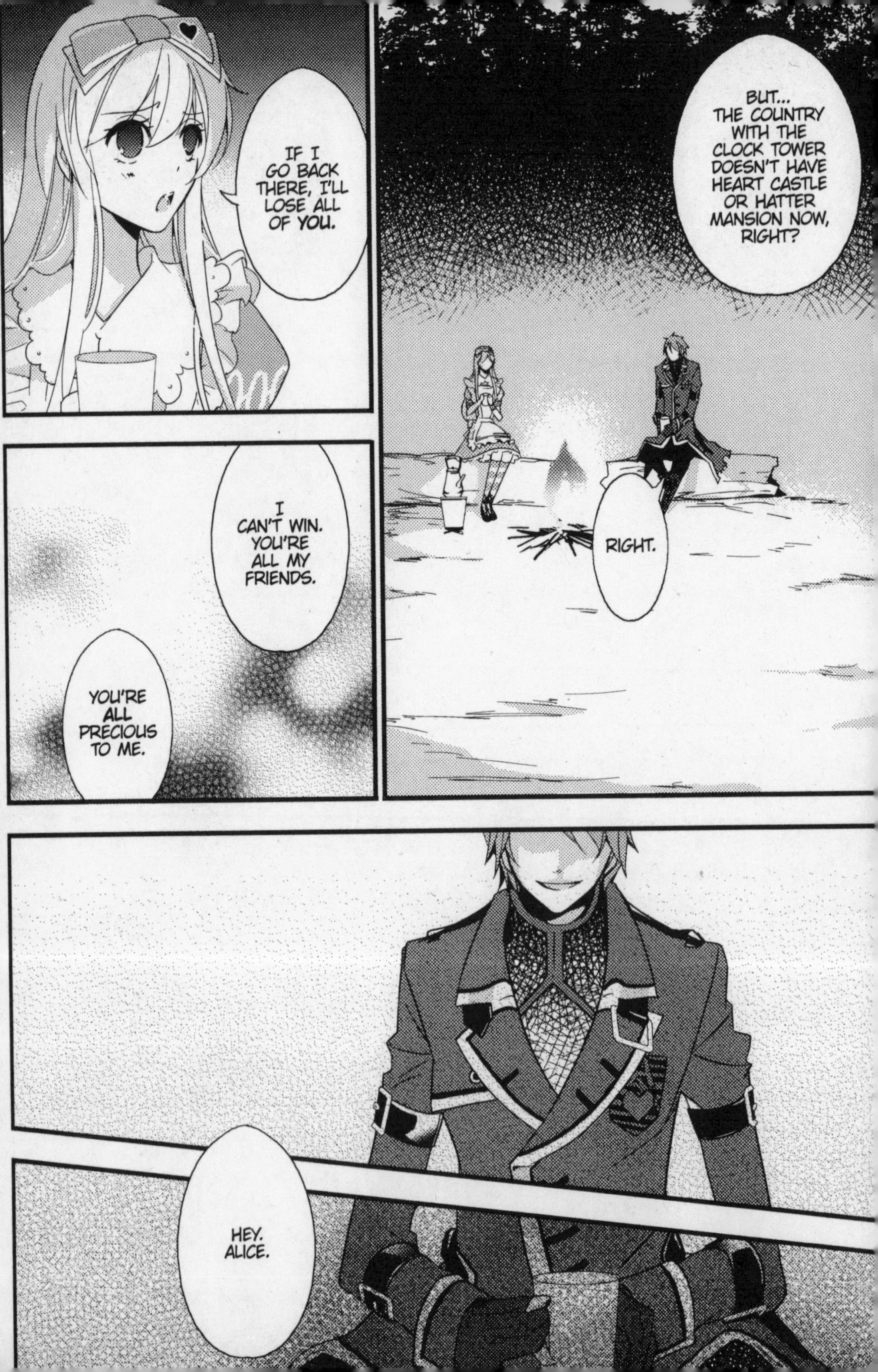
BUT... THE COUNTRY WITH THE CLOCK TOWER DOESN'T HAVE HEART CASTLE OR HATTER MANSION NOW, RIGHT?
RIGHT.
IF I GO BACK THERE, I'LL LOSE ALL OF YOU.
I CAN'T WIN. YOU'RE ALL MY FRIENDS.
YOU'RE ALL PRECIOUS TO ME.
HEY. ALICE.

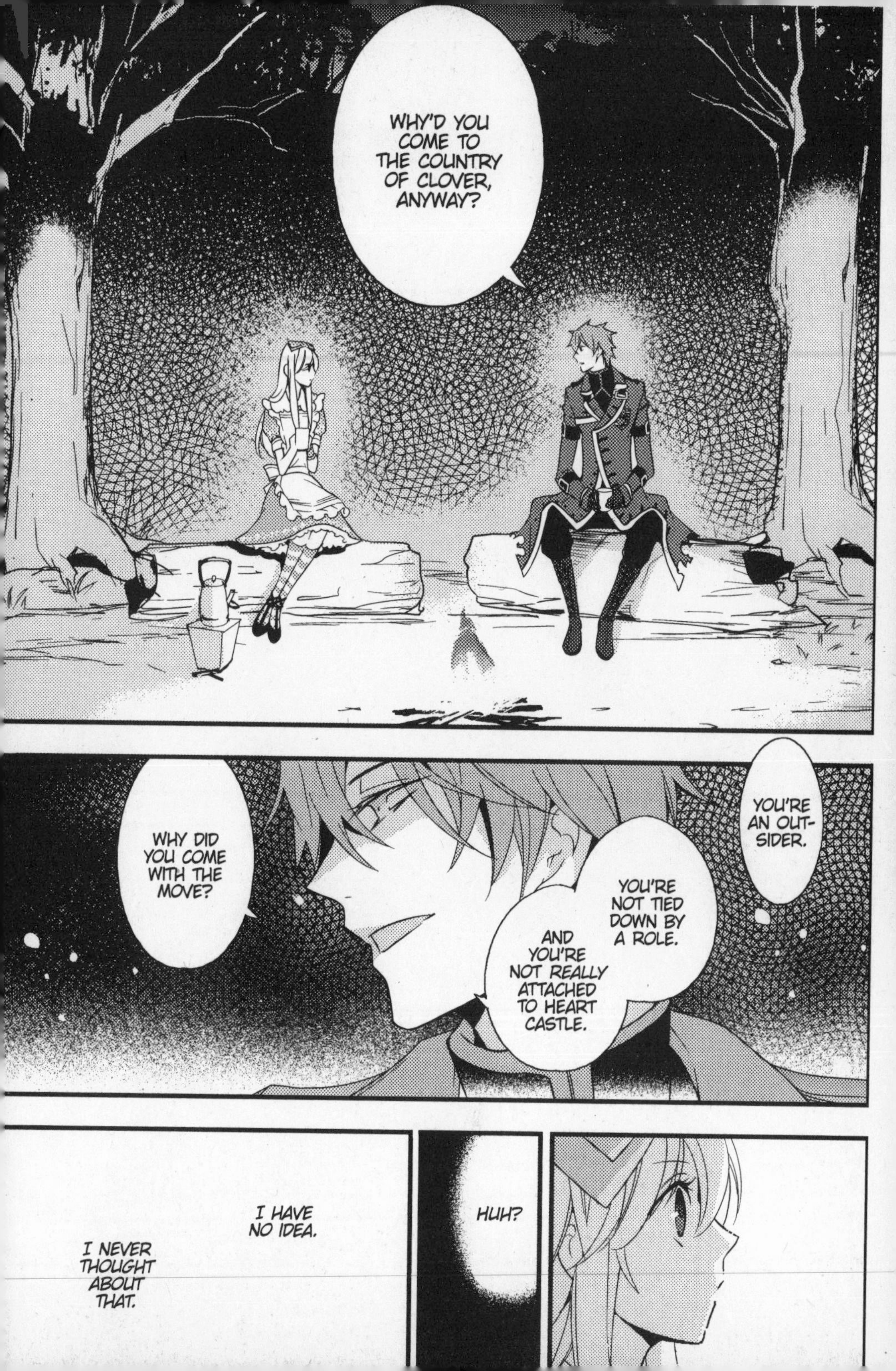
WHY'D YOU COME TO THE COUNTRY OF CLOVER, ANYWAY?
YOU'RE AN OUT-SIDER.
YOU'RE NOT TIED DOWN BY A ROLE.
AND YOU'RE NOT REALLY ATTACHED TO HEART CASTLE.
WHY DID YOU COME WITH THE MOVE?
HUH?
I HAVE NO IDEA.
I NEVER THOUGHT ABOUT THAT.

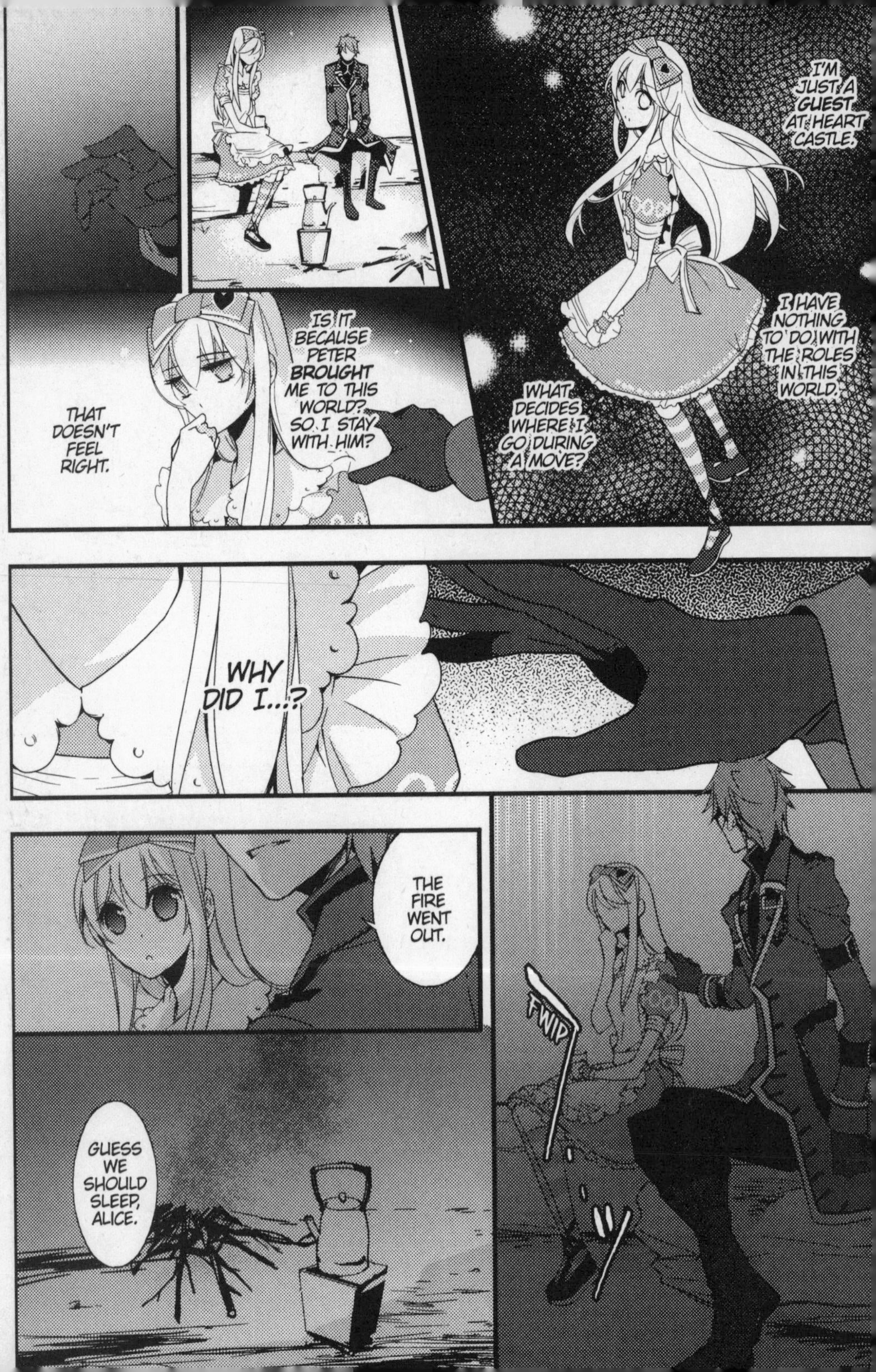
I'M JUST A GUEST AT HEART CASTLE.
I HAVE NOTHING TO DO WITH THE ROLES IN THIS WORLD.
WHAT DECIDES WHERE I GO DURING A MOVE?
IS IT BECAUSE PETER BROUGHT ME TO THIS WORLD? SO I STAY WITH HIM?
THAT DOESN'T FEEL RIGHT.
WHY DID I...?
FWIP
THE FIRE WENT OUT.
GUESS WE SHOULD SLEEP, ALICE.

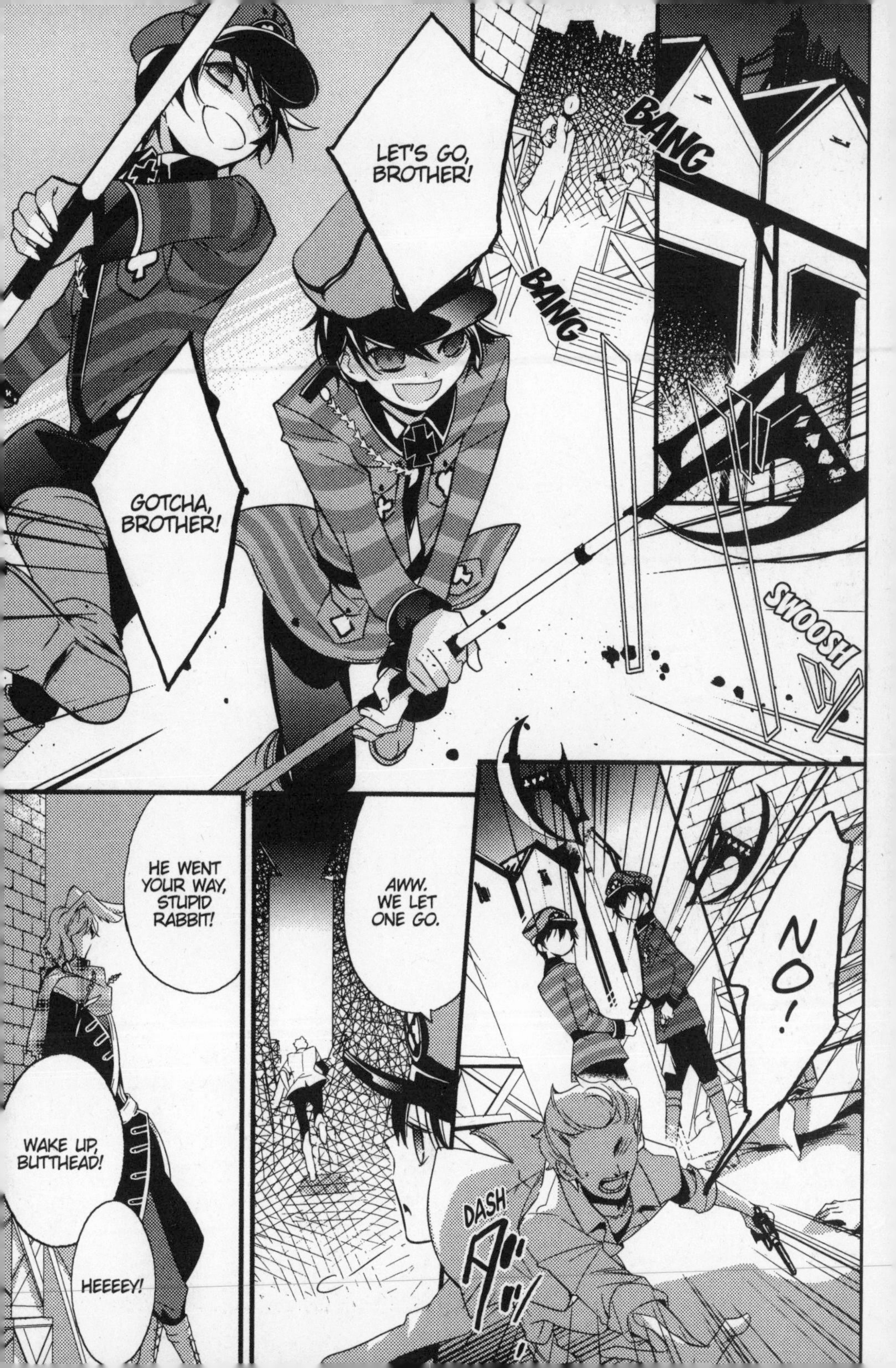
BANG
BANG
SWOOSH
LET'S GO, BROTHER!
GOTCHA, BROTHER!
NO!
DASH
AWW. WE LET ONE GO.
HE WENT YOUR WAY, STUPID RABBIT!
WAKE UP, BUTTHEAD!
HEEEEY!

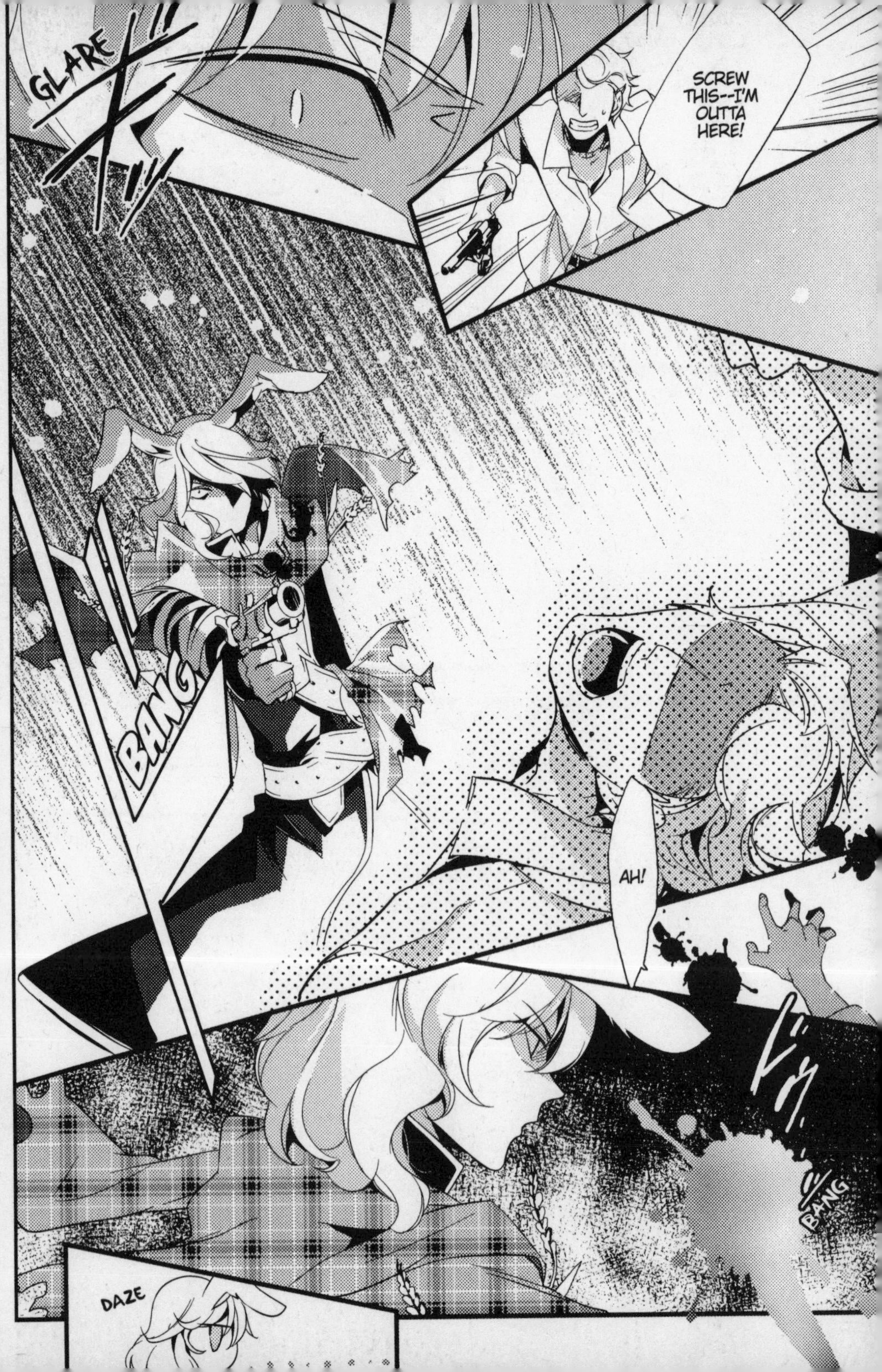
SCREW THIS--I'M OUTTA HERE!
GLARE
BANG
AH!
BANG
DAZE

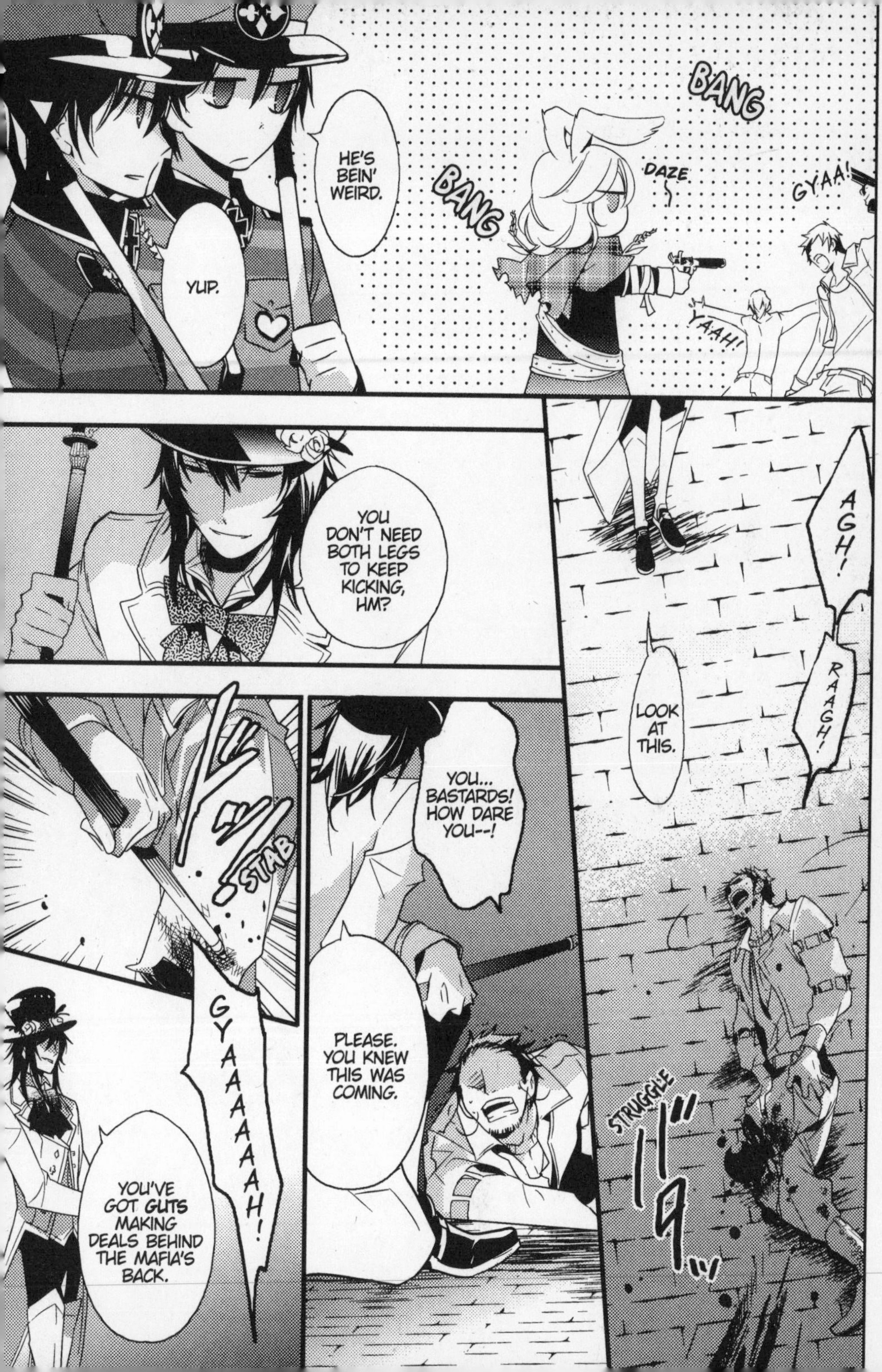
BANG
BANG
DAZE
GYAA!
YAAAH!
HE'S BEIN' WEIRD.
YUP.
AGH!
RAAAGH!
LOOK AT THIS.
STRUGGLE
YOU DON'T NEED BOTH LEGS TO KEEP KICKING, HM?
YOU... BASTARDS! HOW DARE YOU--!
PLEASE. YOU KNEW THIS WAS COMING.
STAB
GYAAAAAAH!
YOU'VE GOT GUTS MAKING DEALS BEHIND THE MAFIA'S BACK.

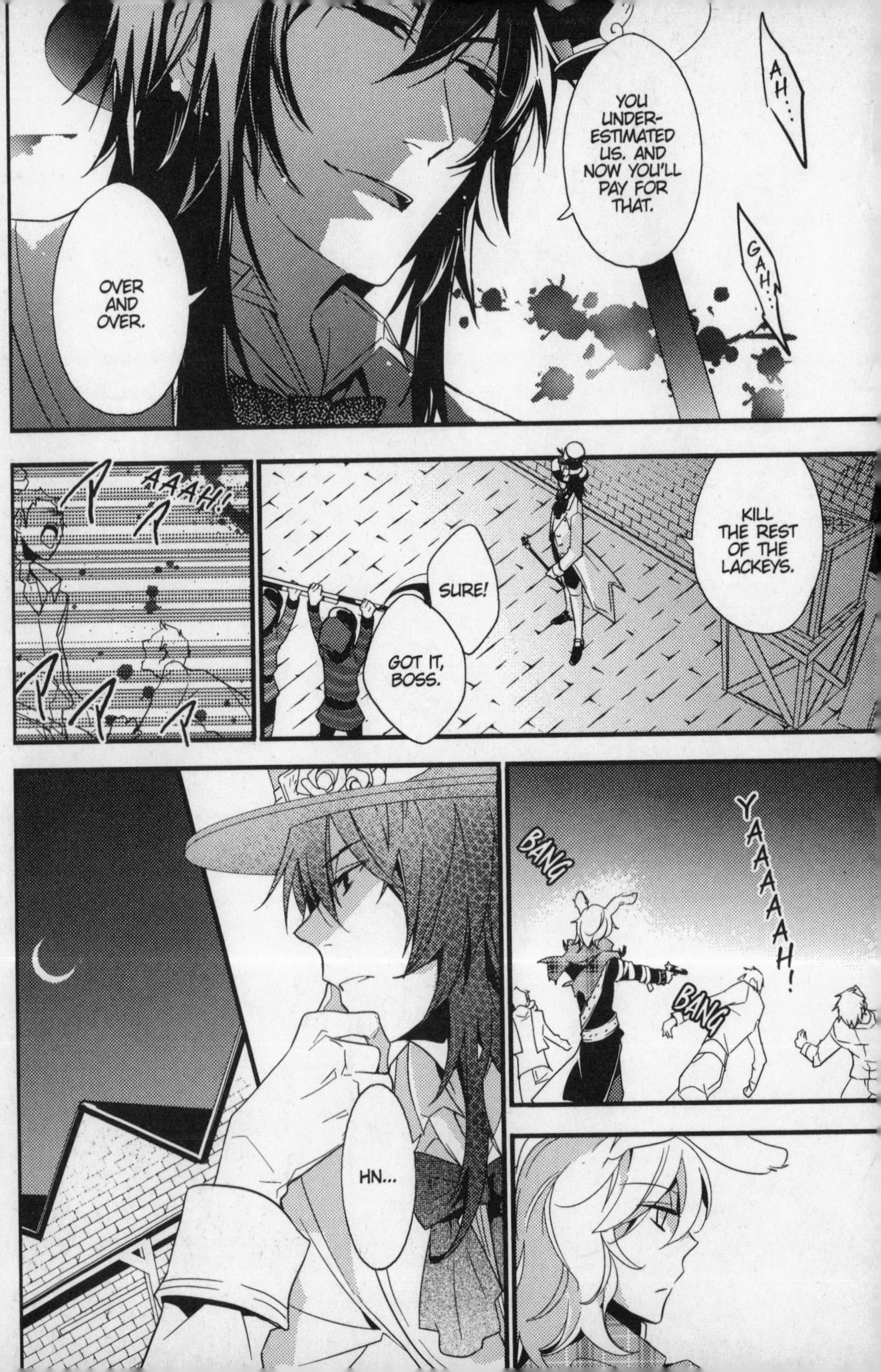
AH...
YOU UNDER-ESTIMATED US. AND NOW YOU'LL PAY FOR THAT.
GAH...
OVER AND OVER.
KILL THE REST OF THE LACKEYS.
SURE!
GOT IT, BOSS.
AAAH!
BANG
YAAAAAAH!
BANG
HN...

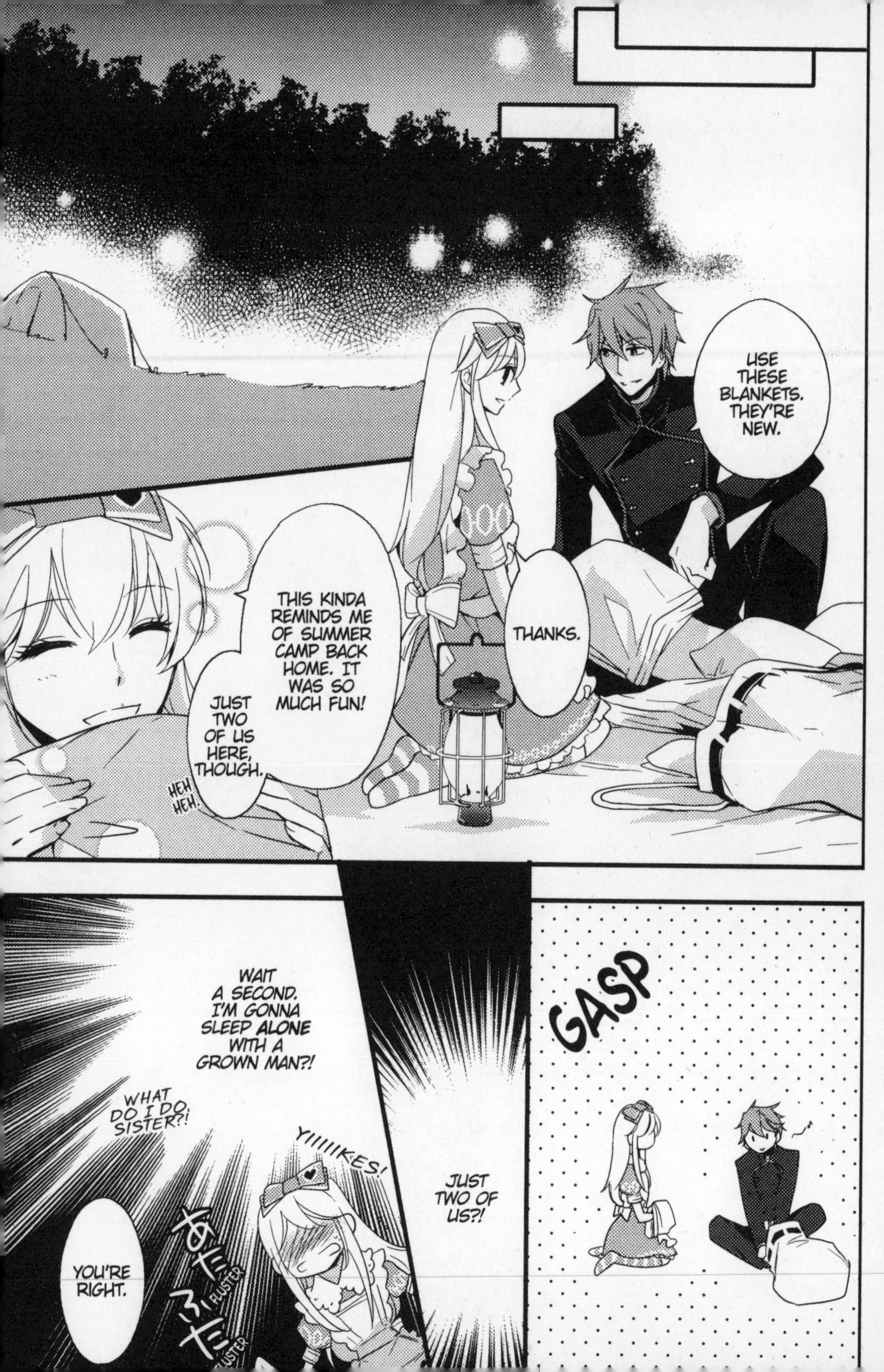

USE THESE BLANKETS. THEY'RE NEW.
THANKS.
THIS KINDA REMINDS ME OF SUMMER CAMP BACK HOME. IT WAS SO MUCH FUN!
JUST TWO OF US HERE, THOUGH.
HEH HEH
GASP
JUST TWO OF US?!
WAIT A SECOND. I'M GONNA SLEEP ALONE WITH A GROWN MAN?!
WHAT DO I DO SISTER?!
YIIIIIKES!
あたふた FLUSTER FLUSTER
YOU'RE RIGHT.

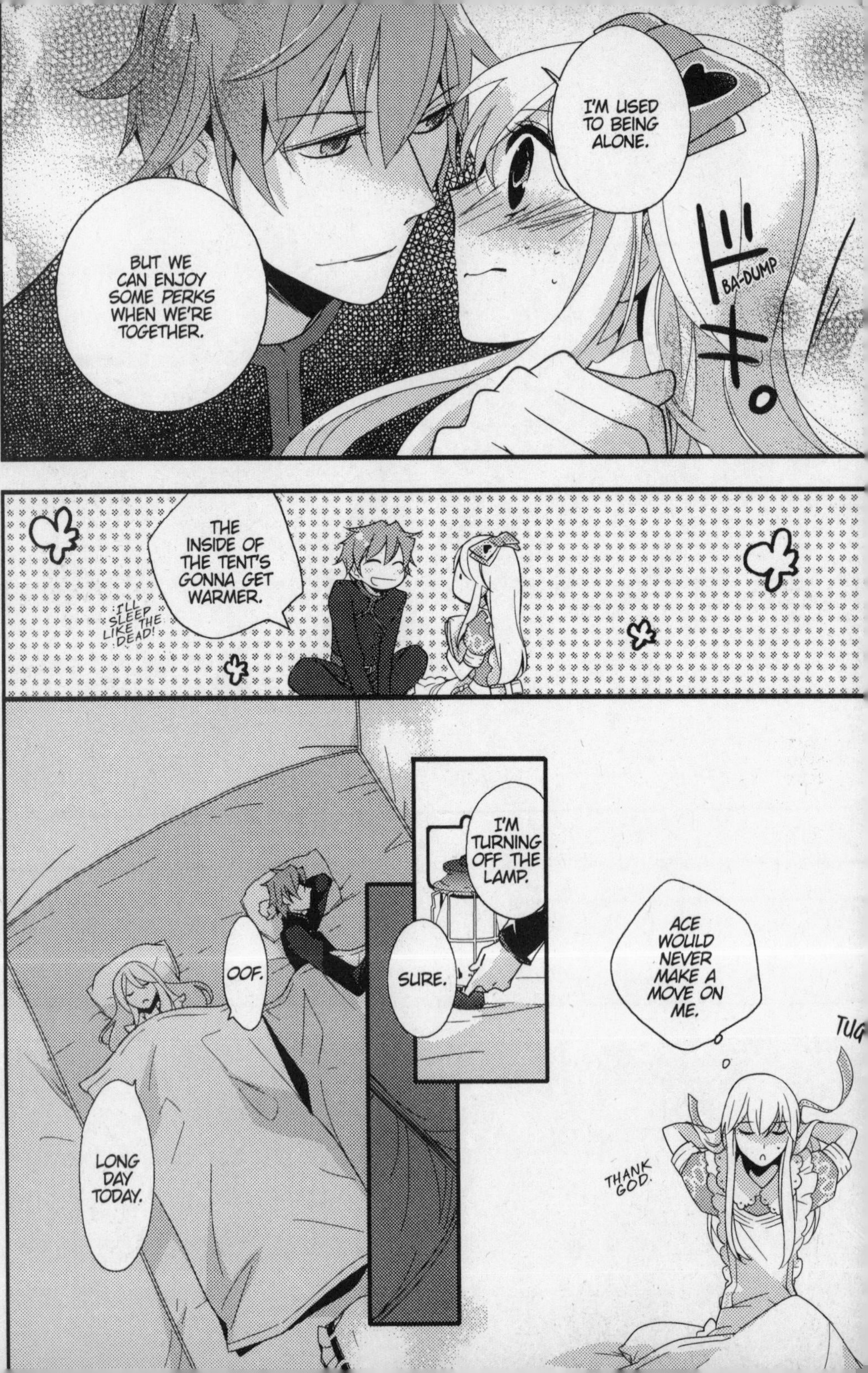

I'M USED TO BEING ALONE.
BUT WE CAN ENJOY SOME PERKS WHEN WE'RE TOGETHER.
BA-DUMP
THE INSIDE OF THE TENT'S GONNA GET WARMER.
I'LL SLEEP LIKE THE DEAD!
ACE WOULD NEVER MAKE A MOVE ON ME.
TUG
THANK GOD.
I'M TURNING OFF THE LAMP.
SURE.
OOF.
LONG DAY TODAY.

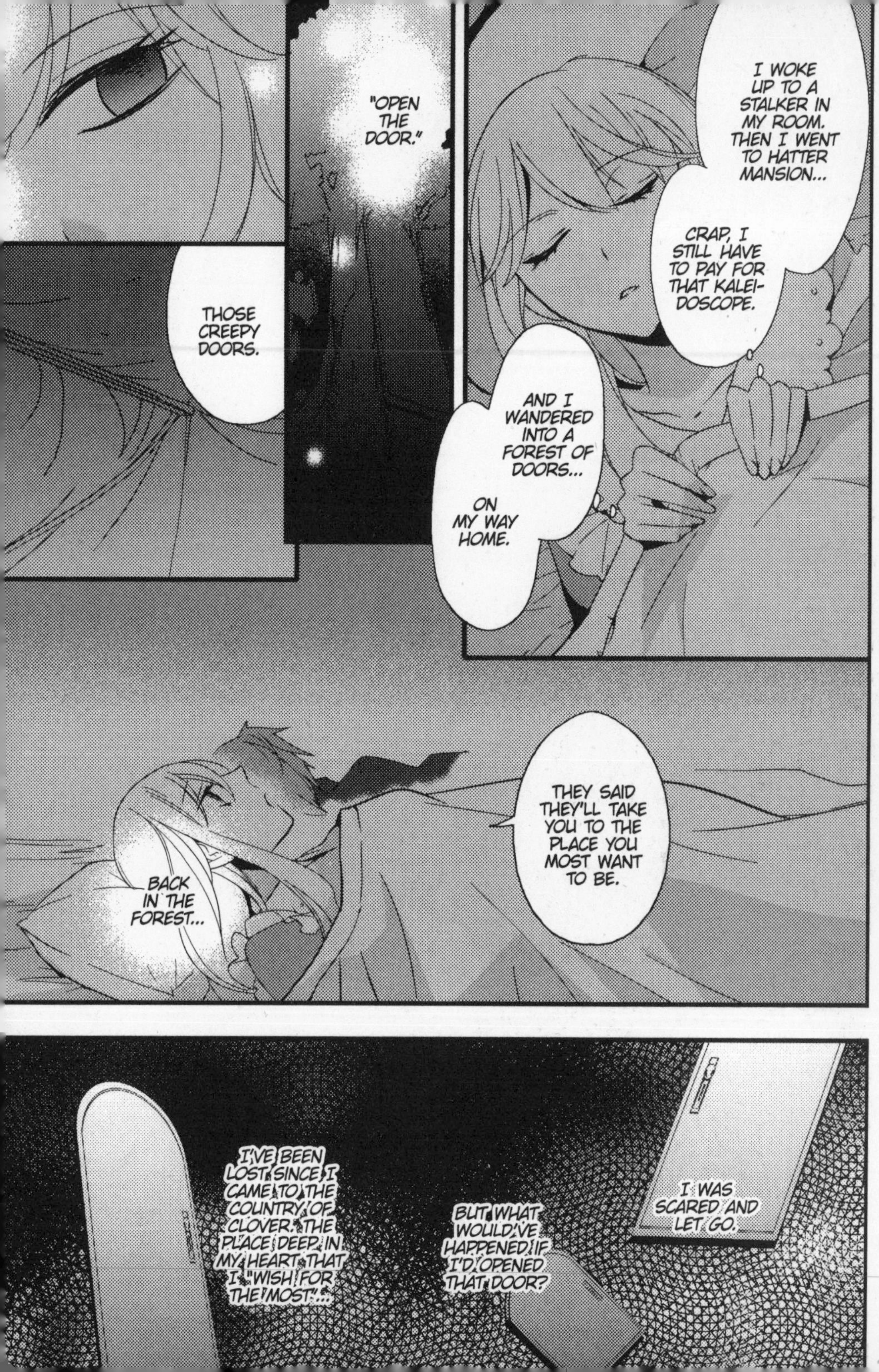
I WOKE UP TO A STALKER IN MY ROOM. THEN I WENT TO HATTER MANSION...
CRAP, I STILL HAVE TO PAY FOR THAT KALEI-DOSCOPE.
AND I WANDERED INTO A FOREST OF DOORS...
ON MY WAY HOME.
"OPEN THE DOOR."
THOSE CREEPY DOORS.
THEY SAID THEY'LL TAKE YOU TO THE PLACE YOU MOST WANT TO BE.
BACK IN THE FOREST...
I WAS SCARED AND LET GO.
BUT WHAT WOULD'VE HAPPENED IF I'D OPENED THAT DOOR?
I'VE BEEN LOST SINCE I CAME TO THE COUNTRY OF CLOVER, THE PLACE DEEP IN MY HEART THAT I "WISH FOR THE MOST"...

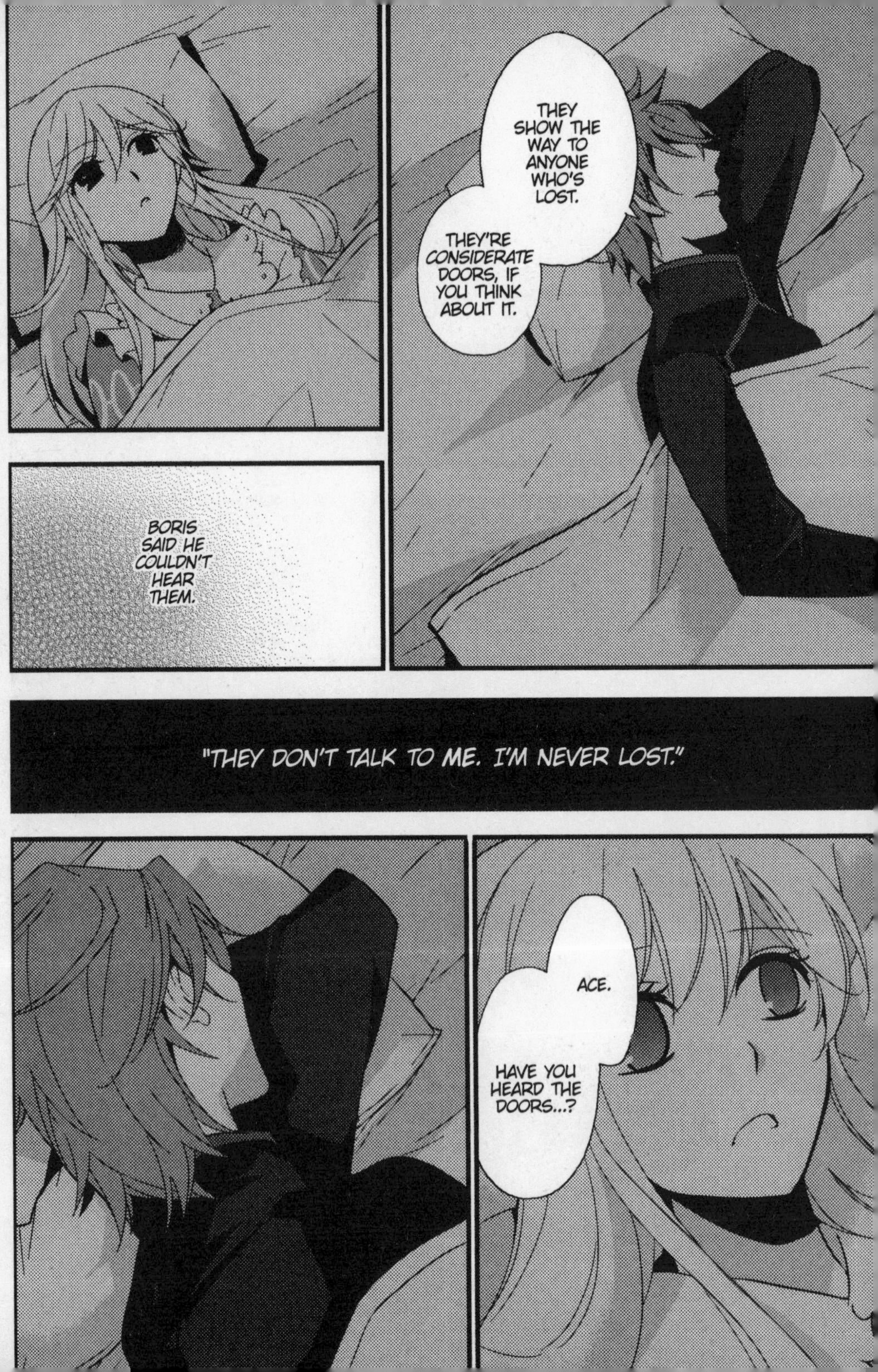
THEY SHOW THE WAY TO ANYONE WHO'S LOST.
THEY'RE CONSIDERATE DOORS, IF YOU THINK ABOUT IT.
BORIS SAID HE COULDN'T HEAR THEM.
"THEY DON'T TALK TO ME. I'M NEVER LOST."
ACE.
HAVE YOU HEARD THE DOORS...?

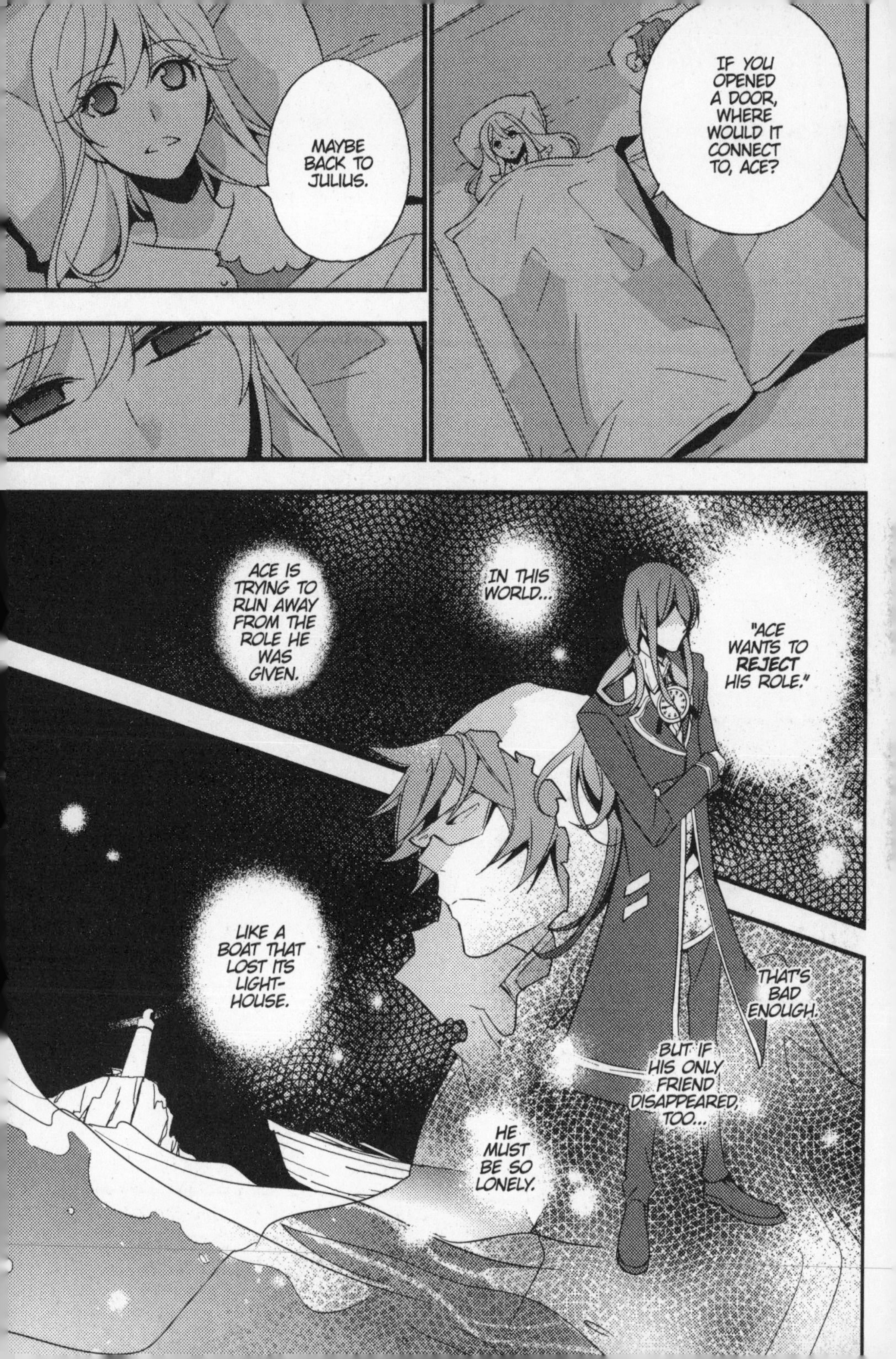
IF YOU OPENED A DOOR, WHERE WOULD IT CONNECT TO, ACE?
MAYBE BACK TO JULIUS.
"ACE WANTS TO REJECT HIS ROLE."
IN THIS WORLD...
ACE IS TRYING TO RUN AWAY FROM THE ROLE HE WAS GIVEN.
THAT'S BAD ENOUGH.
BUT IF HIS ONLY FRIEND DISAPPEARED, TOO...
HE MUST BE SO LONELY.
LIKE A BOAT THAT LOST ITS LIGHT-HOUSE.

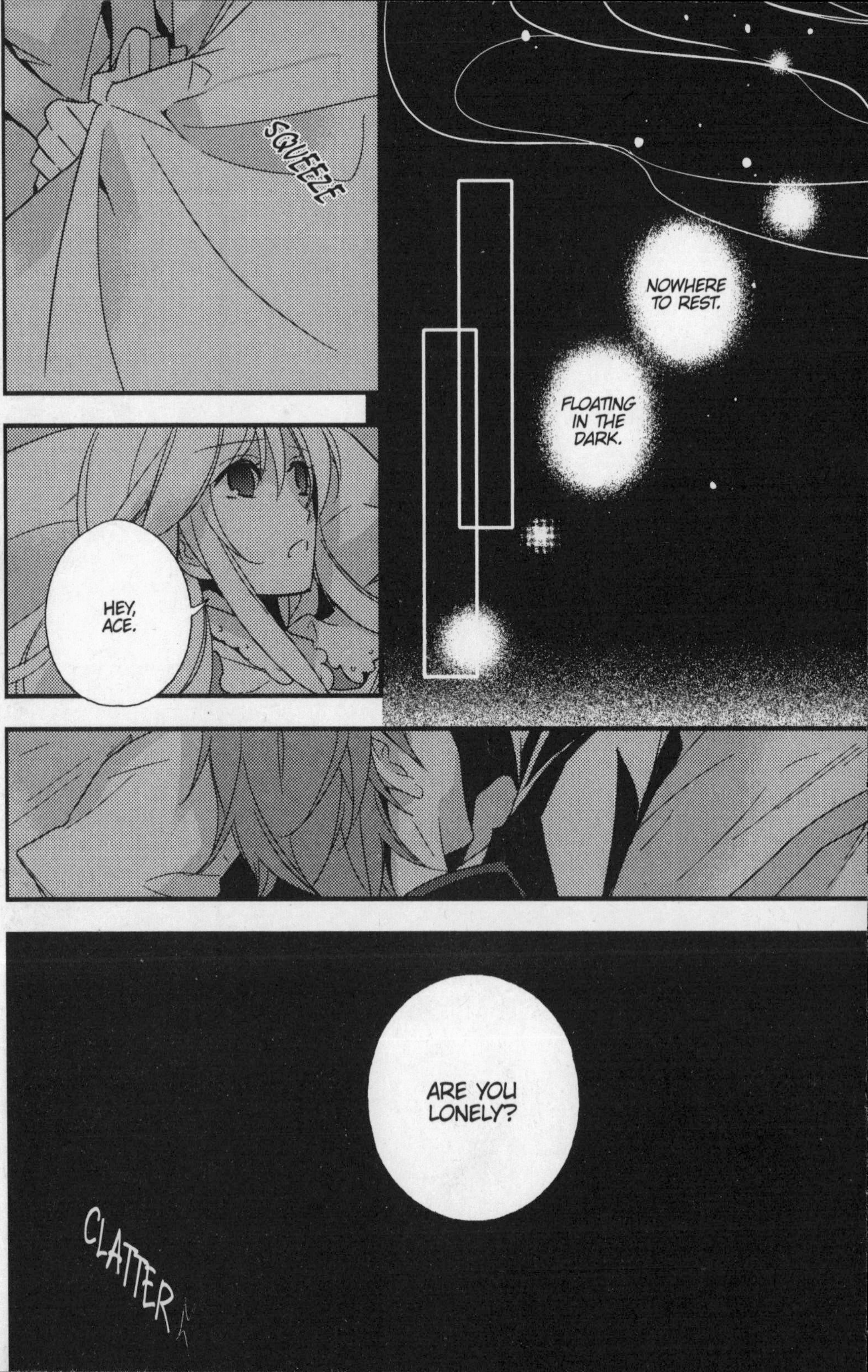
NOWHERE TO REST.
FLOATING IN THE DARK.
SQUEEZE
HEY, ACE.
ARE YOU LONELY?
CLATTER

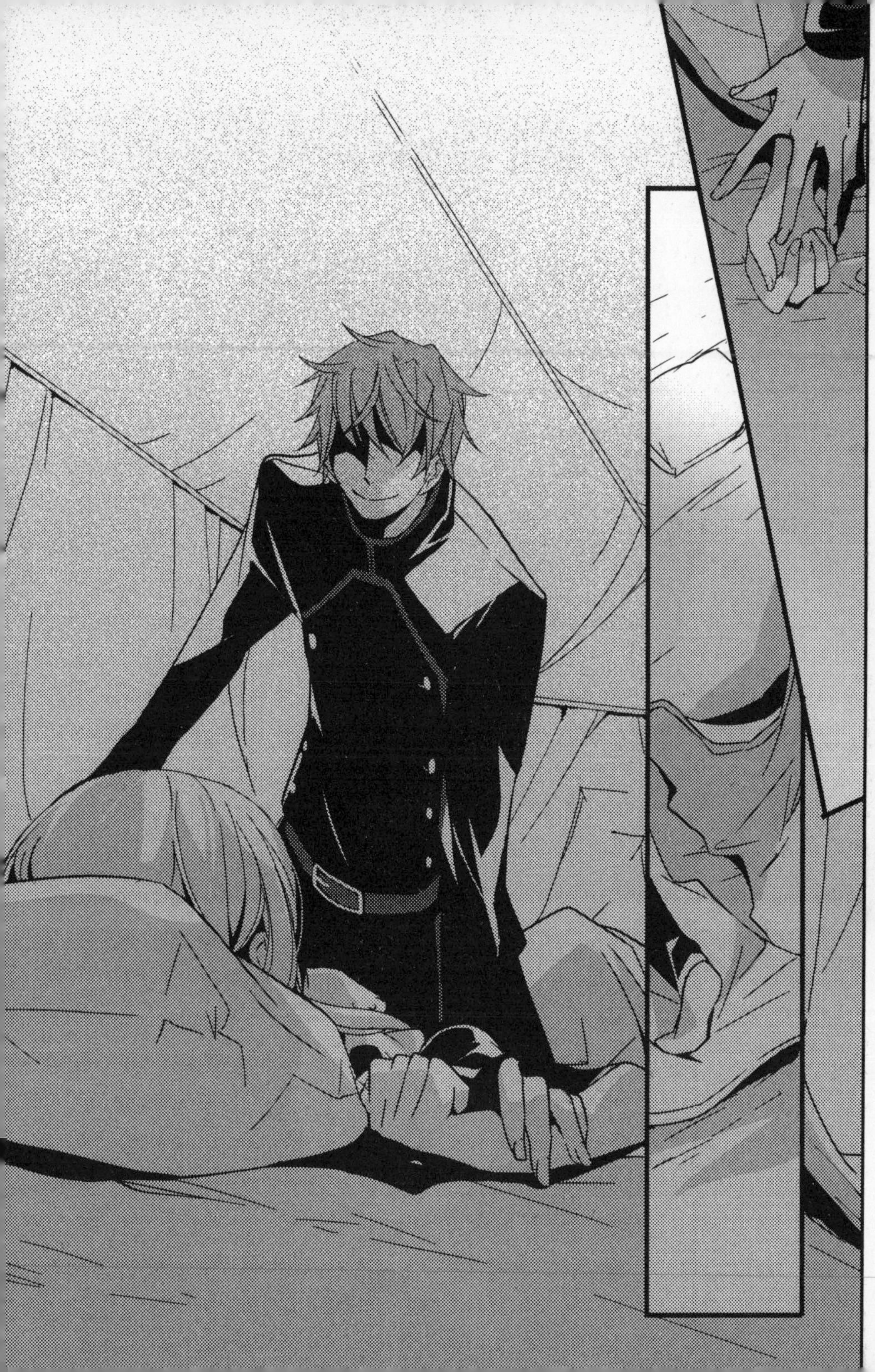

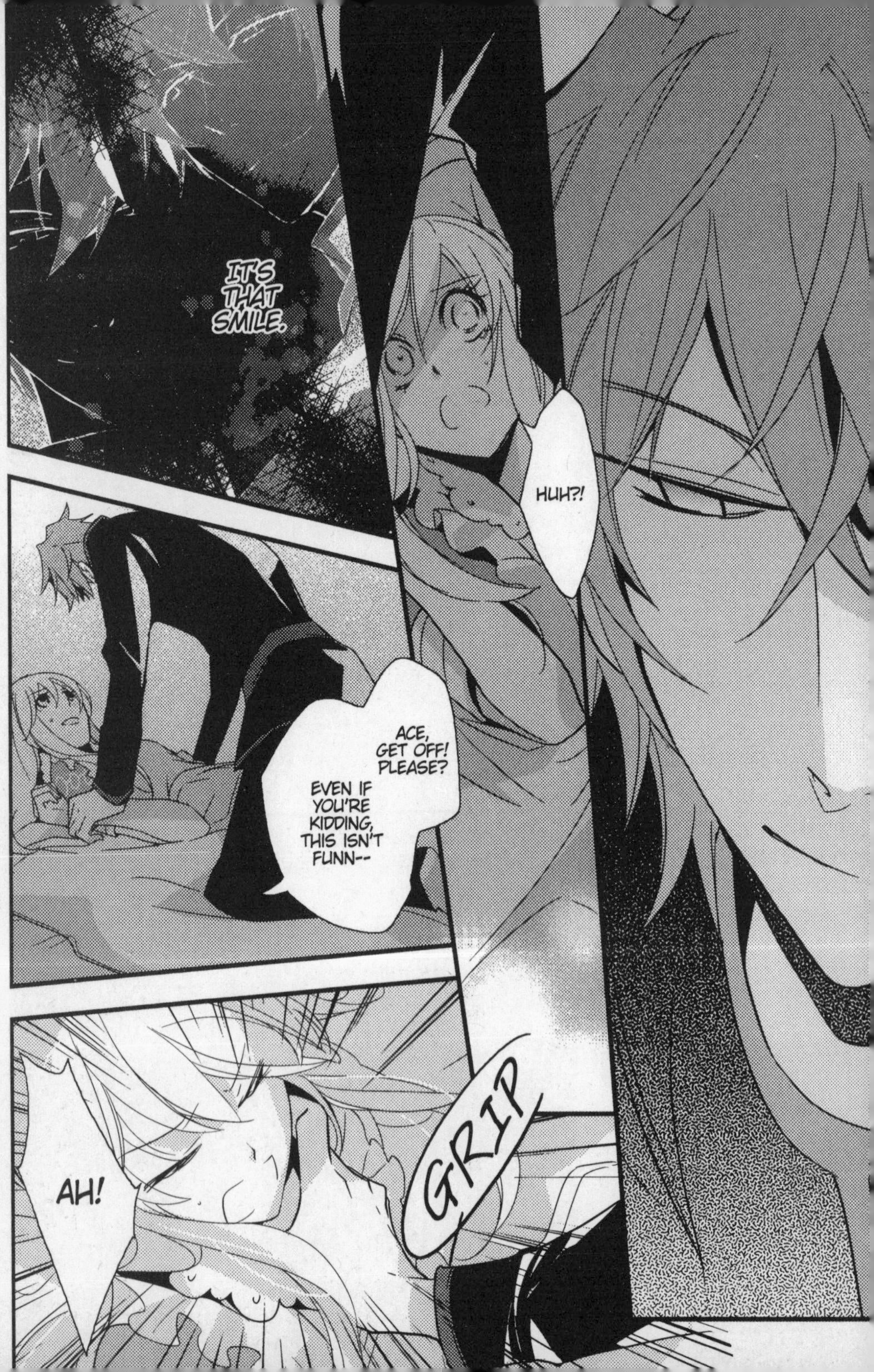
HUH?!
ACE, GET OFF! PLEASE?
EVEN IF YOU'RE KIDDING, THIS ISN'T FUNN--
IT'S THAT SMILE.
GRIP
AH!

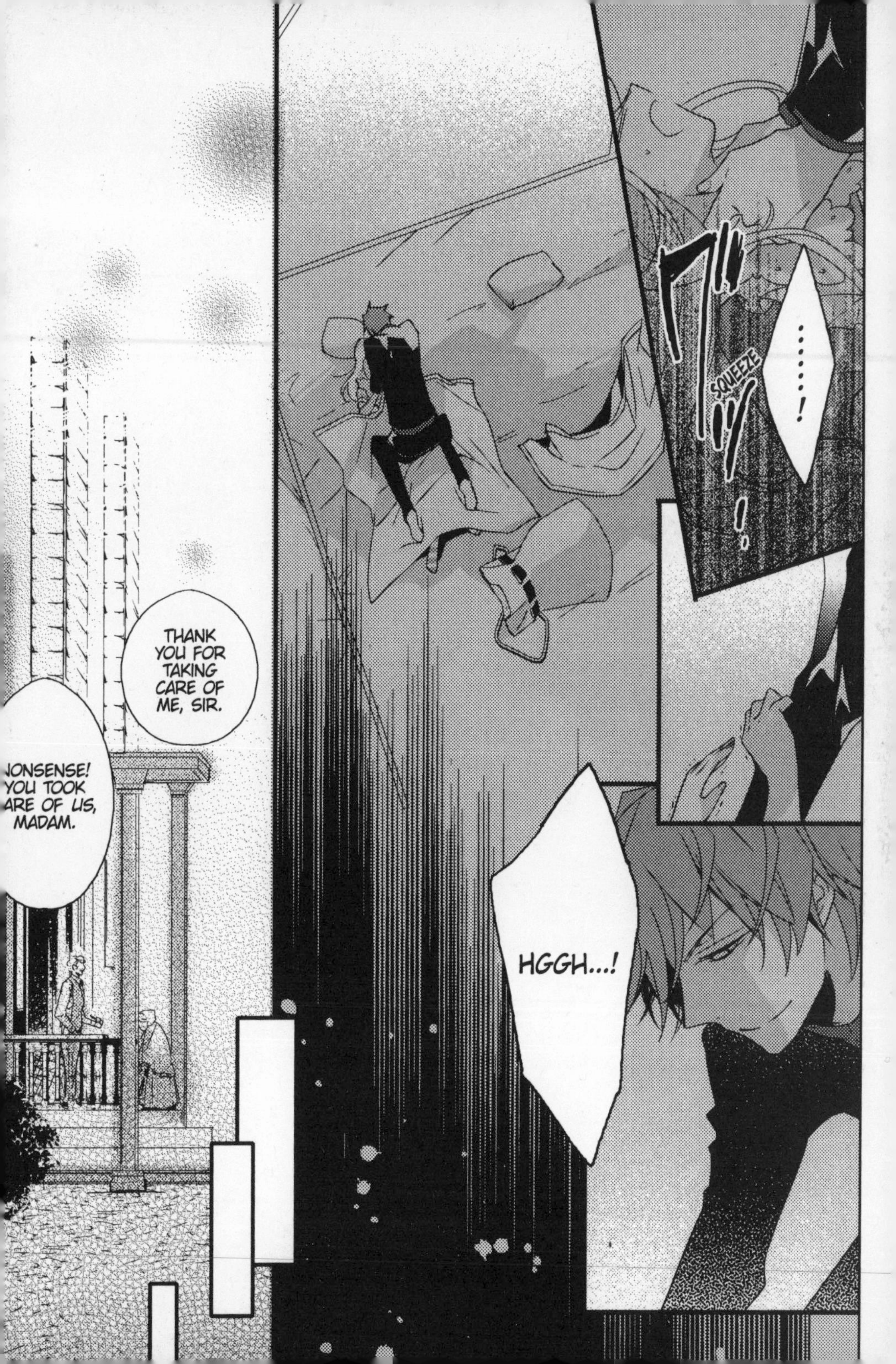
SQUEEZE
......!
HGGH...!
THANK YOU FOR TAKING CARE OF ME, SIR.
JONSENSE! YOU TOOK ARE OF US, MADAM.

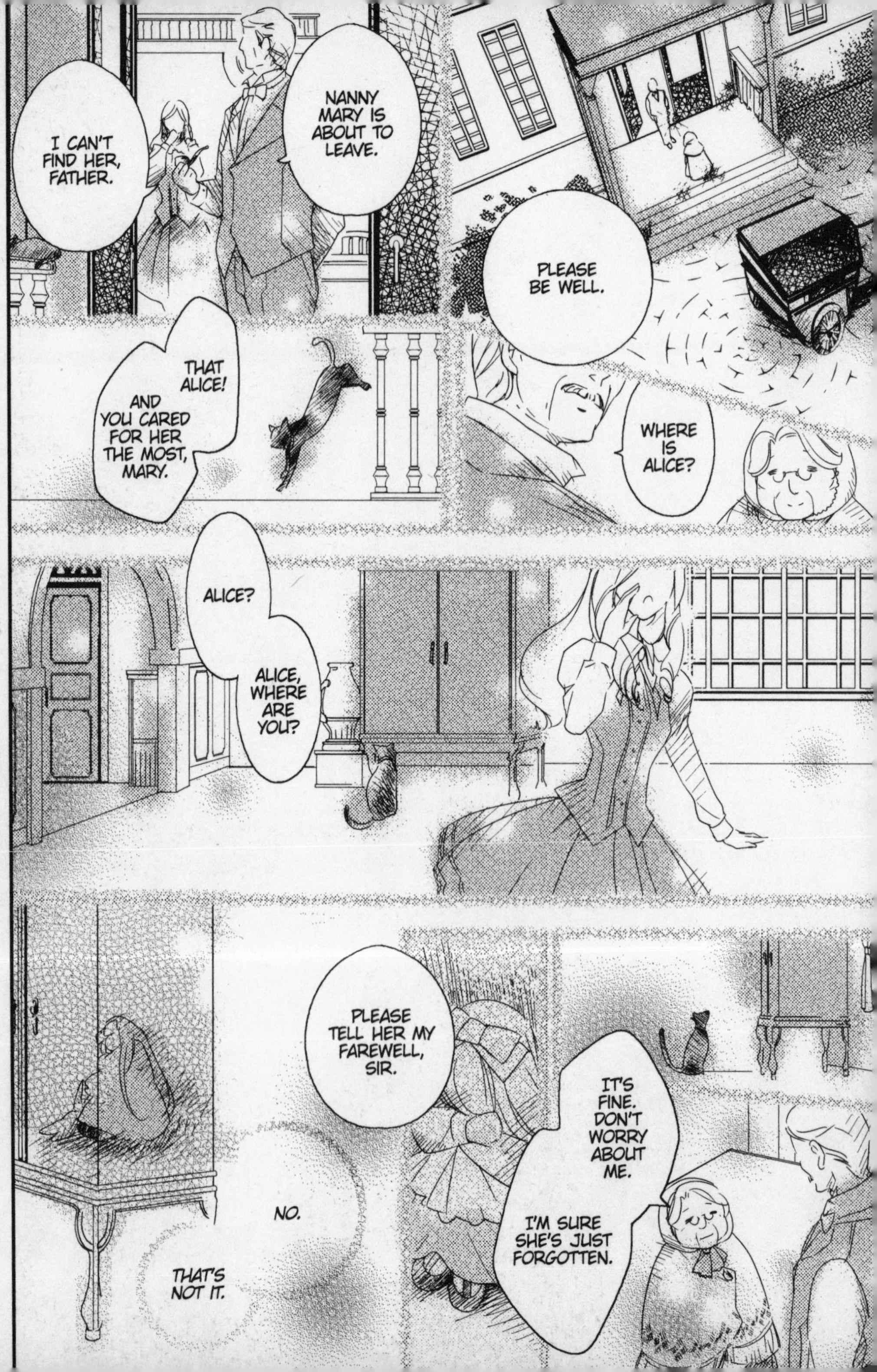
NANNY MARY IS ABOUT TO LEAVE.
I CAN'T FIND HER, FATHER.
PLEASE BE WELL.
WHERE IS ALICE?
THAT ALICE! AND YOU CARED FOR HER THE MOST, MARY.
ALICE?
ALICE, WHERE ARE YOU?
PLEASE TELL HER MY FAREWELL, SIR.
IT'S FINE. DON'T WORRY ABOUT ME.
I'M SURE SHE'S JUST FORGOTTEN.
NO.
THAT'S NOT IT.

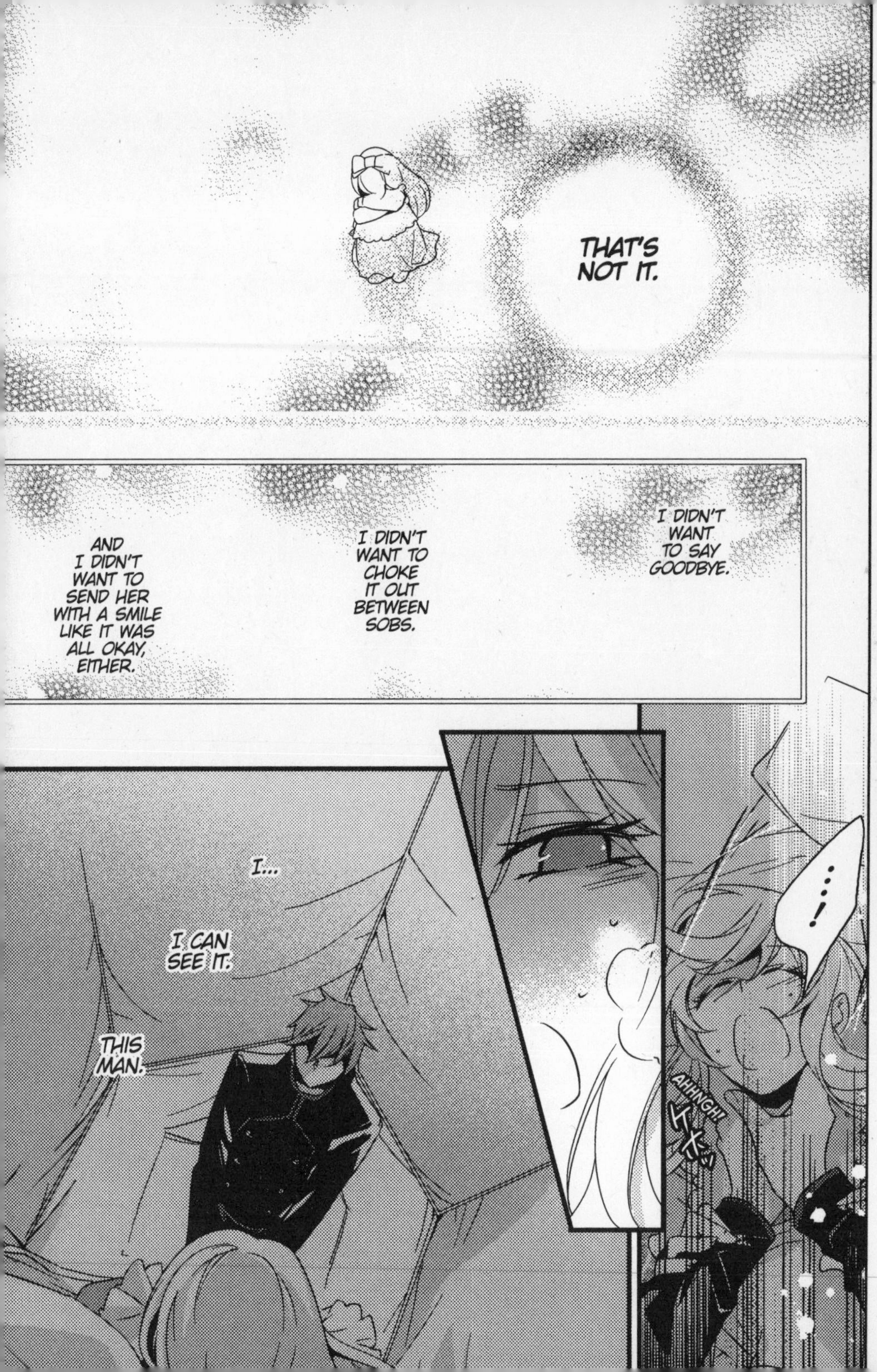
THAT'S NOT IT.
I DIDN'T WANT TO SAY GOODBYE.
I DIDN'T WANT TO CHOKE IT OUT BETWEEN SOBS.
AND I DIDN'T WANT TO SEND HER WITH A SMILE LIKE IT WAS ALL OKAY, EITHER.
...!
AHHNGH!
I...
I CAN SEE IT.
THIS MAN.

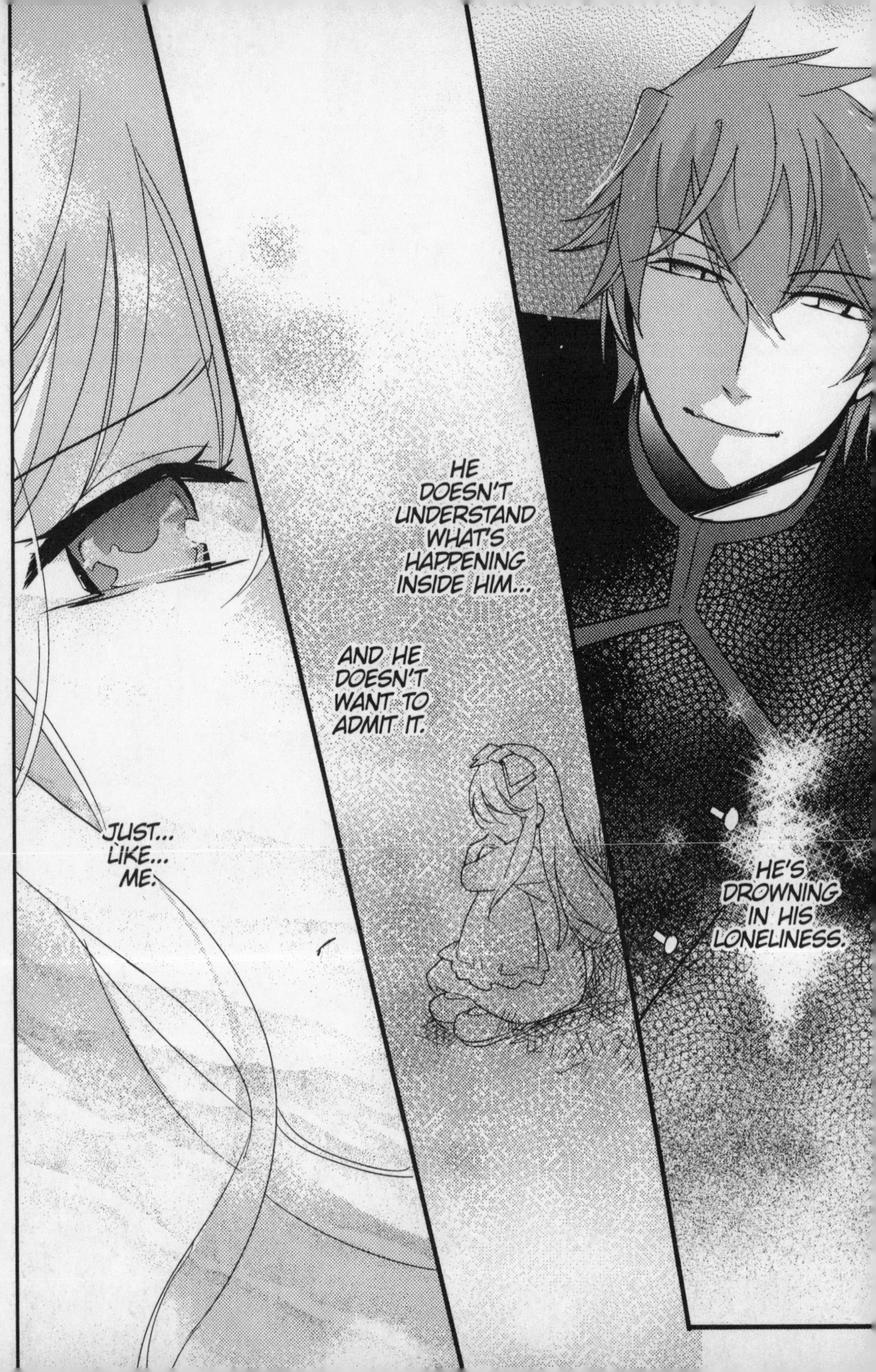
HE'S DROWNING IN HIS LONELINESS.
HE DOESN'T UNDERSTAND WHAT'S HAPPENING INSIDE HIM...
AND HE DOESN'T WANT TO ADMIT IT.
JUST... LIKE... ME.

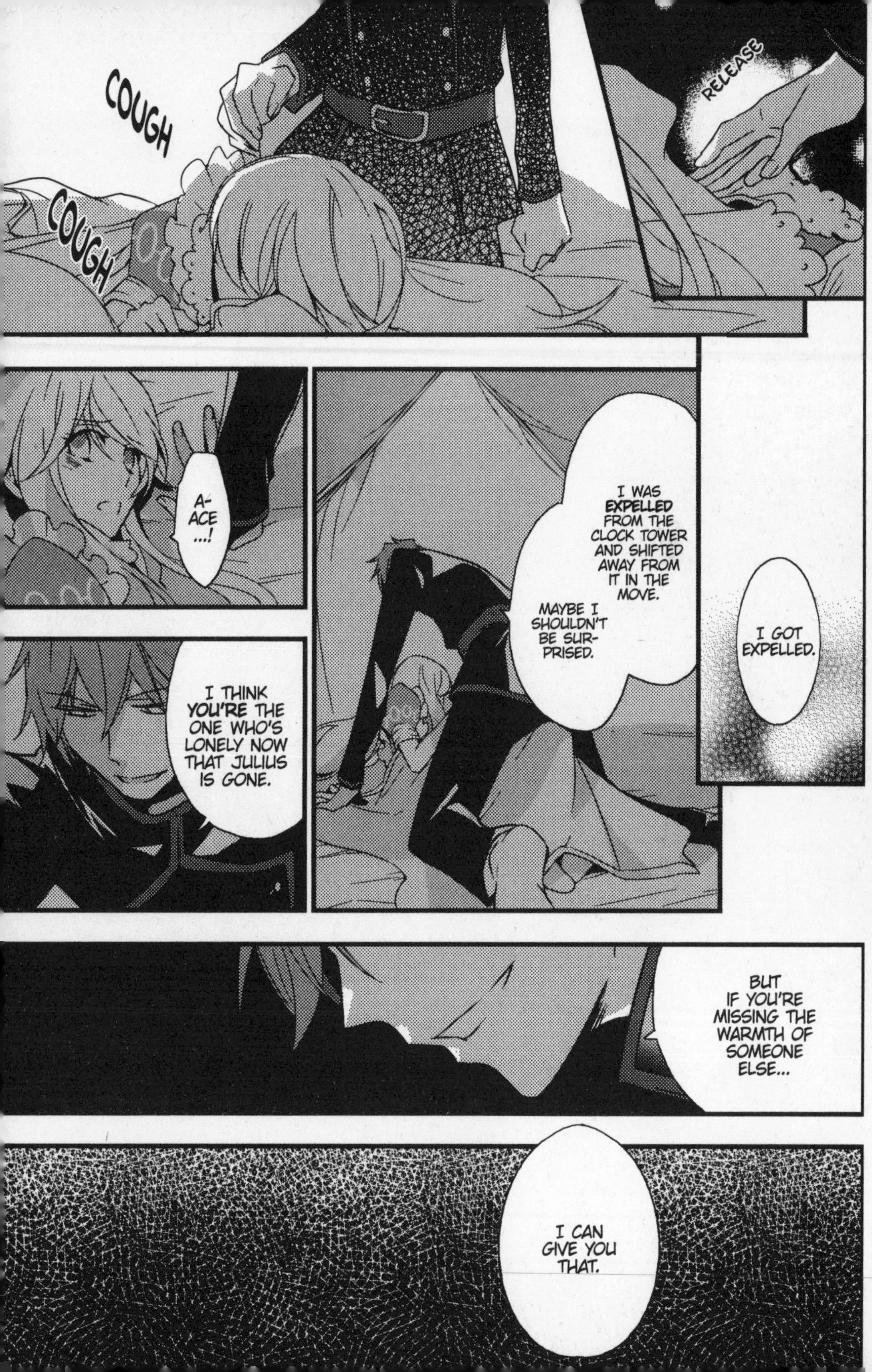
RELEASE
COUGH
COUGH
I GOT EXPELLED.
I WAS EXPELLED FROM THE CLOCK TOWER AND SHIFTED AWAY FROM IT IN THE MOVE.
MAYBE I SHOULDN'T BE SUR-PRISED.
A-ACE ...!
I THINK YOU'RE THE ONE WHO'S LONELY NOW THAT JULIUS IS GONE.
BUT IF YOU'RE MISSING THE WARMTH OF SOMEONE ELSE...
I CAN GIVE YOU THAT.

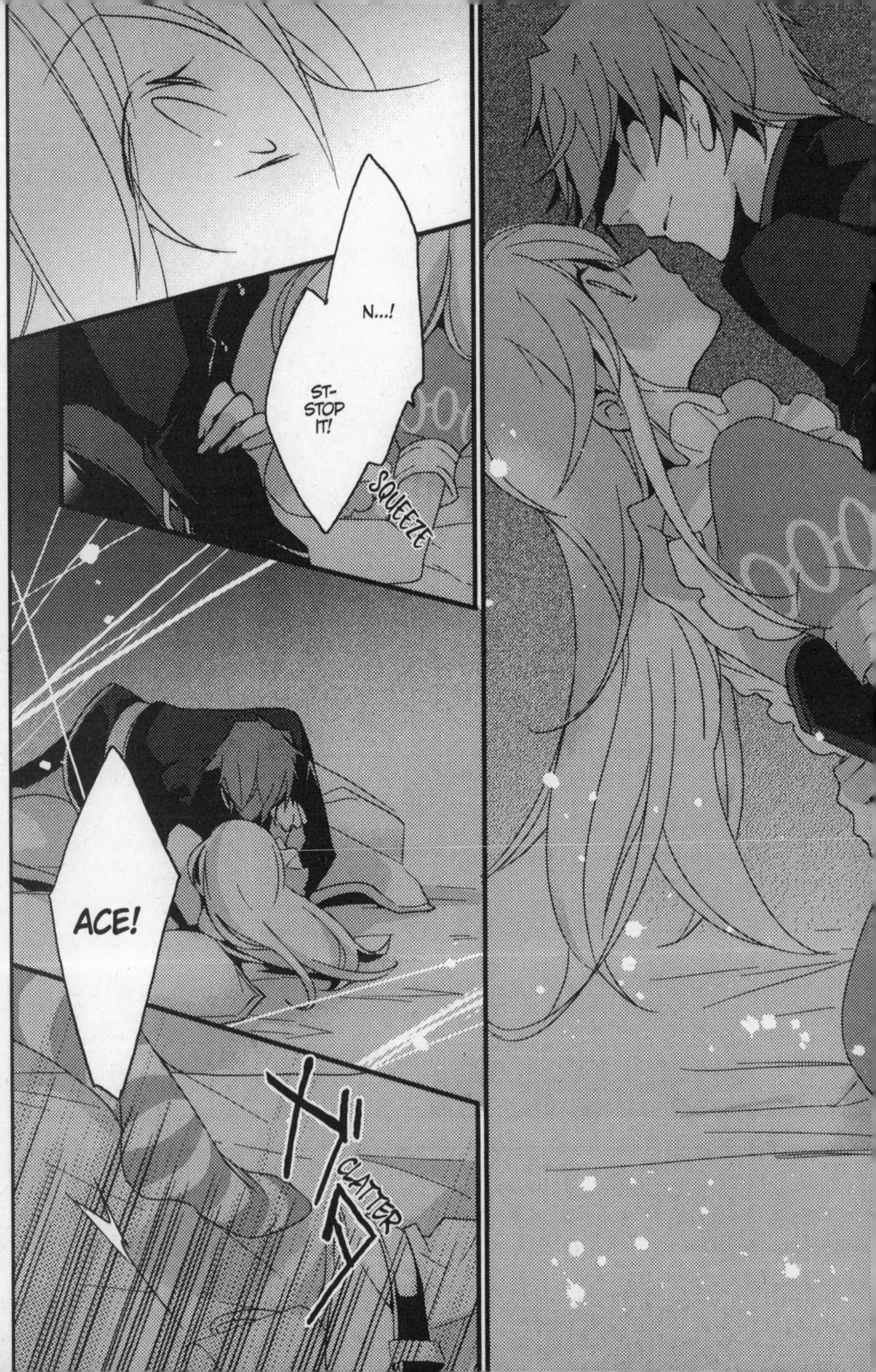
N...!
ST-STOP IT!
SQUEEZE
ACE!
CLATTER

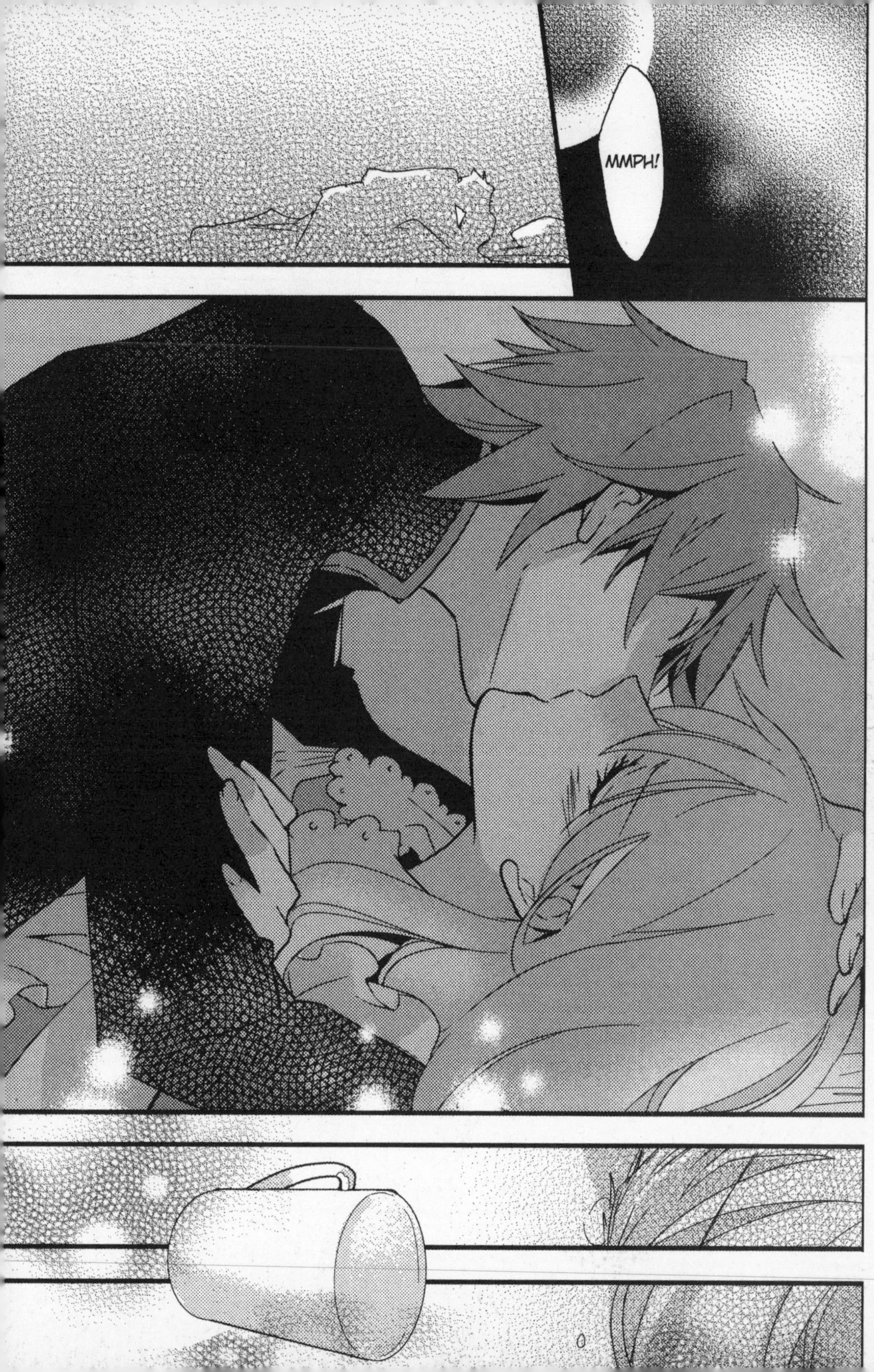
MMPH!

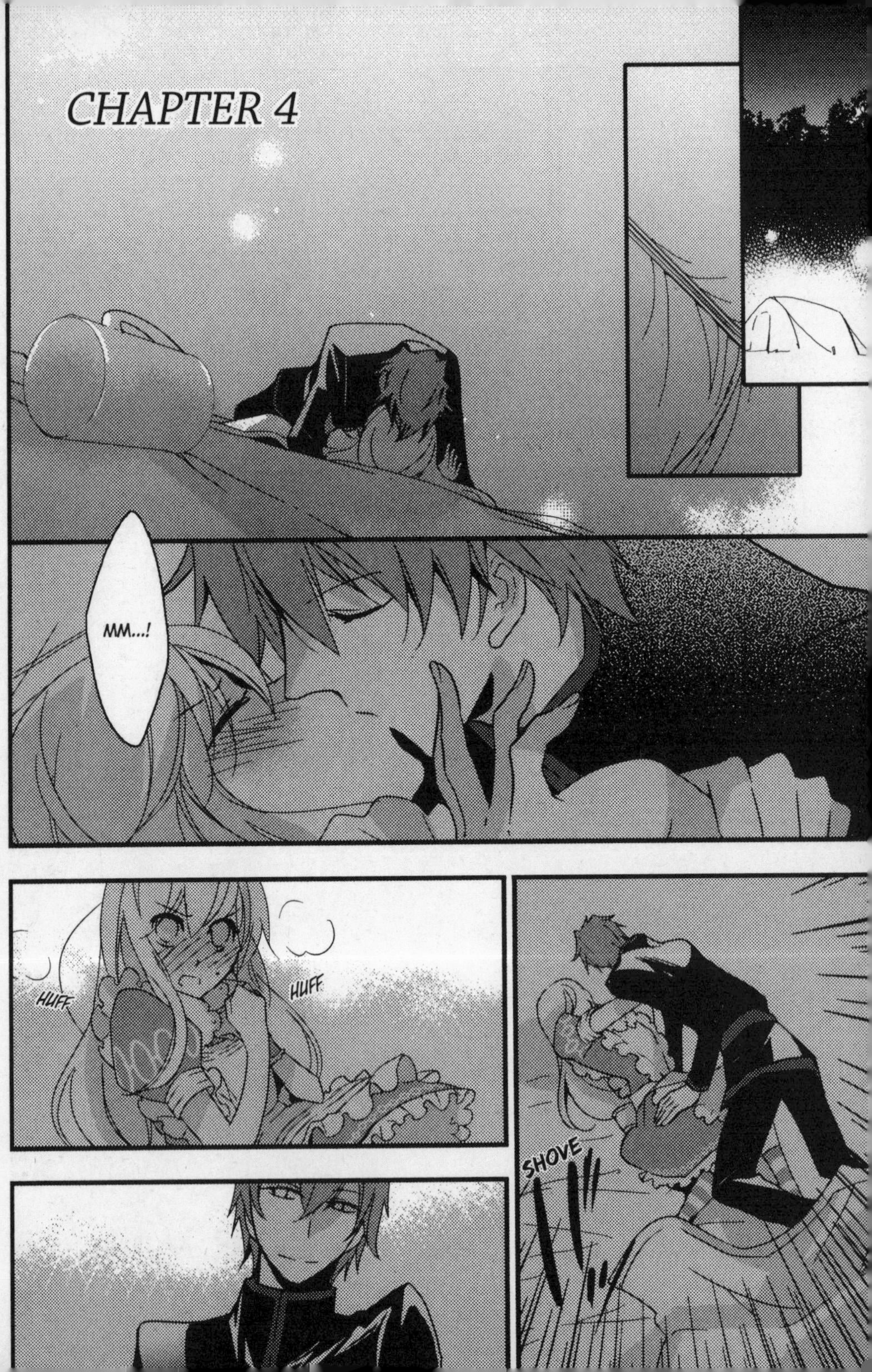
CHAPTER 4
MM...!
HUFF
HUFF
SHOVE

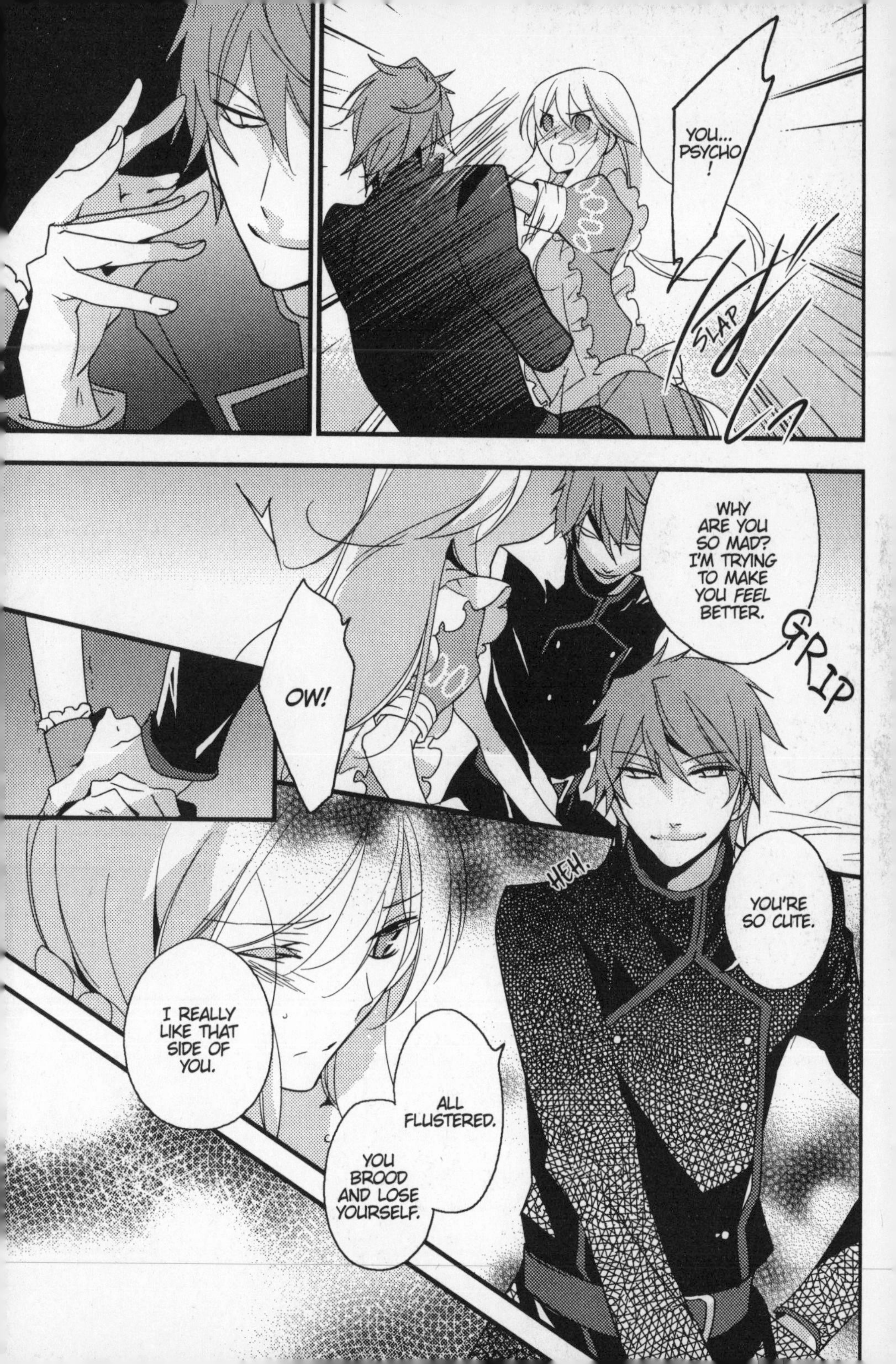
YOU... PSYCHO!
SLAP
WHY ARE YOU SO MAD? I'M TRYING TO MAKE YOU FEEL BETTER.
GRIP
OW!
HEH.
YOU'RE SO CUTE.
I REALLY LIKE THAT SIDE OF YOU.
ALL FLUSTERED.
YOU BROOD AND LOSE YOURSELF.

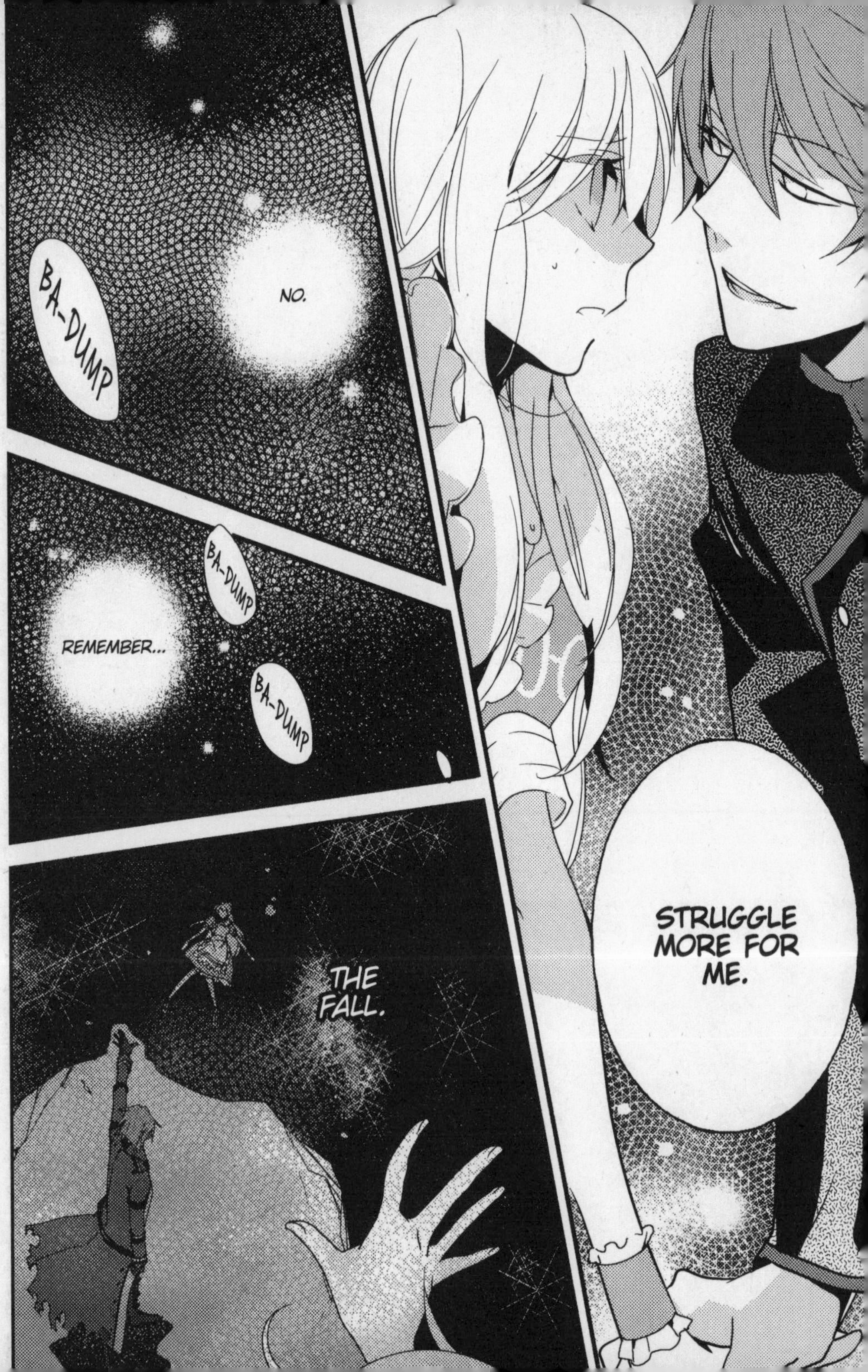
STRUGGLE MORE FOR ME.
NO.
BA-DUMP
BA-DUMP
BA-DUMP
REMEMBER...
THE FALL.

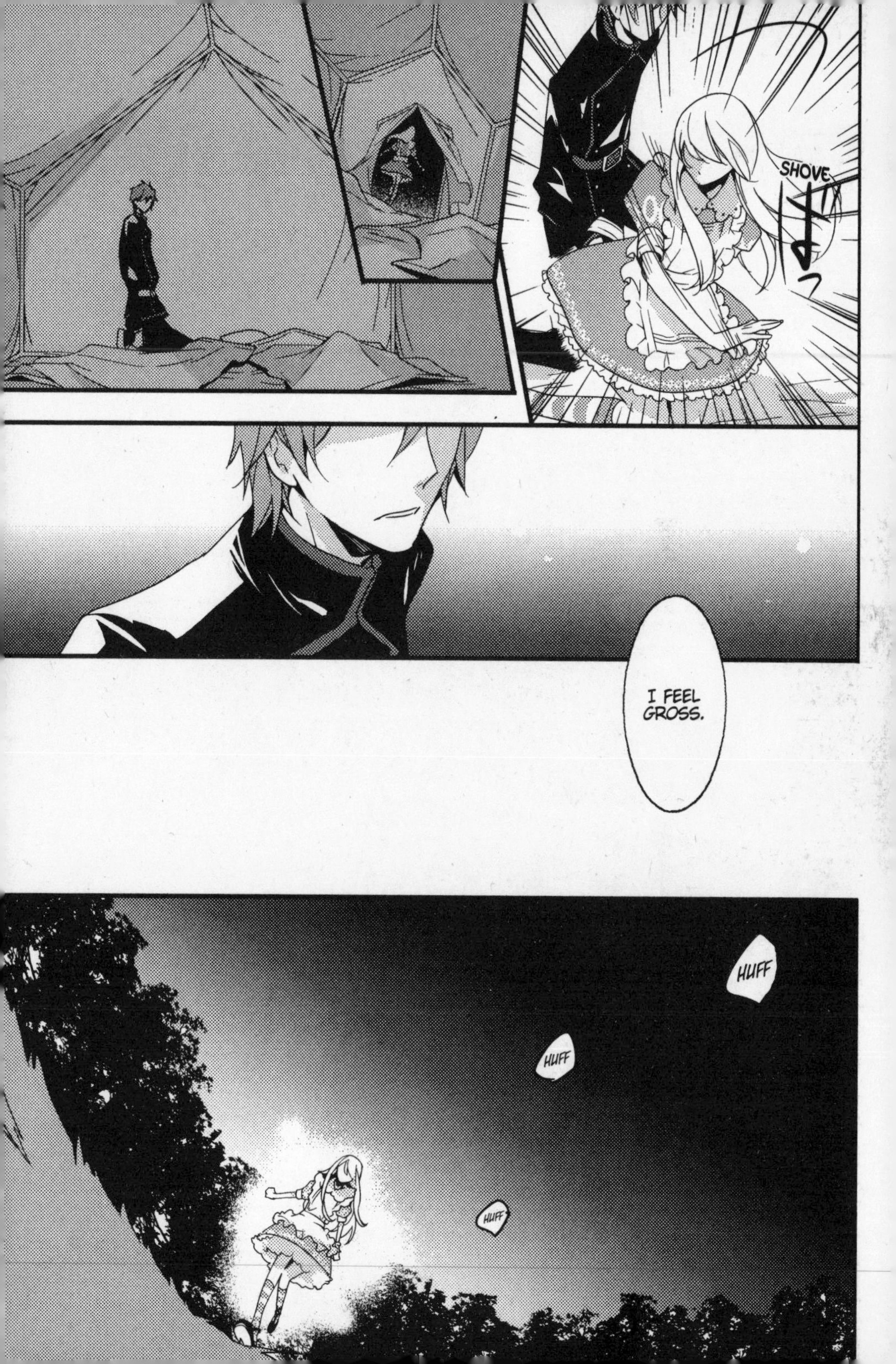
SHOVE
I FEEL GROSS.
HUFF
HUFF
HUFF

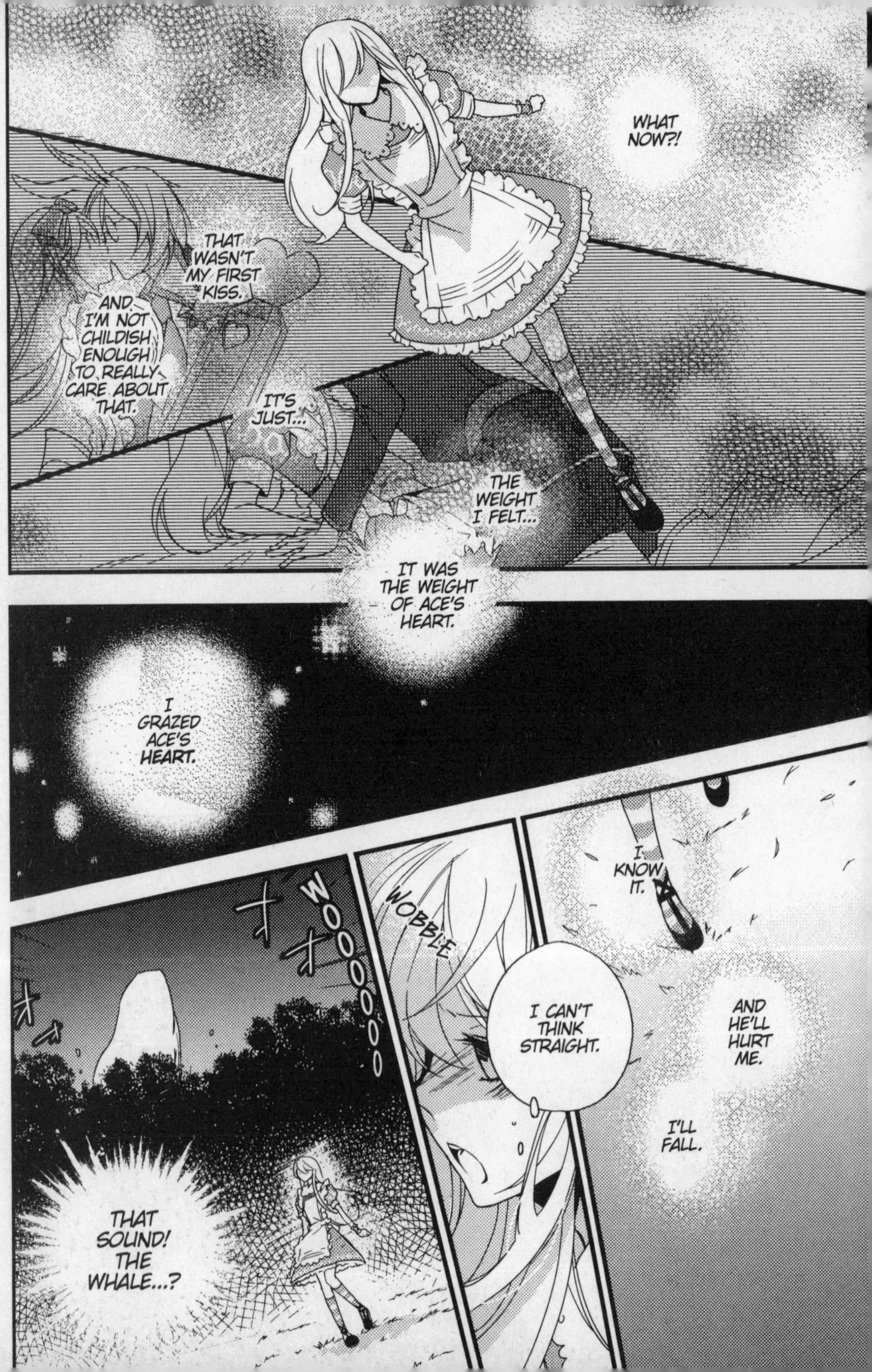
WHAT NOW?!
THAT WASN'T MY FIRST KISS.
AND I'M NOT CHILDISH ENOUGH TO REALLY CARE ABOUT THAT.
IT'S JUST...
THE WEIGHT I FELT...
IT WAS THE WEIGHT OF ACE'S HEART.
I GRAZED ACE'S HEART.
I KNOW IT.
AND HE'LL HURT ME.
I'LL FALL.
WOBBLE
I CAN'T THINK STRAIGHT.
WOOOOOOOO
THAT SOUND! THE WHALE...?

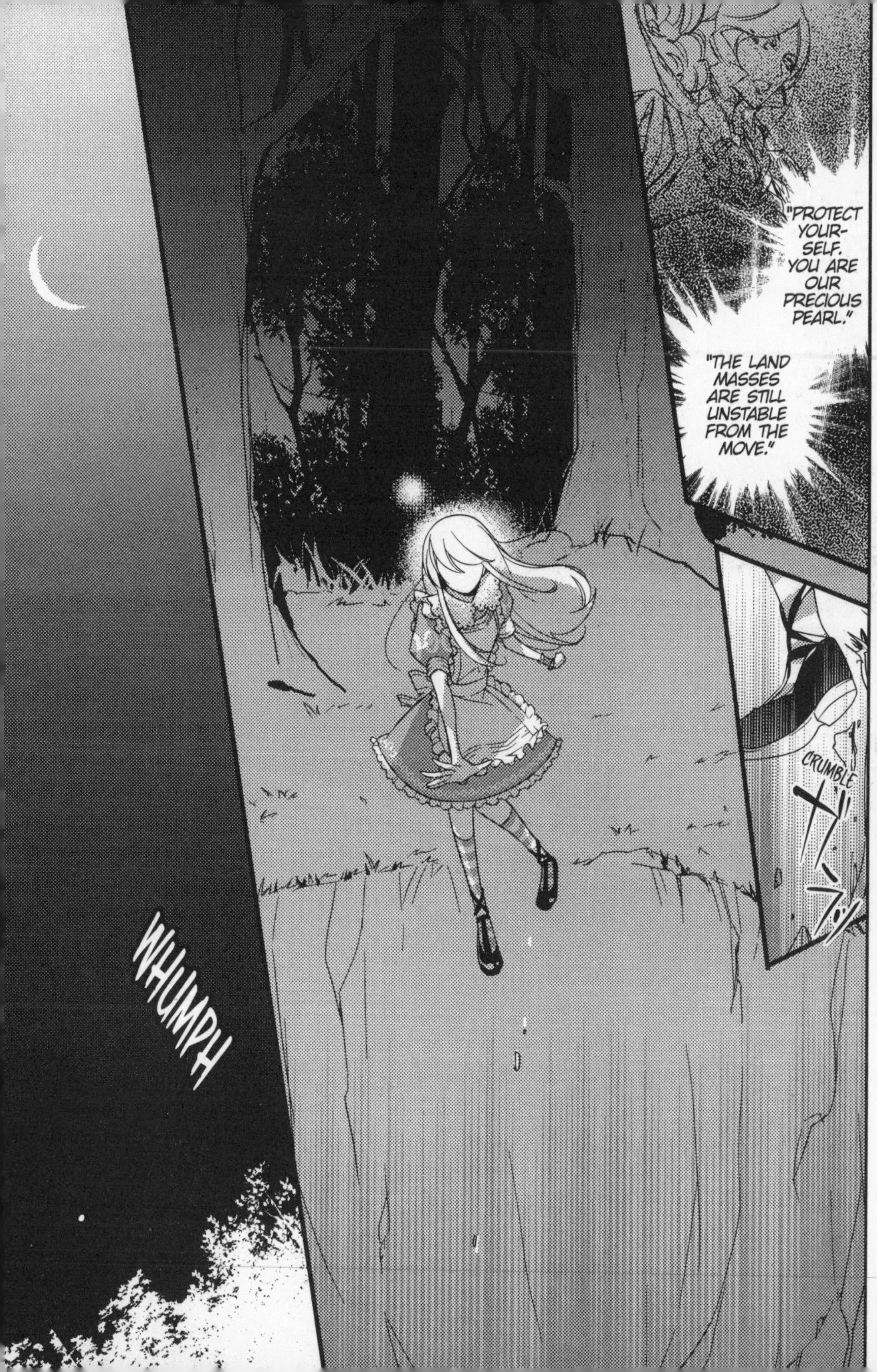
"PROTECT YOUR-SELF. YOU ARE OUR PRECIOUS PEARL."
"THE LAND MASSES ARE STILL UNSTABLE FROM THE MOVE."
CRUMBLE
WHUMPH

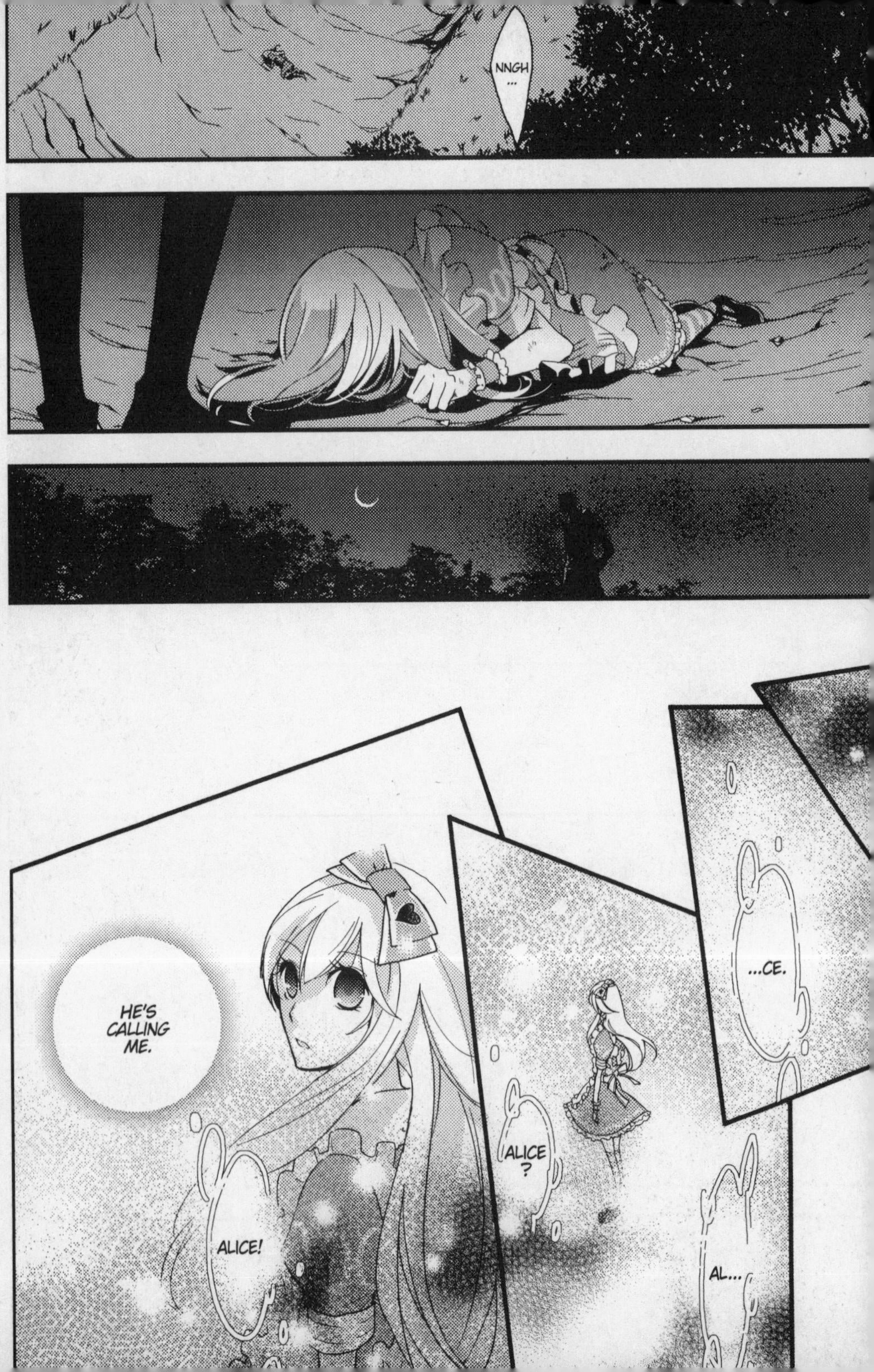
NNGH...
...CE.
AL...
ALICE?
ALICE!
HE'S CALLING ME.

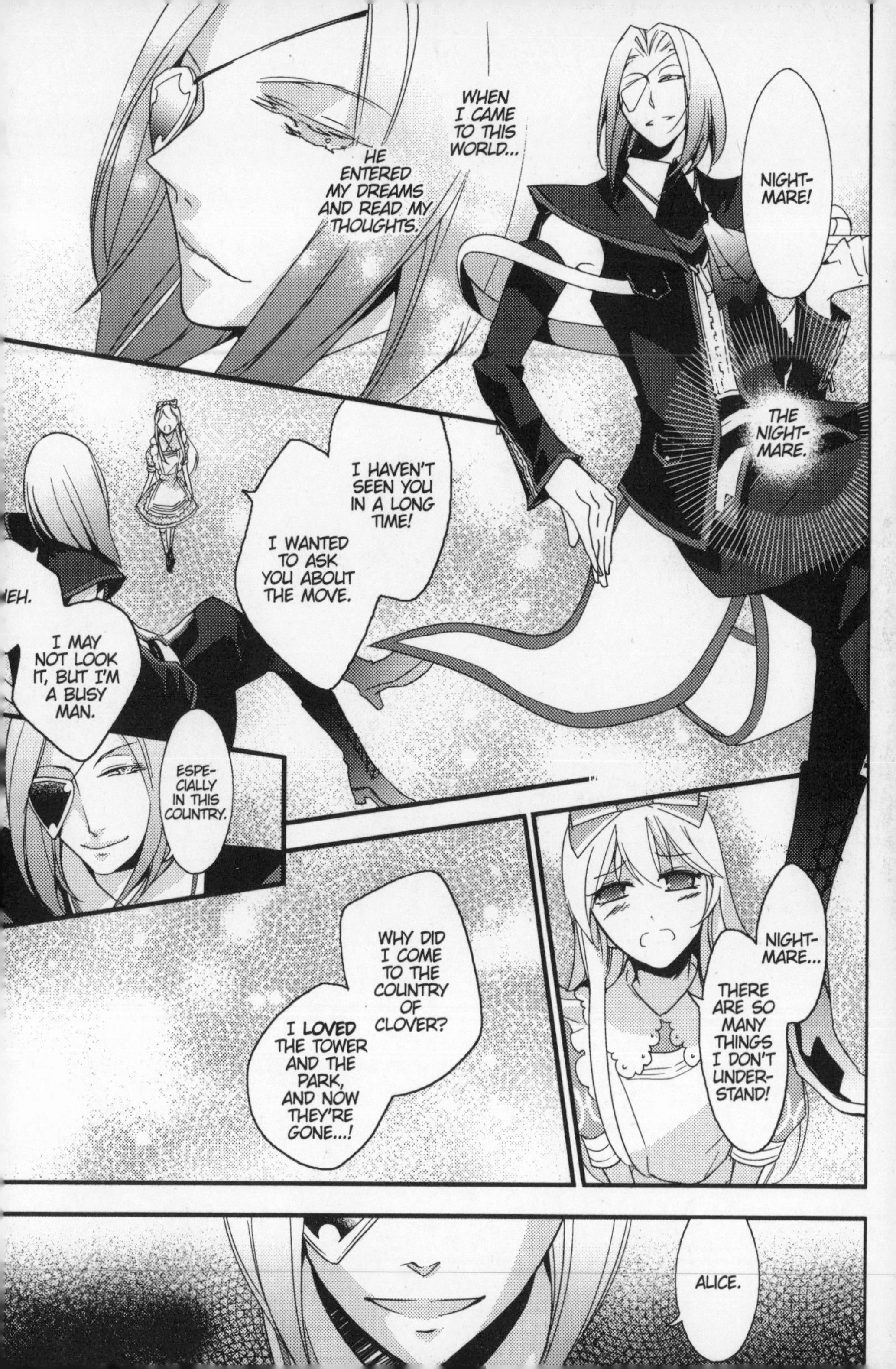
WHEN I CAME TO THIS WORLD...
HE ENTERED MY DREAMS AND READ MY THOUGHTS.
NIGHT-MARE!
THE NIGHT-MARE.
I HAVEN'T SEEN YOU IN A LONG TIME!
I WANTED TO ASK YOU ABOUT THE MOVE.
HEH.
I MAY NOT LOOK IT, BUT I'M A BUSY MAN.
ESPE-CIALLY IN THIS COUNTRY.
NIGHT-MARE...
THERE ARE SO MANY THINGS I DON'T UNDER-STAND!
WHY DID I COME TO THE COUNTRY OF CLOVER?
I **LOVED** THE TOWER AND THE PARK, AND NOW THEY'RE GONE...!
ALICE.

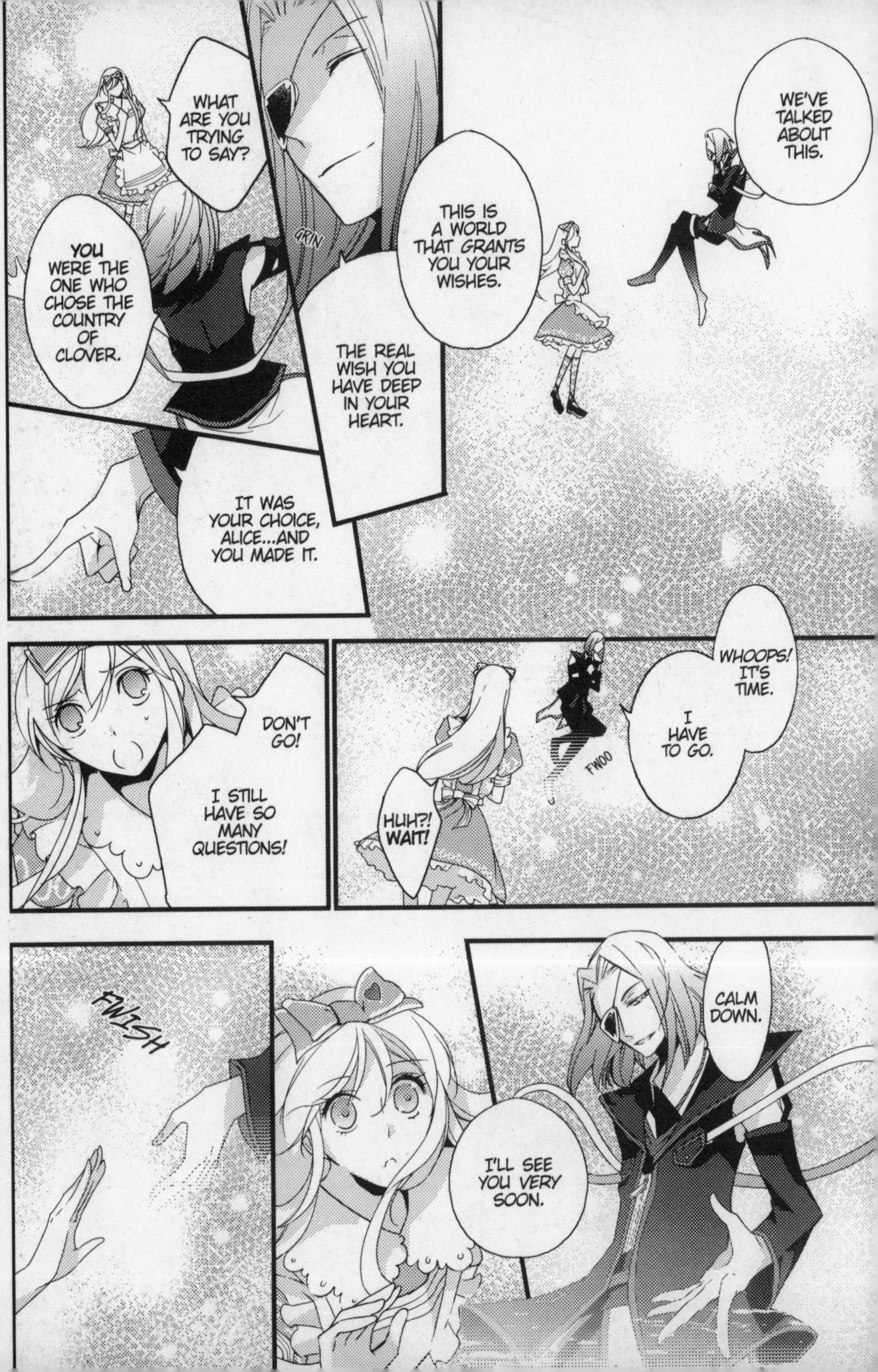
WE'VE TALKED ABOUT THIS.
THIS IS A WORLD THAT GRANTS YOU YOUR WISHES.
THE REAL WISH YOU HAVE DEEP IN YOUR HEART.
GRIN
WHAT ARE YOU TRYING TO SAY?
YOU WERE THE ONE WHO CHOSE THE COUNTRY OF CLOVER.
IT WAS YOUR CHOICE, ALICE...AND YOU MADE IT.
WHOOPS! IT'S TIME.
I HAVE TO GO.
FWOO
HUH?! WAIT!
DON'T GO!
I STILL HAVE SO MANY QUESTIONS!
CALM DOWN.
I'LL SEE YOU VERY SOON.
FWISH

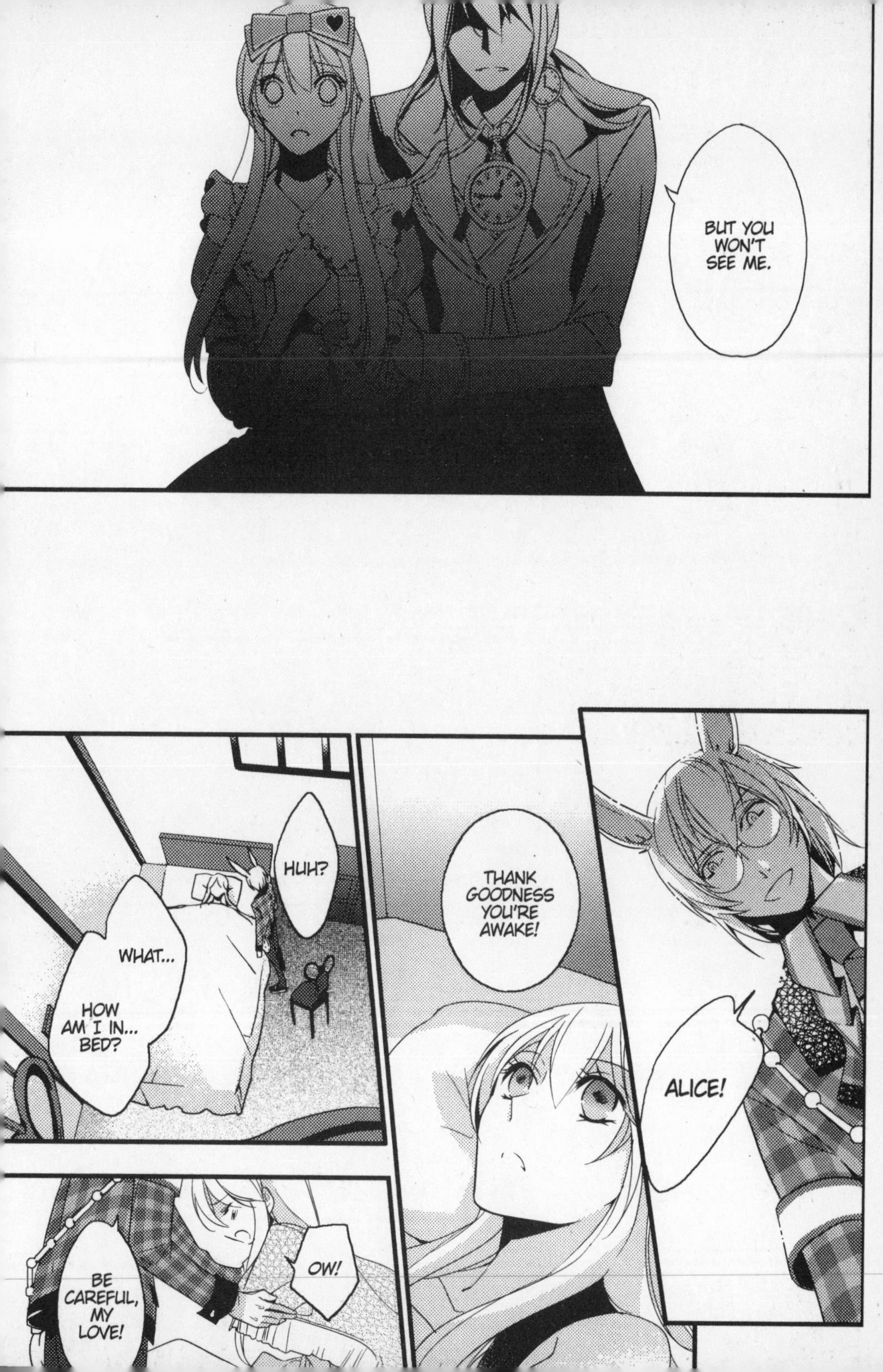
BUT YOU WON'T SEE ME.
ALICE!
THANK GOODNESS YOU'RE AWAKE!
HUH?
WHAT...
HOW AM I IN... BED?
OW!
BE CAREFUL, MY LOVE!

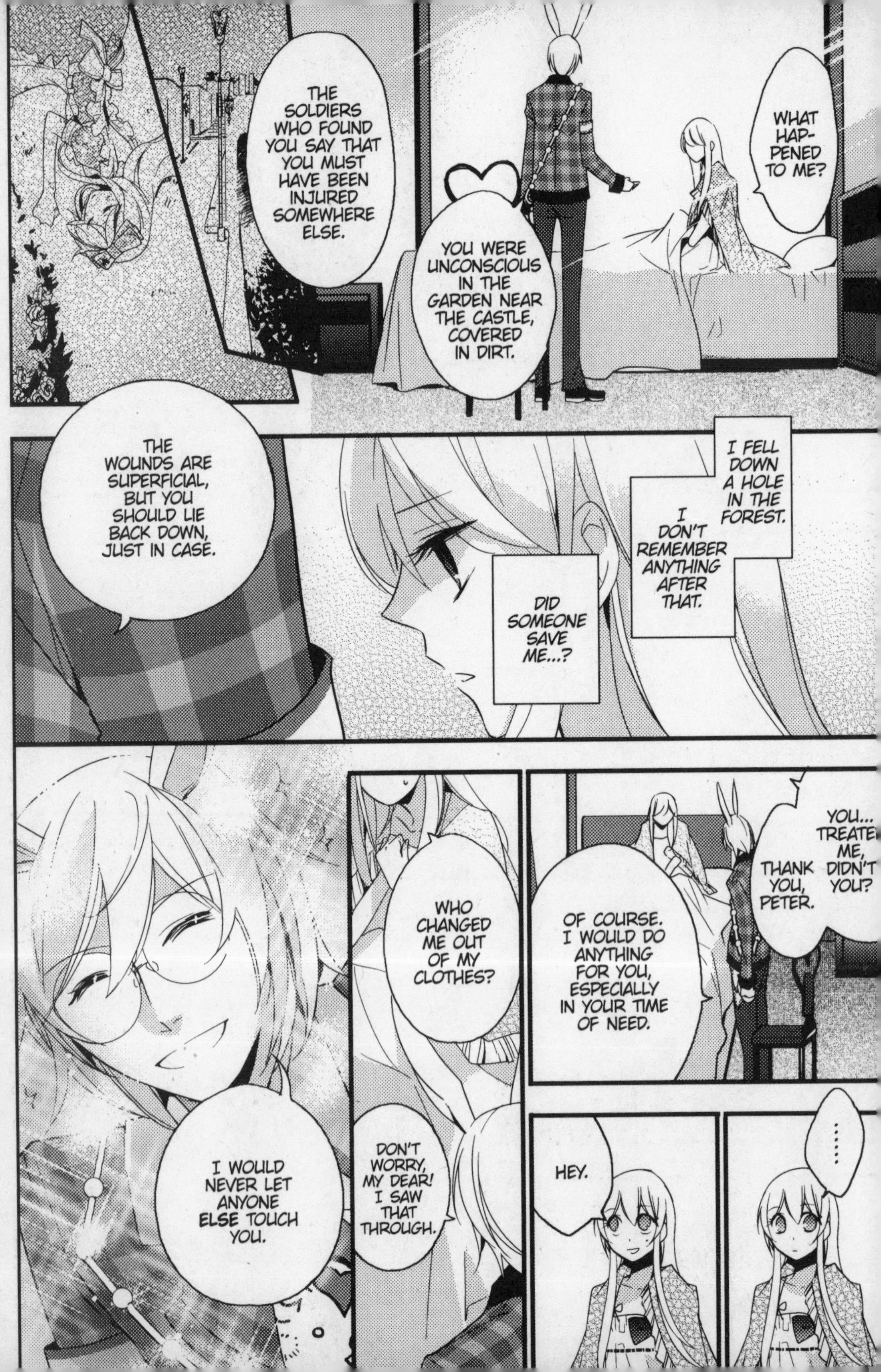
WHAT HAP-PENED TO ME?
YOU WERE UNCONSCIOUS IN THE GARDEN NEAR THE CASTLE, COVERED IN DIRT.
THE SOLDIERS WHO FOUND YOU SAY THAT YOU MUST HAVE BEEN INJURED SOMEWHERE ELSE.
I FELL DOWN A HOLE IN THE FOREST.
I DON'T REMEMBER ANYTHING AFTER THAT.
DID SOMEONE SAVE ME...?
THE WOUNDS ARE SUPERFICIAL, BUT YOU SHOULD LIE BACK DOWN, JUST IN CASE.
YOU... TREATE ME, DIDN'T YOU?
THANK YOU, PETER.
OF COURSE. I WOULD DO ANYTHING FOR YOU, ESPECIALLY IN YOUR TIME OF NEED.
WHO CHANGED ME OUT OF MY CLOTHES?
DON'T WORRY, MY DEAR! I SAW THAT THROUGH.
I WOULD NEVER LET ANYONE ELSE TOUCH YOU.
......
HEY.

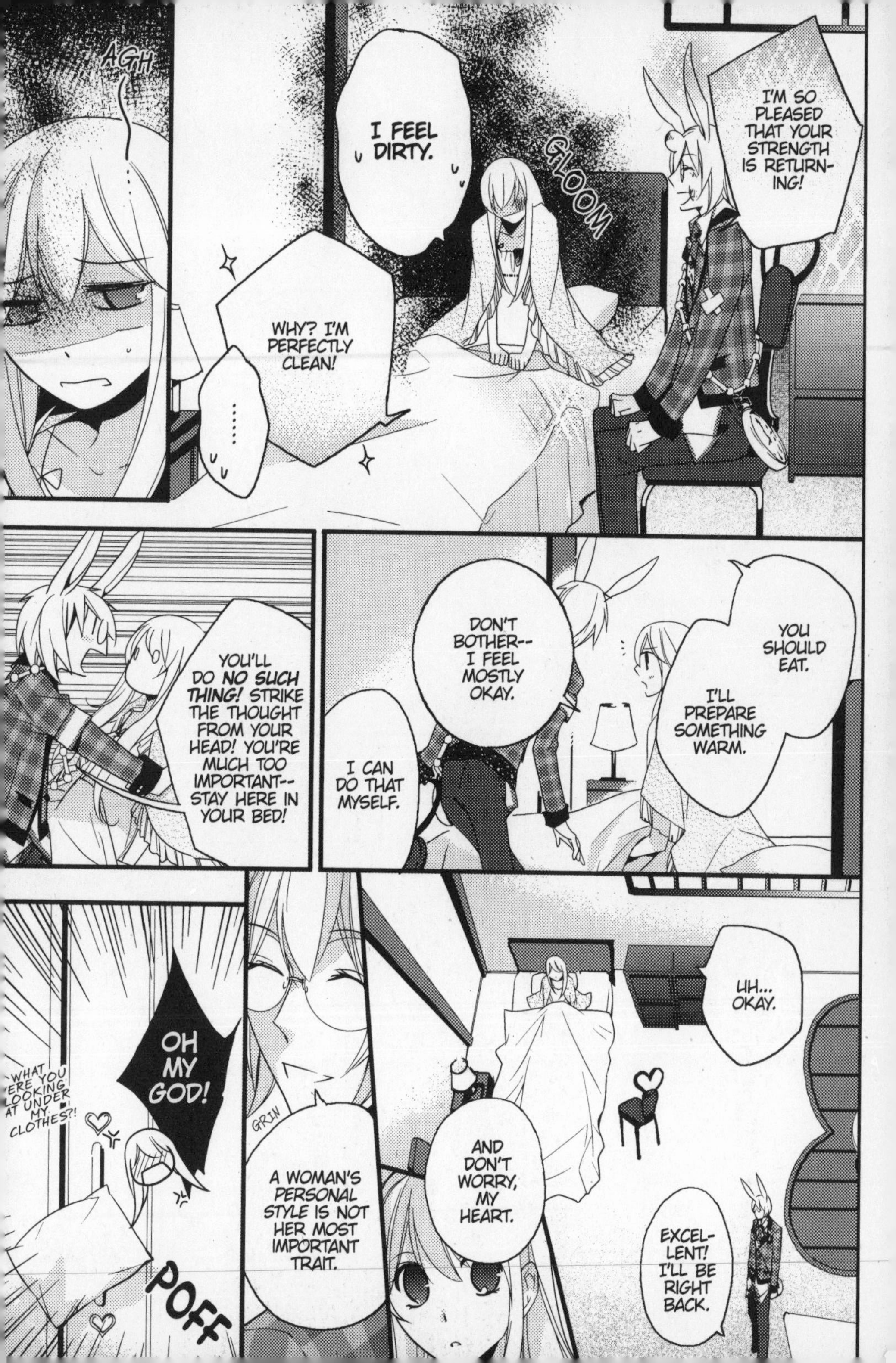
I'M SO PLEASED THAT YOUR STRENGTH IS RETURNING!
I FEEL DIRTY.
GLOOM
WHY? I'M PERFECTLY CLEAN!
......
AGH
YOU SHOULD EAT.
I'LL PREPARE SOMETHING WARM.
DON'T BOTHER-- I FEEL MOSTLY OKAY.
I CAN DO THAT MYSELF.
YOU'LL DO NO SUCH THING! STRIKE THE THOUGHT FROM YOUR HEAD! YOU'RE MUCH TOO IMPORTANT-- STAY HERE IN YOUR BED!
UH... OKAY.
EXCEL-LENT! I'LL BE RIGHT BACK.
AND DON'T WORRY, MY HEART.
GRIN
A WOMAN'S PERSONAL STYLE IS NOT HER MOST IMPORTANT TRAIT.
OH MY GOD!
WHAT ERE YOU LOOKING AT UNDER MY CLOTHES?!
POFF

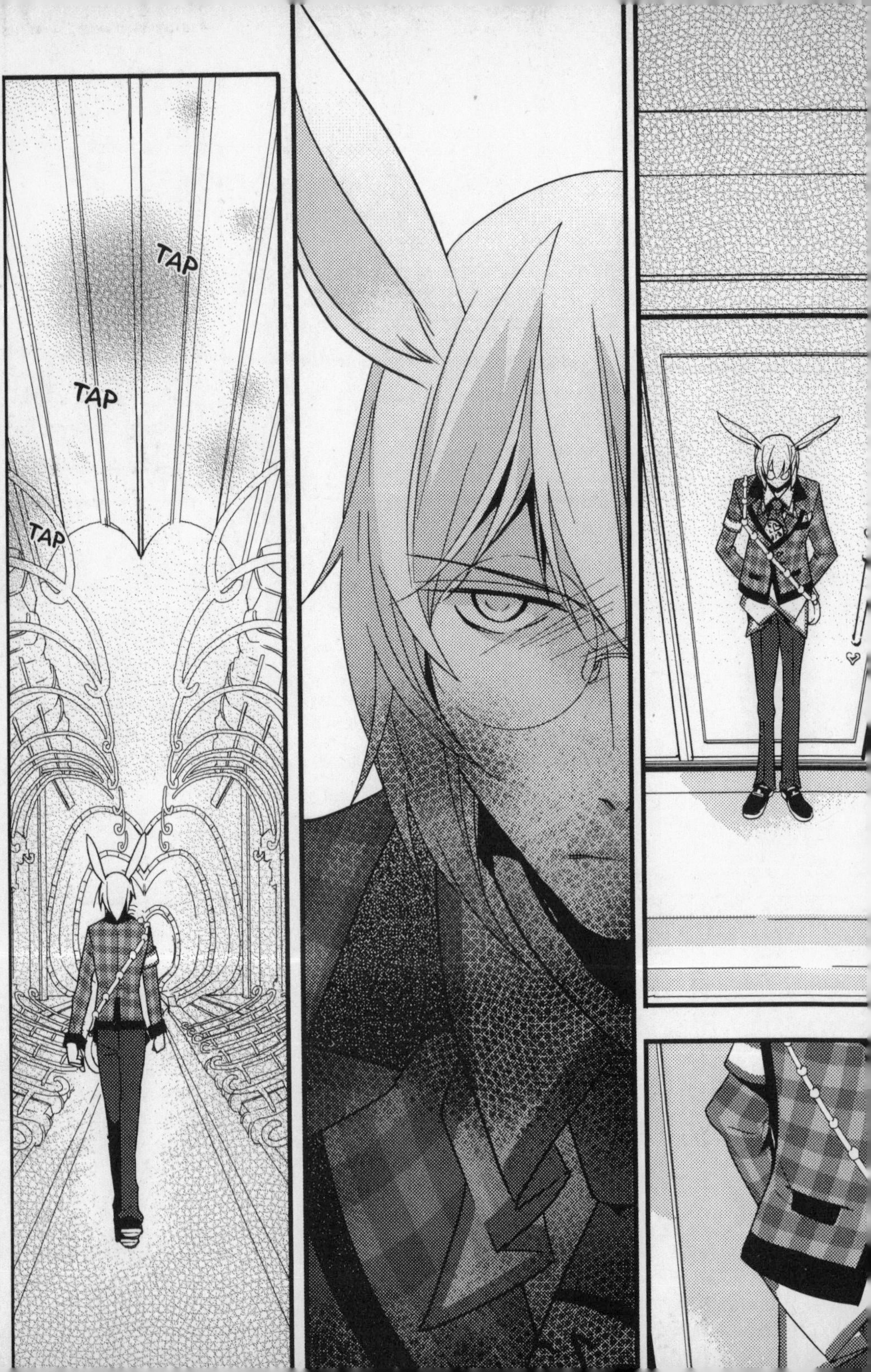
TAP
TAP
TAP

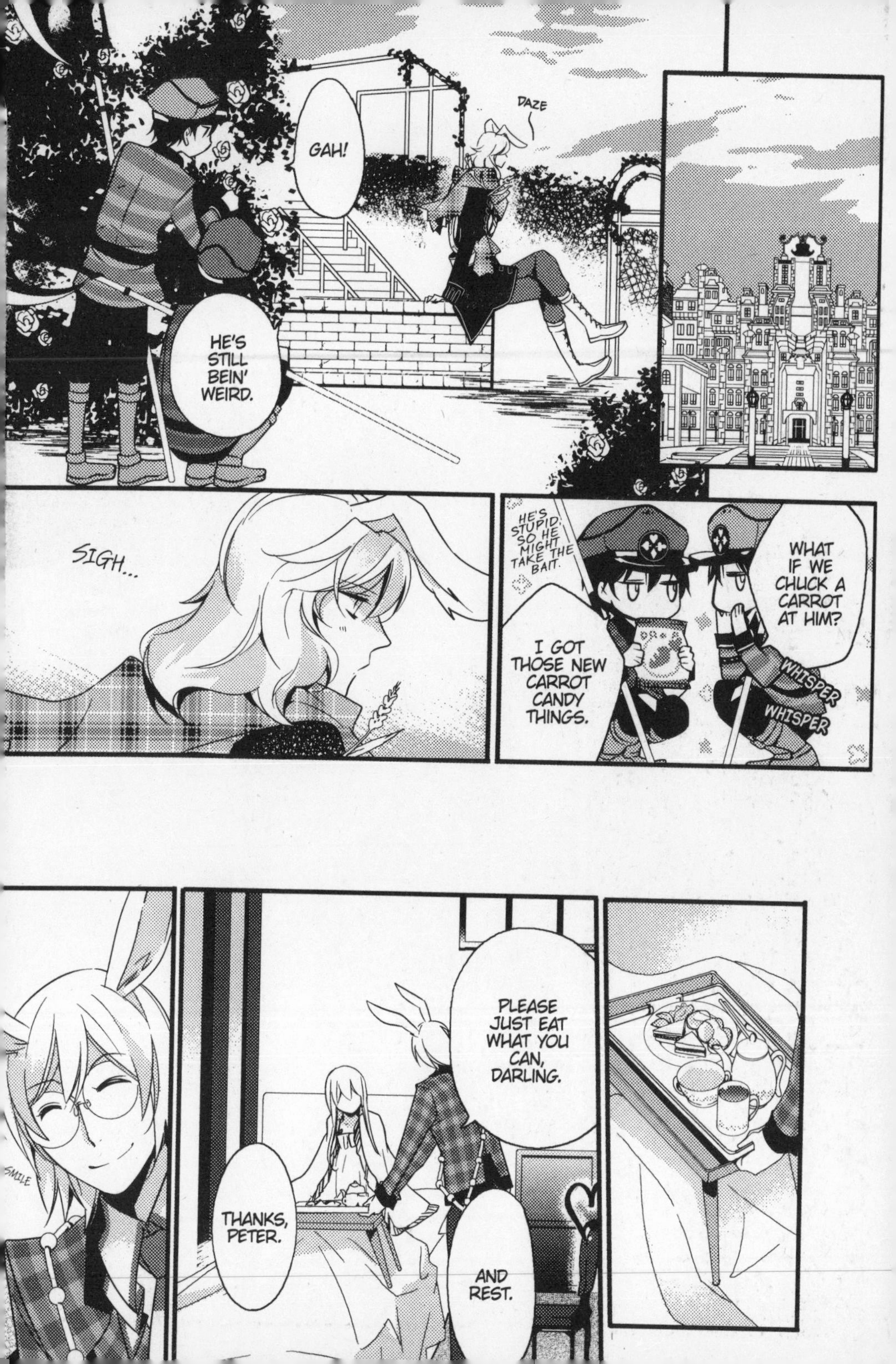
DAZE
GAH!
HE'S STILL BEIN' WEIRD.
WHAT IF WE CHUCK A CARROT AT HIM?
WHISPER
WHISPER
HE'S STUPID, SO HE MIGHT TAKE THE BAIT.
I GOT THOSE NEW CARROT CANDY THINGS.
SIGH...
PLEASE JUST EAT WHAT YOU CAN, DARLING.
AND REST.
THANKS, PETER.
SMILE

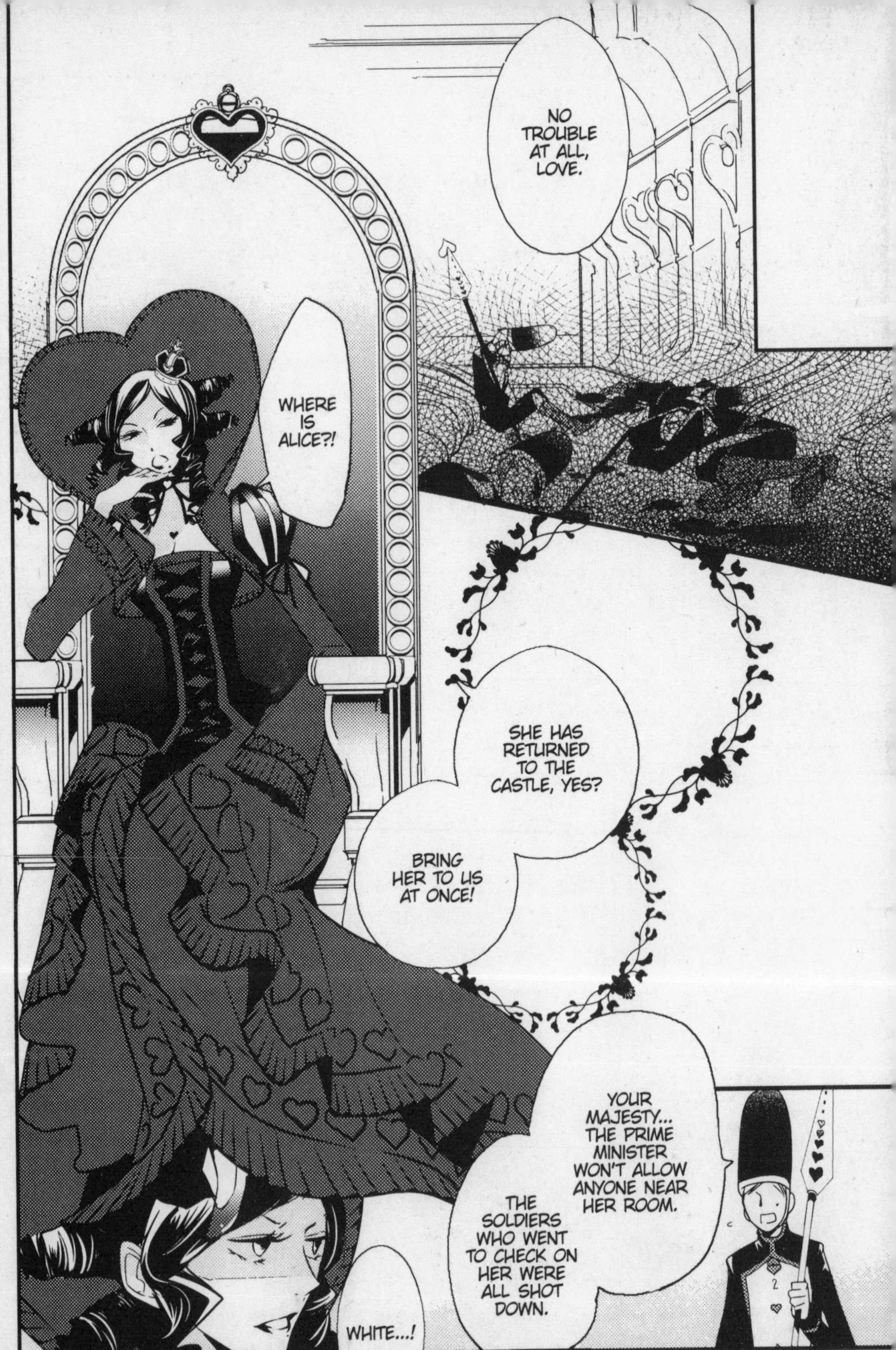
NO TROUBLE AT ALL, LOVE.
WHERE IS ALICE?!
SHE HAS RETURNED TO THE CASTLE, YES?
BRING HER TO US AT ONCE!
YOUR MAJESTY... THE PRIME MINISTER WON'T ALLOW ANYONE NEAR HER ROOM.
THE SOLDIERS WHO WENT TO CHECK ON HER WERE ALL SHOT DOWN.
WHITE...!

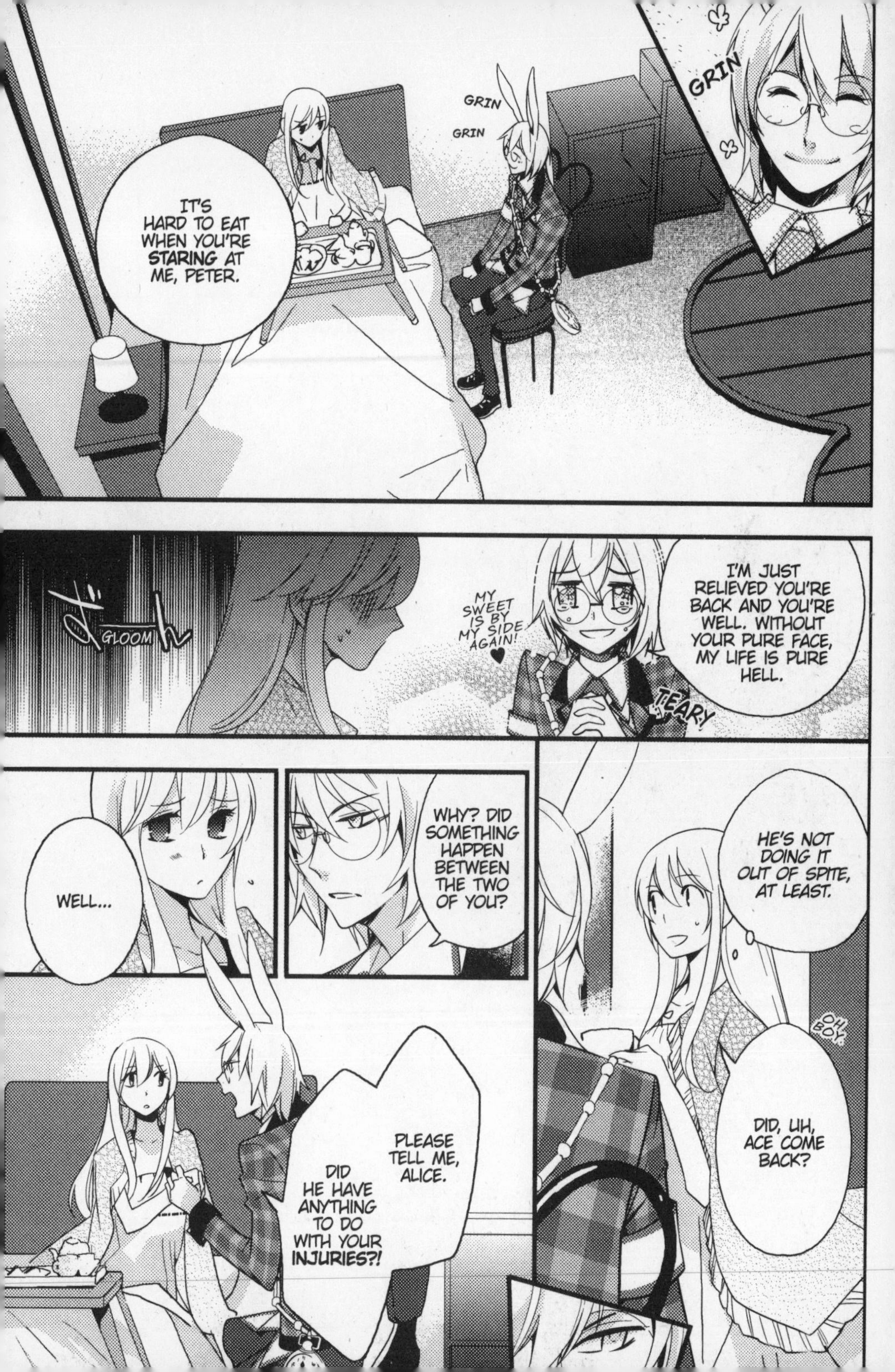
GRIN
GRIN
GRIN
IT'S HARD TO EAT WHEN YOU'RE STARING AT ME, PETER.
I'M JUST RELIEVED YOU'RE BACK AND YOU'RE WELL. WITHOUT YOUR PURE FACE, MY LIFE IS PURE HELL.
MY SWEET IS BY MY SIDE AGAIN! ♥
TEARY
GLOOM
HE'S NOT DOING IT OUT OF SPITE, AT LEAST.
OH, BOY.
DID, UH, ACE COME BACK?
WHY? DID SOMETHING HAPPEN BETWEEN THE TWO OF YOU?
WELL...
PLEASE TELL ME, ALICE.
DID HE HAVE ANYTHING TO DO WITH YOUR INJURIES?!

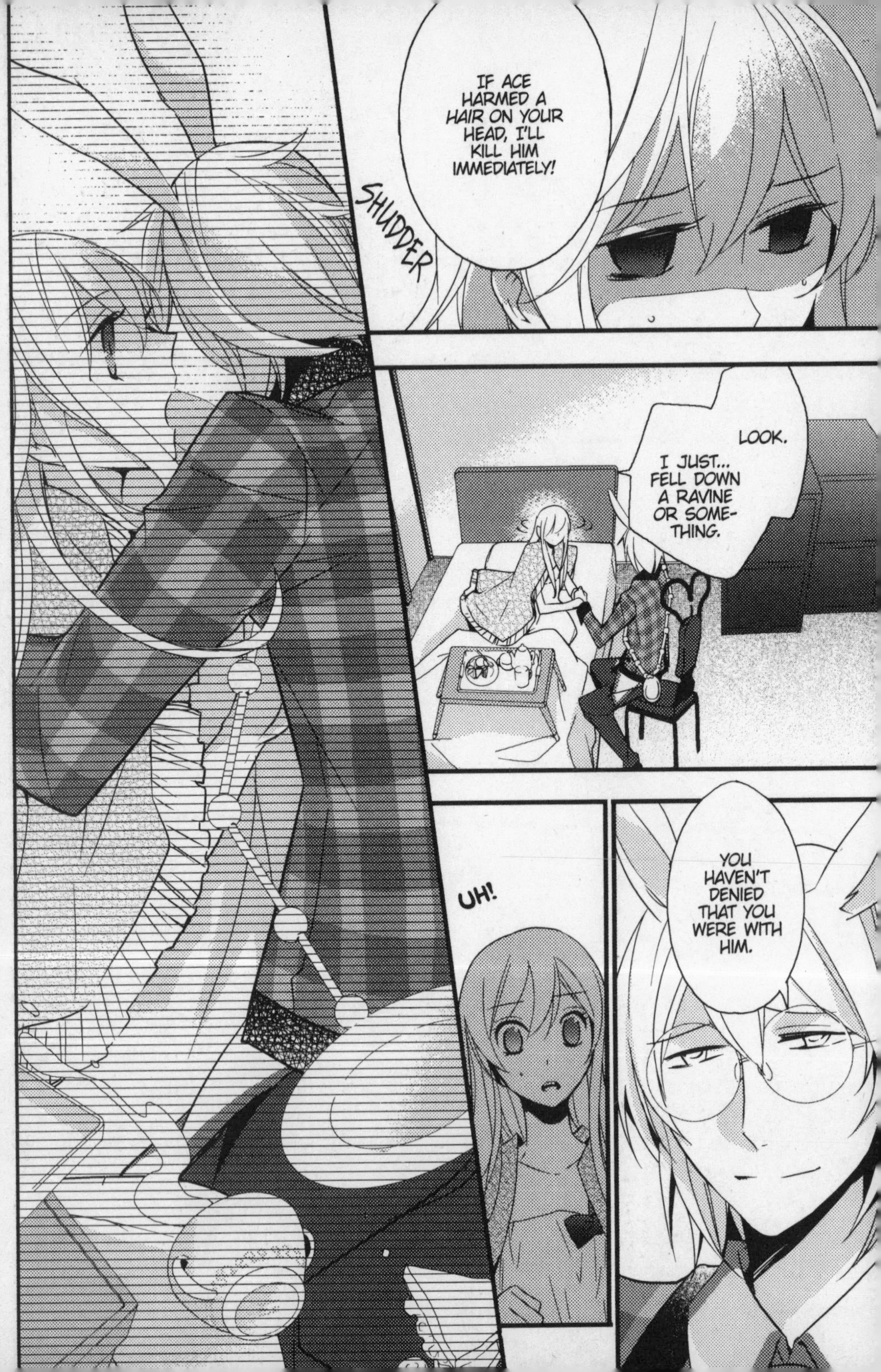
IF ACE HARMED A HAIR ON YOUR HEAD, I'LL KILL HIM IMMEDIATELY!
SHUDDER
LOOK.
I JUST... FELL DOWN A RAVINE OR SOME-THING.
YOU HAVEN'T DENIED THAT YOU WERE WITH HIM.
UH!

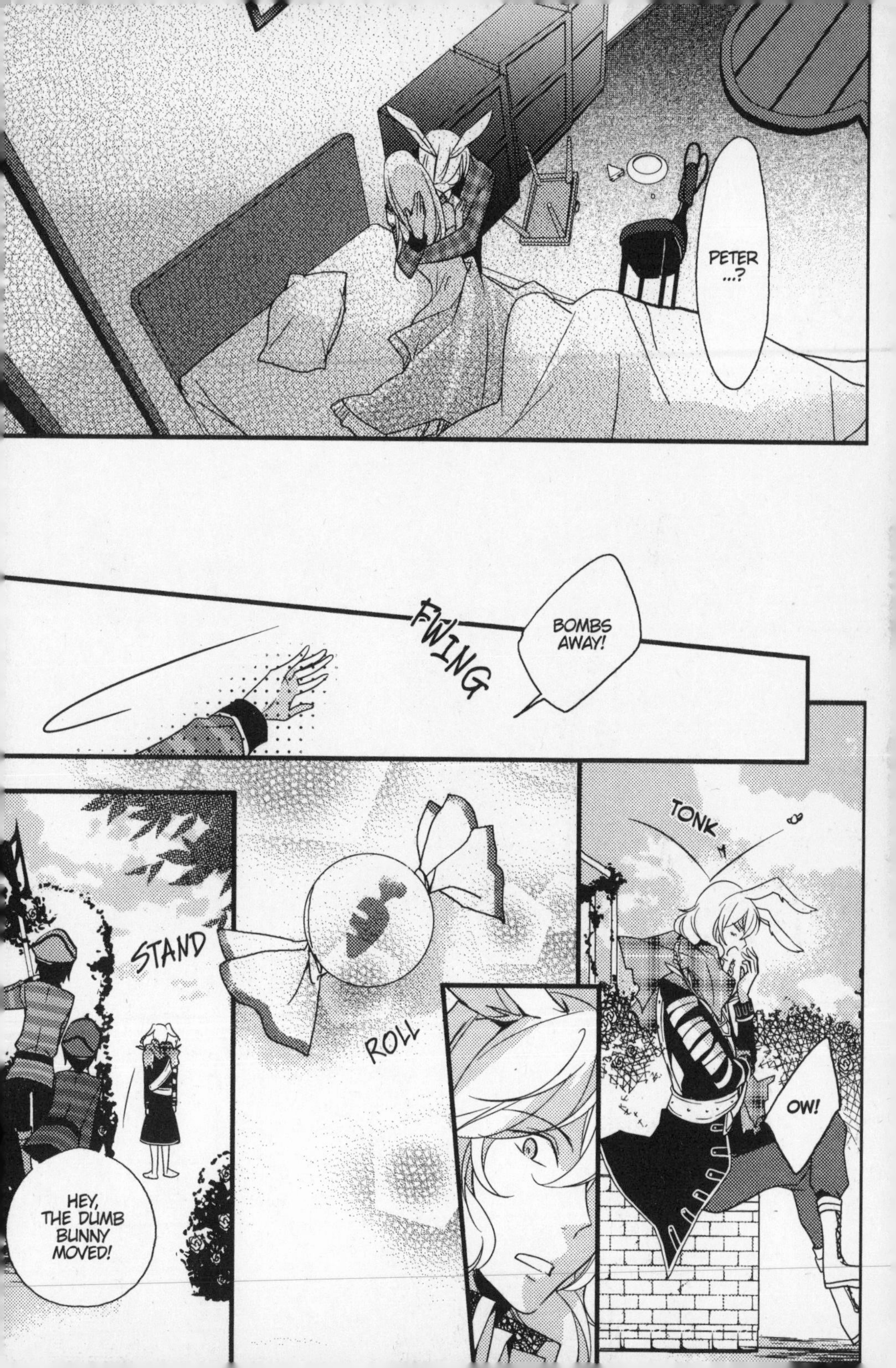
PETER ...?
FWING
BOMBS AWAY!
TONK
OW!
ROLL
STAND
HEY, THE DUMB BUNNY MOVED!

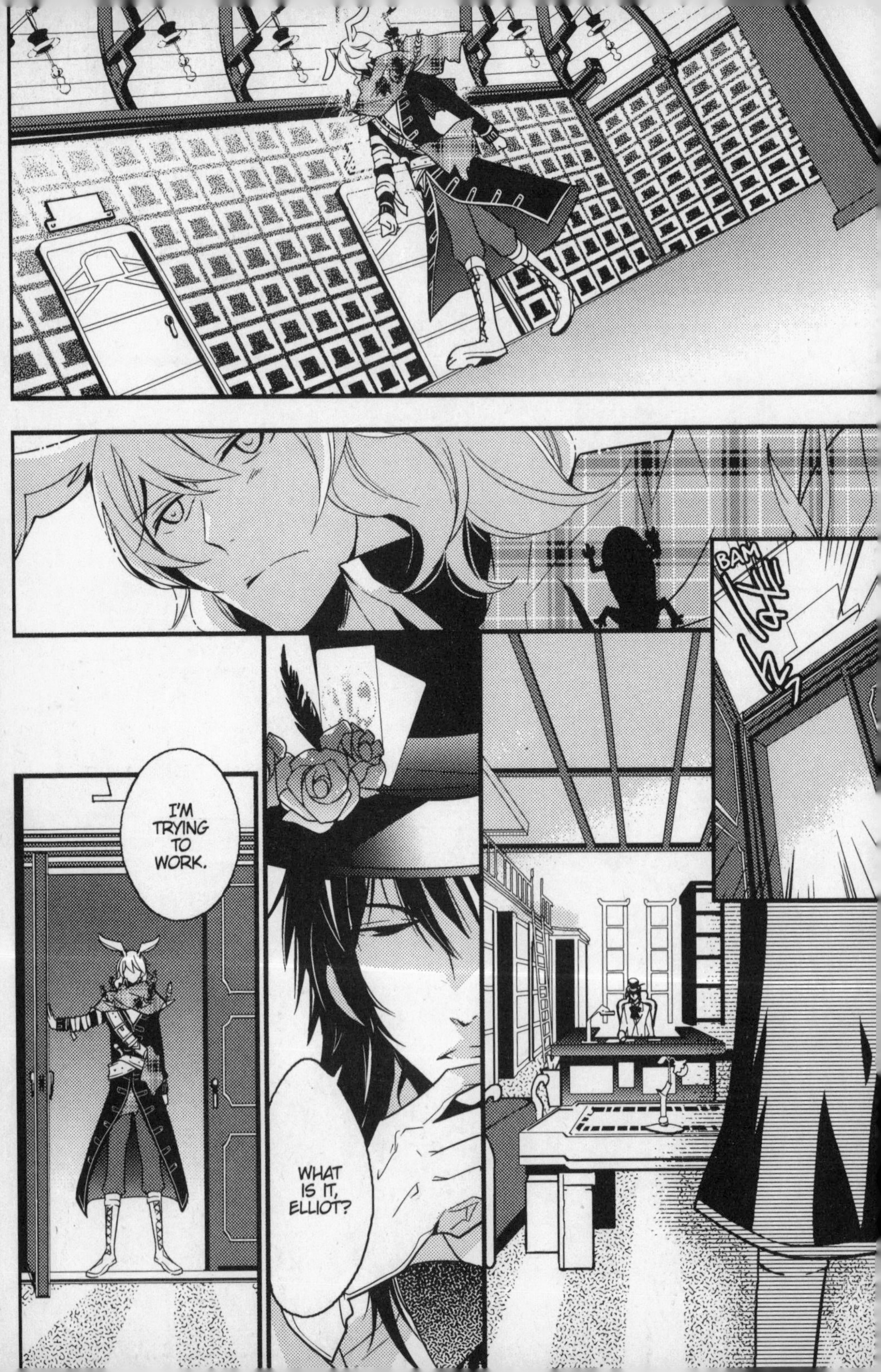
BAM
WHAT IS IT, ELLIOT?
I'M TRYING TO WORK.

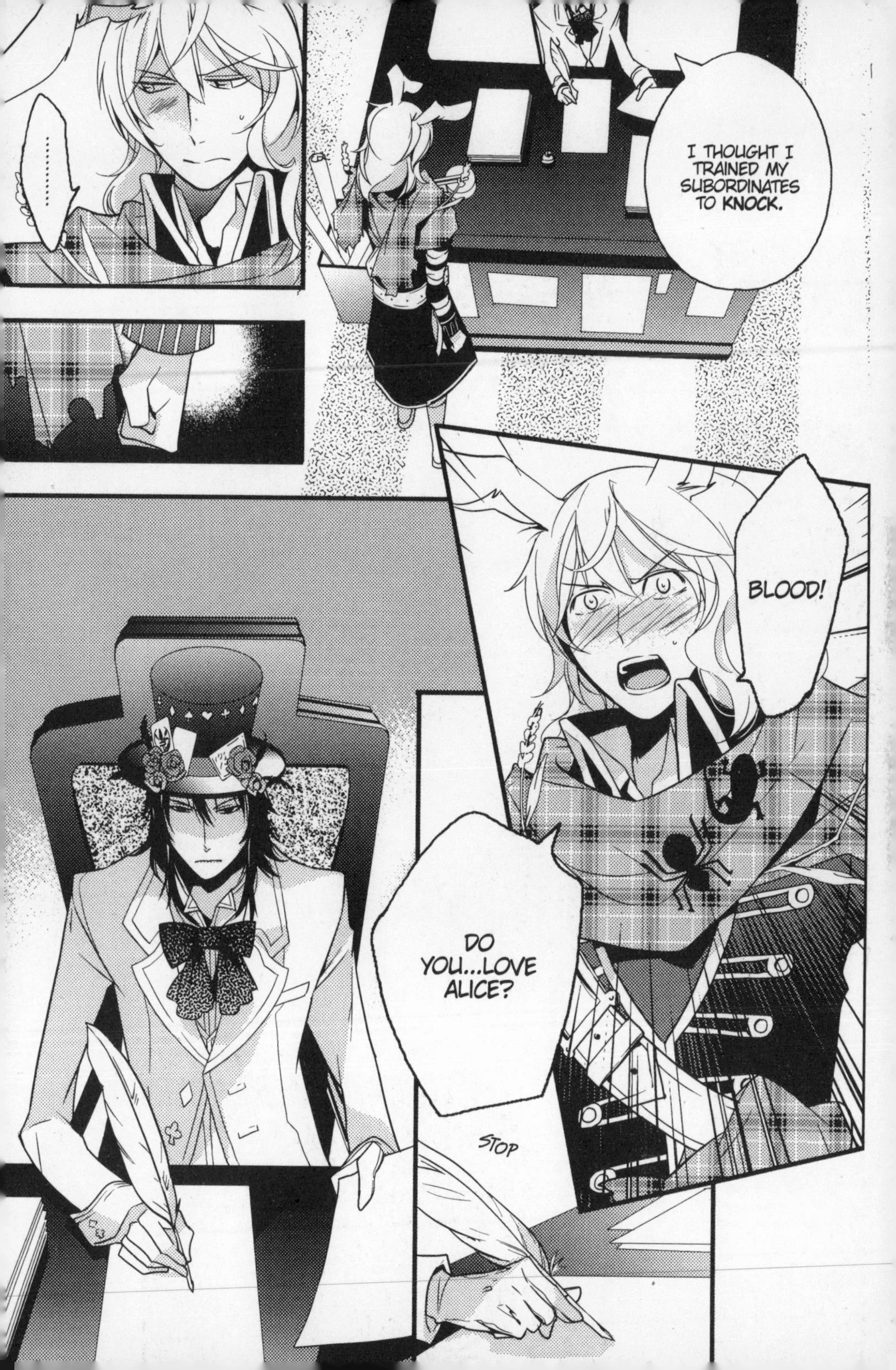
I THOUGHT I TRAINED MY SUBORDINATES TO KNOCK.
......
BLOOD!
DO YOU...LOVE ALICE?
STOP

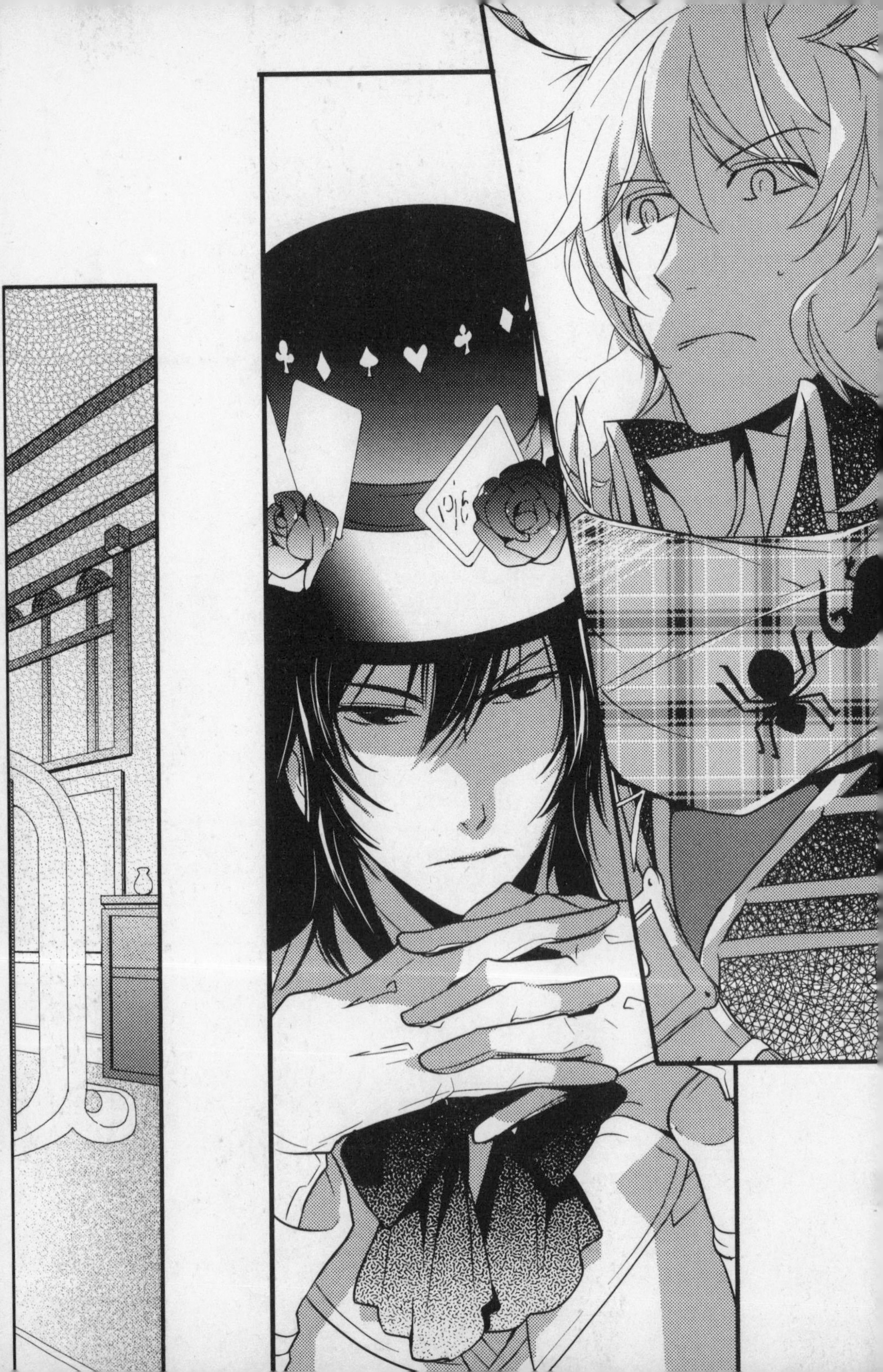

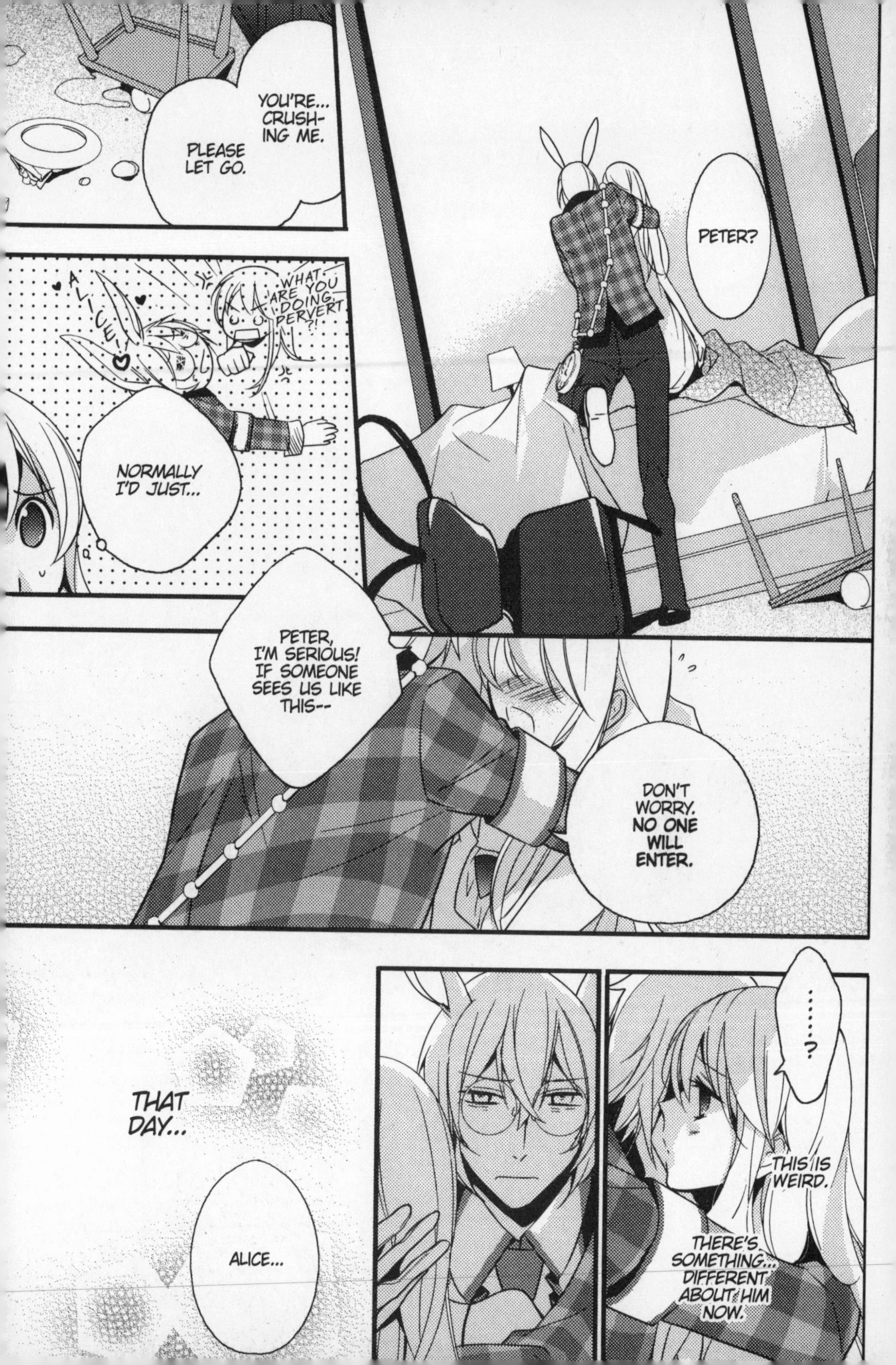
PETER?
YOU'RE... CRUSHING-ING ME.
PLEASE LET GO.
WHAT ARE YOU DOING, PERVERT?!
ALICE!
NORMALLY I'D JUST...
PETER, I'M SERIOUS! IF SOMEONE SEES US LIKE THIS--
DON'T WORRY. NO ONE WILL ENTER.
......?
THIS IS WEIRD.
THERE'S SOMETHING... DIFFERENT ABOUT HIM NOW.
THAT DAY...
ALICE...

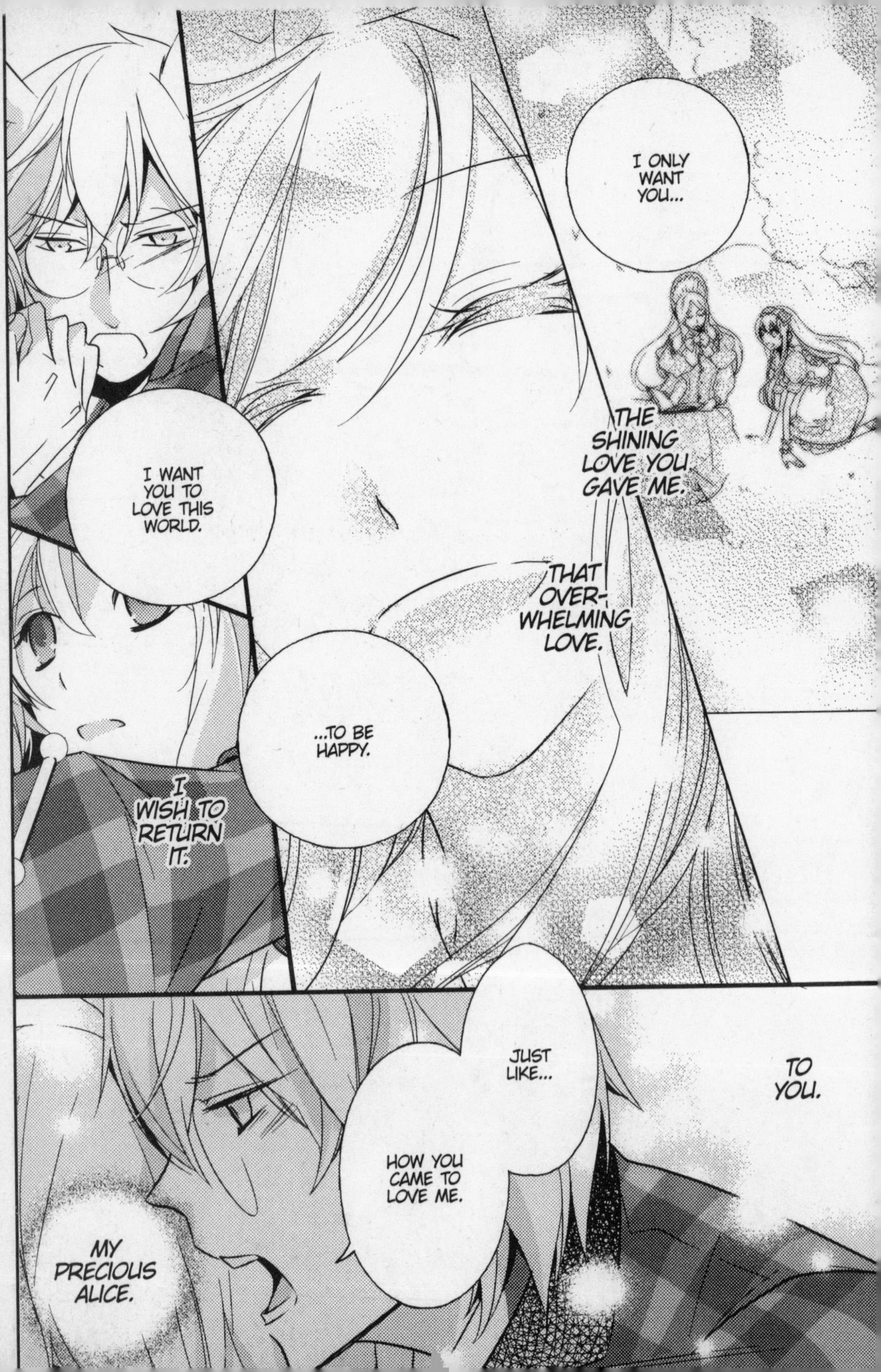
I ONLY WANT YOU...
THE SHINING LOVE YOU GAVE ME.
THAT OVER-WHELMING LOVE.
I WANT YOU TO LOVE THIS WORLD.
...TO BE HAPPY.
I WISH TO RETURN IT.
TO YOU.
JUST LIKE...
HOW YOU CAME TO LOVE ME.
MY PRECIOUS ALICE.

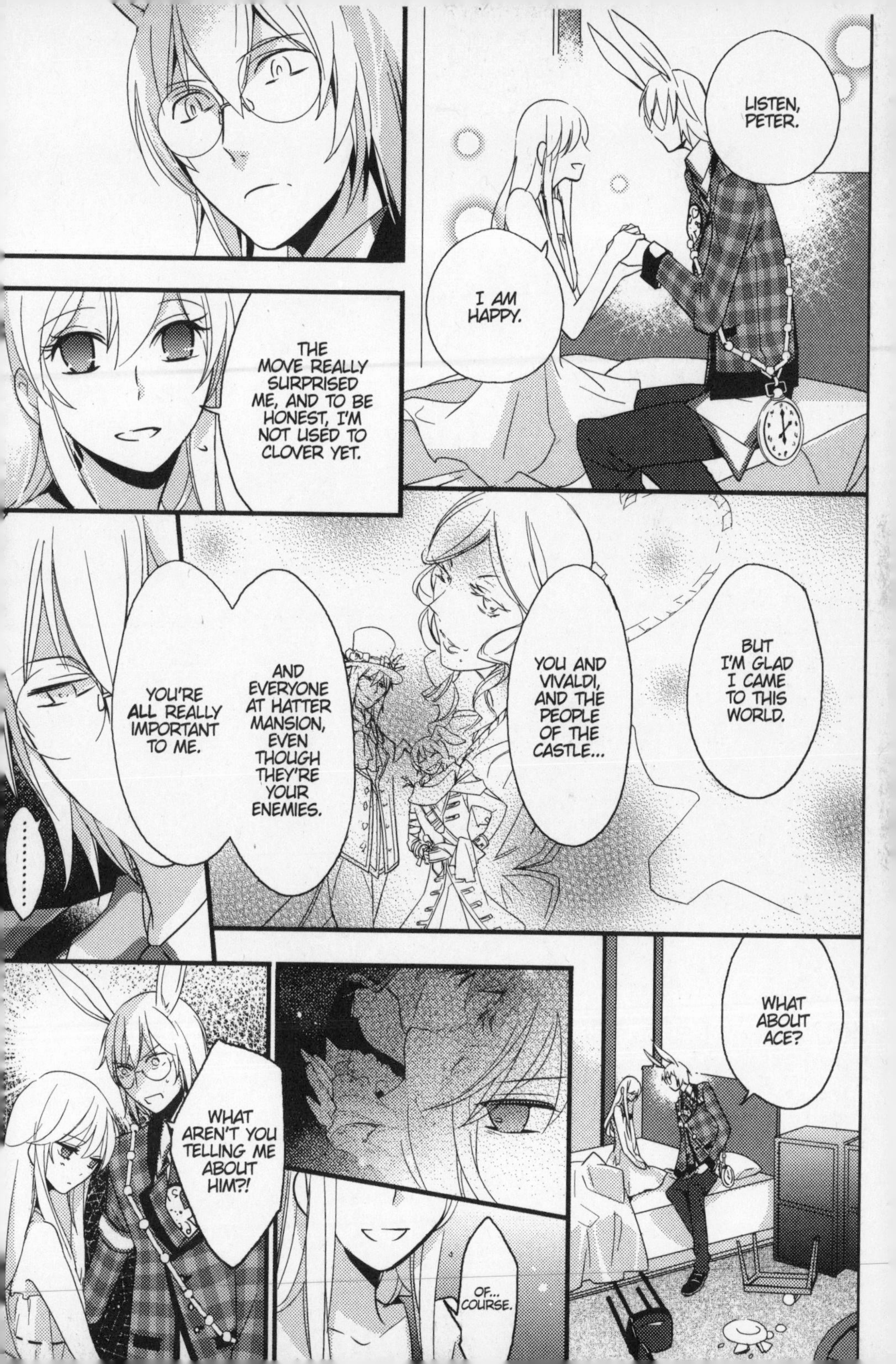
LISTEN, PETER.
I AM HAPPY.
THE MOVE REALLY SURPRISED ME, AND TO BE HONEST, I'M NOT USED TO CLOVER YET.
BUT I'M GLAD I CAME TO THIS WORLD.
YOU AND VIVALDI, AND THE PEOPLE OF THE CASTLE...
AND EVERYONE AT HATTER MANSION, EVEN THOUGH THEY'RE YOUR ENEMIES.
YOU'RE ALL REALLY IMPORTANT TO ME.
......
WHAT ABOUT ACE?
OF... COURSE.
WHAT AREN'T YOU TELLING ME ABOUT HIM?!

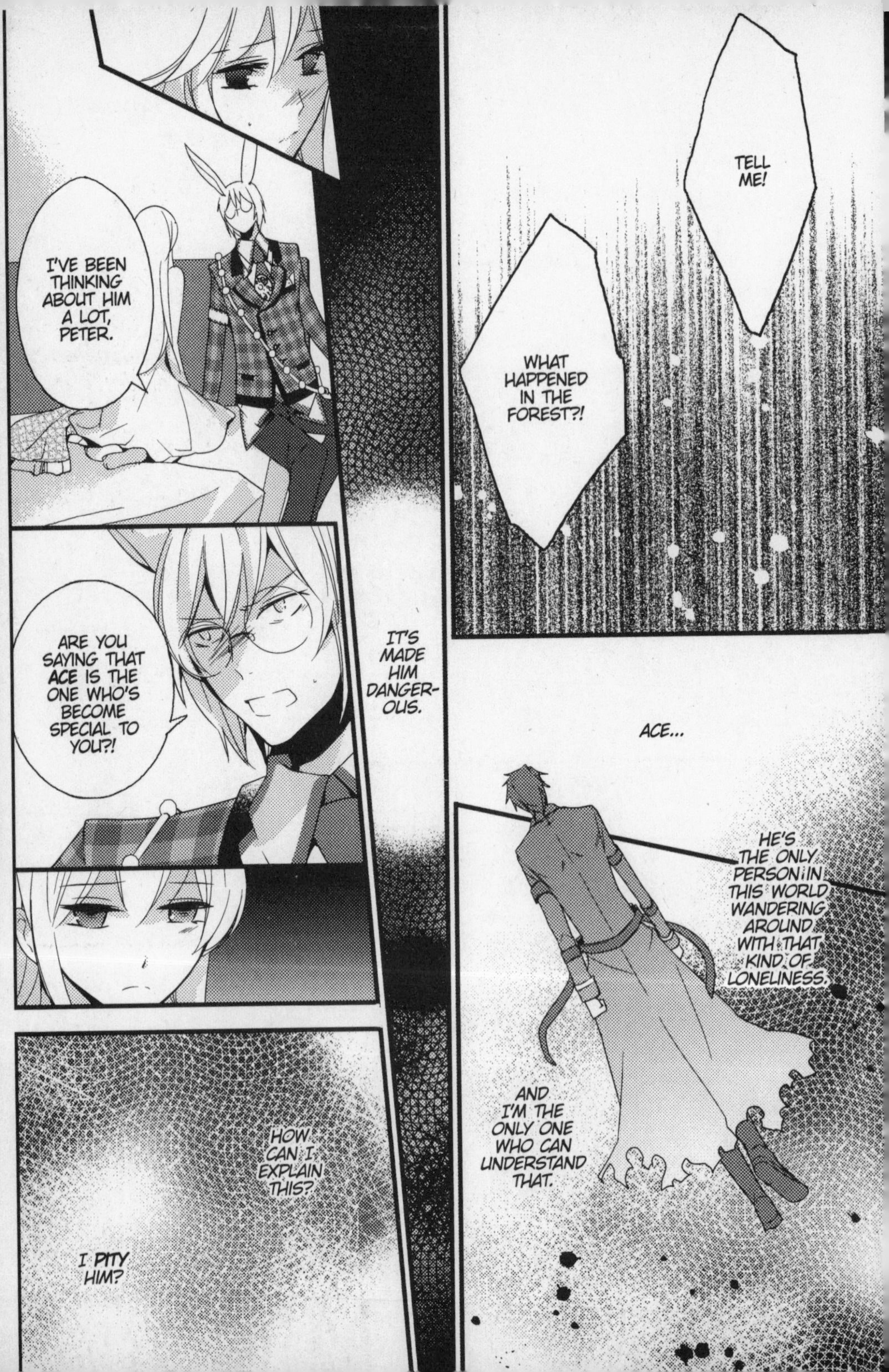
TELL ME!
WHAT HAPPENED IN THE FOREST?!
ACE...
HE'S THE ONLY PERSON IN THIS WORLD WANDERING AROUND WITH THAT KIND OF LONELINESS.
AND I'M THE ONLY ONE WHO CAN UNDERSTAND THAT.
I'VE BEEN THINKING ABOUT HIM A LOT, PETER.
IT'S MADE HIM DANGEROUS.
ARE YOU SAYING THAT ACE IS THE ONE WHO'S BECOME SPECIAL TO YOU?!
HOW CAN I EXPLAIN THIS?
I PITY HIM?

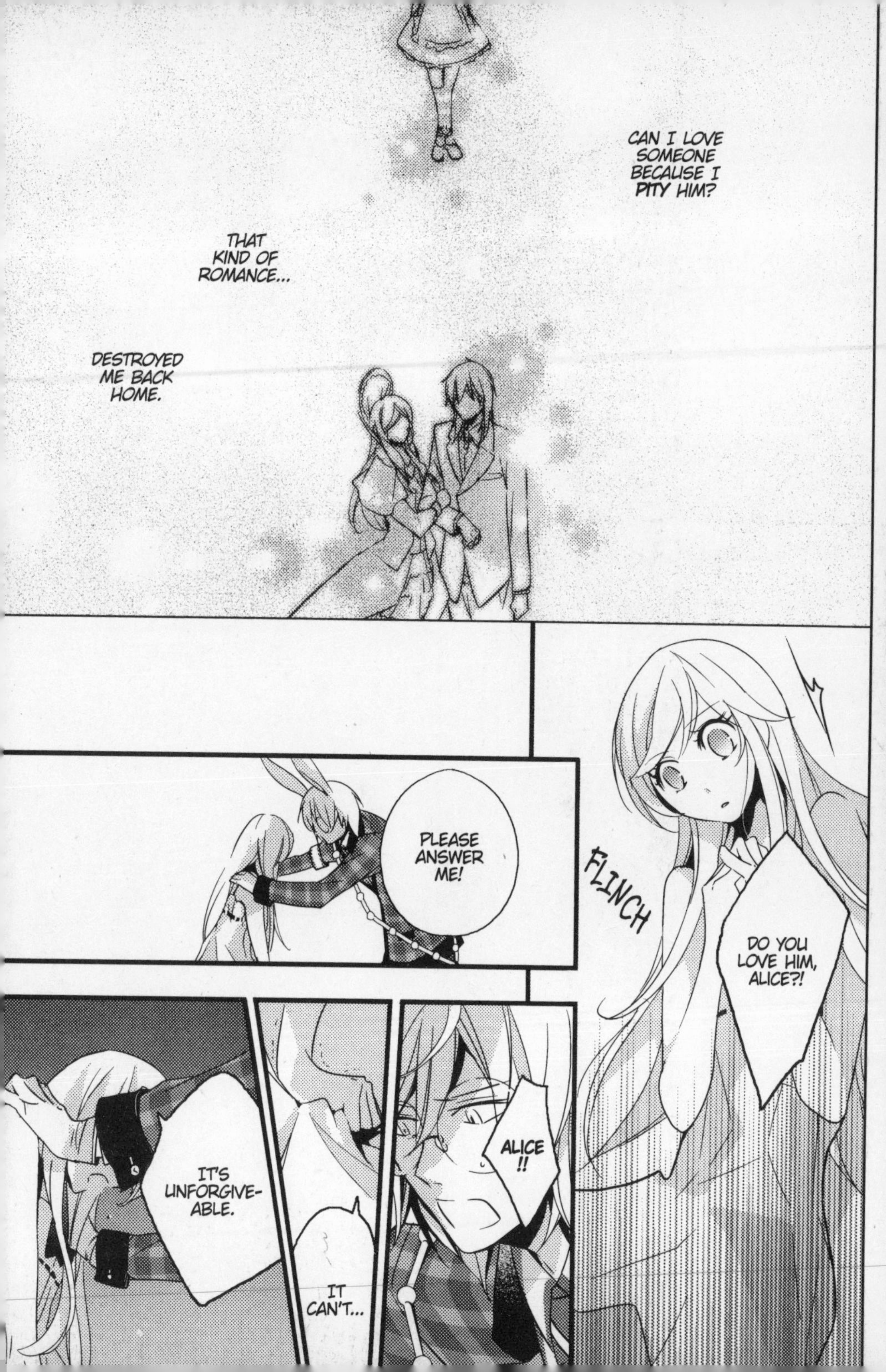
CAN I LOVE SOMEONE BECAUSE I PITY HIM?
THAT KIND OF ROMANCE...
DESTROYED ME BACK HOME.
FLINCH
DO YOU LOVE HIM, ALICE?!
PLEASE ANSWER ME!
ALICE!!
IT CAN'T...
IT'S UNFORGIVE-ABLE.

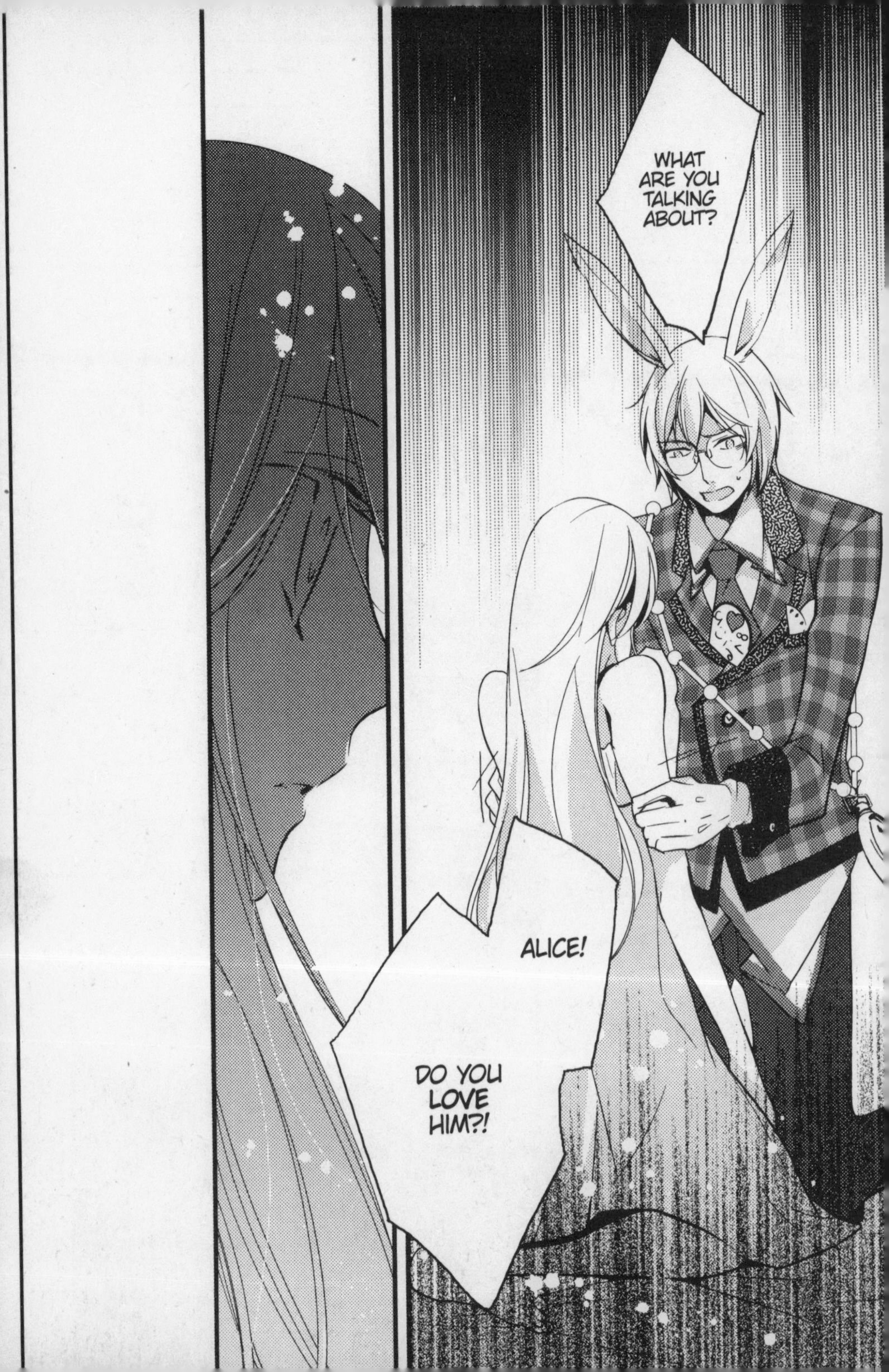
WHAT ARE YOU TALKING ABOUT?
ALICE!
DO YOU LOVE HIM?!

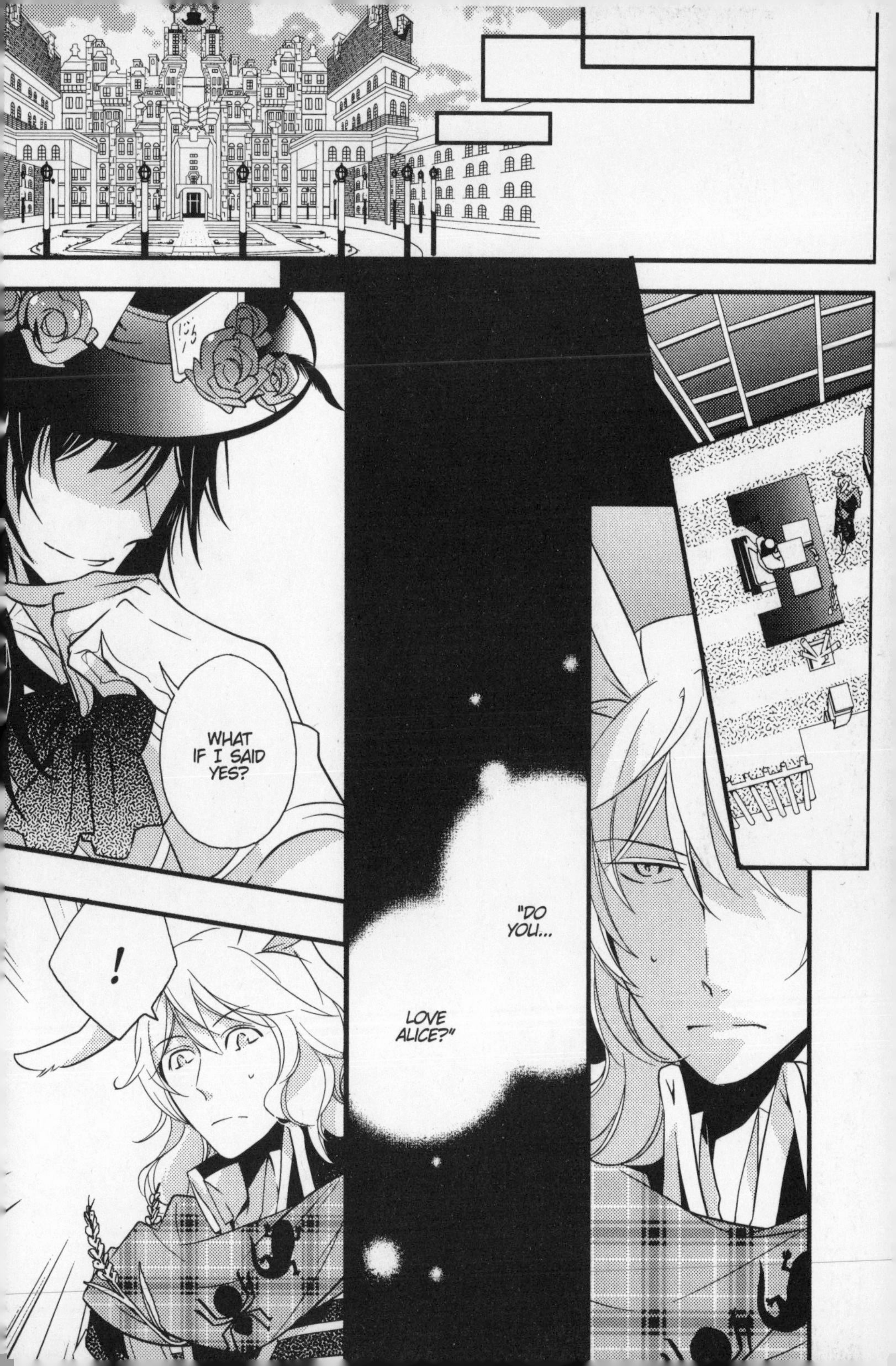
"DO YOU...
LOVE ALICE?"
WHAT IF I SAID YES?
!

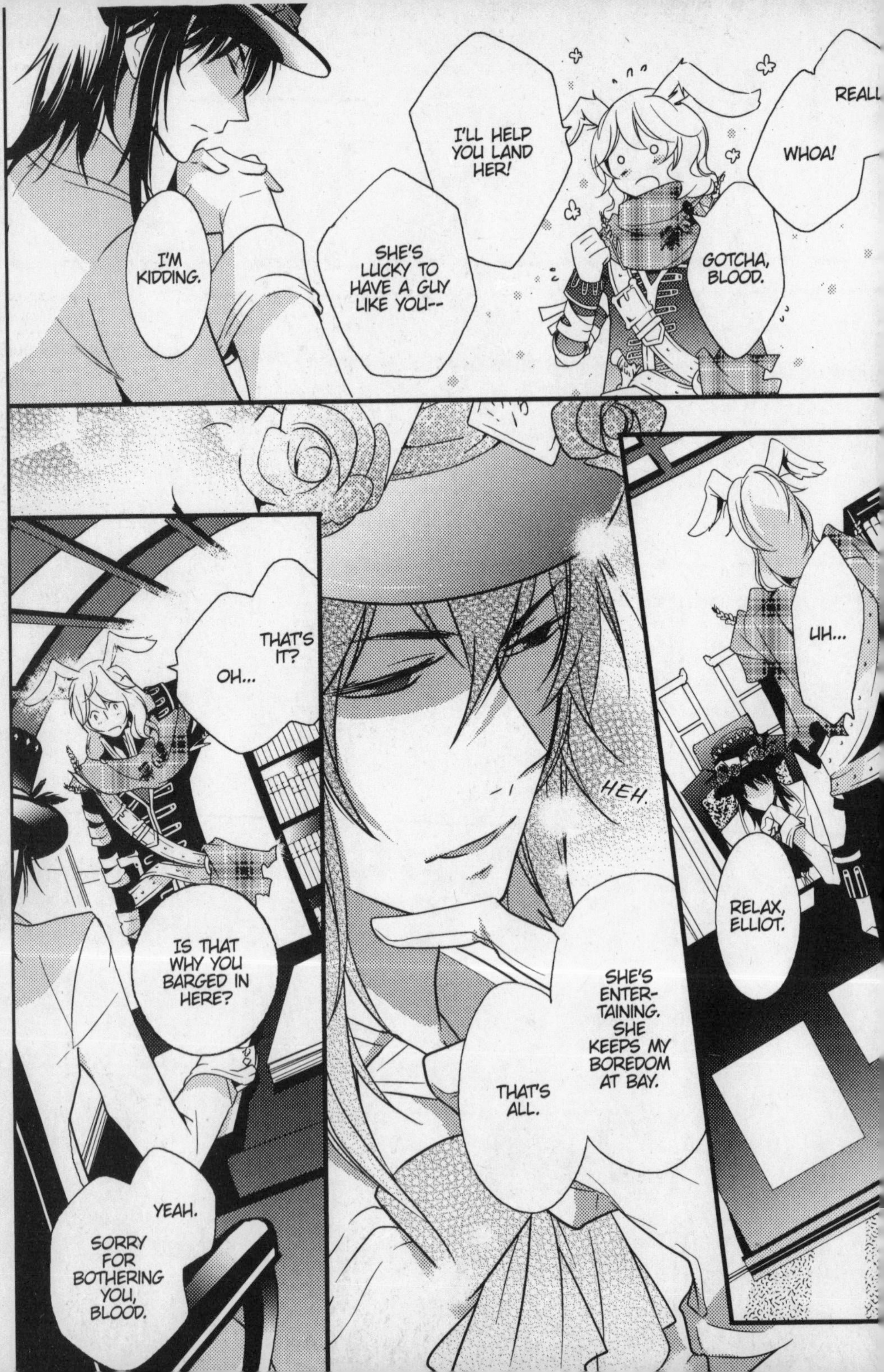
REALL
WHOA!
GOTCHA, BLOOD.
I'LL HELP YOU LAND HER!
SHE'S LUCKY TO HAVE A GUY LIKE YOU--
I'M KIDDING.
UH...
RELAX, ELLIOT.
HEH.
SHE'S ENTER-TAINING. SHE KEEPS MY BOREDOM AT BAY.
THAT'S ALL.
THAT'S IT?
OH...
IS THAT WHY YOU BARGED IN HERE?
YEAH.
SORRY FOR BOTHERING YOU, BLOOD.

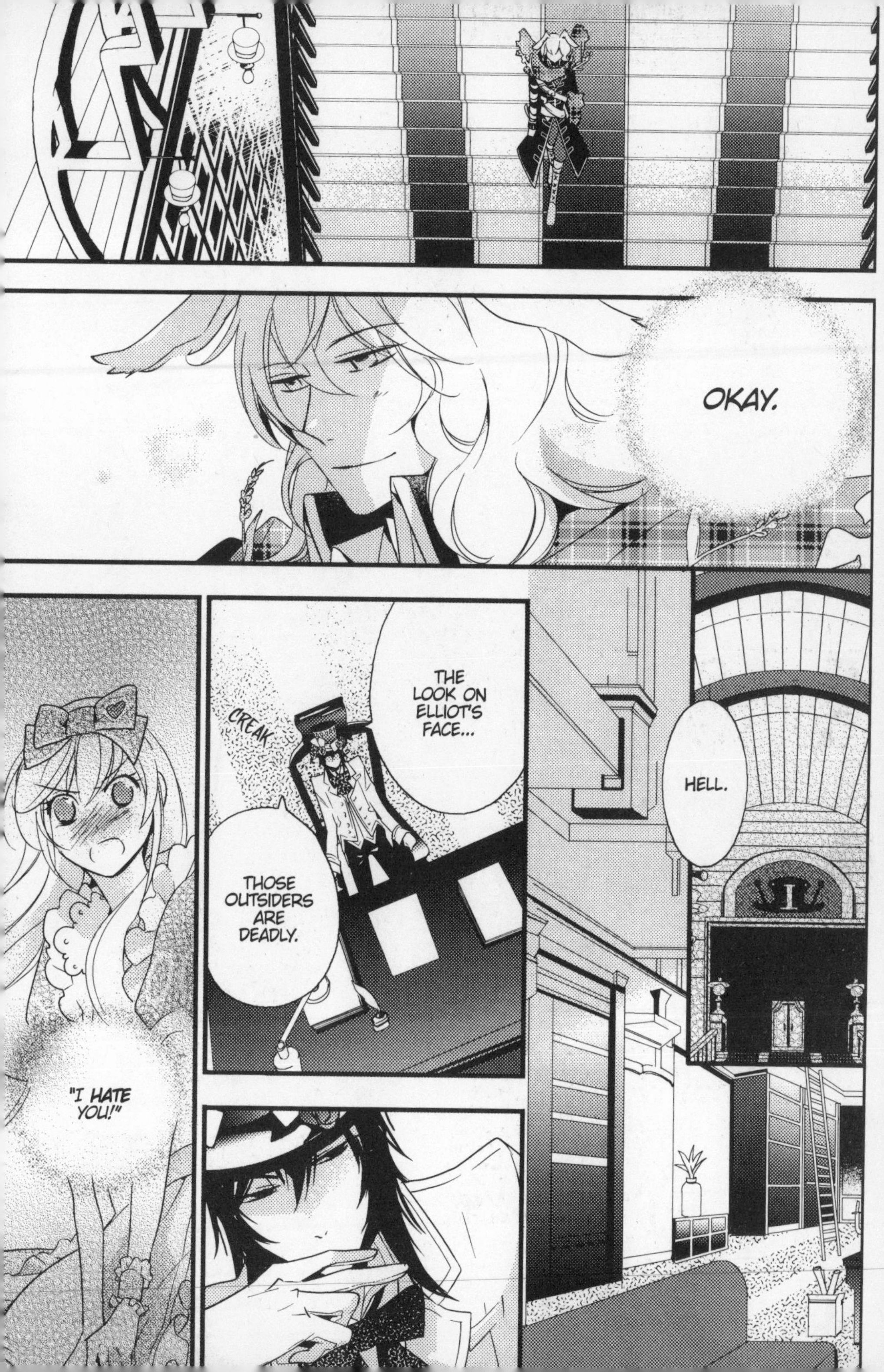
OKAY.
HELL.
THE LOOK ON ELLIOT'S FACE...
CREAK
THOSE OUTSIDERS ARE DEADLY.
"I HATE YOU!"

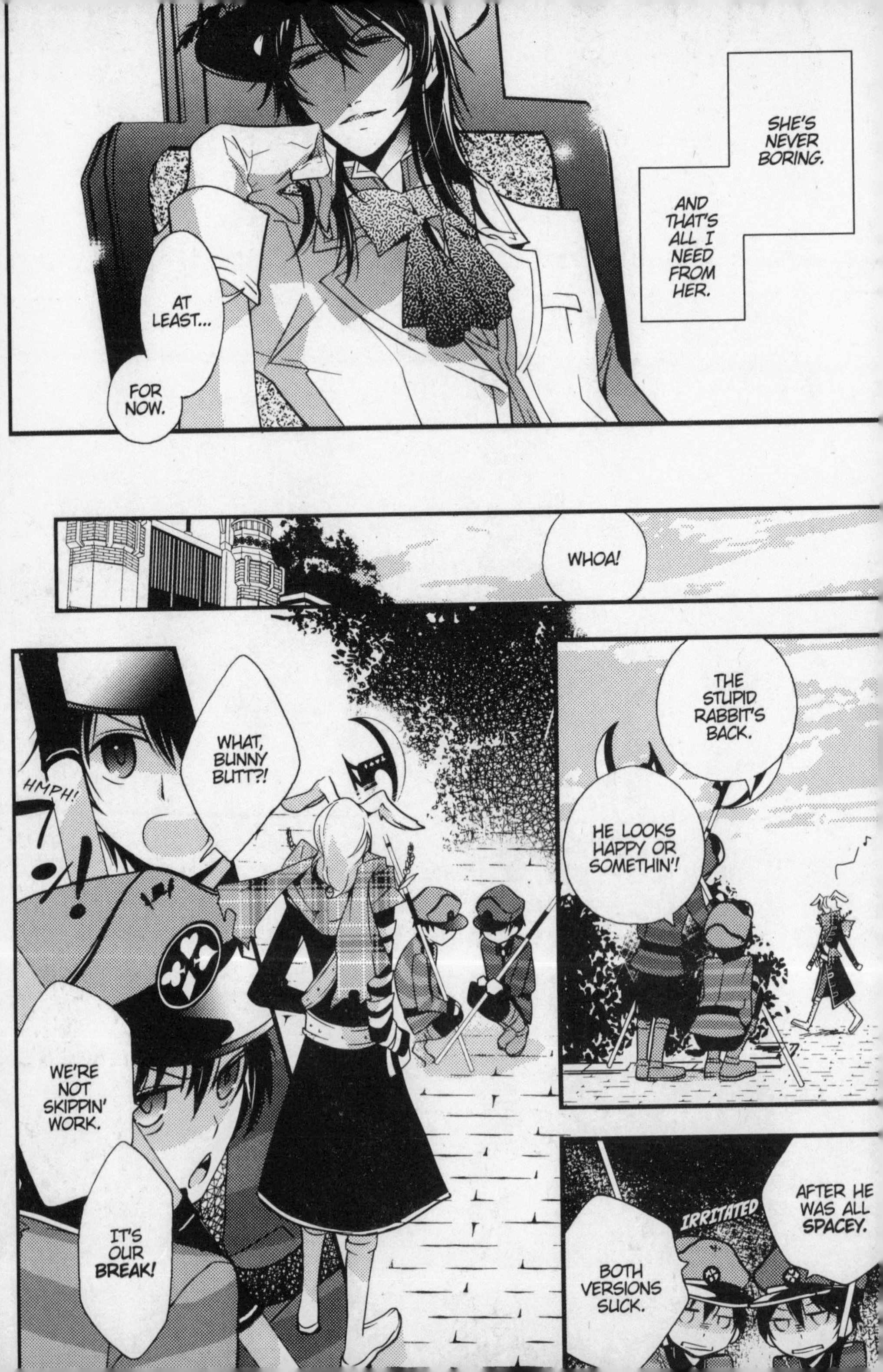
SHE'S NEVER BORING.
AND THAT'S ALL I NEED FROM HER.
AT LEAST...
FOR NOW.
WHOA!
THE STUPID RABBIT'S BACK.
HE LOOKS HAPPY OR SOMETHIN'!
AFTER HE WAS ALL SPACEY.
IRRITATED
BOTH VERSIONS SUCK.
WHAT, BUNNY BUTT?!
HMPH!
WE'RE NOT SKIPPIN' WORK.
IT'S OUR BREAK!

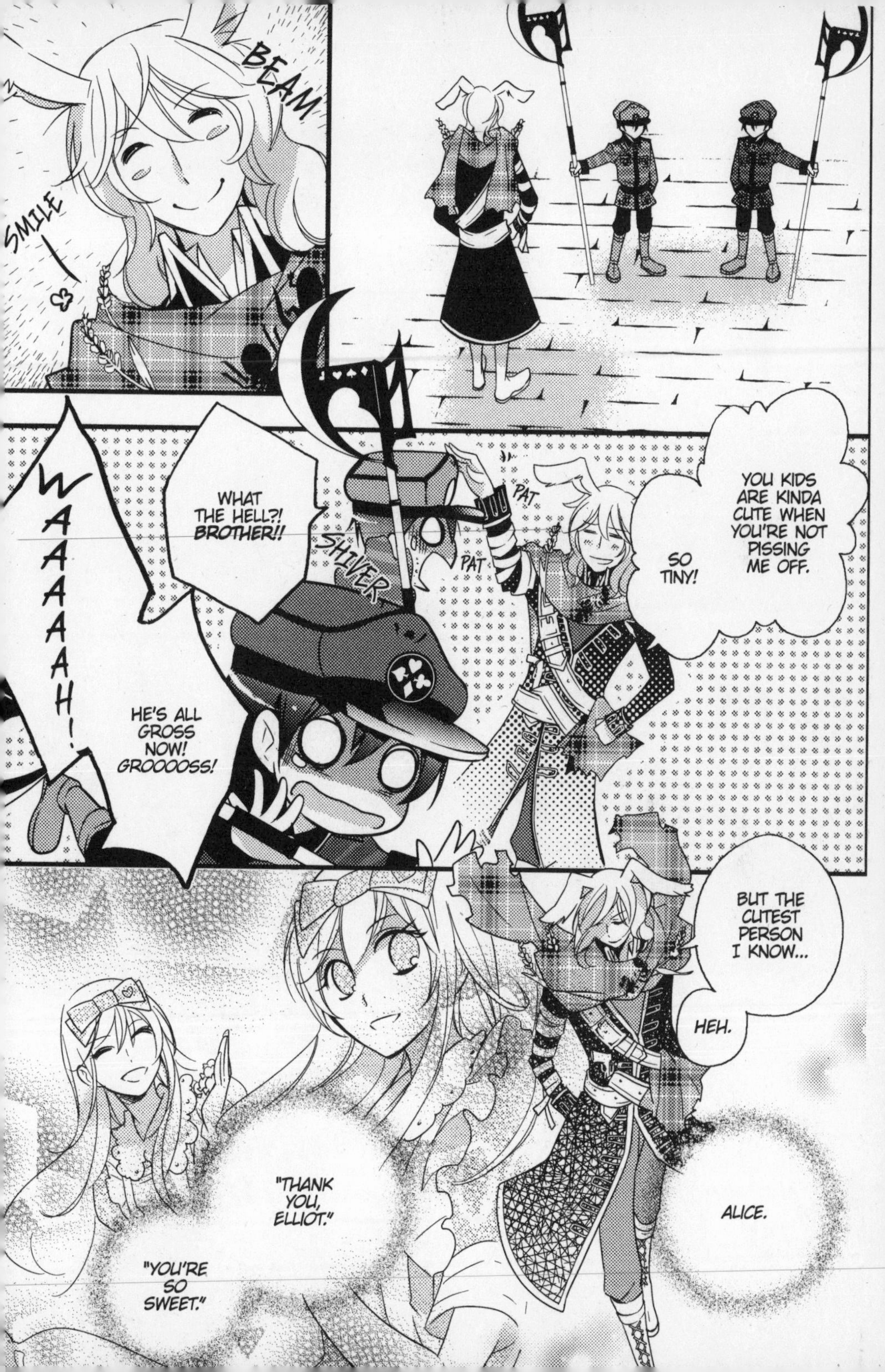

BEAM
SMILE
YOU KIDS ARE KINDA CUTE WHEN YOU'RE NOT PISSING ME OFF.
SO TINY!
PAT
PAT
SHIVER
WHAT THE HELL?! BROTHER!!
HE'S ALL GROSS NOW! GROOOOSS!
WAAAAAAH!
BUT THE CUTEST PERSON I KNOW...
HEH.
ALICE.
"THANK YOU, ELLIOT."
"YOU'RE SO SWEET."

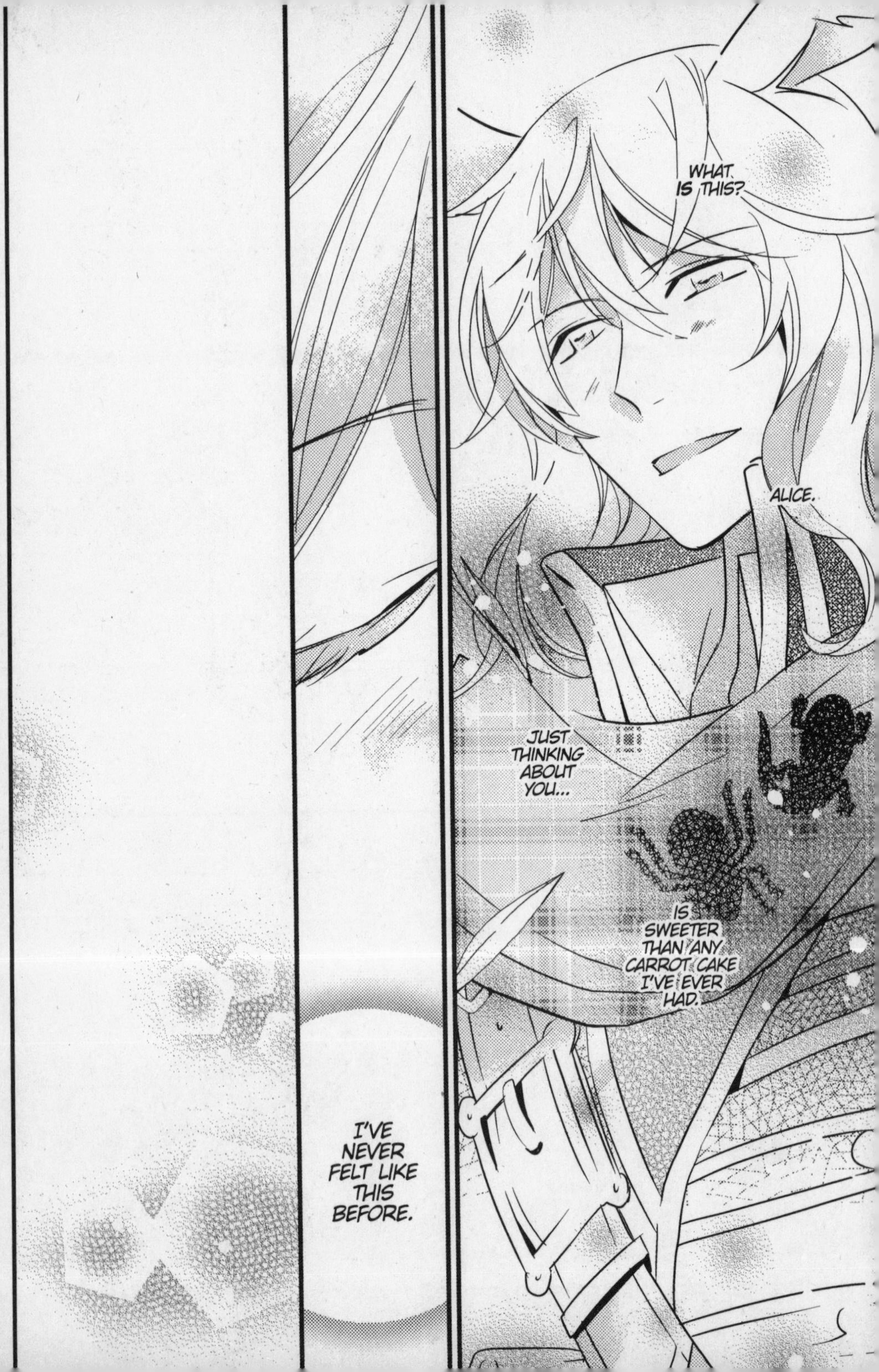
WHAT IS THIS?
ALICE.
JUST THINKING ABOUT YOU...
IS SWEETER THAN ANY CARROT CAKE I'VE EVER HAD.
I'VE NEVER FELT LIKE THIS BEFORE.

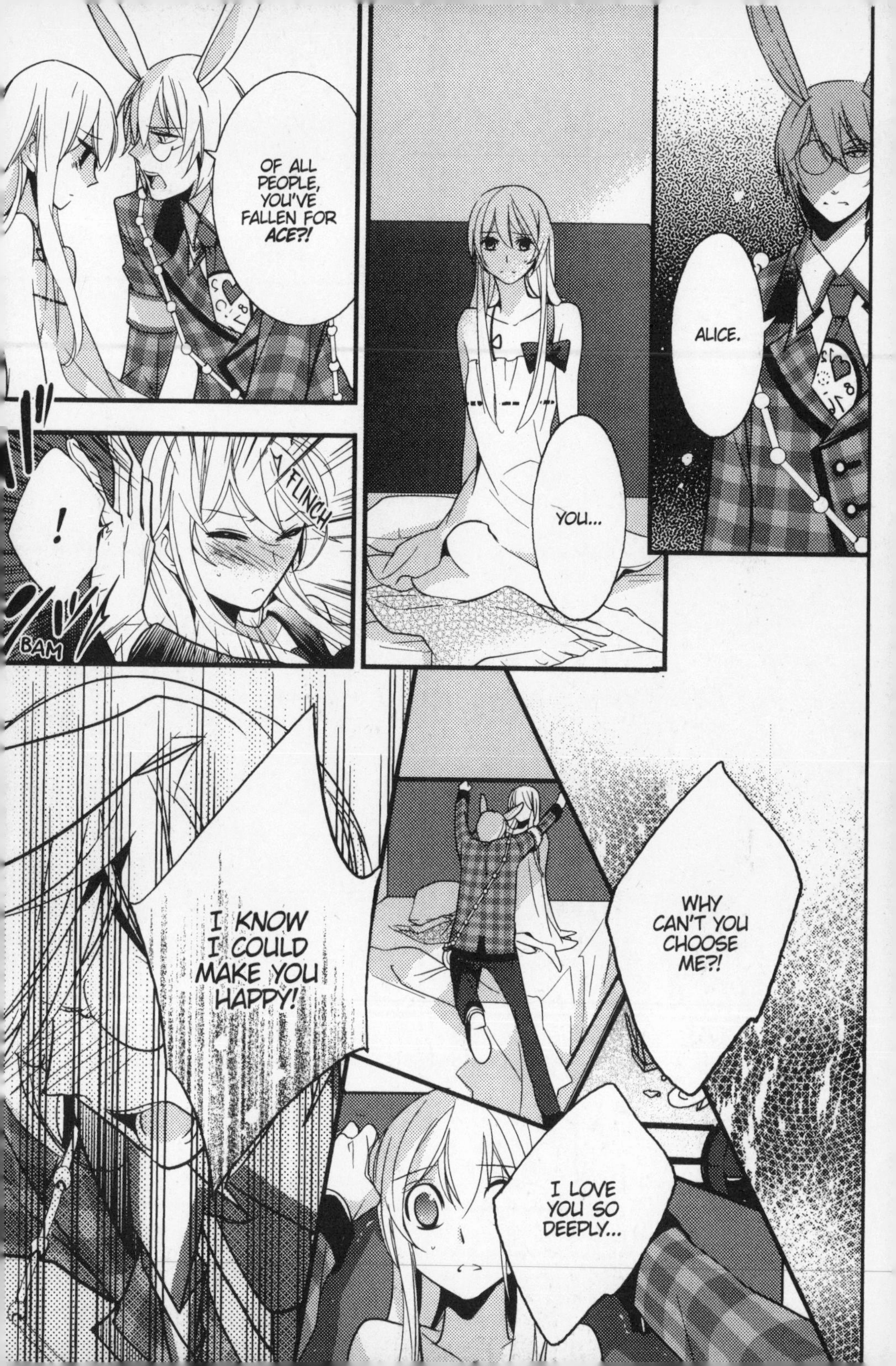
ALICE.
YOU...
OF ALL PEOPLE, YOU'VE FALLEN FOR ACE?!
!
FLINCH
BAM
WHY CAN'T YOU CHOOSE ME?!
I LOVE YOU SO DEEPLY...
I KNOW I COULD MAKE YOU HAPPY!

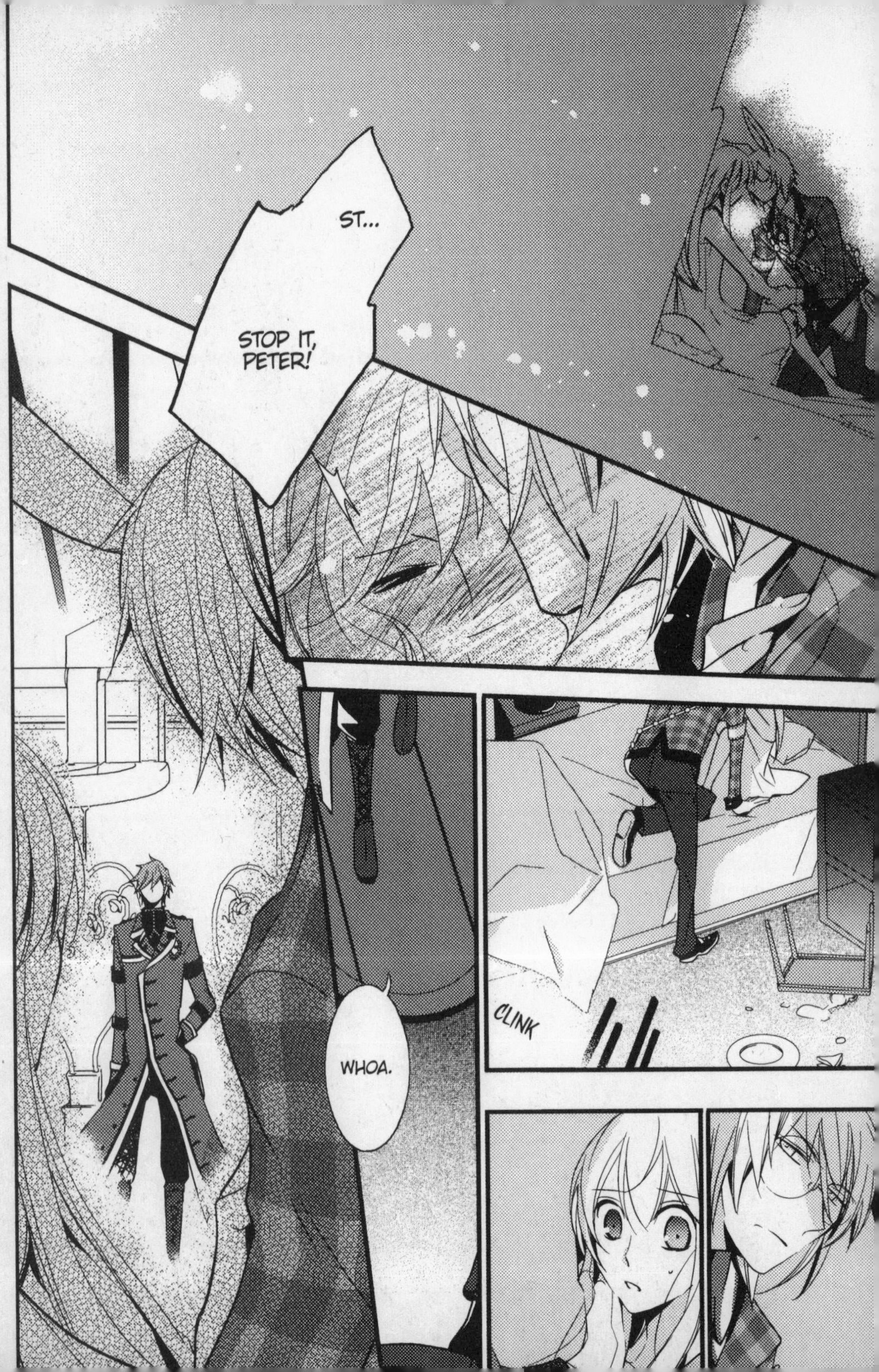
ST...
STOP IT, PETER!
CLINK
WHOA.

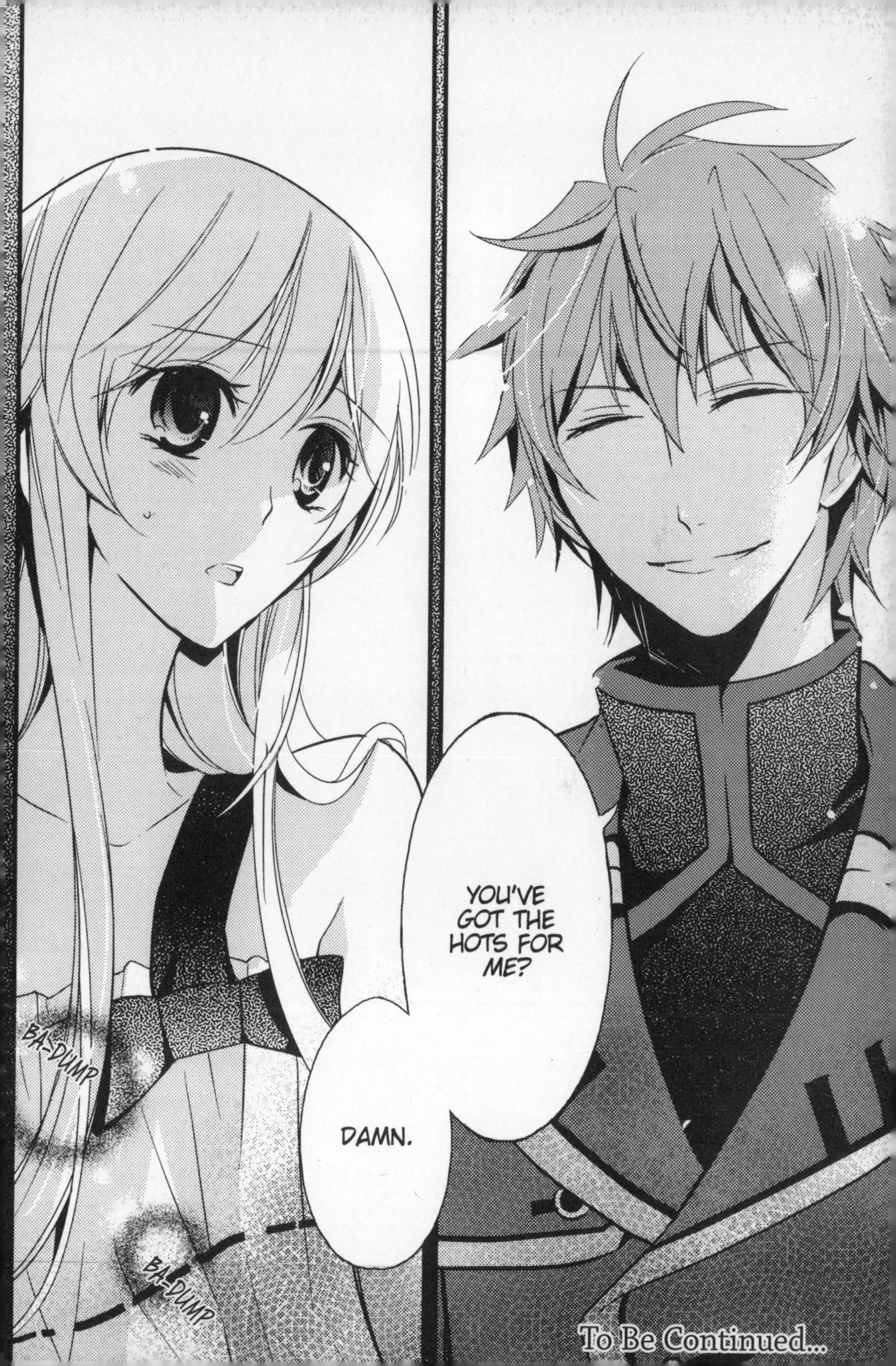
YOU'VE GOT THE HOTS FOR ME?
DAMN.
BA-DUMP
BA-DUMP
To Be Continued...

Thank you very much!

Alice, lost as always, and Ace, who's even more lost in the Country of Clover. I'm sorry their love isn't blooming very fast. I plan for them to be pretty mushy in the next volume, so I'd appreciate it if you stick with me until then.

Thanks!

QuinRose
Tama-zou
Taku-zou

Sai Asai

↑

My first name (西) is read as Sai. I received it from my grandmother's name.

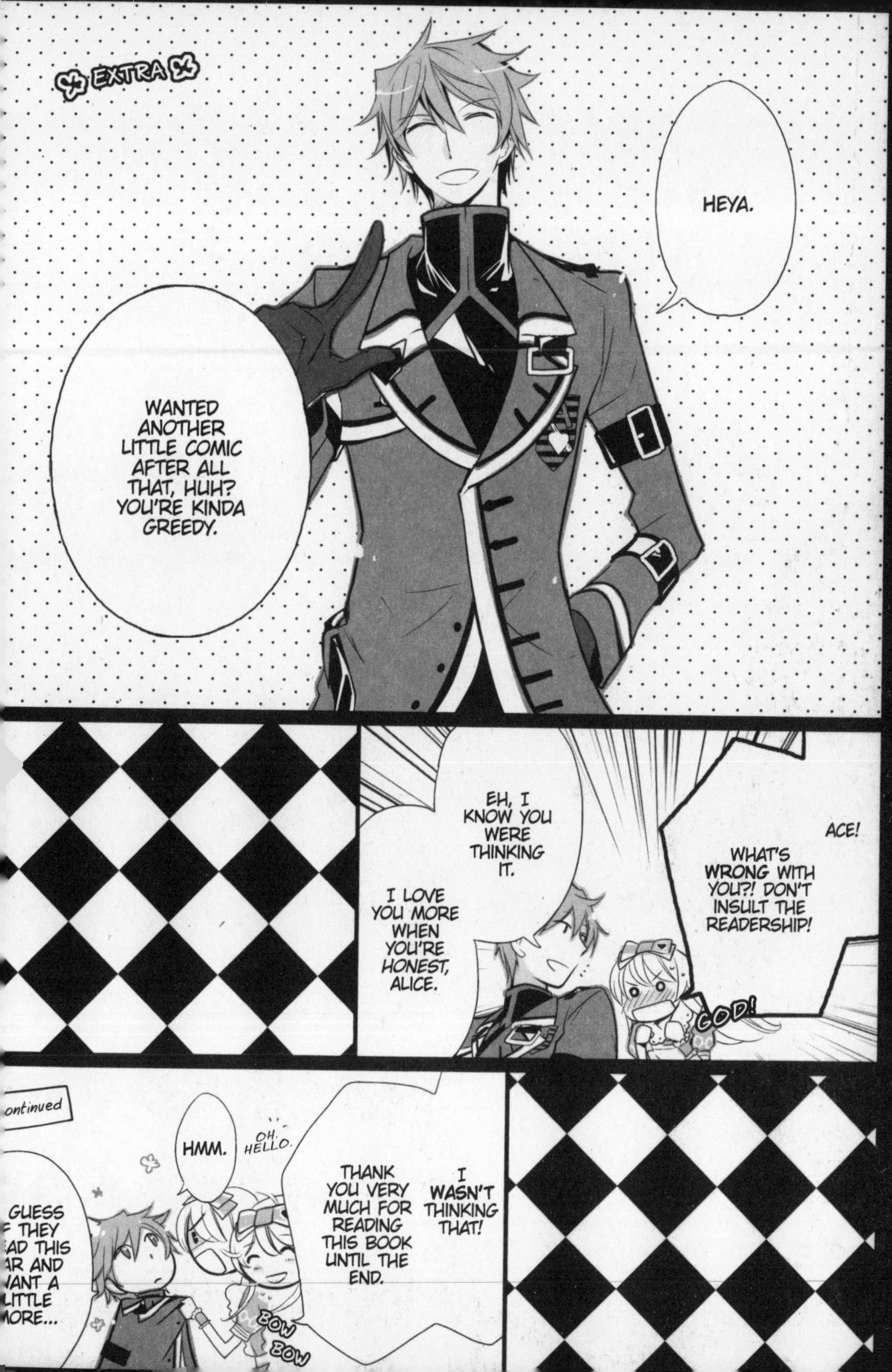
EXTRA
HEYA.
WANTED ANOTHER LITTLE COMIC AFTER ALL THAT, HUH? YOU'RE KINDA GREEDY.
ACE!
WHAT'S WRONG WITH YOU?! DON'T INSULT THE READERSHIP!
GOD!
EH, I KNOW YOU WERE THINKING IT.
I LOVE YOU MORE WHEN YOU'RE HONEST, ALICE.
I WASN'T THINKING THAT!
THANK YOU VERY MUCH FOR READING THIS BOOK UNTIL THE END.
BOW BOW
OH. HELLO.
HMM.
GUESS F THEY EAD THIS AR AND ANT A LITTLE MORE...
ontinued

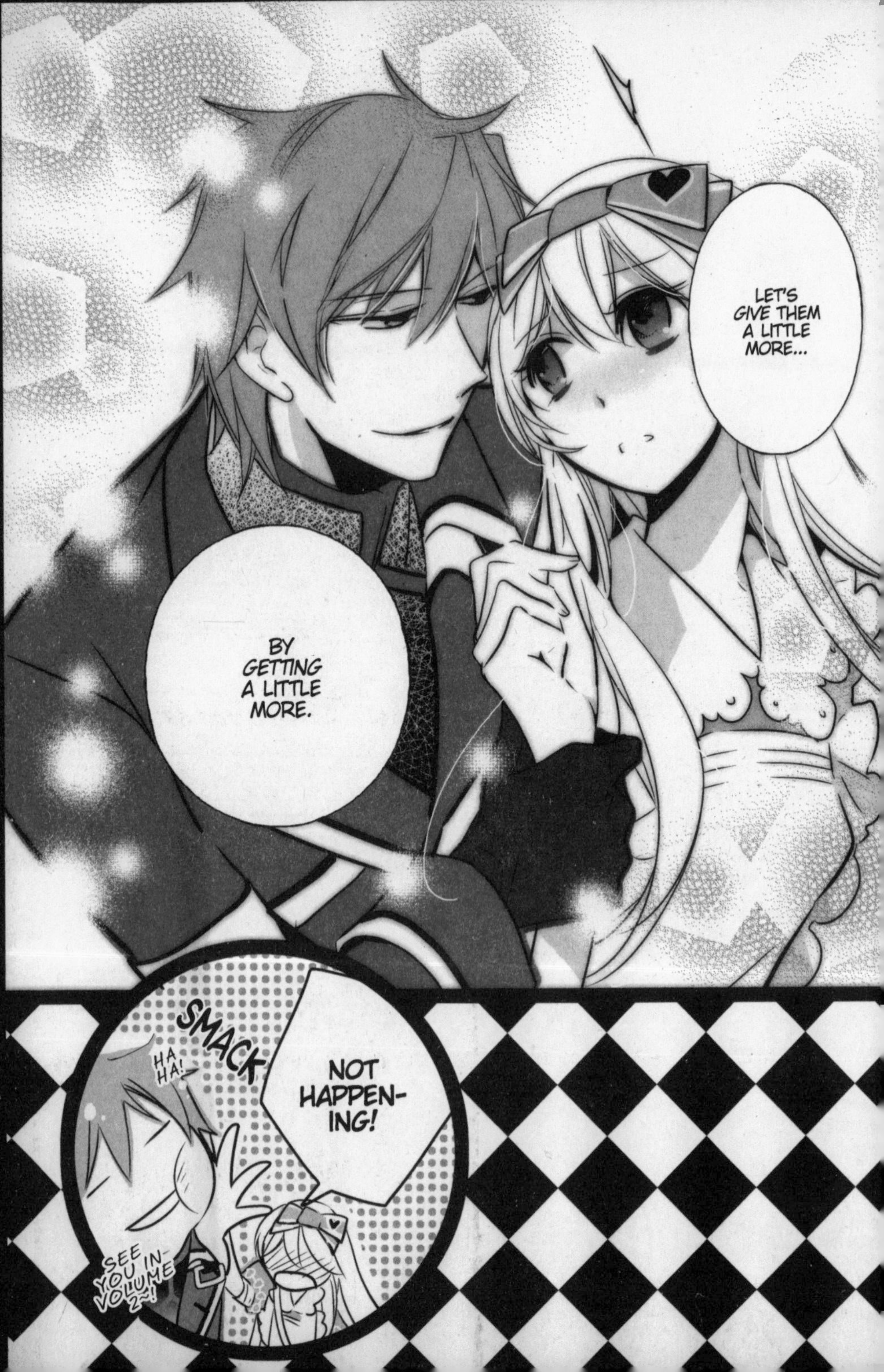
LET'S GIVE THEM A LITTLE MORE...
BY GETTING A LITTLE MORE.
NOT HAPPEN-ING!
SMACK
HA HA!
SEE YOU IN-VOLUME 2~!

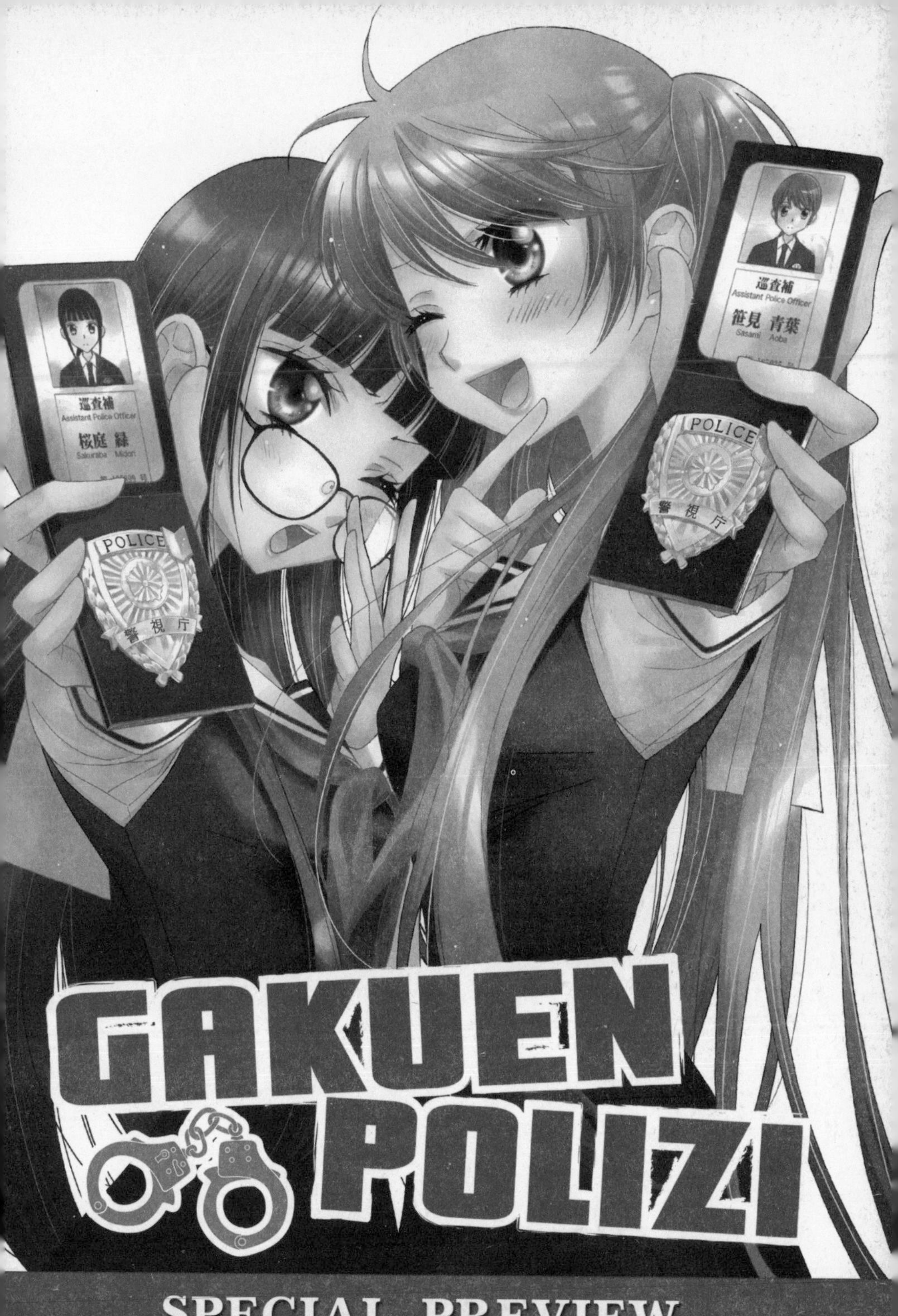
巡査補
Assistant Police Officer
笹見 青葉
Sasami Aoba
POLICE
警視庁
巡査補
Assistant Police Officer
桜庭 緑
Sakuraba Midori
POLICE
警視庁
GAKUEN POLIZI

SPECIAL PREVIEW

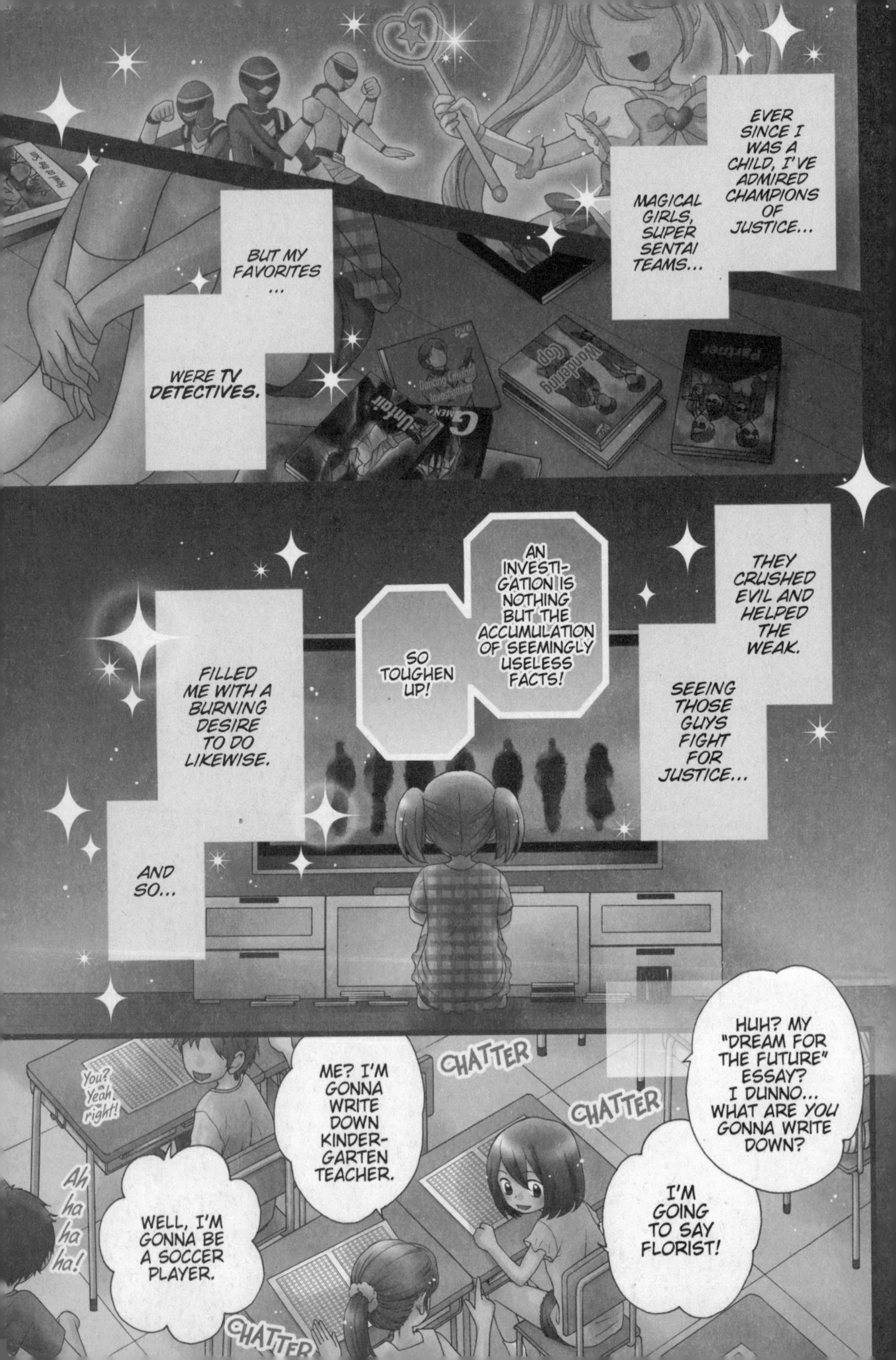
EVER SINCE I WAS A CHILD, I'VE ADMIRED CHAMPIONS OF JUSTICE...
MAGICAL GIRLS, SUPER SENTAI TEAMS...
BUT MY FAVORITES ...
WERE TV DETECTIVES.
Partner
Wandering Cop
Dancing Criminal Investigation
THEY CRUSHED EVIL AND HELPED THE WEAK.
SEEING THOSE GUYS FIGHT FOR JUSTICE...
AN INVESTIGATION IS NOTHING BUT THE ACCUMULATION OF SEEMINGLY USELESS FACTS!
SO TOUGHEN UP!
FILLED ME WITH A BURNING DESIRE TO DO LIKEWISE.
AND SO...
HUH? MY "DREAM FOR THE FUTURE" ESSAY? I DUNNO... WHAT ARE YOU GONNA WRITE DOWN?
I'M GOING TO SAY FLORIST!
CHATTER
CHATTER
ME? I'M GONNA WRITE DOWN KINDER-GARTEN TEACHER.
You? Yeah right!
WELL, I'M GONNA BE A SOCCER PLAYER.
Ah ha ha ha!
CHATTER

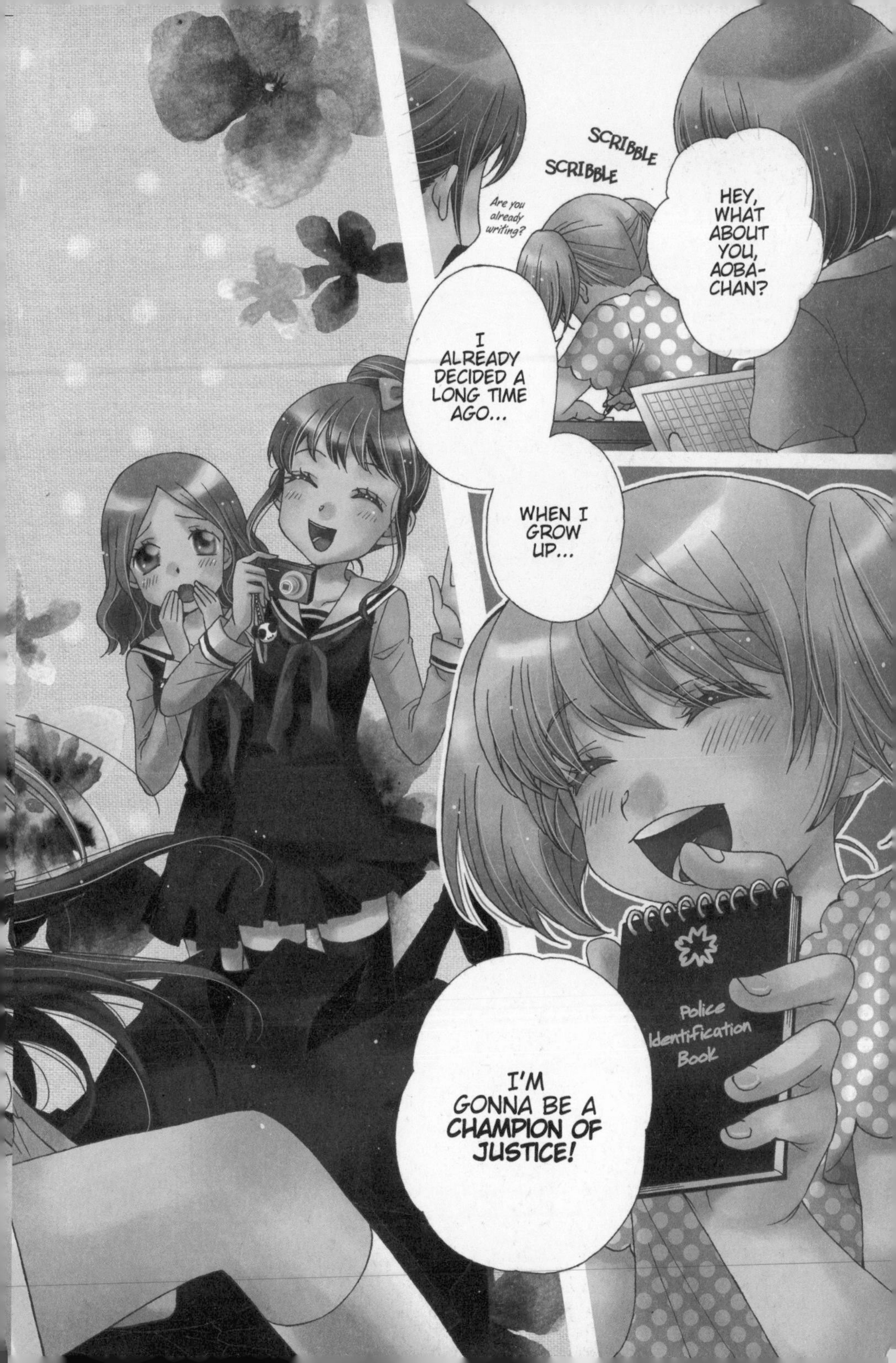
SCRIBBLE
SCRIBBLE
HEY, WHAT ABOUT YOU, AOBA-CHAN?
Are you already writing?
I ALREADY DECIDED A LONG TIME AGO...
WHEN I GROW UP...
I'M GONNA BE A CHAMPION OF JUSTICE!
Police Identification Book

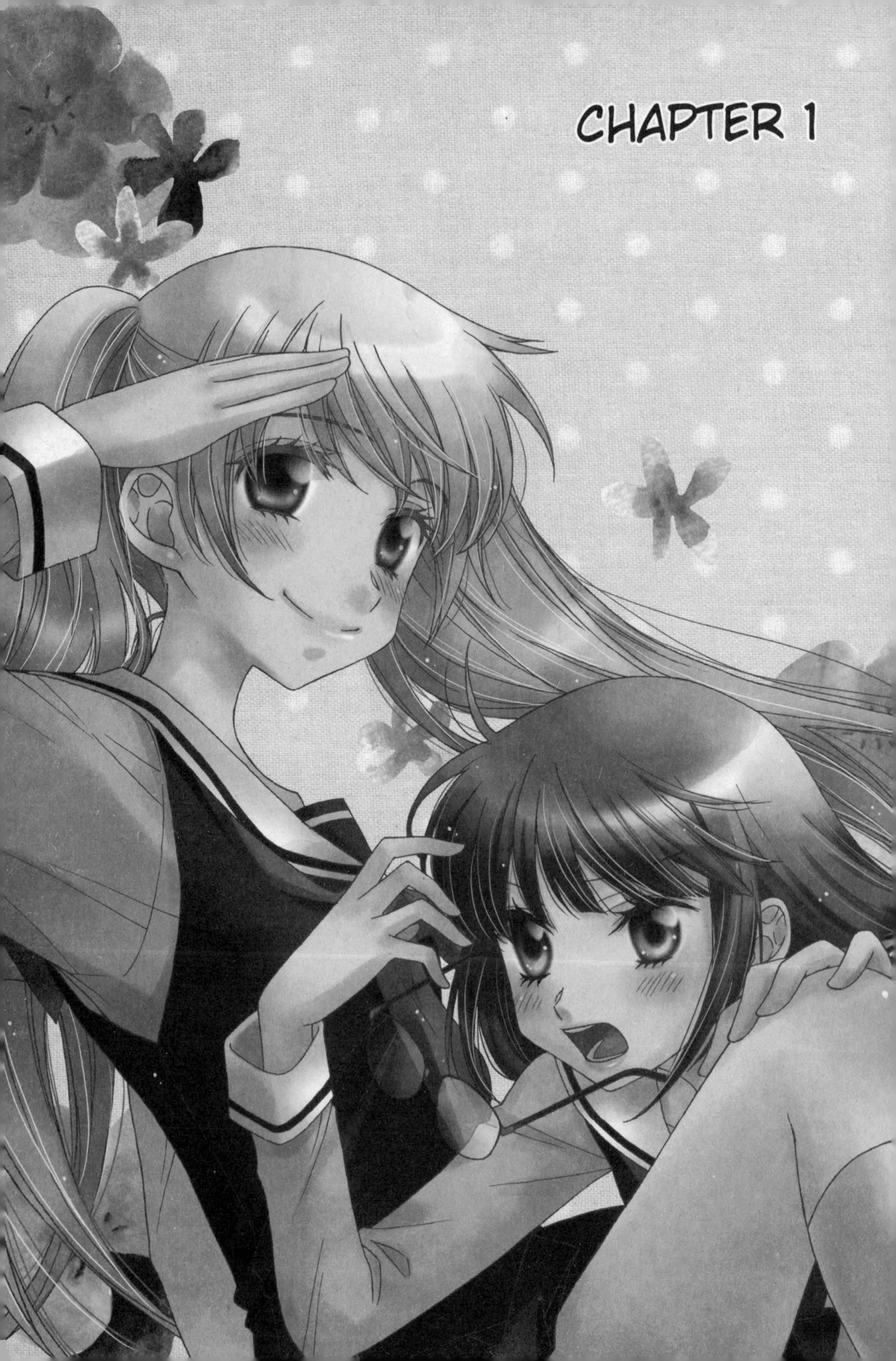
CHAPTER 1

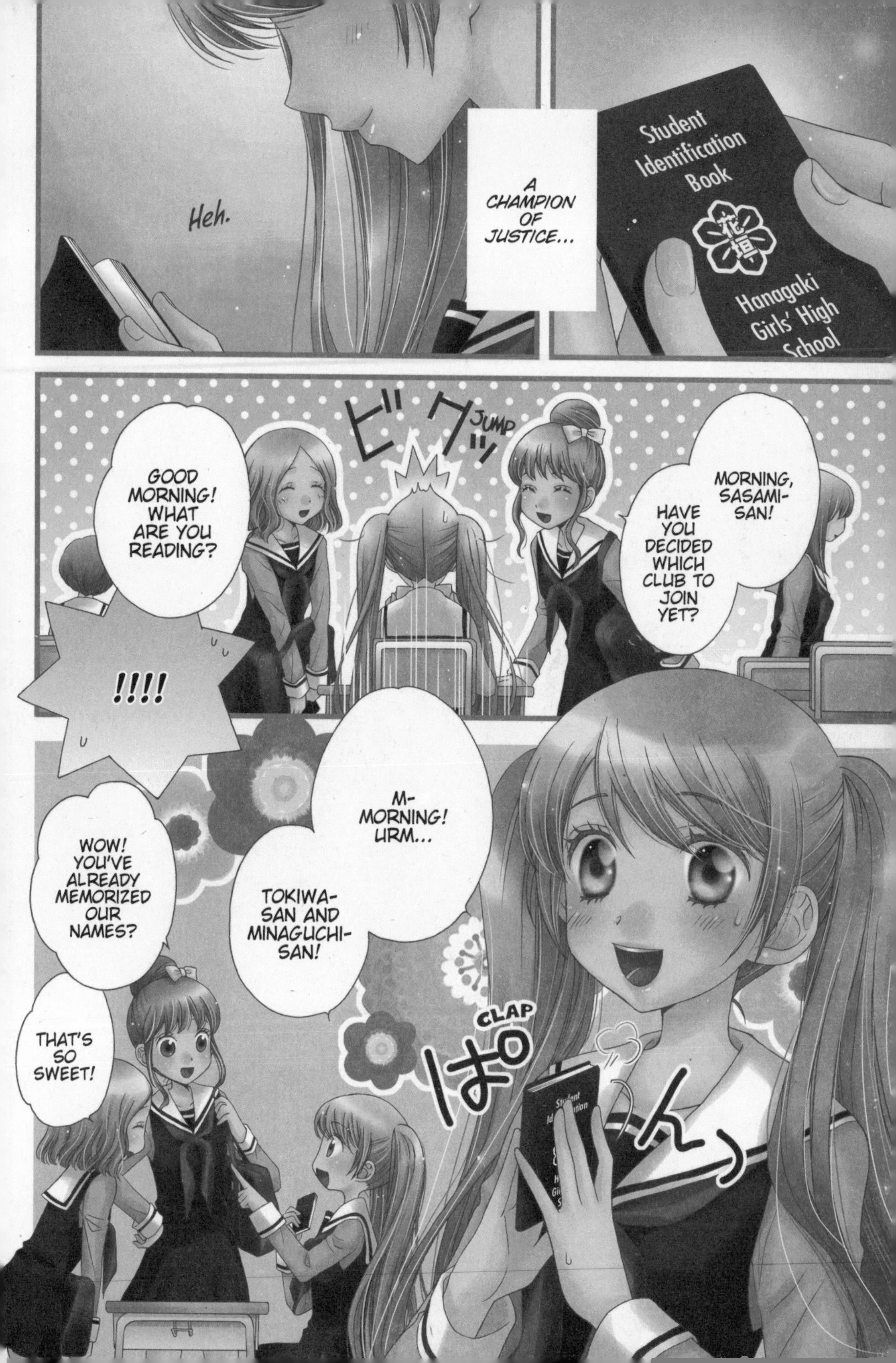
Student Identification Book
Hanagaki Girls' High School
A CHAMPION OF JUSTICE...
Heh.
MORNING, SASAMI-SAN!
HAVE YOU DECIDED WHICH CLUB TO JOIN YET?
JUMP
GOOD MORNING! WHAT ARE YOU READING?
!!!!
M-MORNING! URM...
TOKIWA-SAN AND MINAGUCHI-SAN!
CLAP
WOW! YOU'VE ALREADY MEMORIZED OUR NAMES?
THAT'S SO SWEET!

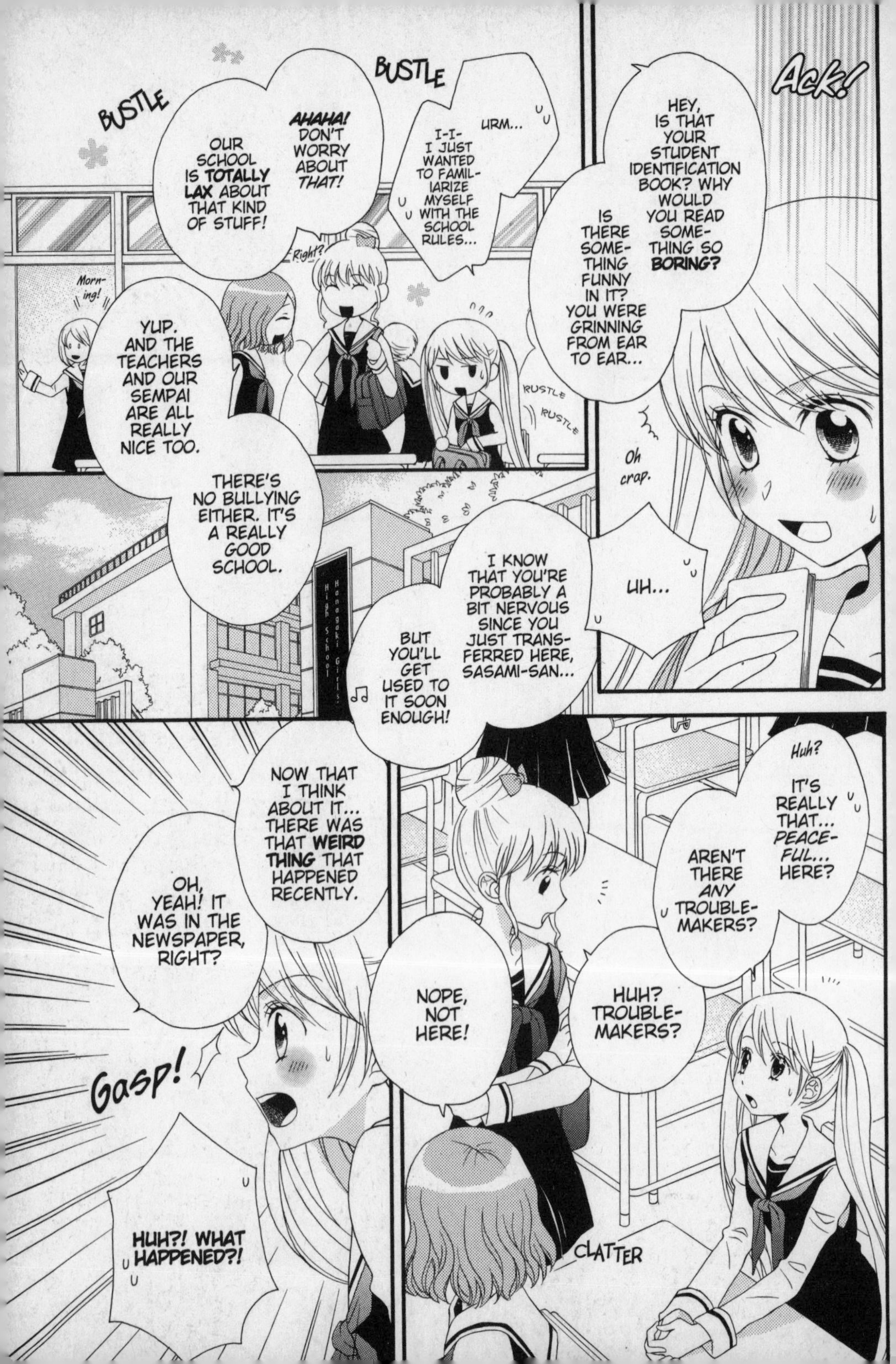
Ack!
HEY, IS THAT YOUR STUDENT IDENTIFICATION BOOK? WHY WOULD YOU READ SOMETHING SO BORING?
IS THERE SOMETHING FUNNY IN IT? YOU WERE GRINNING FROM EAR TO EAR...
Oh crap.
UH...
URM...
I-I- I JUST WANTED TO FAMILIARIZE MYSELF WITH THE SCHOOL RULES...
BUSTLE
AHAHA! DON'T WORRY ABOUT THAT!
OUR SCHOOL IS TOTALLY LAX ABOUT THAT KIND OF STUFF!
BUSTLE
Right?
RUSTLE
RUSTLE
YUP. AND THE TEACHERS AND OUR SEMPAI ARE ALL REALLY NICE TOO.
Morn-ing!
THERE'S NO BULLYING EITHER. IT'S A REALLY GOOD SCHOOL.
Hanagaki Girls' High School
I KNOW THAT YOU'RE PROBABLY A BIT NERVOUS SINCE YOU JUST TRANSFERRED HERE, SASAMI-SAN...
BUT YOU'LL GET USED TO IT SOON ENOUGH! ♫
Huh?
IT'S REALLY THAT... PEACEFUL... HERE?
AREN'T THERE ANY TROUBLEMAKERS?
HUH? TROUBLEMAKERS?
NOPE, NOT HERE!
NOW THAT I THINK ABOUT IT... THERE WAS THAT WEIRD THING THAT HAPPENED RECENTLY.
CLATTER
OH, YEAH! IT WAS IN THE NEWSPAPER, RIGHT?
Gasp!
HUH?! WHAT HAPPENED?!

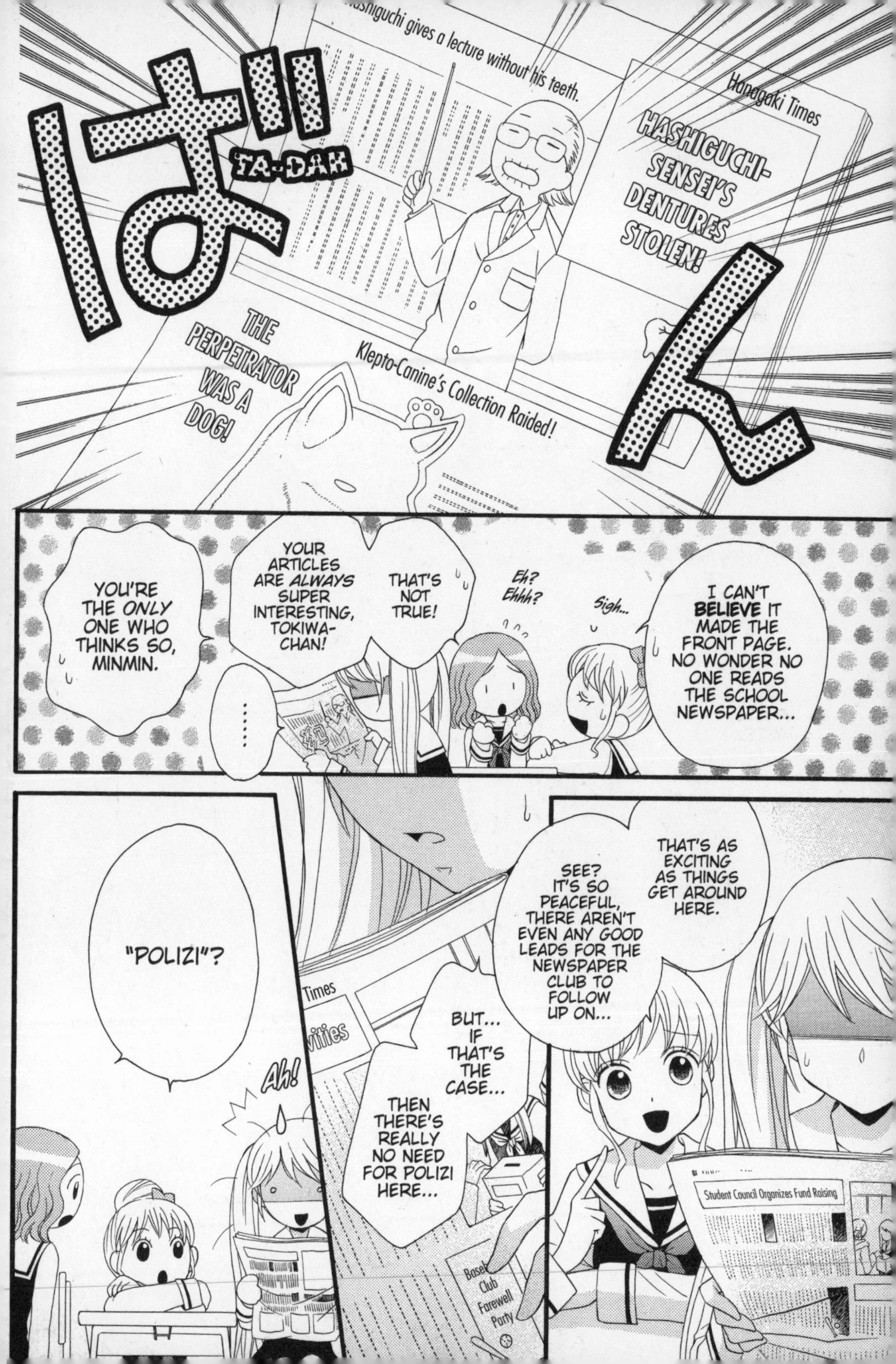
Hashiguchi gives a lecture without his teeth.
Hanagaki Times
HASHIGUCHI-SENSEI'S DENTURES STOLEN!
TA-DAH
THE PERPETRATOR WAS A DOG!
Klepto-Canine's Collection Raided!
I CAN'T BELIEVE IT MADE THE FRONT PAGE. NO WONDER NO ONE READS THE SCHOOL NEWSPAPER...
Sigh...
Eh? Ehhh?
THAT'S NOT TRUE!
YOUR ARTICLES ARE ALWAYS SUPER INTERESTING, TOKIWA-CHAN!
......
YOU'RE THE ONLY ONE WHO THINKS SO, MINMIN.
THAT'S AS EXCITING AS THINGS GET AROUND HERE.
SEE? IT'S SO PEACEFUL, THERE AREN'T EVEN ANY GOOD LEADS FOR THE NEWSPAPER CLUB TO FOLLOW UP ON...
Student Council Organizes Fund Raising
BUT... IF THAT'S THE CASE...
THEN THERE'S REALLY NO NEED FOR POLIZI HERE...
Ah!
"POLIZI"?

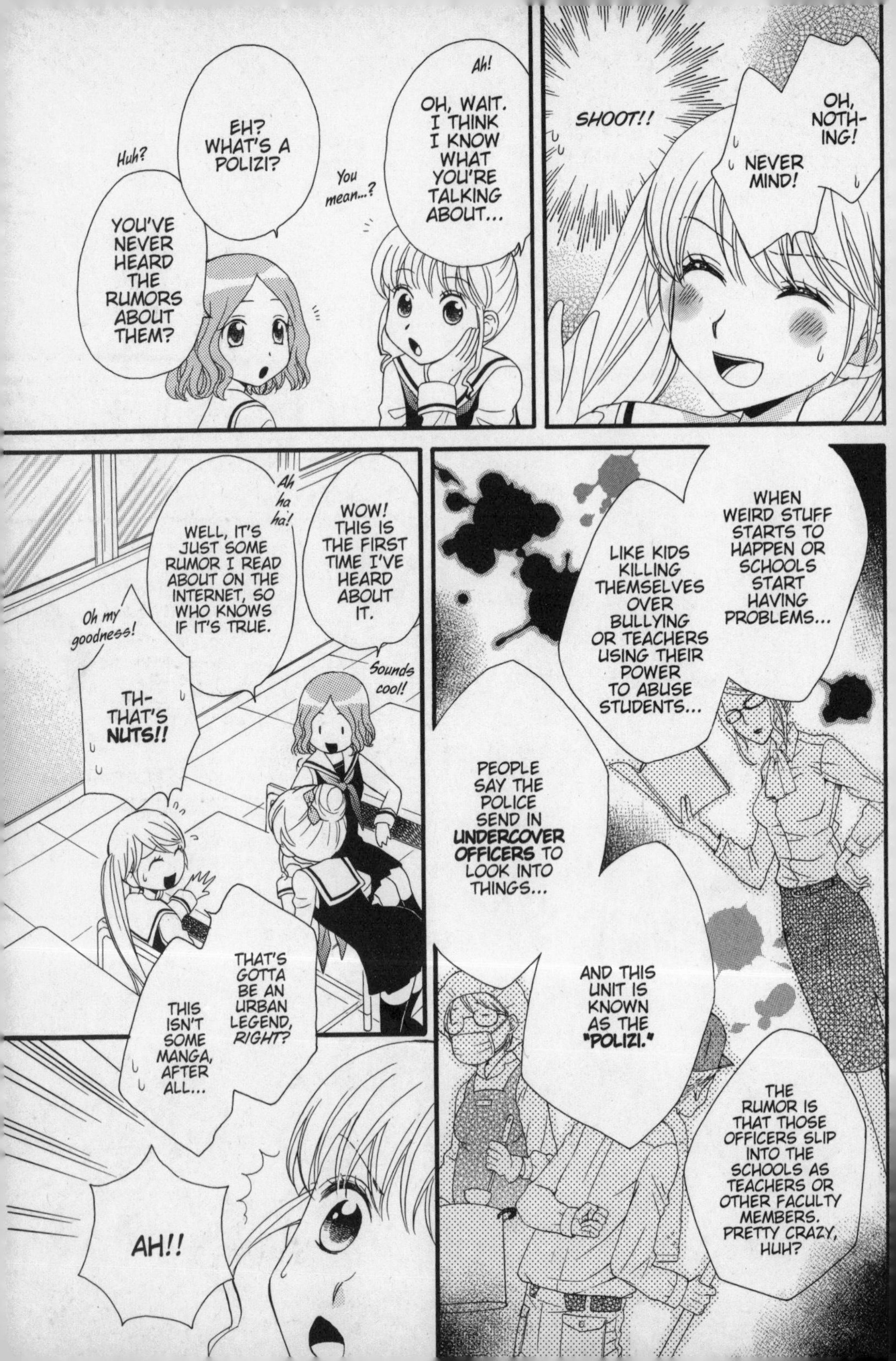
SHOOT!!
OH, NOTHING!
NEVER MIND!
Ah!
OH, WAIT. I THINK I KNOW WHAT YOU'RE TALKING ABOUT...
You mean...?
EH? WHAT'S A POLIZI?
Huh?
YOU'VE NEVER HEARD THE RUMORS ABOUT THEM?
WHEN WEIRD STUFF STARTS TO HAPPEN OR SCHOOLS START HAVING PROBLEMS...
LIKE KIDS KILLING THEMSELVES OVER BULLYING OR TEACHERS USING THEIR POWER TO ABUSE STUDENTS...
PEOPLE SAY THE POLICE SEND IN **UNDERCOVER OFFICERS** TO LOOK INTO THINGS...
AND THIS UNIT IS KNOWN AS THE **"POLIZI."**
THE RUMOR IS THAT THOSE OFFICERS SLIP INTO THE SCHOOLS AS TEACHERS OR OTHER FACULTY MEMBERS. PRETTY CRAZY, HUH?
WOW! THIS IS THE FIRST TIME I'VE HEARD ABOUT IT.
Ah ha ha!
WELL, IT'S JUST SOME RUMOR I READ ABOUT ON THE INTERNET, SO WHO KNOWS IF IT'S TRUE.
Sounds cool!
Oh my goodness!
TH-THAT'S **NUTS!!**
THAT'S GOTTA BE AN URBAN LEGEND, *RIGHT?*
THIS ISN'T SOME MANGA, AFTER ALL...
AH!!

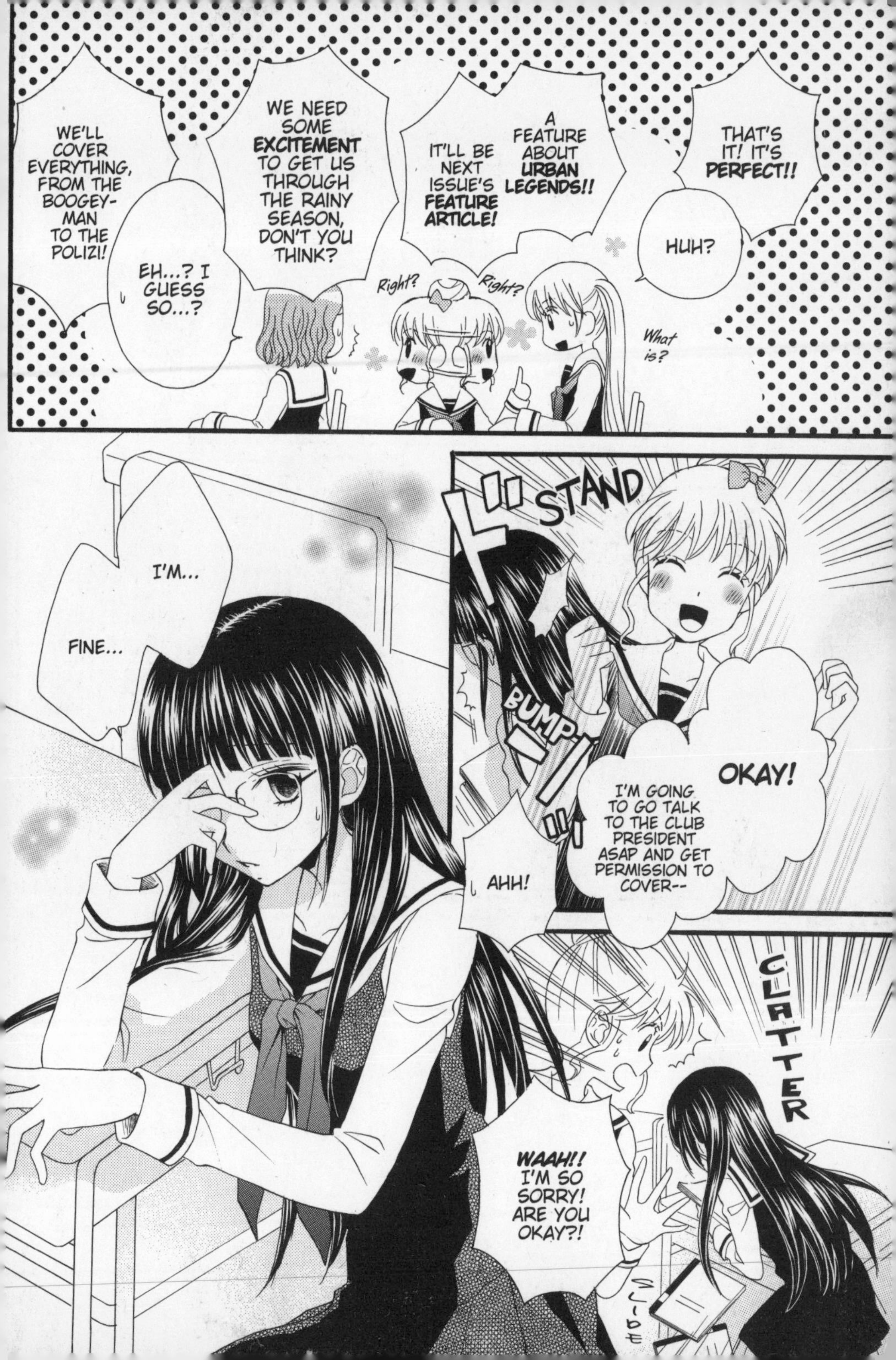

THAT'S IT! IT'S PERFECT!!
HUH?
What is?
A FEATURE ABOUT URBAN LEGENDS!!
IT'LL BE NEXT ISSUE'S FEATURE ARTICLE!
Right?
Right?
WE NEED SOME EXCITEMENT TO GET US THROUGH THE RAINY SEASON, DON'T YOU THINK?
WE'LL COVER EVERYTHING, FROM THE BOOGEY-MAN TO THE POLIZI!
EH...? I GUESS SO...?
STAND
OKAY!
I'M GOING TO GO TALK TO THE CLUB PRESIDENT ASAP AND GET PERMISSION TO COVER--
BUMP
AHH!
CLATTER
WAAH!! I'M SO SORRY! ARE YOU OKAY?!
SLIDE
I'M...
FINE...

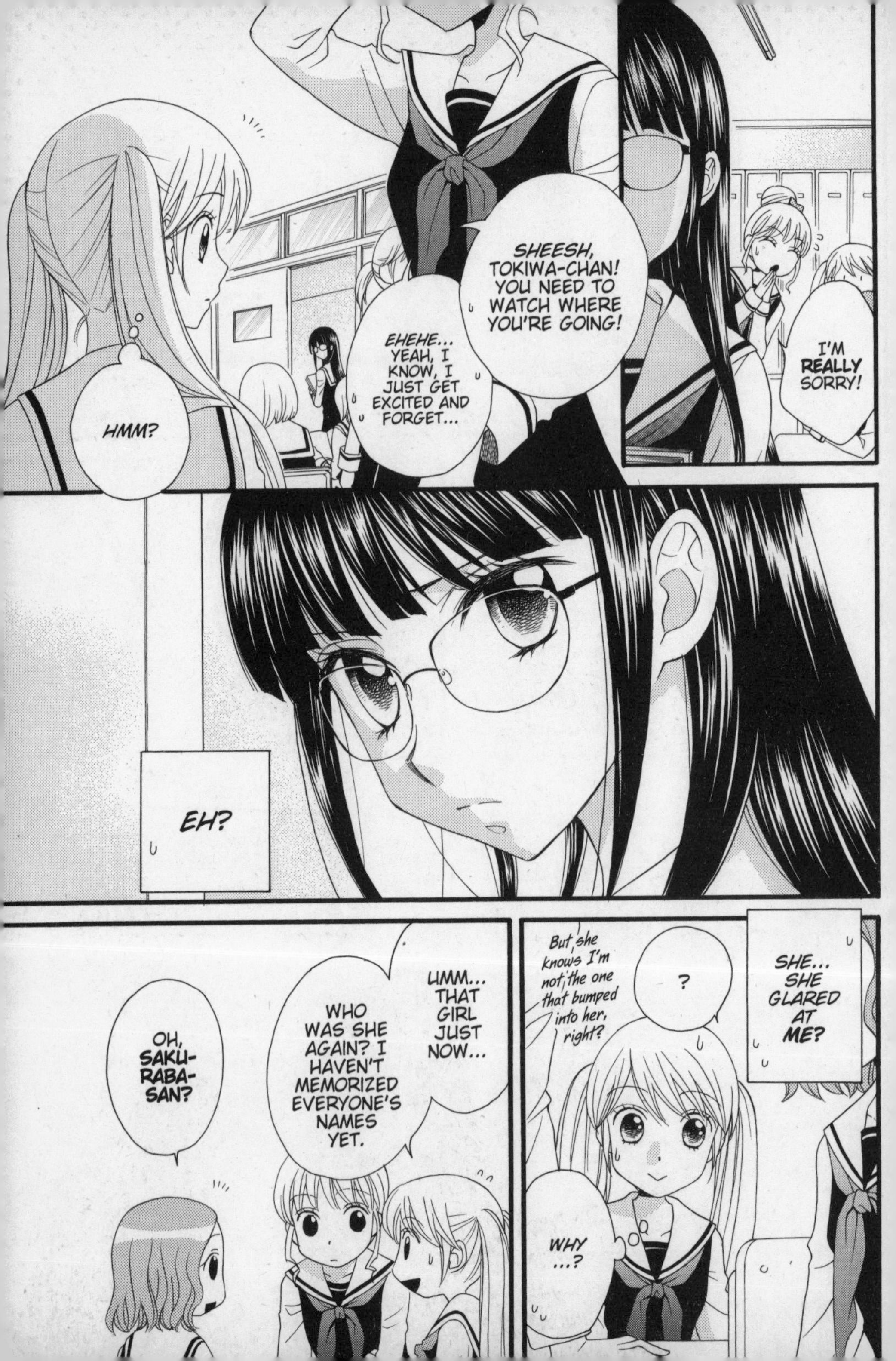

I'M REALLY SORRY!
SHEESH, TOKIWA-CHAN! YOU NEED TO WATCH WHERE YOU'RE GOING!
EHEHE... YEAH, I KNOW, I JUST GET EXCITED AND FORGET...
HMM?
EH?
SHE... SHE GLARED AT ME?
?
But, she knows I'm not the one that bumped into her, right?
WHY...?
UMM... THAT GIRL JUST NOW...
WHO WAS SHE AGAIN? I HAVEN'T MEMORIZED EVERYONE'S NAMES YET.
OH, SAKU-RABA-SAN?

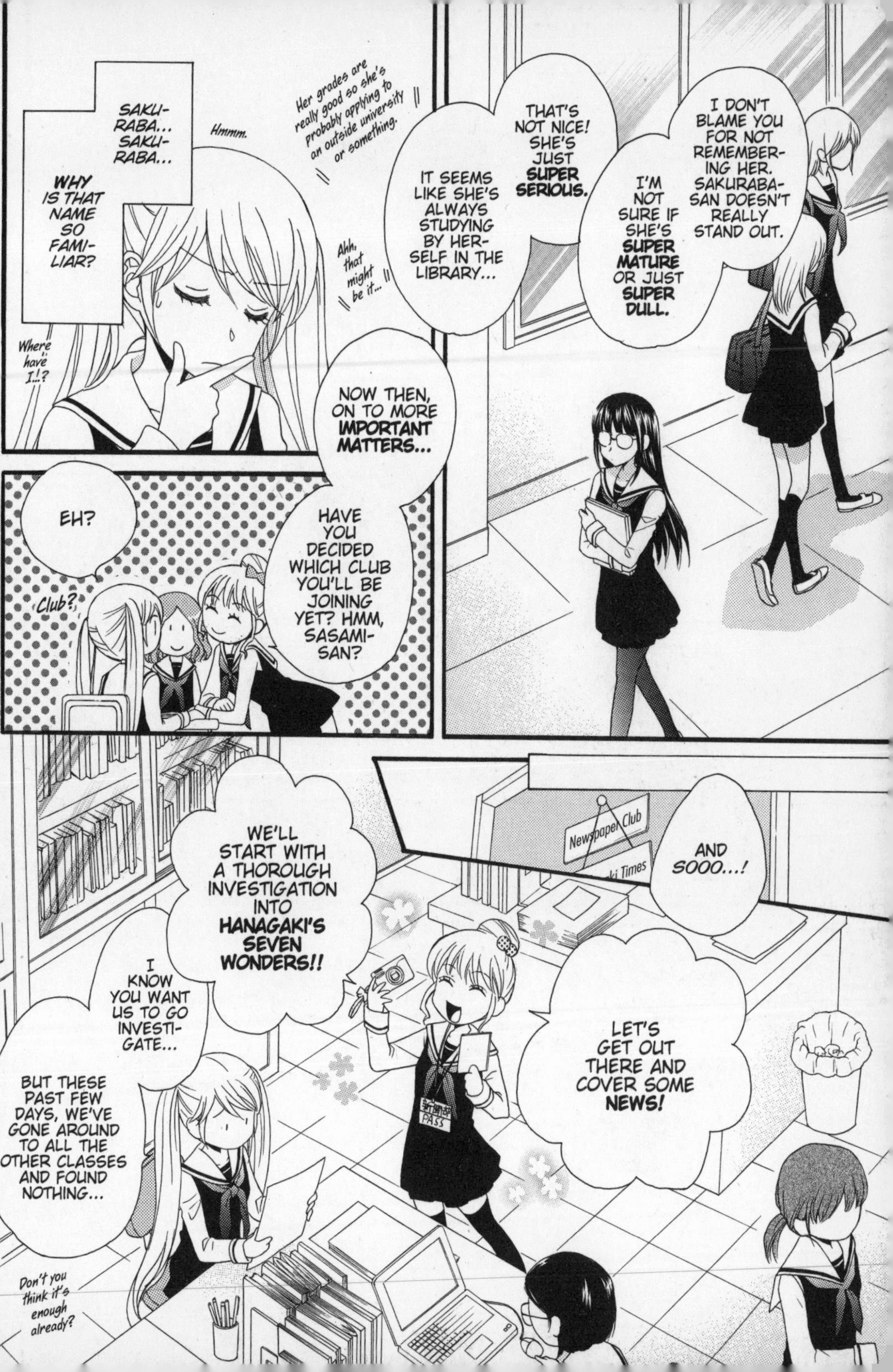
I DON'T BLAME YOU FOR NOT REMEMBERING HER. SAKURABA-SAN DOESN'T REALLY STAND OUT.
I'M NOT SURE IF SHE'S SUPER MATURE OR JUST SUPER DULL.
THAT'S NOT NICE! SHE'S JUST SUPER SERIOUS.
IT SEEMS LIKE SHE'S ALWAYS STUDYING BY HERSELF IN THE LIBRARY...
Her grades are really good so she's probably applying to an outside university or something.
Ahh, that might be it...
SAKURABA... SAKURABA...
WHY IS THAT NAME SO FAMILIAR?
Hmmm.
Where have I...?
NOW THEN, ON TO MORE IMPORTANT MATTERS...
HAVE YOU DECIDED WHICH CLUB YOU'LL BE JOINING YET? HMM, SASAMI-SAN?
EH?
Club?
Newspaper Club
AND SOOO...!
WE'LL START WITH A THOROUGH INVESTIGATION INTO HANAGAKI'S SEVEN WONDERS!!
LET'S GET OUT THERE AND COVER SOME NEWS!
PASS
I KNOW YOU WANT US TO GO INVESTIGATE...
BUT THESE PAST FEW DAYS, WE'VE GONE AROUND TO ALL THE OTHER CLASSES AND FOUND NOTHING...
Don't you think it's enough already?

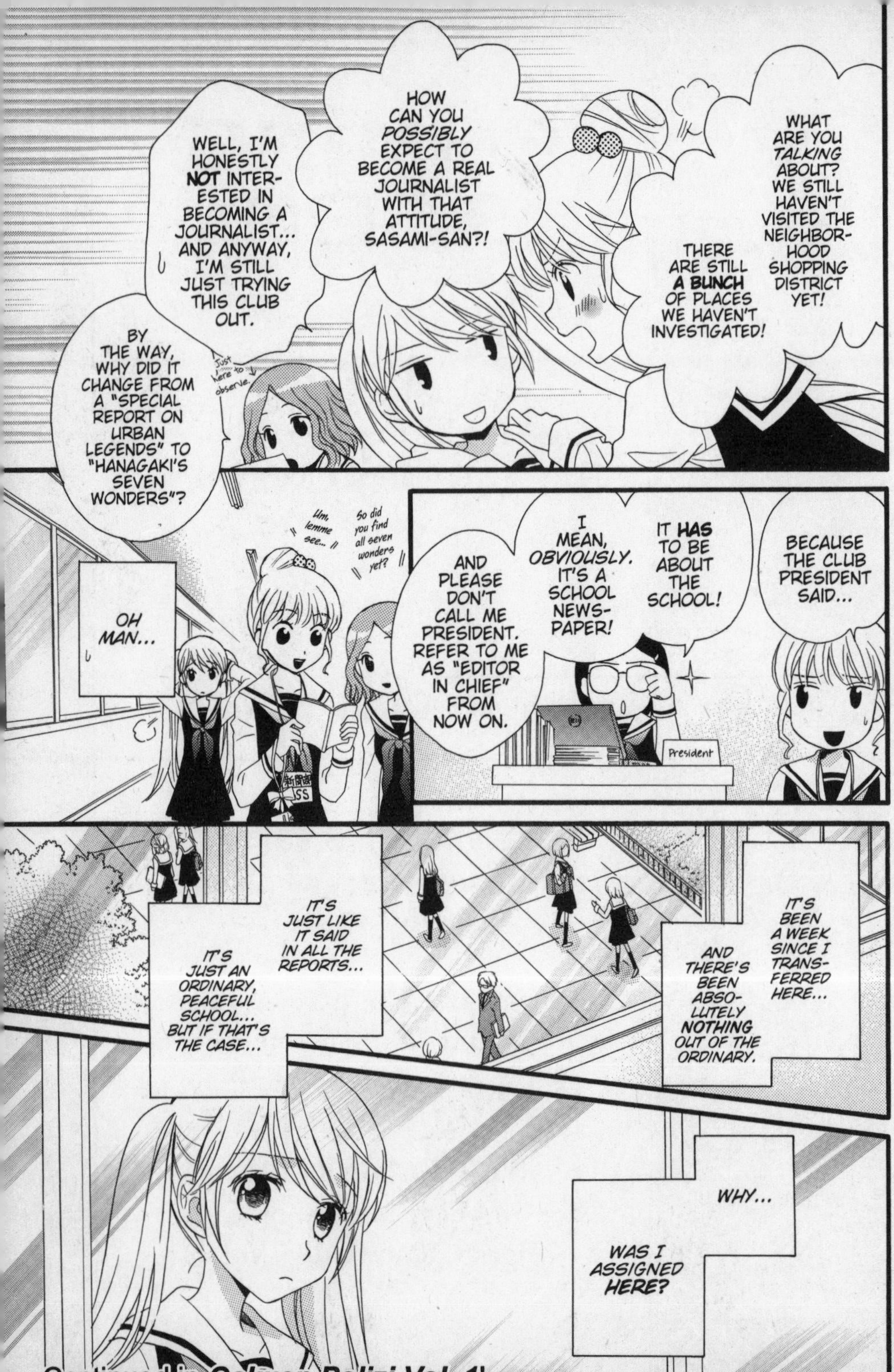
WHAT ARE YOU *TALKING* ABOUT? WE STILL HAVEN'T VISITED THE NEIGHBOR-HOOD SHOPPING DISTRICT YET!
THERE ARE STILL **A BUNCH** OF PLACES WE HAVEN'T INVESTIGATED!
HOW CAN YOU *POSSIBLY* EXPECT TO BECOME A REAL JOURNALIST WITH THAT ATTITUDE, SASAMI-SAN?!
WELL, I'M HONESTLY **NOT** INTER-ESTED IN BECOMING A JOURNALIST... AND ANYWAY, I'M STILL JUST TRYING THIS CLUB OUT.
Just here to observe.
BY THE WAY, WHY DID IT CHANGE FROM A "SPECIAL REPORT ON URBAN LEGENDS" TO "HANAGAKI'S SEVEN WONDERS"?
BECAUSE THE CLUB PRESIDENT SAID...
IT **HAS** TO BE ABOUT THE SCHOOL!
I MEAN, *OBVIOUSLY.* IT'S A SCHOOL NEWS-PAPER!
AND PLEASE DON'T CALL ME PRESIDENT. REFER TO ME AS "EDITOR IN CHIEF" FROM NOW ON.
President
So did you find all seven wonders yet?
Um, lemme see...
OH MAN...
IT'S BEEN A WEEK SINCE I TRANS-FERRED HERE...
AND THERE'S BEEN ABSO-LUTELY ***NOTHING*** *OUT OF THE ORDINARY.*
IT'S JUST LIKE IT SAID IN ALL THE REPORTS...
IT'S JUST AN ORDINARY, PEACEFUL SCHOOL... BUT IF THAT'S THE CASE...
WHY...
WAS I ASSIGNED ***HERE?***

Continued in *Gakuen Polizi Vol. 1*!

COMING SOON

AUGUST 2014
Alice in the Country of Joker:
The Nightmare Trilogy Vol. 1

SEPTEMBER 2014
Alice in the Country of Clover:
Knight's Knowledge Vol. 2

OCTOBER 2014
Alice in the Country of Diamonds:
Bet On My Heart

Alice in the Country of Joker:
Circus and Liar's Game Vol. 6

NOVEMBER 2014
Alice in the Country of Clover:
Knight's Knowledge Vol. 3

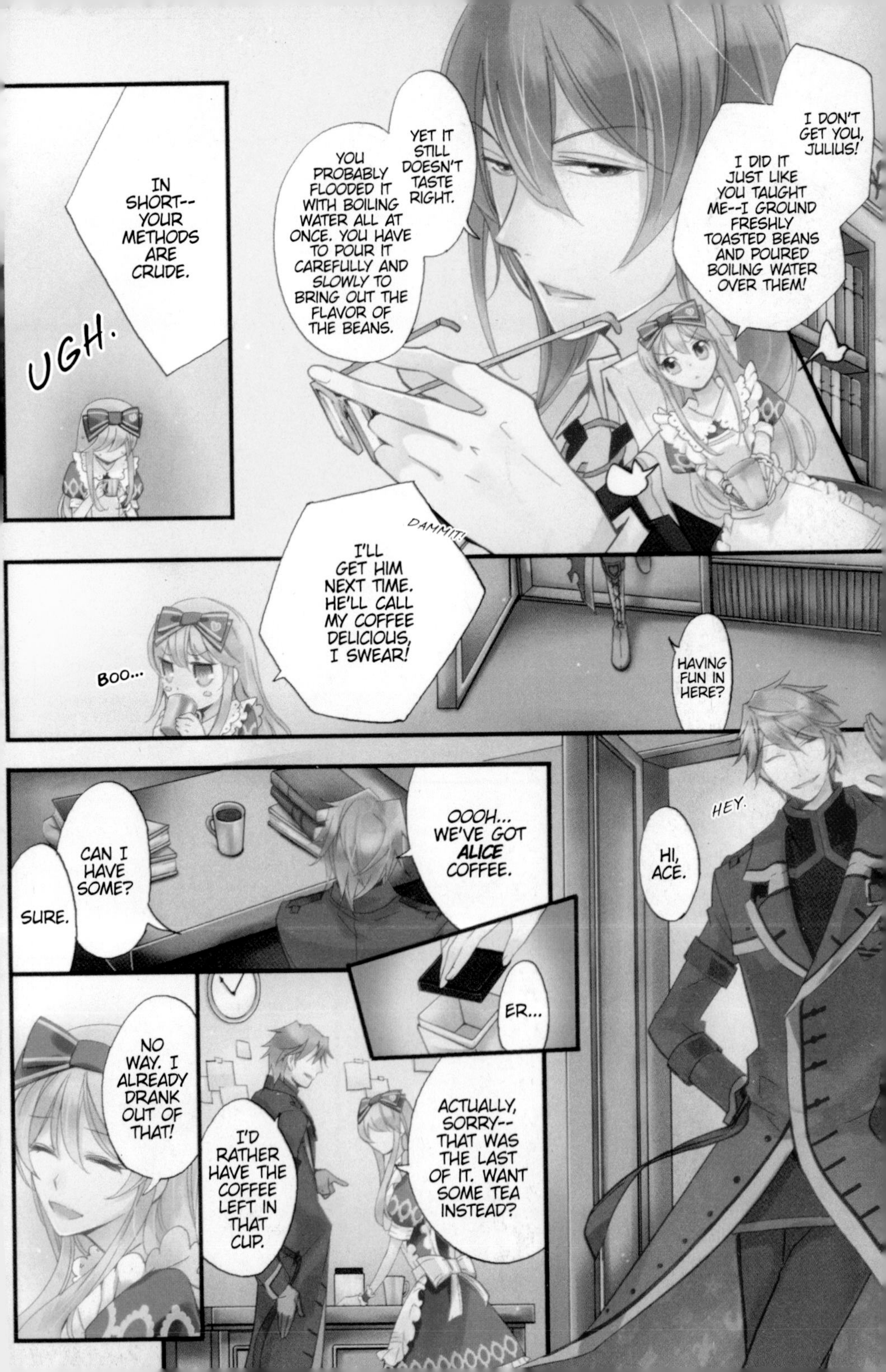
I DON'T GET YOU, JULIUS!
I DID IT JUST LIKE YOU TAUGHT ME--I GROUND FRESHLY TOASTED BEANS AND POURED BOILING WATER OVER THEM!
YET IT STILL DOESN'T TASTE RIGHT.
YOU PROBABLY FLOODED IT WITH BOILING WATER ALL AT ONCE. YOU HAVE TO POUR IT CAREFULLY AND SLOWLY TO BRING OUT THE FLAVOR OF THE BEANS.
IN SHORT-- YOUR METHODS ARE CRUDE.
UGH.
DAMMIT!
I'LL GET HIM NEXT TIME. HE'LL CALL MY COFFEE DELICIOUS, I SWEAR!
BOO...
HAVING FUN IN HERE?
HEY.
HI, ACE.
OOOH... WE'VE GOT **ALICE** COFFEE.
CAN I HAVE SOME?
SURE.
ER...
ACTUALLY, SORRY-- THAT WAS THE LAST OF IT. WANT SOME TEA INSTEAD?
I'D RATHER HAVE THE COFFEE LEFT IN THAT CUP.
NO WAY. I ALREADY DRANK OUT OF THAT!

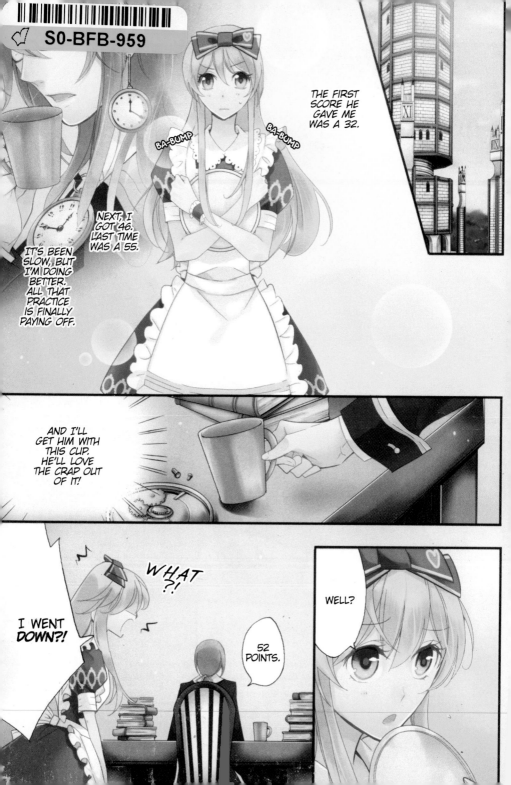

S0-BFB-959

THE FIRST SCORE HE GAVE ME WAS A 32.

BA-BUMP BA-BUMP

NEXT, I GOT 46. LAST TIME WAS A 55.

IT'S BEEN SLOW, BUT I'M DOING BETTER. ALL THAT PRACTICE IS FINALLY PAYING OFF.

AND I'LL GET HIM WITH THIS CUP. HE'LL LOVE THE CRAP OUT OF IT!

WHAT ?!

I WENT DOWN?!

52 POINTS.

WELL?